The American Shotgun

The American Shotgun

David F. Butler

WINCHESTER PRESS

Library of Congress Catalog Card Number: 72-96094
ISBN 0-87691-104-1

Published by Winchester Press
460 Park Avenue, New York 10022

Acknowledgments

I am indebted to many shooting friends and gun experts who have consulted with me over the past twenty years. I particularly want to mention Tom Hall, curator of the Winchester Gun Museum, who provided valuable information and many illustrations of early shotguns and ammunition; Ed Lowry, Winchester's Director of Exploratory Research, who taught me a great deal about shotgun ballistics; and Fred Parsi, who is as avid a gun collector as I am, and has been a companion on many jaunts to gun shows and shooting expeditions.

There are many others in the gun industry who provided technical information and illustrations. Ted McCawley and Sam Alvis were particularly helpful with data on Remington firearms.

I am also grateful to *The American Rifleman*, for giving me an excuse to begin the research that led to this book by commissioning a series of articles on shotguns and ammunition that the magazine published in 1953; and to *The Rifleman*, for permission to use data from my article "The Design of Semi-Automatic Shotguns," published in 1967.

Finally, I must thank Carolyn Chesto, who converted countless belts of dictation into typescript and helped with the many revisions.

May 1973   —David F. Butler

Contents

Chapter 1

THE EARLIEST SMOOTHBORES

Where should our story begin? Probably with a definition of an American shotgun, for it makes a difference whether we think of the term as meaning "used in America," or "entirely manufactured in America." In manufacturing technology the Colonies were far behind England and the continent during the entire Colonial period and only by enormous effort during the early nineteenth century did America catch up. Indeed it was not until late in the 1800s that American-made shotguns became fully competitive with their European counterparts.

Although the Colonists depended heavily on Europe for gun components—and even for complete firearms—there was, by the early eighteenth century a strong American influence on shotgun design, featuring long smallbored barrels and slim, graceful stocks, often of curly maple. (The purpose of the small barrel was to conserve powder and shot, which were scarce and expensive.)

American skill with these flintlock weapons has become legendary. They were in continual use during the French and Indian Wars of the 1750s and 1760s, and later in the Revolution. What is not well known is that fully half of the long "Kentucky" and "Pennsylvania" flintlocks were smoothbores, and that more than three quarters of the Colonial troops who fought in the Revolution were armed with smoothbore flintlocks. These weapons could be fired with single ball, buckshot, finer shot, or a favorite combination of "buck and ball" consisting of a single ball about ⅝ inch in diameter plus several buckshot—in case the main ball missed. So, while the major focus of this book is on the specialized smoothbore, intended for use primarily with shot rather than ball, and manufactured in the United States, much of the book's first part will describe other weapons that were more or less widely used in the U.S., and sketch their origins abroad.

There is no record as to the first gunsmith in Colonial America or the first blacksmith or farrier who produced firearms as a sideline, but the chances are that he would have been primarily an assembler or fitter who imported the metal elements of his products, including barrels and lock assemblies, from the old country.

Some aristocratic European sportsmen were demanding specially designed double-barrel shotguns, many with remarkably advanced features for the 17th century. These complex firearms could be created only by extremely skilled craftsmen working with the best tools, most likely on a Royal Grant. The double-barrel Miquelet shotguns and early flintlocks probably cost the equivalent of $100,000 in skilled labor at today's rates. Before deriding this figure as ridiculous keep in mind that to make *one* experimental shotgun to an entirely new design today, even with the best modern toolmaking machinery, can cost $15,000, and the workers of the 17th century had no jig borers, precision lathes, or milling machines with micrometer controls to work with. Just the preparation of reliable metal took months of tedious effort, and the gold inlay and wood carving to complete the weapons took months more.

The first American shotgun was nowhere near so elaborate. Many were built to the same design as a rifle, so that the owner had the flexibility of using either single ball or shot. However, it was likely to have been a smoothbore, for the rifling of barrels, though well known in Europe by the 16th century, did not come into wide use in America during the Colonial period because of the crude tooling available. Later, shotguns evolved as long, single-barreled, light firearms with a thin barrel wall, often octagonal at the breech, changing to a rounded barrel forward. They were usually full stocked to the muzzle, and were much cruder in construction and ornamentation than were their aristocratic European counterparts. Hence our proper story starts in a murky haze of conjecture, and we can show only typical examples of the sort of thing the first American shotgun would have been.

To set the stage, however, let us briefly recapitulate the story of long-arm development in Europe, so that we will understand the origins of our story.

EARLY FIREARMS

The invention of firearms is generally credited to the Chinese during the 11th or 12th century. By 1350 crude cannon had been manufactured by casting and forging processes in both Europe and China. Progress with this dramatic new weapon was rapid. Models were developed that could be carried by foot soldiers and larger caliber weapons were designed to be mounted on wooden carriages (for use on land) or on ships.

The explorations of Columbus during the 1490s opened a period of intense and competitive exploration. The Spanish and Portuguese quickly established colonies, ports, and garrisons extending through the islands of the Caribbean, the east coast of South America, Mexico, and as far north as Florida. This forced the English, Dutch, and French to limit their explorations to the northern hemisphere or fight the Spanish. They did both. In such a power struggle, colonists needed the best weapons they could secure—and by modern standards the best were incredibly crude. A typical matchlock of the 16th century is shown in Figure 1-1. This heavy, clumsy, slow-loading smoothbore musket was the result of 250 years of development. It had many drawbacks in Europe, and even more in the New World. The musketeer required a great deal of equipment, as shown in Figure 1-2, a Dutch illustration of 1607. To support his heavy matchlock, which was often over five feet in length and weighed more than 15 pounds, the musketeer carried a forked rest. The sling across his left shoulder carried much of his equipment. Powder charges were contained in small hollow carved wooden holders, each containing sufficient powder for one shot. A leather or cloth bag containing spherical lead bullets was attached to the sling right under the shooter's right arm. Low down on the right side was a separate powder horn containing fine-grained powder for priming the musket. The looped

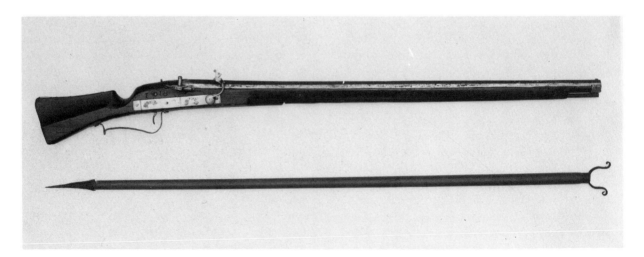

Figure 1-1 Typical matchlock of the early Colonial period.

Figure 1-2   The musketeer of 1607.

strings hanging from the sling were "slow matches." Since loading was so slow and cumbersome, the musketeer carried a long sword for last-ditch defense.

The musket was ignited by the "slow match"—a long piece of soft rope that had been dipped in an oxygen-rich chemical, such as saltpeter. Both ends were lit by flint and steel or from a fire and the "match" smouldered slowly, much like a modern cigar. When expecting combat the musketeer normally carried the match as shown in the illustration, with both ends clasped between the fingers of his left hand. The forked stick, used to support the muzzle of the musket, he jammed into the ground a few feet in front of him.

The loading procedure was complex. The butt end of the musket was placed on the ground, one of the wooden powder chargers opened and its contents poured into the barrel of the musket, keeping the ends of the slow match well away from the powder. A bullet was removed from the leather pouch and pushed into the muzzle of the musket. The "scouring-stick," or ramrod, was removed from a channel beneath the barrel and used to ram the bullet down onto the powder charge. If the bullet fitted poorly, wadding was often rammed in to hold it in position. The scouring-stick was then returned to its slot beneath the barrel, a small quantity of priming powder placed in a shallow pan on the right side of the barrel and a pivoted lid swung over to cover the priming pan and keep the powder from blowing away.

To fire the matchlock the gunner blew on his match to brighten the glowing ends, and clamped one end into a moveable jaw on the matchlock mechanism. The musket was then lifted and placed onto the forked stick and aimed at the enemy. The pivoted cover to the pan was swung open and the gunner took aim through crude sights (which may be seen at the muzzle and on the breech tang of Figure 1-1.) At the crucial moment the musketeer pulled the trigger, which was hooked to the movable jaw through a series of levers, causing the glowing end of the match to be dipped into the fine powder in the pan. This powder flashed in all directions with some of the flash passing through a small diameter "touchhole" drilled through the side of the barrel into the main powder charge. This ignited the main charge in the barrel, hurling the bullet at a moderate velocity in the general direction of the enemy. The reloading procedure involved remov-

ing the slow match from the mechanism, going through the entire loading procedure again and reclamping the match in the holder.

As accuracy was poor and reloading incredibly slow, why were such cumbersome and inaccurate weapons worth anything at all? Indians, generally poor shots with bows and arrows, could, after all, get off five arrows in the time it took to reload a matchlock. Part of the anwer lies deep in European history. During the early Middle Ages knights in armor were virtually impregnable. There are some recorded battles where knights charged up and down, wreaking great havoc without a single one on either side being killed! Such an arrangement was dandy for the nobility—they had all the fun of raising an army and taking a whack at their neighbor's land with little risk to themselves or to other members of the knightly order. Unfortunately the peasants and common soldiers were on the receiving end of the frolic and didn't enjoy it anywhere near as much.

There were few ways of stopping the knights. Archers with long bows could penetrate the normal 65 to 70 pound suit of armor at short range, but the power and skill necessary to do so required a lifetime of practice. Crossbows were developed during the 11th and 12th centuries to concentrate enough power in an extremely short, stiff bow to penetrate armor. These weapons were slow and difficult to reload but they posed such a threat to the nobility that the knights complained to the Pope, who issued a papal order forbidding their use against Christians!

The cannon or hand gun, no matter how crude, offered the best opportunity to equalize the odds. As power was supplied by chemical energy rather than muscle, the foot soldier at last had a weapon that could stop the knights in their rampage across the battlefields. The knights, of course, did not like this new game at all. First they tried increasing the thickness of the metal in their breastplate to fend off the bullets. Their other response was to deal savagely with any enemy gunners captured during a battle. Neither solution worked, and by the time Columbus landed in the New World knighthood was on its way out and firearms had become the predominant instruments in deciding the outcome of Europe's quarrels.

In the New World, guns were essential to survival. Despite their slowness, inconvenience, and inaccuracy, they possessed fantastic magic power in the eyes of the natives. Furthermore, these crude matchlocks provided a means of defense against representatives of rival European powers and a tool for harvesting game.

Hunters in England and on the Continent used the matchlock loaded with a round lead ball to stalk large animals in the forests and royal preserves. When loaded with fine lead shot the matchlock was found to be superb against wild fowl. Since there was often a delay of close to a second between pulling the trigger and the gun going off, it was virtually impossible to use the matchlock shotgun against birds in flight, but fens and marshes in season were filled with resting, wintering birds. A careful gunner could creep within shotgun range and often kill two or three birds floating on the water with one carefully aimed shot—a feat impossible with bow and arrow. Moreover, winters were a time of starvation in Europe and the fresh meat that the matchlocks made possible was often the difference between health and starvation.

The situation was similar in the New World. The Colonists who landed in Plymouth, Massachusetts, in 1620, lost more than half of their number to disease and starvation during that first terrible winter. There is some question as to whether the first Thanksgiving celebrated in November 1621 was truly a Thanksgiving for the bounty of the past year, for there was precious little, or an earnest prayer to the Almighty to deliver the Colonists from disease and starvation in the approaching New England winter.

Some Colonists tried to survive with insufficient weapons. French Huguenots started a colony called Fort Caroline on the St. John's River in Florida in 1564. A year later, near starvation, they succumbed to Spanish forces who massacred every one to show both their dislike of French incursions into Spanish territory and their intolerance of the Huguenot's religious practices.

MATCHLOCK DESIGN

The matchlocks used by colonists in America differed from cannon in many important respects. Siege cannon were usually fired by igniting the powder grain with a burning stick, a red hot coal, or a piece of heated wire. Any of these required that a small fire be kept burning near the cannon. The "slow match" proved a useful source of ignition for portable firearms, and was an important improvement.

A second major improvement was to move the touchhole, drilled into the chamber of the barrel, from the top of the barrel to the right side, and place the priming powder in a shallow pan adjacent to it. A vertical plate or "fence" was often constructed at the rear of the flash pan to prevent the priming powder from flashing back in the gunner's face.

A third major improvement came about when some ingenious soul designed a mechanical holder for the slow match that would automatically dip the smoldering end into the flash pan when the trigger, or "tricker," was pulled. The first designs were crude indeed. The match holder, or serpentine, was simply a long S-shaped bar, pivoted in the center and mounted in a slot in the stock of the musket. The slow match was clamped to the upper end of the S, and the long trigger projected below the stock with the tail of the S beneath the shooter's hand. The tail was weighted so that gravity held it downwards, away from the wooden stock. As the gunner lifted the trigger, the slow match was pivoted downwards into the flash pan, igniting the powder. This mechanism was soon improved by the addition of a spring, which held the trigger downwards with the match well away from the flash pan until the gunner made a conscious effort to pull upwards and discharge his matchlock.

Experiments continued throughout Europe and an improved lock was developed in the 15th century. The improved matchlock mechanism, shown in Figure 1-3 was mounted on a metal plate fastened to the right side of the musket. The long trigger, or tiller, was screwed into a sear or "scear" lever pivoted in the center of the lock plate. The scear had a hook at one end which engaged a tumbler or cam, which, in turn, was fastened to the match holder, or "cock." The match holder was split at its upper end and the slow match was clamped in between the split ends by a match screw. The flash pan was improved by giving it a cover, which held the priming in place until the gunner was ready to fire.

The matchlock, shown in Figure 1-1, has almost all these features and is fairly typical of those used by the early American colonists. The long heavy barrel was mounted on a wooden stock with a slightly curved butt to better fit the shoulder, and a deep cut behind the lock plate to fit the gunner's hand. The lock mechanism was attached to a rectangular flat plate set into the

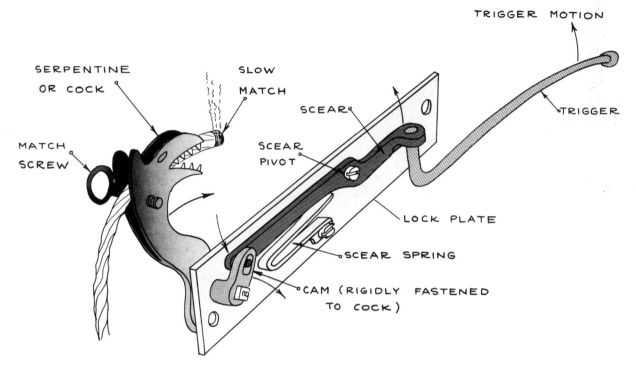

Figure 1-3   Improved matchlock mechanism of the 15th century.

side of the wooden stock. This particular match-lock retains the long trigger guard designed for the long trigger shown in Figure 1-3, but has a separate trigger, a later development that did not require anywhere near so long a guard.

The matchlock was still a heavy, cumbersome gun. But the new matchlock mechanism had two advantages over the old. One was that the match holder had been reversed so that the gunner could keep a continuous eye on the match and be sure that it remained lighted while he was wait-ing to fire his shot. The second was that the short camming arm on the tumbler, or cam, enabled the match to move rapidly as the trigger was pulled. Still, there was often a delay of as much as a second between the time the trigger was pulled and the time the match ignited the powder within the barrel.

LATE MATCHLOCK MECHANISMS

The development of improved matchlock mech-anisms was an intensely competitive activity throughout Europe. Designs were created in which a powerful spring was used to rotate the serpentine rapidly into the flash pan. The serpen-tine was held in a cocked position by a trigger and sear arrangement. These mechanisms did not

prove successful, however, for they were prone to accidental discharge, and the fast motion of the match as it was snapped downwards into the pan sometimes extinguished the fire. During the 17th century the final development in matchlock mech-anisms evolved as shown in Figure 1-4, with many refinements from the designs shown in Figures 1-1 and 1-3. For one, the lockplate was made smaller and more graceful, with rounded surfaces and a curved, tapered tail. The plate was even reduced in size until it was barely sufficient to enclose the linkage and levers fastened to its inner surface. A second major change was the use of a separate trigger, which was either pivoted in the wooden stock or in a metal trigger plate set into the underside of the stock. As the trigger was pulled, it rotated about the pivot point and a blade at the rear of the trigger rose, contacting the crossbar shown in the lower illustration of Figure 1-4. The crossbar was part of the sear, which was pivoted on the second screw from the right in the figure.

A small upward motion of the crossbar was translated into a large motion at the cam. The distance from crossbar to sear pivot is 1.55 inches, while the distance from the pivot point to the small finger that engages the cam is 3.6 inches. The trigger motion is further amplified by the arrangement of the cam and serpentine. The end

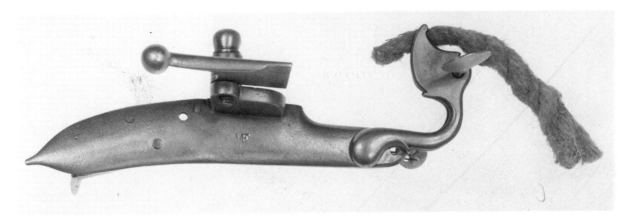

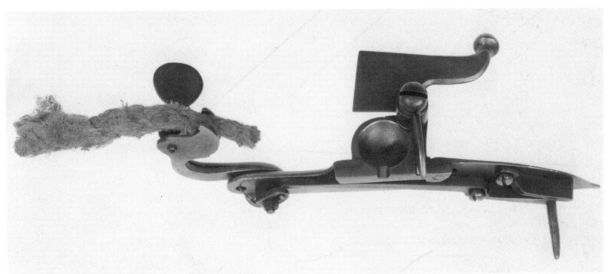

Figure 1-4 Late matchlock mechanism (17th century).

result is that a small vertical motion of the cross-bar on the sear of .165 inches causes the match holder to move a distance of 3.5 inches—a magnification of more than 20 to 1.

Another major change was the incorporation of the flash pan into the lock mechanism, instead of its being welded separately to the barrel. The pan is relatively flat and shallow, so that the stubby end of the glowing match would strike the pool of powder whether the match was long or short at the time the trigger was pulled. On the example shown in Figure 1-4, the pan is .950 inches in diameter and only .200 inches deep. A groove was cut on the inside of the pan to communicate with the touchhole. To protect the powder, a pivoted pan cover could be rotated to completely cover the pan. Although this lock mechanism is in excellent condition, the crude workmanship of the 17th century left a gap of about .030 inches between the flat upper surface of the pan and the cover.

Protection for the shooter had been added in

the form of a vertical plate forming a shield at the rear of the pan. This is visible in the lower view of Figure 1-4, although the actual plate is much bigger than it appears: Its size is ⅞ of an inch high by 1¼ inches wide at the upper surface. It is cut on the inner surface to match the contour of the barrel so that the powder that flashed in the pan was thoroughly blocked from flashing back in the shooter's face. The lock mechanism shown in Figure 1-4 is ready to fire, with the match clamped in the serpentine and the flash pan uncovered.

The serpentine was held in this open position by a powerful V spring, fastened to the lock plate with the right-hand screw in the lower illustration. This was the only spring required for the entire matchlock musket, and was the only component that had to be heat-treated. All of the other elements would work properly and give long service if carefully forged of wrought iron and filed to smooth surfaces before assembly into the mechanism.

Chapter 2

THE WHEEL LOCK AND TRANSITION

THE WHEEL LOCK

As we have seen in the previous chapter, the principal disadvantage of the matchlock was the need for a lighted match to ignite the powder, which meant that the musketeer in situations of danger had to carry lighted matches. Otherwise he was virtually defenseless until he had taken out flint and steel and kindled his match.

It was obvious that a great improvement could be made if the gun mechanism itself could provide the sparks needed to ignite the powder. Inventors struggled with this problem until late in the 15th century when the first designs for wheel-lock firearms were created. The idea was basically quite simple. Linkages were arranged so that a powerful spring would rotate a serrated and grooved wheel. A second spring pressed a lump of iron pyrites firmly against the wheel and a quantity of fine priming powder was placed at the area of contact. As the spring was released the serrated wheel rotated rapidly, creating a shower of sparks that ignited the fine powder in the priming pan.

This was a brilliant solution to the ignition problem even though the manufacture of such mechanisms was difficult and expensive by 15th- and 16th-century techniques.

The usual wheel lock used a powerful V-shaped spring, the lateral movement of which was converted to rotary motion by wrapping links of a chain, similar to a bicycle chain, around a small diameter drum affixed to the wheel, with one end

of the chain attached to the spring. The wheel was wound up about ¾ of a turn and then locked in the wheel. The general arrangement of the mechanism with the parts all cocked and ready to fire is shown in the main drawing of Figure 2-1. The wheel in this example is 1.35 inches in diameter and .200 inches wide. It has three V-shaped grooves cut into the outside surface, and diagonal serrations to roughen its periphery. The pan is quite small—only .45 inches wide, .70 inches long, and .150 inches deep. The lower working arm of the mainspring is 4⅛ inches long and the chain, which is wrapped around the drum inside the wheel, has three links. The sliding cover for the pan protected the powder against the weather or from being shaken out. The operation of the pan is shown in the left hand illustration of Figure 2-1. The pan cover has been moved to cover the pan, with the iron pyrites lowered on top of the pan cover. The wheel is unwound, with the chain hanging vertically and the mainspring down against the spring's top surface.

As the gunner cocked the wheel into the position shown in the main illustration, the cam struck the pivoted link holding the pan cover and snapped it into the fully open position. The wheel-lock musket was then completely ready to fire.

This was an unusual wheel-lock mechanism. A much more common arrangement allowed the gunner to cock the wheel using a spanner, place the priming powder in the small pan, then slide

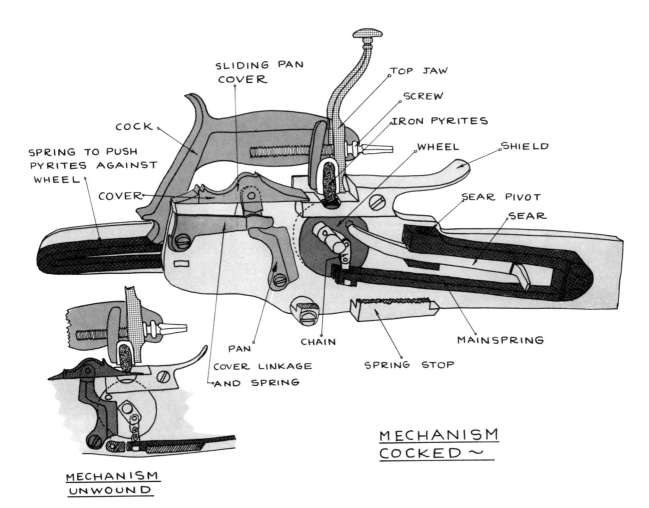

SLIDING PAN
COVER

TOP JAW

SCREW

IRON PYRITES

COCK

WHEEL

SHIELD

SPRING TO PUSH
PYRITES AGAINST
WHEEL

SEAR PIVOT

COVER

SEAR

PAN

CHAIN

MAINSPRING

COVER LINKAGE

SPRING STOP

AND SPRING

MECHANISM
COCKED ~

MECHANISM
UNWOUND

Figure 2-1 Sectional drawing of wheel-lock mechanism.

the cover shut and lower the iron pyrites onto the cover. In this way the mechanism could be carried, cocked, for long periods with the priming powder fully protected. Most mechanisms were designed so that when the trigger was pulled, the very first motion of the wheel cammed the pan cover forward, allowing the iron pyrites to drop onto the wheel and generate the shower of sparks.

The sear arrangement for this wheel lock is fairly intricate. The sear, pivoted upon a vertical screw, has a small cylindrical end that drops into a hole in the wheel, locking it in the fully cocked position. Linkages were arranged so that when the trigger was pulled the rear end of the sear bar was pushed inwards thus disengaging it from the wheel and allowing the mainspring to snap the chain downwards. The rapid acceleration of the wheel generated sparks, and the excess mainspring energy was absorbed by the "mainspring stop," fastened to the lock plate. As the motion of the wheel tended to throw glowing red embers of iron pyrites towards the shooter's face, another

stop was machined into the rear of the pan. Any embers that got by this were deflected by the "shield," which caused them to scoot up and over the shooter's head.

Three illustrations of this wheel-lock mechanism are shown in Figure 2-2. The upper illustration shows the outside view of the lock. The square shaft, which was used to cock the wheel, is immediately below the pan and cock. A second plate has been used to enclose the spring holding the cock down against the main wheel. The middle illustration shows the interior view of the lock with the mechanism unwound. The exact arrangement of the components is a little difficult to see for the "bridle," which formed the inside bearing for the wheel shaft, covers up the cam, the chain and the connection of the chain to the mainspring, which is ornately engraved with flower-like designs. The pan cover is shown in a forward position with the iron pyrites dropped down onto the wheel. The interior arrangement of the components is also shown in the lower illustration of

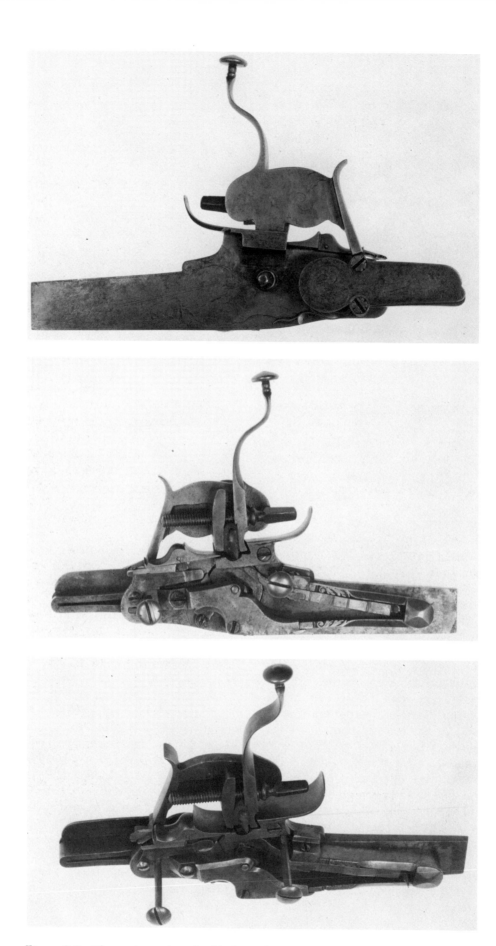

Figure 2-2 Three views of a wheel-lock mechanism.

Figure 2-2. The quality of workmanship required to manufacture locks of this complexity in the 16th century made them extremely expensive.

A heavy smoothbore wheel-lock musket is shown in Figure 2-3. This is a typical European design with a 12-gauge barrel pinned to a full-length wooden stock. It was reloaded with a wooden ramrod contained in a single guide beneath the stock. The wheel-lock mechanism was set into the right side of the stock, and the spring that held the iron pyrites against the wheel is visible in the illustration at the front end of the lock plate. Although there were no sights fitted to the wheel lock, it was fitted with a double-set trigger mechanism to reduce the heavy trigger pull. The linkages to these trigger mechanisms were often arranged so that the force of the main wheel acting on the sear tended to release the sear, which was held in a locked position by a small step on the lateral sear bar. A slight rearward motion of the sear bar when struck by the set trigger would allow the sear to swing inward, thus firing the musket.

Wheel-lock muskets and rifles were desirable firearms for the New World. They gave the hunter or colonist a weapon greatly improved over the matchlock, for there was no telltale smoke or glow from the burning match to give away the hunter's approach. For protection or defense, the wheel lock could be kept cocked and ready for instant use in case of attack.

There was a close alliance between the design of wheel locks and that of clock mechanisms. Both represented extremes of sophistication for their time and both were so expensive that the number manufactured was limited. There was another major problem with wheel locks in the New World and that was the lack of skilled gunsmiths capable of keeping them in good working order. Since the mainspring was powerful and as fast motion of the wheel was required to make sparks, the stresses on the small link chain were severe. The powerful mainspring slammed into the mainspring stop on every shot, tending to wear out and loosen the poor-quality materials then available. Careful examination of the wheel-lock mechanism shown in Figure 2-2 shows how the soft metal has worn in many places. One side of the hole in the wheel has worn, as has the sear itself. Although the mechanism is still in excellent working order, part of the main bearing bracket on the outside of the lock plate has broken away and some of the interior surfaces show evidence of fractures.

A comparatively minor accident could render a wheel lock completely useless. One particular hazard was the crystalline property of iron pyrites, which tends to break into small pieces. If a piece of broken pyrites was carried downwards by the wheel, it could jam between the wheel and the frame of the lock, and removing this jammed material was no easy task. The small chains were, in addition, subject to breakage, and if water got into the mechanism while it was in the cocked position (shown in Figure 2-1) the mechanism could rust fast in the position shown and not fire at all. Such mechanical difficulties posed great problems in Europe, particularly in military campaigns, but far greater problems on the American frontier. The wheel lock became a favorite weapon of the landed gentry in Europe and many beautifully engraved specimens can be seen in European museums. They were used only to a limited extent in the New World and were replaced in the early 18th century by the simpler flintlock.

Figure 2-3 A typical smoothbore wheel lock.

12

THE SNAPHANCE

The next step in the evolution of the gunlock first appeared about 1540, probably in Holland. This was the snaphance, the word itself a corruption of the Dutch for "Snapping Hen," no doubt because the hammer motion resembles just that as it snaps downward and and slams into the frizzen.

Several views of a typical snaphance lock are shown in Figure 2-4. Although simpler to construct than the wheel lock, it had many points of similarity, similarities that may be seen by comparing this figure with Figure 2-1. The snaphance also included the sliding cover protecting the priming powder in the pan; it was moved back and forth by a long slender bar, which may be seen in the middle illustration of Figure 2-4 running from the screw below the pan cover to a small hole in the tumbler. The tumbler was rigidly mounted on a square shaft that was part of the hammer or cock. A powerful mainspring pressing downwards on the L-shaped extension of the tumbler tended to rotate the hammer or cock and cause it to slam into the battery. In these illustrations the battery is shown in a fully forward position. With the hammer cocked, the battery was rotated until it stood vertically ready to be struck by the flint. The curved surface of the battery was designed to send the sparks downwards into the pan.

The searing system on the snaphance also evolved from the wheel lock. The sear, shown on the left hand side of the middle illustration of Figure 2-4, was pivoted about a vertical axis and projected through a hole in the lock plate. This square hole, with the sear in place, may be seen in the upper illustration of Figure 2-4 just to the rear of the hammer. As the hammer was drawn to a full-cocked position the sear moved outwards, projecting beyond the face of the lock plate and locking the hammer in a fully cocked position by projecting over the L-shaped extension on the hammer. As the trigger was pulled the sear was withdrawn through the lock plate and the hammer was released. The mainspring rotated the tumbler which in turn forced the hammer into the battery or frizzen. The motion of the tumbler also moved the small bar shown in the middle illustration of Figure 2-4 to the right, moving the pan cover off of the pan and exposing the powder. The pan cover was kept fully closed or fully opened by a small retainer spring, shown fastened by the extreme right hand screw in the illustration.

The snaphance lock represented such an improvement and its use spread so rapidly that there are records of them before 1550 in Holland, Italy, Sweden and other European countries. The Germans never took to them, preferring the wheel lock until the true flintlock finally took over in the early 18th century, but the Moors and Arabs continued to manufacture snaphances until late in the 19th century after which Belgian manufacturers continued production into the 20th century to meet the continuing demand from North African countries. Aside from Germany, the only major arms-producing country to regard the snaphance coolly was Spain, where an action with rival claims was developed at about the same time: the Miquelet.

THE MIQUELET

Spanish designers differed from others in their approach to develop an inexpensive firearm with self-contained ignition. Their design became known as the Miquelet or Spanish lock, sometimes referred to as the Mediterranean lock. It is generally dated from the second half of the 16th century and was a design with many solid virtues. A careful study of the beautiful Miquelet double-barreled shotgun in the Winchester Gun Collection in New Haven, Connecticut, can provide many clues to the reasoning behind its design.

An overall view of the shotgun is shown in Figure 2-5, and a closeup of the breech and left-hand lock in Figure 2-6. The overall shotgun weighs 6¾ pounds--amazingly low for a double-barreled shotgun constructed this early. Many of the most highly considered firearms in the world were made in Spain and this one shows much of the skill and artistry on which the Spanish reputation was based.

The overall length of the shotgun is 49½ inches; the barrels, 33½ inches long, are almost exactly .600 inches in diameter or slightly under 20 gauge. Wear at the muzzle has opened up the left barrel to .609 inches, the right to .617 inches. The barrels are extremely thin at the muzzle with outside diameters of .693 on the left and .700 on the right. The breech details shown in Figure 2-6 show the octagonal breech sections with a slightly sunken rib between the two bar-

Figure 2-4 Three views of a snaphance lock.

Figure 2-5   A Miquelet double-barreled shotgun.

Figure 2-6   Closeup of the Miquelet lock.

rels. The octagonal shape extends 10 inches from the breech with a double-banded ornamental transition to a rounded section for the remainder of the length. A small brass front sight is mounted in the center of the rib, about one inch back from the muzzle. There is a U-shaped rear sight forged into the tang at the breech. The stock, made of dark walnut, is 31½ inches long. The steel ramrod is held in two ramrod pipes and a ramrod guide inset into the lower forearm of the shotgun. The ramrod itself is beautifully tapered with a mushroom head .515 inches in diameter, and an ornamental design with a necked-down section followed by a swelling and then a gradual taper to .200 inches in diameter in the center and then .140 inches at the small end. A thread has been cut on the small end to take a cleaning patch or worm.

The lock details are shown in Figure 2-6. The touchhole, bushed with silver, connects directly to the lower surface of the pan. The frizzen is L shaped, eliminating the separate pan cover and need for internal linkage. Deep grooves have been cut in the face of the frizzen to guide the flint sparks downwards into the pan. A vertical curved baffle has been forged onto the rear of the pan to provide a shield to protect the shooter from flying sparks. (This construction is known as a "fence to the rear.") The frizzen is held in a fully open or fully shut position by the small V spring which presses upwards upon its curlicue tail.

The most important distinguishing element of the Spanish lock, however, is the outside mainspring, which is clearly shown in the illustrations. The lower surface of this large V-shaped spring is thoroughly anchored, whereas the long upper surface moves vertically. The spring gradually tapers from the thickness of ⅛ of an inch at its midpoint to .105 inches just forward of the hammer and .090 inches thick at the extreme rear end. The hammer pivot is located immediately under the bracket that looks like a lion's paw. The end of the mainspring presses upwards upon a curved extension of the hammer. Another extension to the front of the hammer is the searing surface, which is held in a locked position by the small flat bar projecting through the face of the

lock plate. This seems like a curious and complex construction until one realizes that the gunsmiths of the time had only relatively soft materials to work with. Designs had to be created which kept bearing pressures sufficiently low that the searing surface would not rapidly wear and become unsafe. In addition to the main searing surface, which holds the hammer, there is a safety, the square stud in the cutout portion of the mainspring. This safety had a deep V notch. If the hammer was held and the trigger pulled and then released, the safety notch came back out to the position in Figure 2-6. If the hammer was carefully lowered, the sear surface was locked rigidly into the safety notch providing an excellent way to carry the gun fully loaded and ready for shooting but quite safe.

There is an obvious question: why was the large, bulky mainspring mounted *outside* the lock plate when the wheel lock and snaphance had the spring mounted inside? The answer is simple. Because of the relatively weak steels, springs were large and bulky. The use of horizontal searing surfaces meant that some wood had to be cut away inside the action so that the inclusion of such a large mainspring inside the lock would have seriously cut away the remaining wood, requiring that the entire breech assembly be made much more bulky to provide adequate wood strength. The Mediterranean lock also put all of the operating forces directly on the hammer, eliminating the tumbler, square shaft and locking pin.

This Miquelet shotgun has beautiful balance and is stocked with a rather large drop at the comb as if designed for deliberate shooting. Such a shotgun would provide a superb and long-lasting wildfowl gun for its aristocratic owner. The small gold inlays on the lock plate and barrels and the artistic shaping of the metal components show extreme attention to detail and the investment of untold hours of skilled labor in its creation.

While few Miquelet firearms are of such extraordinary quality as this example, the Mediterranean or Spanish lock became widely used throughout southern Europe and remained in manufacture for several hundred years.

Chapter 3

THE FLINTLOCK

Competition to develop better firearms continued, and early in the seventeenth century a major development occurred—the flintlock. Historians generally credit Marin leBourgeoys as the inventor of the flintlock, sometime between 1610 and 1620. The leBourgeoys family had for many years manufactured clocks, weapons and locks and Marin leBourgeoys operated a shop in the village of Lisieux in Normandy, France, where he manufactured wheel locks, snaphances, and crossbows in addition to musical instruments and mechanical devices. He was also a noted sculptor and painter.

FLINTLOCK DESIGN

The basic invention in the flintlock consisted of combining the one piece hand cover and frizzen of the Miquelet with the inside mainspring of the snaphance. To this combination a new searing system was added, located entirely within the lockplate and operated on the tumbler.

A good example of a true flintlock mechanism is shown in Figure 3-1. This lock is from the famous British Brown Bess musket and contains all of the basic elements of leBourgeoys' invention together with many detailed refinements of 120 years of development. The one piece frizzen is shown in a closed position covering the pan in the upper illustration. The position of the frizzen was controlled by the frizzen spring, a U-shaped spring with the lower end screwed to the lockplate. The free end of the spring pushed upwards

against two tails on the frizzen, which were so designed that the frizzen was held tightly closed until struck by the flint. Then it was driven to a fully open position where it was held by the frizzen spring until the soldier was ready to reload.

This particular Brown Bess lock mechanism was manufactured by a British contractor in 1729 and the details were beautifully done. The frizzen is gracefully shaped, its ornamental curlicues carefully finished with smooth sweeping curves. The pan is forged integrally with the lock plate, which required heavy machinery for the eighteenth century, and the lockplate itself is rounded and has an engraved border. The lock is stamped with an engraved crown with the initials "GR" beneath, identifying it as a British government purchase and at least nominally the property of King George, whose Latin name was Georgius Rex. After the lock was manufactured and inspected, it was stamped with a broad arrow and second crown to indicate that it fully met the specifications and had been accepted by the government. The hammer was designed with long sweeping curves and is far more ornate than would be required simply for functioning—it has been designed like a piece of metal sculpture, its spur rising like a post out of the gooseneck of the hammer. The cap and cap screw have also been designed with rounded contours.

The mainspring, shown in the upper illustration of Figure 3-1, was a powerful U-shaped spring with one end screwed fast to the lock-

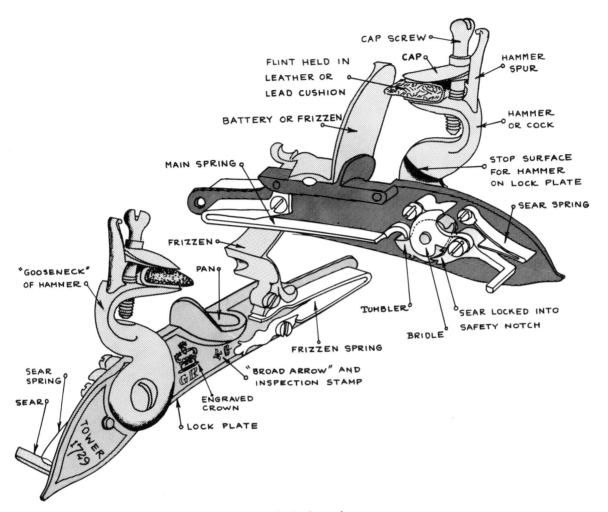

CAP SCREW

FLINT HELD IN
LEATHER OR
LEAD CUSHION

CAP

HAMMER
SPUR

BATTERY OR FRIZZEN

HAMMER
OR COCK

MAIN SPRING

STOP SURFACE
FOR HAMMER
ON LOCK PLATE

SEAR SPRING

FRIZZEN

"GOOSENECK"
OF HAMMER

PAN

TUMBLER

SEAR LOCKED INTO
SAFETY NOTCH

BRIDLE

FRIZZEN SPRING

SEAR
SPRING

"BROAD ARROW" AND
INSPECTION STAMP

SEAR

ENGRAVED
CROWN

LOCK PLATE

Figure 3-1   The lock mechanism of a Brown Bess flintlock musket.

plate. The free end had an arched hook, which contacted an extension on the tumbler. These springs were sufficiently powerful to exert a downward force on the tumbler of as much as 100 pounds. As the tumbler was driven counterclockwise by the mainspring, the hammer was carried forward and the flint gripped in the jaws struck the battery or frizzen. The excess energy of the hammer was absorbed by the hammer stop surface, which struck the upper surface of the lockplate at the end of the hammer motion.

The hammer is shown in a half cocked or safety position in both of the illustrations of Figure 3-1. The rotation of the tumbler was controlled by the sear, which pivoted upon a screw fastened through the bridle and into the lockplate. A sear spring rotated the sear clockwise, holding the searing surface firmly against the tumbler. In this illustration the sear is caught in a deep safety notch, which was used when loading or

when carrying a fully loaded flintlock. In this position no amount of force on the trigger could disengage the sear, making the flintlock relatively safe. In order to fire, the hammer was drawn back to a shallower notch, shown just under the bridle. As the trigger was pulled it lifted the right-angle tail on the sear, disengaging the sear from the tumbler and allowing the hammer to fall. As the hammer drove home, a piece of hard flint clamped in the hammer jaws and surrounded by a piece of leather or lead struck the upper surface of the frizzen, driving the frizzen forward and sending a weak shower of sparks downwards into the pan. These sparks ignited the small priming charge in the pan and as with earlier muskets flame passing through the small conical touchhole ignited the main charge in the chamber. The remainder of the flash was wasted and in fact posed a hazard to the shooter which prompted the addition of a small raised lip known as the "fence to the rear" behind the pan to deflect burning fragments of powder from the shooter's face.

The flintlock had such a relatively weak ignition system that if the hammer spring was weak, the flint dull or the powder damp too few sparks would be generated and the gun would misfire. If the small touchhole into the barrel was rusted the gun would misfire even though the powder in the pan ignited properly, a problem so annoying that it gave rise to the expression "a flash in the pan" signifying much smoke and fire but no real action. For reasonably reliable functioning, flintlocks had to be carefully adjusted and provided with good quality flint and fine, dry powder.

CIVILIAN FLINTLOCKS

Three views of a much more common quality of flintlock are shown in Figure 3-2. This lock is similar in overall design to that of the Brown Bess but of much cruder construction. The hammer and lock plate are flat with beveled edges, compared to the rounded contours of the Brown Bess lock, the surface finishes are nowhere near as smooth and the curves are not so carefully formed. The lock is shown in the fired position with the hammer down and the frizzen fully forward. The hammer stop surface can be seen resting on top of the lock plate in the middle illustration. The flint is shown held in a pad of leather, clamped hard between the cap and the hammer by the cap screw. The components required for a complete flintlock are shown in Figures 3-3 and 3-4. This lock is similar to that shown in Figure 3-2 but the design of the hammer and cap reflect developments of the late 18th century.

Any home craftsman can see that fabrication of these components with hand tools or even simple machine tools would be difficult and time consuming. The tools available in the American colonies during the 18th century were not very sophisticated—in fact, many machines for boring and rifling barrels and for turning metal components were still made of wood. Forging a lock plate with an integral pan, as shown in these illustrations, was an enormous job, as was drilling the holes in the lock plate and tapping the threads after the forging and machining were finished. Fabrication of such items as the frizzen and hammer required a tremendous amount of

hand forging and filing until these complex shapes were achieved. The lock contained three springs—for the hammer, frizzen, and sear—all three very tricky to manufacture. They had to be made of a high-carbon steel that was difficult to work. After forging rather carefully to rough shape they were then heat treated to a hard, relatively brittle condition by heating them red hot, then quenching them in oil or water. If in the heat treatment they became too hard they would be brittle and snap. If they became too soft they would tend to lose their spring temper. The hammer spring was particularly powerful—at full cock the curved end often pressed down on the tumbler with almost 100 pounds of force—increasing the difficulty of its manufacture.

When the Colonial blacksmith tempered his springs some came out as shown in the drawing, some came out with a wider angle at the bend and some with a smaller angle. Once a spring was tempered, it was difficult to change the angle, for it was brittle after heat treatment and tended to crack through the bend. At the same time if the gunsmith assembled these various angle springs to his lock mechanisms, the springs with a very tight angle at the bend would give very little force, resulting in a hammer that was easy to cock but would often misfire, whereas the springs with a wide open angle would make a hammer not only difficult to cock, but have a tendency to break flints rapidly and cause excessive damage to the frizzen.

There were two ways to solve the problem. One was to anneal the spring to a dead soft condition again, bend it to a slightly better angle and heat treat it again, hoping that the final angle would be more nearly correct. The other approach was to file the surfaces on the tumbler or move the location of the hammer spring screw so that the deflection was in the proper range for functioning.

The design of the ornate hammer is shown in Figure 3-4. This is basically a flat forging and on the better guns was formed into an artistically pleasing S shape with smooth flowing lines and carefully sculptured contours. The curves swirled around and flared out to form the lower jaw, which held the flint. Rising from the back of the S shape was the hammer spur, which served to guide the cap and also prevented the cap screw from bending out of shape under the heavy blows of the flint.

The cap is shown in the upper right-hand illus-

Figure 3-2   Three views of a flintlock mechanism.

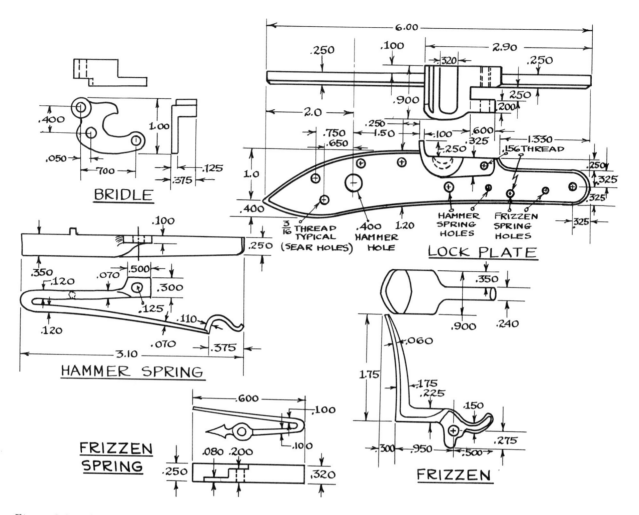

Figure 3-3 Flintlock components.

tration. There were two basic designs of cap. In the earlier design, shown in Figure 3-1, a small groove was cut in the face of the hammer spur inside of which rode a matching projection on the cap. The design shown in Figure 3-4 first appeared before 1750 and became increasingly common in the latter part of the eighteenth century. In this design a groove, cut into the cap, surrounded the hammer spur. The slot and the screw holding the cap in place aligned the axis of the cap with the axis of the hammer. The flint slid into an opening between cap and hammer and the cap screw was tightened down holding it firmly in place.

The sear and frizzen springs are shown in the lower left side of Figure 3-3. They were not as critical as the mainspring, but were tricky to make with the methods available in the eighteenth century. The sear design remained virtually unchanged for 200 years and is a typical design used in all side-lock mechanisms, appearing even on many breech-loading rifles.

The tiny tumbler, shown on the lower right of Figure 3-4, provided the transfer of powerful forces within the flintlock mechanism and had to be forged and machined most carefully. It can be seen in its proper position in the right side of Figure 3-1 slightly hidden behind the bridle.

The mainspring pushed down on the sloping surface forward of the pivot. On the lower surface a deep safety notch was cut, with a shallower firing notch to the rear. There was a .200-inch diameter pivot on the inboard side which passed through the bridle and positioned the inboard end of the tumbler. A shaft .400 inch in diameter passed through the lock plate, and flats were filed onto the outer end of the shaft so that the rotational torque developed by the mainspring could be transferred to the hammer, making it rotate and slam the flint into the frizzen. In addition the square-ended shaft had a hole drilled and tapped to hold the hammer screw. The tumbler was small but absolutely essential to the functioning of the flintlock mechanism.

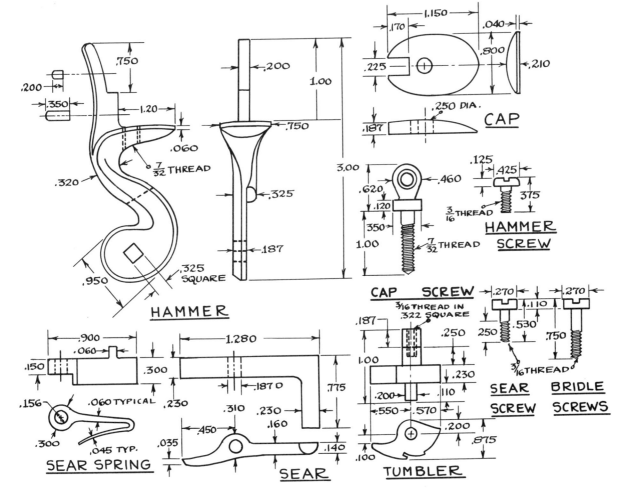

Figure 3-4 Flintlock components.

MILITARY FLINTLOCKS

The improvements offered by the flintlock were so important that by 1700 all of the leading nations of Europe had adopted it for military use. For the next 140 years—a time of turbulent expansion and competition—the flintlock remained the undisputed master of the battlefield and was carried to the four corners of the globe.

The seventeenth-century practice was to order a quantity of muskets from independent contractors with the design defined by general specifications. As the contractors incorporated many of their own ideas into the musket, there were wide variations in both appearance and performance. The French and British moved towards standardizing designs early in the eighteenth century. The French started manufacture of their standard model of 1717 at three royal armories. About the same time the British developed the ordnance system of manufacture for their new "Long Land Service Musket" affectionately known as "Brown Bess," which became the standard military weapon used in the American Colonies from the early 1700s until the Revolution. Under the ordnance system long-term contracts were issued to private firms that specialized in the manufacture of locks, barrels or "furniture," such as triggers, trigger guards, butt plates, ramrods and ramrod pipes. Some of the contracts extended over four or five years and involved more than 10,000 components. The barrels were tested by the government with a heavy charge of powder and then stamped with the broad arrow of government ownership and sent to the Tower of London for storage. Other components were as rigorously inspected and also stored in the Tower. In times of national emergency, the necessary components were withdrawn from storage and delivered to gunmakers in the London area who made the wooden stocks and assembled the finished muskets "lock, stock and barrel."

A typical Long Land Service Musket, shown in Figure 3-5, was fitted with a .75 caliber barrel

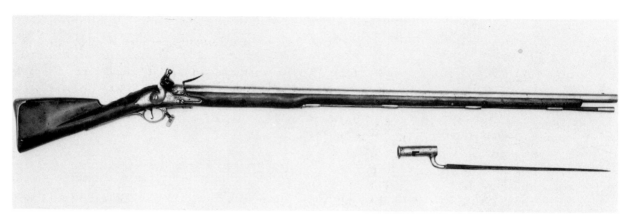

Figure 3-5 The Brown Bess musket.

about 46 inches in length. The stock was of walnut cut off four inches short of the muzzle to leave room for the bayonet. There were some variations in the design of the furniture, but most Brown Bess muskets were fitted with cast-brass butt plates which extended up along the heel of the stock giving good protection. A long cast-brass trigger guard was set into the underside of the stock, with a long tail extending down through the thin section of the grip. A brass medallion set into the upper section of the grip usually had the regimental and rack numbers engraved on it. The barrel was cross pinned to the stock and four cast-brass ramrod pipes were set into the underside of the stock, also held in place with cross pins. The channel cut into the underside of the stock held the wooden ramrod, which was fitted with a brass tip.

The British experimented with changes to improve the design. For example, the very early muskets had iron furniture. The change to brass started about 1725 but was not complete until nearly 1740. Steel ramrods were tried in 1724 and yet British troops during the American Revolution still had many muskets with wooden ramrods.

In the middle of the eighteenth century an improved Brown Bess musket with a 42-inch barrel was designed, known as the Short Land Service Musket. First adopted by the marines and some militia in 1756, it was standardized for the British service after 1768. Both short and long models were widely used during the Revolution.

Ammunition for the Brown Bess Musket

Though flintlocks were the standard infantry weapon they were also often employed as shotguns resulting in there being some four basic types of ammunition. The one normally associated with the musket was the widely used single round ball. For example, the standard cartridge for the Brown Bess contained a ball slightly under .700 inches in diameter which was listed as "14 to the pound." An enormous powder charge of 163 grains was contained in the paper cartridge of which about 10 grains was placed in the pan and the remainder poured down the barrel. The paper cartridge and bullet were wadded up together and rammed down the smoothbore barrel. Obviously a lead ball of slightly under .700 inches is a fairly loose fit in a barrel of .750 inches diameter. This difference was necessary because powder fouling built up rapidly near the breech of the firearm, reducing its diameter, and neither the bullets nor the barrels were perfectly round or uniform in dimensions. This added up to dreadful accuracy. A British officer, Colonel Hanger, writing in 1814 stated: "A soldier's musket, if not exceedingly ill-bored (as many are) will strike the figure of a man at 80 yards; it may even at 100 but a soldier must be very unfortunate indeed who shall be wounded by a common musket at 150 yards, providing his antagonist aims at him; and, as to firing at a man at 200 yards, with a common musket, you may just as well fire at the moon. No man was ever killed by a musket at 200 yards by the person who aimed at him."[1] Official tests with the Brown Bess showed that with the barrel held horizontally the musket ball struck the ground at distances varying from 116 to 218 yards. In a test at 200 yards the vertical spread of the musket balls was 9 feet 4 inches and the horizontal spread was so great that it could not be determined accurately.

[1]B. R. Lewis, *Small Arms and Ammunition in the United States Service*, Smithsonian Institution.

The poor accuracy of the flintlock musket led towards two obvious solutions. One was to utilize rifles which were more accurate, but also much slower to load. The other was to use different ammunition. The rifles were generally designed with smaller caliber barrels, lighter bullets, and higher muzzle velocities. It was essential that the lead bullets be a tight fit in the barrel in order that the rifling spin the bullet so as to provide accuracy. Unfortunately the rifle became difficult to load after only a few shots, due to the build up of black powder fouling on the inside of the barrel near the breech. This slowed up loading so severely that only about 10 percent of the troops were armed with rifles.

The second solution was to accept the poor accuracy of the military musket and develop tactics and ammunition which would minimize these difficulties. One answer was to develop the "buck and ball" load (the standard musket ball with four buckshot, generally about .30 inches in diameter). This was normally loaded with the same powder charge as the ball, but sent five projectiles toward the enemy. The recoil must have been savage, for the recoil of the standard single-ball cartridge was itself relatively heavy and this cartridge added an additional four buckshot to the ejected mass. As a result, soldiers often quietly dumped part of the powder charge on the ground before pouring the remainder into the barrel of the musket. The authorities didn't like this, but there wasn't much they could do about it, particularly in the heat of battle.

A third style of ammunition was composed entirely of buckshot. Normal American, British, and French cartridges were loaded with 12 buckshot, thus sending a shotgun pattern in the direction of the enemy. Buckshot loads were particularly useful in close engagements, where heavy smoke obscured targets. Buckshot was also useful for guard duty and night patrols. The fourth style of cartridge was the blank, used for training and ceremonial purposes. Surprisingly two of the three standard service cartridges were designed to use the flintlock musket more as a shotgun than as a point fire weapon.

FRENCH MUSKETS

When the design of the flintlock musket was standardized in France in 1717, their manufacture was concentrated at three royal armories—Charleville, Maubeuge, and St. Etienne. The French, with a .690 inch bore selected a slightly smaller caliber than did the British. This allowed French muskets to be of a slimmer profile than the Brown Bess, and to fire a lighter bullet at a higher velocity. The French continued experimentation with their flintlock designs, incorporating new models much more frequently than the British. By 1728 the French started fastening the barrel to the stock with iron bands, which made the stock stronger without increasing weight. Other improvements followed, and by 1763 France had what many considered the best musket of the period in the world.

An important support that the French gave to the American colonists was the sale or gift of over 100,000 muskets, most of which were the Model 1763 design. The Americans found these muskets so satisfactory that their muskets for the next 60 years closely followed the same pattern. The French Model 1763 Charleville musket is shown in Figure 3-6. Its weight, with bayonet, was only 9¾ pounds. Its barrel was 44¾ inches long, and its black walnut stock was approximately 57 inches long. Its total length was just under 60 inches. The Charleville musket fired a light ball, for its time; a typical cartridge of the Rev-

Figure 3-6   The French Model 1763 Charleville flintlock musket.

24

olutionary period contained a .627-inch diameter lead ball weighing 370 grains. Standard French cartridges contained a powder charge of 189 grains—which can only be considered enormous. The charge was so divided that about 10 grains went in the pan, with the remainder in the barrel. Even with the poor quality powders of the Revolutionary period, this charge gave a muzzle velocity of approximately 1400 feet per second and slightly over 1600 foot-pounds of muzzle energy.

There are, furthermore, a number of differences between French and British muskets. Obvious is the use of the iron-barrel bands to hold barrel and stock together on the French musket; also obvious is the smaller caliber of the French .690 compared to .750 of the "Brown Bess." The French musket was also fitted with an iron ramrod and the hammer was designed with a reinforcing loop up to the jaw. This was known as a "double-necked" design as compared with the "goose-neck" hammer of the Brown Bess.

AMERICAN FLINTLOCK MUSKETS

The Americans found the French flintlock musket so satisfactory that their first standard design of 1795 was copied directly from that of the 1763 French design. The appearance was very much like Figure 3-6. By the early 19th century, manufacturing techniques had improved so that the barrels and bullets were manufactured to more accurate dimensions. The typical American bullet was .640 inches in diameter weighing about 400 grains. The better fit between bullet and barrel allowed less gas leakage, which increased both muzzle velocity and the recoil. The American troops objected to the increase in recoil so strongly that the powder charge was cut to 167 grains. Even this smaller charge resulted in a muzzle velocity of about 1400 feet per second and a new musket had a muzzle energy of slightly over 1800 foot-pounds.

America has long been considered a "nation of riflemen" and much historical folklore relates the deadly accuracy of the Kentucky backwoodsman and Pennsylvania rifleman. The facts are that rifles were so slow to load that the great majority of American troops were armed with flintlock muskets. Americans often used their muskets as *shotguns* with the "buck and ball" and "buckshot" loads. There was one proposal during the American Revolution to make all future cartridges

buckshot loads, for the shotgun is an effective weapon in close combat.

During the early years of the nineteenth century the United States went through many difficulties in its transformation from agricultural colony to self-sufficient nation. Flintlock muskets, rifles and shotguns proved difficult to manufacture with the crude machinery available, and early models were not very satisfactory. As a result the American government put great emphasis on developing better manufacturing techniques for flintlock muskets centering its efforts at the national armories at Springfield, Massachusetts, and Harper's Ferry, Virginia. Improved flintlock musket designs were developed in 1808, 1812, 1816, 1824, and 1835. In addition to these basic models there were many minor design variations, and small production quantities of carbines, musketoons, and special light weight muskets for the West Point cadets were manufactured. Special rifle models were also made in small quantities.

The first standardized American flintlock musket, the Springfield U.S. Model 1795, was largely manufactured by hand on crude machine tools, but during the early nineteenth century, better equipment was developed. Water-powered machinery was designed for the heavy operations such as the forging of lockplates, and the manufacture of barrels, a particularly difficult process. The national armories developed an approach of using a long tapered sheet of iron which was heated red hot and then rolled up to form a cylinder. The two edges were hammered or "forge welded" shut over a long mandrel or "core pin" placed inside the barrel. The use of a water-powered hammer allowed much heavier forging blows and better welding of the barrel seam than was otherwise possible. After the entire 42-inch tube was welded shut, the inside was reamed to a straight smooth finish. By 1820 a water-powered grinding machine had been installed at Springfield Armory to grind the outside contour of the barrel concentric with the reamed bore.

Barrel manufacture was so difficult that anyone who could make a strong, safe, high-quality barrel was generally swamped with work. The Remington Arms Company was founded in 1816 by young Eliphalet Remington, who forged his own rifle barrel since he couldn't afford to buy one, although he had to carry the barrel ten miles to a gunsmith who had machinery to finish it. His high-quality workmanship attracted so much attention that he was sought out by neighbors. From this small beginning the Remington Company grew steadily, and by the time of the Civil War Remington and Colt were the two most important firearms manufacturers in the United States. One of the important reasons for Remington's growth was its willingness to accept new ideas and techniques. While Remington made a few flintlock firearms, the company quickly adopted the improved percussion ignition system and became a leading manufacturer of high-quality firearms.

FLINTLOCK FOWLERS

A typical flintlock shotgun used by the average shooter of Europe and the United States is shown in Figure 3-7. A good sturdy shotgun with no fancy frills or extra adornment, it is enormous, with a length of 5 feet 5¾ inches. The barrel is held to the full-length walnut stock by cross pins which pass through the stock and through small lugs welded to the barrel's bottom. (On more expensive firearms the stock and barrel were held together with flat keys, and escutcheons of brass or silver were set into the stock to reinforce the joint.) All of the furniture on this shotgun is plain. For example there is no forearm tip, and the ramrod is held into the stock with only two cylindrical ramrod pipes with no ornamentation. The pipes are also held to the stock with plain round pins. The trigger guard is a brass casting with a long tail extending to the rear along the bottom of the grip. The trigger guard is sturdy and rugged but is not perfectly curved and has a somewhat crude appearance.

The lock is a well-designed, medium quality flintlock similar in construction to the one shown in Figures 3-3 and 3-4. It is relatively large, and similar to those fitted to flintlock muskets. The hammer is of a gooseneck design with flat surfaces and beveled edges. The cap construction indicates that it is a late 18th-century or early 19th-century lock. The fence to rear of the pan is quite small.

The barrel of early firearms was the most-expensive component and this one must have caused the gunsmith many headaches. We think of 30-inch barrels on a modern shotgun as long; this one is a full 49¹³⁄₁₆ inches. It is octagonal at the breech for the first 11¾ inches, then tapers to a rounded section for the remainder of its length, a type of construction commonly used on flintlock shotguns. The barrel is .695 of an inch in inside diameter or slightly larger than 16 gauge.

Since shotgun barrels were so difficult to manufacture, it is interesting to explore the reasons for such excessive length. In the first place, the black powder available in the United States at the time was often of mediocre quality and a long barrel gave more time for the ingredients to churn and burn up. At the same time such a long barrel gave a great deal of friction contact between the shot column and the inside of the barrel, tending to deform the shot. These early guns had cylindrical barrels without choke and it is probable that most shooters chose such an extremely long barrel under the impression that it would give them higher velocity and tighter shot patterns. In actuality such excessive length made the gun unwieldy and poorly suited to wing shooting.

Double-Barreled Flintlock Shotguns

The highest development in flintlock designs was achieved in double-barreled shotguns—some imported—created for an aristocracy that controlled vast areas of land, had plenty of time and

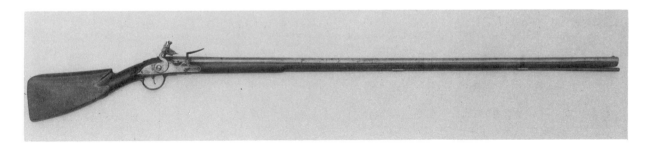

Figure 3-7 A flintlock shotgun.

enough money to enjoy their hobbies. Entertainment of friends was often carried out on a lavish scale, often with elaborate hunts. The shooters were supported by servants who loaded the shotguns and beaters who drove the game in their direction. Game was carefully managed on some of the large preserves so that the guests would have many opportunities for shooting. Bags of 100 birds per day were possible.

Hitting flying birds was extremely difficult with early firearms because of the appreciable time delay between pressing the trigger and the discharge of the shot and a shooter had to carefully track his flying bird, maintaining a proper lead during the long ignition delay. Because even a small improvement in the time lag would be of such great benefit to wing shooters there was tremendous competition among British and European gunsmiths to come up with better designs to gain aristocratic business. This intense competition led to superb firearms. At first small rollers were fitted to the frizzen spring so that the frizzen could snap open more quickly. Rollers were also fitted to the end of the mainspring to reduce the friction between spring and tumbler. During the early 19th century a small swinging stirrup

was interposed between the tumbler and mainspring, to further reduce the heavy force between these two parts.

Four British double-barreled shotguns were shown in Figure 3-8. The upper shotgun was manufactured by Manton of London between 1780 and 1800, with 34-inch Damascus barrels showing a beautiful, twisted pattern typical of these high grade barrels. Bores are approximately 28 gauge, and the overall length of the shotgun is 47½ inches. The locks, also manufactured by Manton, are fitted with rollers on the frizzen to reduce friction. One crucial problem in maintaining good ignition with flintlocks was the touchhole into the barrel. These holes normally had a conical taper with the larger diameter at the pan and the smaller at the chamber. The purpose, of course, was to concentrate the flash inwards. It was extremely important that the touchhole be of small diameter, for once the main charge ignited, gas pressure would drive a blast of flame out the touchhole all the time pressure remained in the barrel. However, since the touchhole had gas flow in both directions, it was prone to rusting and this caused serious misfires. The solution on very high quality firearms was to put a silver,

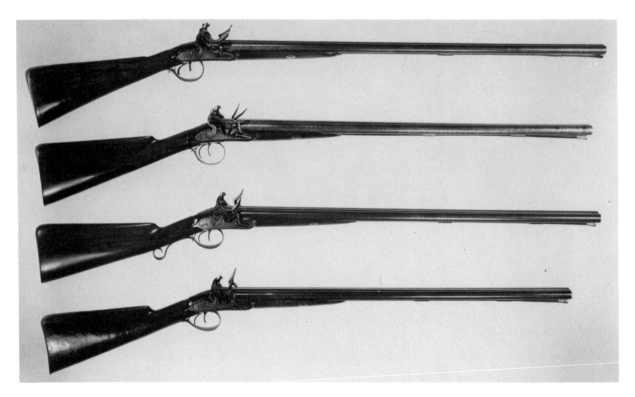

Figure 3-8 Four Manton double-barreled flintlock shotguns, spanning possibly half a century (c. 1780-1834), top to bottom.

gold or platinum bushing in the touchhole so that it could not corrode. On the uppermost shotgun in Figure 3-8, the right touchhole has been bushed with platinum, the left with gold.

The second shotgun from the top in Figure 3-8 was manufactured by Joseph Manton between 1806 and 1820. The 16-gauge barrels are 30½ inches long; the overall length of the shotgun is 47½ inches. The shotgun has been fitted with an elevated rib marked "Joseph Manton Patent." This design was patented in September 1806, clearly establishing the manufacture of this gun after that date. The shotgun is also fitted with a special breech plug to improve the ignition, which was covered by Manton's patent No. 1865 issued in 1792. The shotgun otherwise has an ornate trigger guard with a brass pineapple at the forward extension of the guard, has neat brass forearm tips and is extensively engraved. Rollers have been fitted to the frizzens and both touchholes are bushed with gold.

The third shotgun from the top in Figure 3-8 is also a Joseph Manton design, marked "Manton, London." It was manufactured between 1806 and 1812. The Damascus barrels are 31⅛ inches long and the overall length is 48 inches. The shotgun also has the elevating Manton-patented rib.

The bottom gun is a very late flintlock shotgun manufactured between 1832 and 1834. It is marked "John Manton & Son, Dover Street." John Manton took over from Joseph Manton about 1815. Research by Tom Hall, Curator of the Winchester Gun Museum, has established that this gun was made between 1832, when John Manton's son joined the firm, and 1834, when the elder John Manton died. This is an extremely late flintlock shotgun, for the percussion designs be-

gan to take favor about 1820. After 1825 comparatively few flintlock shotguns were made.

The Manton family was responsible for much of the superb reputation of British gunsmiths. The four shotguns illustrated all exhibit the highest quality of manufacture and the most careful refinement of features that were possible in the early 19th century.

Double-Barreled Flintlocks in America

Most double-barreled flintlock shotguns in America were imported from abroad, for generally by the time American gunsmiths became skilled enough to manufacture these sophisticated firearms the flintlock had been replaced by the percussion ignition system. A high quality flintlock imported into the United States in 1791 is shown in Figures 3-9 and 3-10. This is a beautifully designed and manufactured shotgun that weighs a mere 5¾ pounds even though fitted with 30-inch barrels. Its overall length is 45½ inches and it is fitted with a wooden ramrod .320 inches in diameter held in two ramrod pipes beneath the barrels. The ramrod, which then fits into a silver escutcheon that forms the forearm tip, is fitted with a worm at the rear end and is also threaded for an extension for cleaning. The barrels have an inside diameter of .516 inches (32 gauge) but have been worn to about .015 inches larger in diameter at the muzzle through use. The outside diameters of the barrel average .580 inches at the muzzle. The walls are extremely thin. The stock is made of walnut and is carefully checkered in the pistol grip area, the checkering worn smooth by a great deal of use.

Details of this shotgun are shown in Figure 3-10. A silver escutcheon plate has been set into

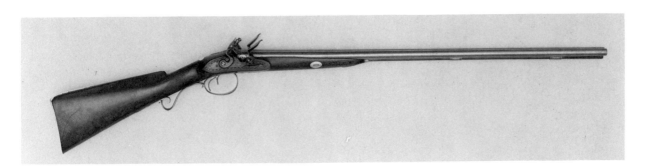

Figure 3-9 W. Allen double-barreled flintlock shotgun.

Figure 3-10 Closeup of the W. Allen flintlock.

the top of the grip just forward of the checkering. The lock plates are engraved with an ornamental border of leaves and a sunburst around the main screw just forward of the hammer. The right lock is marked "W. Allen," the left "New York." W. Allen was a gun dealer in New York City. The hammers are of a gooseneck design with carving and engraving on the surfaces. The pan construction on this shotgun is known as "rainproof," and was included on all the Manton shotguns shown in Figure 3-8. The idea was to form a small pan with a narrow sealing surface around the outside. The area immediately outside of this surface was cut away, so that in rainy weather, water striking the frizzen or the fence to the rear of the pan would not run into the pan, but would be deflected downwards around the outside of the sealing surface and drop to the ground.

Ignition of flintlocks became difficult in damp weather but the rainproof pans gave about the best protection that could be invented. The frizzens were an ornamental design and the frizzen spring is fitted with a roller so that the frizzen would snap quickly from closed to open thereby speeding up ignition. The breech plug at the rear of the barrel is heavily engraved with leaf patterns and the barrels have silver bands inlaid into the surfaces for ornamentation.

This gun was so elaborate that it even had a silver butt plate, silver trigger guard and silver furniture on the forearm. The trigger guard had a long extension to the rear to form a sort of pistol grip for the shooter. It also had an extension of about two inches to the front, which was heavily ornamented and engraved in a pineapple pattern. The forearm tip, another elaborately formed silver component, served as a ramrod guide and also had an ornamental pineapple detail inletted flush with the wood. The elaborate cross pin that held the barrels to the stocks is shown in Figure 3-9 and silver escutcheons were fitted around the cross pin where it passed through the wood.

This elegant shotgun was far beyond the financial reach of the average sportsman, but its wealthy American owner apparently had many years of excellent service from it before it ended up in the Winchester Gun Museum.

Over-Under Flintlock Firearms

Two unusual firearms are shown in Figure 3-11. These are over-under designs and represent an ingenious solution to frontier problems. Many of them were designed as combined shotguns and rifles, providing flexibility no matter what kind of game was encountered. Since the barrels were superposed, the ramrod guides were placed on the side and in each case there were two ramrod pipes as well as a ramrod retainer near the breech. Both firearms have the "Roman nose" butt stock typical of 18th-century design. Both have excessive drop to the stock, but this was not too important as they were heavy firearms and would have relatively little recoil. If a lightweight firearm were designed with this much drop its recoil would be such that it would have a tendency to rise rapidly as it was fired, and the stock would also rise and smack the shooter in the cheek.

However, on these firearms recoil was no problem because of their weight compared to the power of their loads. The upper flintlock for example weighs 11 pounds 6 ounces. The two barrels are 37½ inches long, and the overall length is 52½ inches. The upper smooth-bore barrel is .420 of an inch in diameter, the lower rifled barrel .460 of an inch.

This firearm really consisted of two halves. The rear half stopped immediately forward of the hammer, the front half (containing the two barrels) being a completely independent unit that rotated upon a shaft permanently fixed to the rear half of the gun. There are two barrels, two pans and two frizzens and frizzen spring assemblies. The pan for the upper barrel is shown in the open position. After the shot had been fired, the catch on the left hand side of the flintlock was released and the barrels were rotated 180° bringing the lower barrel on top. Note in the upper illustration that the frizzen on the lower barrel is in a closed position, where it would retain the priming charge in the pan. With the hammer cocked and the barrel rotated to the new position the shooter was ready for a fast second shot—an important consideration in the far frontier, for the hunter was probably in no shape to go through a fast reloading exercise after dragging 11 pounds 6 ounces around all day.

Both stocks have been given the tiger-flame design and both have a brass patch box in the butt to carry spare flints, grease patches and cleaning equipment. Both flintlocks have a flat beveled lock plate, and flat beveled hammers. The upper flintlock has all 18th-century features with a long tail on the lock plate and no roller on the frizzen spring. The lower flintlock has all 18th-century details on the lock except for the rounded rear to the lock plate.

The lower flintlock in Figure 3-11 has even longer barrels, at 38¼ inches, with an overall

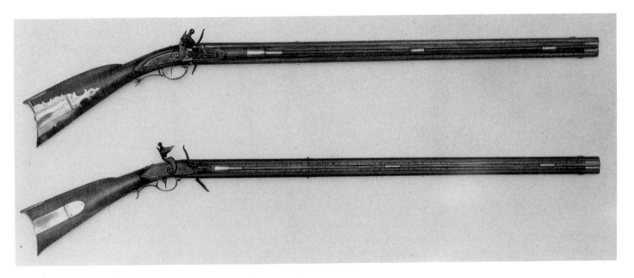

Figure 3-11   Two 18th-century over-under flintlock shotguns.

length of 53½ inches. Despite these longer barrels the gun weighs less, at only 7 pounds 5 ounces. The barrels are octagonal for their full length and again the ramrod is set in a strip of wood between the two barrels. This flintlock is shown ready for the second shot, the pan open on the lower barrel and the hammer in the cocked position, ready to fire the second barrel. The upper barrel has a .350-inch bore, and the lower barrel a .400-inch bore.

Over-under flintlock firearms are extremely rare. Most of the cost of an 18th century firearm was in the extraordinary amount of labor required to manufacture a barrel. These firearms required not only two barrels, but also careful joining operations and relatively difficult mechanical construction in the breech area where the barrels join the butt stock. Barrel diameters were limited to very small sizes in order to keep the weight within reasonable limits. Thus even as a shotgun these would be relatively ineffective firearms with bore diameters of less than ½ inch.

Chapter 4

THE DEVELOPMENT OF AMERICAN SINGLE- AND DOUBLE-BARRELED SHOTGUNS

During the 1830s and 1840s inventors began experimenting seriously with breechloading percussion firearms, often using loose powder and ball. During the Civil War these inventions were perfected, the highest development represented by the Sharps percussion rifles and carbines, which saw very wide and successful service in the War. It was in that war that the first really successful repeating rifle actions were developed and manufactured, especially the Spencer and Henry lever action mechanisms for metallic ammunition.

After the Civil War, American inventors and manufacturers focused primarily on adapting these repeating actions to the shotgun, but it was only after World War I that American ingenuity was brought to bear on the twin-tubed gun, as exemplified by the Browning, the Winchester Model 21 and the Remington Model 32. Nonetheless, our review of American-manufactured single and double-shot scatterguns begins in the early nineteenth century, for it was in this period that American manufacturers caught up with Europe, and by the end of the Civil War became world leaders in many aspects of firearm-manufacturing technology.

As we have seen, high costs and the relative lack of sophistication of American gunsmiths of the eighteenth and early nineteenth centuries tended to keep Americans out of the business of making fine side-by-side shotguns. Most such guns consequently were imported from abroad, primarily from England and Belgium, and American production was restricted more or less to handmade, custom-built firearms.

The early nineteenth century saw a great ferment in the industry, with a transition from flintlock to percussion, muzzle-loading firearms. Feelings ran high, with traditionalists holding firmly to the flintlocks and deriding percussion as a cheap and inferior substitute to such an extent that some American frontiersmen continued to use flintlocks long into the percussion era. The practical reason for this was that percussion caps were hard to get on the frontier, whereas a flintlock required only powder and ball.

Still, the advantages of percussion were strong and by the 1840s all first-line armies and most sportsmen had adopted it. These advantages included simplicity and lower cost and more reliable ignition in damp and rainy weather, when the flintlock was at a particular disadvantage.

THE PERCUSSION CAP

In the turbulent period between 1810 and 1825 many inventors were moving toward a true percussion cap. The credit for it is often given to an English painter named Joshua Shaw, who claimed to have invented it between 1814 and 1815. In his first experiments, he placed detonating powder in a heavy steel cup. The story goes that he idly placed one of these cups over the end of an ivory drawing pen and when this was accidentally knocked on the floor the cap exploded, shattering the ivory point. This suggested to him the idea of using it as a gun ignition system. He then performed other experiments, first with pewter cups, and claimed to have developed the copper percussion cap in late 1814 or early 1815. Shaw made no effort to secure a patent in England, however, and emigrated to the United States in 1817. At that time American patent law stated that an alien could not secure a patent until he had resided in the United States for two years. There is some evidence that Shaw actually did secure a patent in June 1822. Documentation of these early patent records is not complete, however, and this may be due to Shaw's negligence in supplying working drawings and models to fully support his claims.

The earliest recorded patent showing a percussion cap and nipple is by a Frenchman named Prelat issued in 1818. This is not definitive, for French patent law permitted citizens to patent foreign ideas even if they had nothing to do with the invention. Prelat was a gun dealer in France who regularly imported firearms from abroad. He scoured these for new ideas and applied for French patents on ideas he felt worthy of protection in France.

In Britain, leading gunsmiths such as Joseph Manton tried to cover all the bases. Manton had patented, and was pushing, his tube lock design, but at the same time was aware that the percussion cap might well be cheaper and more convenient. So when approached by the leading British writer on sport shooting, Colonel Hawker, with some ideas for a percussion cap ignition shotgun, Manton allowed himself to be persuaded that this might be worth investigation. Colonel Hawker was delighted when Manton developed a rough design within a few weeks based on his sketches. Manton thereby secured support in the public press through Colonel Hawker and had a second line of products to offer his aristocratic clientele. He freely gave credit to Colonel Hawker for suggesting the idea, and Hawker in turn did not claim that he was the original inventor—he only claimed to have invented the system independently of anyone else. The percussion cap was such a logical development that it probably was developed simultaneously in many places. Americans, British, French and others could all—with justification—claim their champion as having created this excellent approach to the ignition problem.

The construction of a typical percussion cap is shown in Figure 4-1. It consisted of a small cup of copper with a flanged rim. The detonating powder was placed in the end of the cup and was usually retained by a paper disk and shellac. The priming was well protected from rough handling and the shellac prevented damage from damp weather.

The small cap was far easier to handle than a loose pill of detonating powder and was so cheap that it was discarded after a single use.

The gun mechanism was thereby greatly simplified. All that was required was a heavy boss welded to the side of the barrel with a horizontal touchhole. A vertical hole was drilled and tapped to hold a removable nipple. The nipples were normally designed with a double conical hole that would tend to concentrate the flame so that it would easily blast into the main charge in the barrel causing rapid ignition. The restriction at the lower end of the hole limited the back pressure from the barrel, and the hammer and cap closed off the top of the nipple, so that gas leakage was much less than with flintlock firearms.

There were of course problems with these early percussion designs. Many manufacturers made their caps of too thin material and serious eye injuries resulted. Even well-designed caps often split upon firing sending loose pieces of copper flying around. With proper design, however, the cap expanded so that it fell off the nipple when the hammer was recocked, allowing for very fast reloading.

Still, as with any drastic change, there was much dispute about its merits. By 1825 arguments in the press had reached vitriolic proportions and all sorts of nonsense was claimed for the two systems. Traditionalists stated that the percussion was too violent, tending to shake the guns to pieces. Some even claimed that the new development was a plot on the part of the manufacturers to wear guns out more quickly and thereby increase their business. Other experienced shooters claimed that the softer ignition of the flintlock led to less pellet deformation and better long-range accuracy, although they conceded that percussion, with its quicker ignition, was superior for wing shooting. Some of these arguments had excellent basis in fact. For example, if a flintlock and a percussion shotgun were loaded with exactly the same charge the percussion would shoot at a higher velocity and would kick more, simply because there was less leakage at the breech. Since the shooter had no way of measuring the velocity, he often came to the conclusion that percussion was a more violent and uncomfortable load to shoot.

In addition, many old timers had spent years learning to wing shoot properly with the flintlock shotgun. They had learned how to fit the flints carefully, adjust the mechanism, place the powder

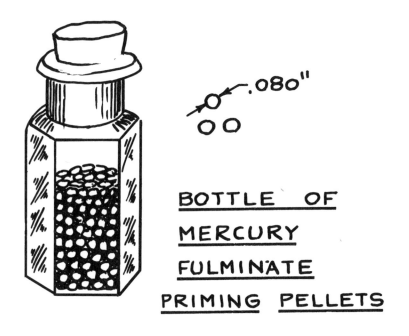

.080"

OO

BOTTLE OF
MERCURY
FULMINATE
PRIMING PELLETS

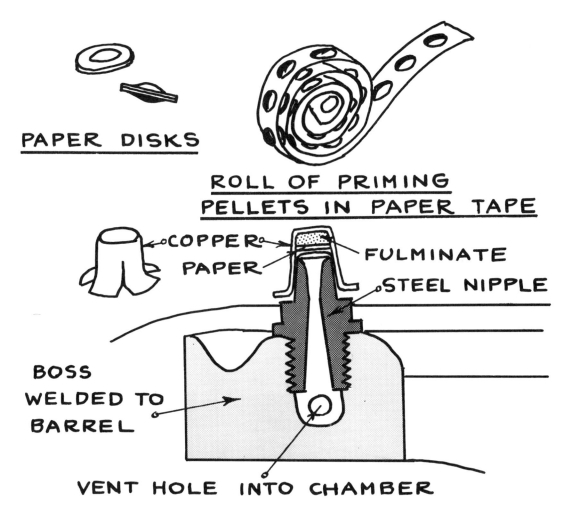

PAPER DISKS

ROLL OF PRIMING
PELLETS IN PAPER TAPE

COPPER
PAPER
FULMINATE
STEEL NIPPLE

BOSS
WELDED TO
BARREL

VENT HOLE INTO CHAMBER

Figure 4-1 Percussion ignition systems.

34

and priming charges properly, and then follow through smoothly and steadily during the long ignition delay of the flintlock mechanism. What they really objected to was that newer and younger shooters could skip the arduous years of work and become good wing shooters more quickly with percussion shotguns.

DOUBLE-BARRELED PERCUSSION SHOTGUNS

The breech detail of a high-quality percussion shotgun is shown in Figure 4-2. This graceful shotgun, manufactured by W. & C. Scott & Son of London, was of a type imported into the United States for wealthy American shooters who wanted the best money could buy. This particular one has an overall length of 48¼ inches and weighs only 7½ pounds. The barrels are 32¼ inches long and

are bored out to 10 gauge. The left barrel actually measures .780 inches in diameter and the right barrel .784. The beautifully finished walnut stock is 25¼ inches long and is carefully checkered at the grip and forearm. The locks are extensively engraved and are marked "W. & C. Scott & Son." The elevated rib between the barrels is marked "W. & C. Scott & Son, Dorset Place, Pall Mall, London." The barrels are also marked "Laminated Steel."

Comparison of this breech detail with the high-quality flintlock shown in the previous chapter underscores the simplification of the percussion system. Safety details on this shotgun have been carefully thought out. A fence to the rear of the nipple provides a shield against flying copper fragments. The face of the hammers are recessed so that a rim of steel surrounds the percussion cap at the time of ignition and the lower rim of the ham-

Figure 4-2   Closeup of breech of W. & C. Scott double-barreled percussion shotgun.

mer is below the shield. By this construction, copper fragments could only fly forward and, at a slight angle, to one side. Another safety feature is the blow-out plug—a platinum plug seen as a light colored disk just forward of the shield. This plug would blow out and relieve pressure in case the shotgun was badly overloaded, which could easily happen with a muzzle-loading double-barreled shotgun. For example, in the excitement of the hunt a shooter might throw both powder charges into one barrel and ram the shot on top of the double charge. Such a mistake could lead to a serious accident but the blow-out plug was the safety valve intended to prevent a catastrophe.

The shotgun shown was fitted with a wooden ramrod that tapered from ½ inch diameter at one end to ⅜ inch at the other. A flared brass end was fitted at one end to ram the charges and a brass ferrule with a worm screw was fitted to the other end. The lock work on this shotgun shows extraordinary attention to detail. Upon first examination it appeared that some of the internal parts were broken. In fact the stirrup and tumbler and other internal parts were machined to interlock like a jigsaw puzzle, eliminating extra pins and screws.

A medium-quality English double-barreled shotgun is shown in Figures 4-3 and 4-4. This type of shotgun was imported into the United States for sportsmen who wanted a solid, reliable gun but were unwilling to pay for a great deal of ornamentation. This was manufactured by a company known as "Onion & Wheelock" and is so marked upon the lock. The shotgun is bored to 12 gauge; the measured diameter of its left barrel is .721 of an inch, the right barrel .725 of an inch. The barrels are 29¾ inches long and the rib is marked "Fine Damascus London Double Proof." These markings reflect that high-quality barrels were the key to a successful shotgun. The Damascus technique particularly required tremendous labor to

form the rods, twist them, heat them and then forge weld the rod in a spiral pattern into a tube. After the forge welding was completed the barrels had to be reamed on the inside and machined on the outside to the slender, thin-walled contours required to hold the weight of the shotgun below seven pounds. The statement "Double Proof" emphasized to the buyer that the barrels had been proven through the standard English proof-house procedure and were fully strong and reliable.

The shotgun shown was also fitted with a one-piece walnut stock, but with coarser checkering on the grip area and no checkering on the forearm. The trigger guard extension was designed to provide a semi-pistol grip for the shooter's hand. A small ornate patch box was set into the right side of the stock—designed to hold enough percussion caps for a day's shooting. Two small silver inserts were set into the bottom of the stock, but both trigger guard and forearm cap were steel, with very modest engraving.

A high-quality native American shotgun is shown in Figure 4-5. This is a Remington double barrel manufactured from 1840 until about 1880. This particular example was manufactured about 1848, and now resides in the Remington Museum at Ilion, New York. This was a deluxe shotgun, made on special order to a customer's specifications. It could be ordered as a combination rifle-shotgun, as was this example. One barrel is a smooth bore 32-gauge shotgun barrel, the other a rifled .45 caliber barrel. The combination explains the addition of front and tang peep sights. The metalwork on the gun has been designed with care and contains ornamental details on trigger guard and patch box. Overall the design is suited to American hunting needs with its strong, solid and simple construction, omitting the ornate engraving of such a high-quality British shotgun as the W. & C. Scott design.

Figure 4-3 Onion & Wheelock double-barreled percussion shotgun.

Figure 4-4   Closeup of breech of Onion & Wheelock shotgun.

Figure 4-5   Remington double-barreled shotgun-rifle (c. 1848).

A significant feature shown in Figure 4-5 was a new type of lock known as the "back-action" or "back" lock. Notice that the hammer is closer to the front of the lock plate when compared to the locks previously illustrated. This represented a significant improvement in design, moving the mainspring from the front of the lock to the rear, and moving away the delicate lock mechanism from the area where all the dirt, flash and flame occurred.

Details of this lock compared with a traditional lock are shown in Figure 4-6. If these two designs are compared with the lock from the Brown Bess flintlock, the improvements over a 200-year span can be readily visualized. The Brown Bess flintlock mechanism had two sub-systems. One, involving pan, battery, battery spring and pivots, kept the powder in the pan dry and covered until the shot was fired—and then the pan was snapped open by the flint striking the battery and sending

a shower of sparks down into the pan. The second sub-system included the springs, pivots and sears that provided power to the hammer, which had a movable jaw in order to clamp the flint (which had to be replaced every 15 or 20 shots). The hammer also had surfaces designed to absorb the excess energy delivered by the mainspring for, as the flint and battery could not be counted on to absorb all the hammer spring energy, there was a stopping surface forged onto the hammer and a matching flat surface on the lock plate to absorb the blow.

The mainspring, which pushed down directly on the tumbler, causing tumbler and hammer to rotate, was extremely powerful, pushing downward with close to 100 pounds of force. Consequently, the contact between spring and tumbler was a source of friction and wear.

By the 1850s, American percussion locks had evolved into the design shown in the left side of

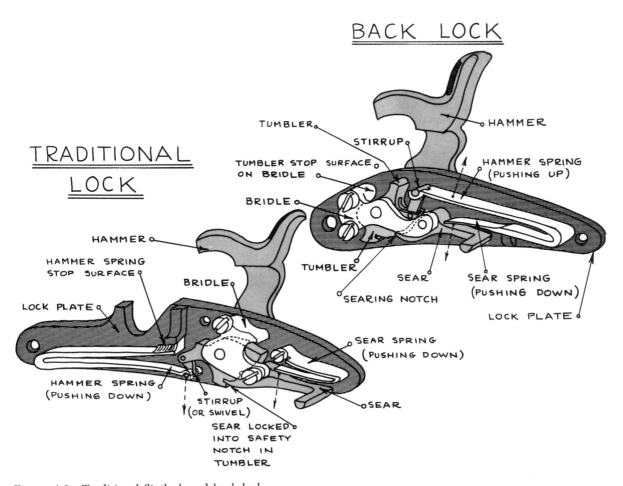

Figure 4-6 Traditional flintlock and back lock.

38

Figure 4-6. The entire mechanism comprising the pan, battery, battery spring and pivots had been eliminated by the substitution of the much simpler percussion ignition system, nonetheless the arrangement of mainspring and hammer mechanism was similar to that of Brown Bess 150 years earlier. The one major area of improvement was the elimination of the heavy bearing contact between mainspring and tumbler. The hammer spring was reduced to 65 to 75 pounds of force, which was transmitted to the tumbler through a little intermediate link known as the stirrup or swivel. The hammer spring had a slot cut in the middle of the end with two hookshaped fingers machined on each side of it. These slipped over a cross bar in the little stirrup which, in turn, could swing freely on a cross shaft in the tumbler. This eliminated the heavy bearing contact between spring and tumbler and substituted a much lower friction of rotating shafts.

The hammer components of the mechanism were held in position by a bridle, which was firmly fixed to the lock plate by two screws. With a properly functioning arm all the hammer energy was absorbed by the percussion cap and cone. If the lock was removed from the rifle or the cone broken off, then a flat surface on the tumbler moved upward as the hammer rotated and slammed into fixed surface at top of bridle. The sear was held in its proper position by the sear spring, small and delicate compared with the hammer spring which provided a limited downward force rotating the sear clockwise and holding it in proper engagement in the notches cut into the tumbler.

The design of a "back lock" is shown in the right side of Figure 4-6. Here the percussion mechanism is reduced to its simplest terms. Whereas the lock from the Brown Bess flintlock had three separate springs, the back-lock percussion mechanism generally had only one. The hammer spring, mounted at the back of the lock plate, pulled upward rather than pushing down. The tumbler was redesigned and the stirrup relocated so that this upward force still provided a powerful movement, tending to rotate the hammer counterclockwise. A small triangular stop surface, forged into the lower part of the lock plate, took the reaction of the hammer spring and then a thin section of hammer spring was extended forward to serve as the sear spring, pushing downward and holding the sear in proper engagement with the tumbler. This drawing shows

the hammer seared up on the firing notch, which is considerably shallower than the safety notch immediately forward.

The back-action lock represented the final design improvement in the percussion era. It was lighter in weight and cheaper to manufacture than the older type of locks and the whole mechanism was moved rearwards in the stock so that there was less chance of dirt and debris working their way into the lock mechanism. These locks proved so satisfactory that their use has continued to the present day and some "hammerless shotguns" have mechanisms very similar to them, but with a small internal hammer that is hidden from view.

During the second half of the nineteenth century many famous companies were started to manufacture breech-loading firearms. The Parker Brothers of Meriden, Connecticut, began about 1865. Their first shotguns were hammer-style, breech-style, with an underlever to control the action. Their first hammerless double-barreled shotgun was manufactured in 1889. The Ithaca Gun Company, founded in 1873, first manufactured double-barreled, hammer-style shotguns in 1880. Over the years the Ithaca Gun Company absorbed the Union Firearms Company, the Lefever Arms Company, and others. The first Winchester repeating rifle was manufactured in 1866, and shotguns were first marketed in 1880. The Iver Johnson Arms and Cycle Works was founded in 1871. In the 1890s they began producing single- and double-barreled shotguns. The Harrington and Richardson Arms Company was founded in 1888 to manufacture hammerless double-barreled shotguns of high quality. The A. H. Fox Gun Company was started in the early 1880s to manufacture double-barreled shotguns. The Stevens Firearms Company of Chickopee Falls, Massachusetts, manufactured a double-barreled hammer-style shotgun as early as 1876.

The Spencer Arms Company, like Winchester, was founded to manufacture lever-action repeating rifles. Starting in 1862 Spencer manufactured over 100,000 lever-action carbines and rifles, the most successful repeaters used in the Civil War. During the 1880s Spencer manufactured the first successful slide-action shotgun. Both of Spencer's designs were milestones in the development of American firearms.

During the late nineteenth century the finest shotguns in the world were manufactured abroad, the finest generally coming from Britain. The British were experimenting with hammerless break-open, double-barreled shotguns in the 1860s. By 1874 Anson and Deeley, two workmen in the Westley Richards Factory, invented the "box lock" hammerless action for double-barreled shotguns, which is still the basic action manufactured today in many factories throughout the world. Other British makers, such as W. W. Greener, continued the development of the "side-lock" action, an older approach in which the lock mechanisms are contained in separate side plates. By the end of the century Westley Richards had developed light-weight perfectly balanced double-barreled shotguns with detachable locks which were of such superb quality that the design has remained unchanged for three quarters of a century. Guns with the detachable locks were manufactured both as shotguns and double-barreled rifles. Experienced hunters of dangerous game consider that these double-barreled rifles are the best firearms to use when hundreds of miles from civilization. The gun can be chambered for extremely heavy cartridges and gives two reliable shots under even the most difficult circumstances. The Westley Richards guns with detachable locks can be disassembled by merely removing the forearm, swinging open the barrels and removing them and then uncovering a small trap door which allows the locks to be removed from the bottom of the action. The locks may be examined, cleaned, and reassembled in a few minutes and the gun is ready for more hunting.

The traditional late-nineteenth-century English shotguns were generally of 12-gauge bore, chambered for 2½ inch long black powder shells loaded with 1 to 1⅛ ounces of shot. It was common practice when shooting grouse, for example, to have beaters drive the game in the direction of the hunters, so the need was for light, beautifully balanced shotguns which could follow the fast, darting birds. Extreme range was not required. Guns of 6½ to 7½ pounds weight were generally found most satisfactory. Continental shooters favored even lighter shotguns of 16 gauge weighing 6 to 7 pounds. Here again, the emphasis was on handling qualities and balance rather than extreme power and range.

During the 1870s trap shooting became popular in England and on the continent. Extremely agile, fast flying blue rock pigeons were selected for the sport. On the better ranges five metal traps were set up. These were usually tent shaped boxes with spring loaded sides. The gunner stood fifteen or twenty yards from the traps and on signal the trap boy would open one of the five traps. The shooter never knew which trap would be opened nor the direction the bird would fly. Generally the traps were designed with three solid sides and one side facing away from the shooter with holes in it. This orientation encouraged the bird to face the light and when the trap was released fly away from the shooter. Whether he flew close to the ground and straight or zig-zagged in a diagonal path was entirely up to chance. Americans who tried the sport were amazed at the difficulty in hitting those fast moving elusive targets. To score a kill the trap shooter had to drop the bird within a fenced area around the traps. Scores of 80 out of 100 birds were considered excellent.

Shotgunning in the United States was a different sport. While there were a few gun clubs for wealthy American sportsmen who set up trap-shooting ranges, the sport did not last long with live birds. The American birds tended to be slower and more predictable in flight and scores of over 90 out of 100 were not uncommon. By 1882 birds suitable for trap shooting were in such short supply in the United States that many matches were cancelled. During the 1880s Americans shifted over, first to glass balls, then to clay birds. Live bird shooting in England remained active until the First World War.

The main interest of Americans was hunting birds to put food on the table. There was little call for extra fancy Damascus-barreled shotguns with elaborate engraving and hand-checkered stocks. The average American hunter wanted a shotgun that was reliable, and had *plenty* of power and range. Until well after the Civil War most American shotguns were simply adaptations of rifle designs. The Sharps lever action and Remington rolling-block shotguns for example, were simple conversions of the rifle designs with smooth-bore barrels. Muzzle-loading shotguns tended to have long, light-weight smooth-bore barrels which gave good range but were rather unwieldy for wing shooting. As most American hunters saw nothing wrong with shooting birds resting on the water enormous punt guns were designed to kill large quantities of birds resting together in flocks. Generally the punt guns were single-barreled muzzle-loading shotguns which were fired from a boat. They weighed from 20 up to 100 pounds. Some of the smaller ones were loaded with three or four ounces of shot but one enormous punt gun is known to have been loaded with 2½ pounds of

40

shot. So-called market gunners would use these cannons from a very low boat, which would be camouflaged with branches and leaves. The gunner quietly sculled his boat to within range of a raft of ducks and then cut loose with his punt gun when he was within 40 or 50 yards and it was not unusual to kill 25 to 50 ducks with a single blast. Market gunners, who provided food for many of the leading hotels in the big cities, generally packed their game in barrels with layers of ice between each layer of ducks. It was not until late in the century that conservation pressure and dwindling supplies of game put an end to this practice.

SINGLE-SHOT SHOTGUNS

During the muzzle-loading period almost all American shotguns were single-barreled, single-shot models. There were a few double-barreled and over-under shotguns, but they were rare and expensive.

Most Americans simply could not afford the elegant refinement of a double-barreled shotgun and had to make do with much simpler ones, such as those shown in Figures 4-7 and 4-8. This simple and sturdy single-barreled percussion shotgun does not even have a maker's name. It is about 16-gauge with a bore diameter of .665 of an inch and a weight of just over 6½ pounds. The overall length is 52½ inches and the barrel is 36¼ inches long. The barrel was not made by the Damascus process but was probably rolled up from a plate of iron and forge welded along one seam. Typically American practice was to make the rear section of the barrel octagonal for a short distance forward of the breech and then have a transition section into a round barrel about a foot from the breech. There is a double-banded ornamental de-

tail at the transition between octagonal and round sections.

This is a moderate-quality single-barreled shotgun with checkering at the grip and a small silver medallion set into the upper section just to the rear of the tang. Brass escutcheons, fitted around the cross keys, locked the barrel to the full-length walnut stock. The ramrod was retained by two ornamental brass ferrules and a third brass pipe was fitted where the ramrod entered the stock. The trigger guard and butt plates were carefully ornamented brass castings showing careful attention to detail, but of nowhere near such high quality as the W. & C. Scott shotgun shown in Figure 4-2. The lock mechanism is a back-lock design, simple and sturdy with no frills. It was held to the gun mechanism with a cross bolt through the left side of the gun and a simple wood screw holding the tail of the lock to the wooden stock. The hammer is held to the tumbler shaft with a large nut—rugged if not very elegant.

While many Americans on the frontier in the early nineteenth century dreamed of an over-under rifle-shotgun combination with rotating barrels, or an all out double-barreled shotgun, the great majority settled for this sort of simple, low-cost single-barreled shotgun.

Remington manufactured a basic muzzle-loading percussion shotgun from 1840 to 1880. The price in 1877 was $8.00, complete. The shotgun was fitted with a butt stock and forearm both attached to a steel receiver which held the hammer and trigger mechanism and into the upper section of which the barrel was solidly screwed. The shotgun had a long ramrod which was retained in the forearm and by three ramrod pipes. It was only in the latter part of the nineteenth century when improved techniques lowered manufacturing costs that the average American shooter could afford to

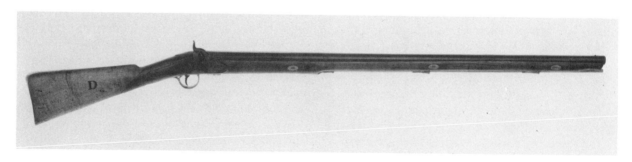

Figure 4-7 American single-shot shotgun.

Figure 4-8 Closeup of breech of American single-shot shotgun.

purchase a double-barreled or repeating shotgun. When this trend became a flood tide in the late nineteenth century the single shot, single-barreled shotgun then became the economy model mostly used by beginning shooters or those with limited budgets.

EARLY BREECHLOADING SHOTGUNS

The idea of breechloading firearms dates back to the fifteenth century when skilled craftsmen, working with the crude tools and soft iron of the Renaissance, designed and laboriously constructed breechloading pistols, muskets and cannon. Some of these early cannon were designed with a barrel rigidly clamped to a wooden carriage. A separate breech section fashioned like a cup provided sufficient space for the powder charge and ball. Usually a conical seal was used between the breech and the barrel. After loading, the chamber was dropped into the carriage and slid into position behind breech and carriage to hold the breech solidly in position as the shot was fired. Since wood is a compressible material the gas leakage at the breech was spectacular unless very light charges were used. With the weak powder of the time the cannoneer needed all the power he could get to extend the range of his cannon, and the breechloading designs never became very popular.

Even though breechloading weapons were of limited use in war, for sport the aristocrats of Europe desired rapid-firing guns in case they missed their first shot. Craftsmen responded with ingenious designs including some breechloading flintlock firearms with separate magazines for round ball and black powder. In some designs both magazines were in the butt stock, in others the powder was stored in the butt stock and the balls in a magazine tube beneath the barrel. A rotating breech was used with a long handle which was cranked around first to pick up a powder charge from the butt stock, then rotated to line up with the magazine full of balls. After a ball had dropped in on top of the powder charge the lever was rotated to its original position, where the chamber lined up with the barrel. Some of these designs even went so far as to have an automatic mechanism to prime the pan. Such firearms were extraordinarily expensive, for they were intricate and required close tolerances for success. Obviously if the gap between barrel and breech was large the flame could escape around the breech and if it reached the powder magazine in the butt

stock the gunsmith was likely to lose a highly valued customer.

The most successful breechloading firearms using loose powder and ball were the Colt revolvers, rifles and shotguns, manufactured between 1838 and 1872, and the Sharps breechloading single-shot rifles manufactured from 1851 through 1865. Both of these designs were successful because of the accumulated skill and knowledge of the inventors and the precision machinery and hardened steels available by the mid-nineteenth century.

The true solution to the breechloading problem, however, lay in another direction. The most basic need was for some kind of flexible container for the powder and shot which could easily be placed in the chamber of the firearm, but which would expand under gas pressure to form a really tight seal—like the cork in a bottle—at the instant of firing. It was also important that this case be designed of a resilient material that would shrink to a smaller size after firing and thereby be removed easily from the chamber. These are not easy conditions to meet. Many of the early designs met the first two, but the cartridge cases would expand against the chamber walls and lock in place under firing. This was particularly true if the chamber walls were rough or dirty or had insufficient taper. Experimenters gradually found that brass and copper were excellent metals for use in cartridge cases. Surprisingly, they also found that if paper were coated with glue and rolled up into a many layered tube, it would also perform in the proper manner. Gradually from many inventors came the general adoption of a rolled paper tube with a metal head crimped over a metal or fiber base wad. Experience showed that even though the paper tube was cylindrical, it was essential that the chamber be tapered so that once the shell broke free the case could be withdrawn. Another essential point was that a seal at the *case mouth* was the secret to success. If the gas was blocked by a flexible case mouth, the chamber would remain relatively clean and the gun could be refired many times without cleaning. If the seal was at the base end of the shell, carbon residue built up rapidly in the chamber making loading and extraction increasingly difficult.

The toughest problem of all was how to provide ignition within this tough resilient package of powder, wads and shot. After hundreds of approaches were tried, the first really successful design was the pinfire cartridge developed by two Frenchmen, Robert and Lefacheaux, in the early

1830s. A schematic drawing of a pin fire shotshell as manufactured in the 1840s is shown in Figure 4-9. The idea was rather ingenious. A rolled and glued tube was used to hold the powder charge, wads and shot. A fiber base wad, developed by another French inventor, Houllier, was pressed into the paper tube, and a brass head reinforcement was formed and crimped to hold them together. Then a hole was drilled through the side of the brass reinforcement, rolled paper tube and base wad. A small percussion cap with a priming charge was slid in from the mouth end of the cartridge and positioned beneath the hole. The tight-fitting firing pin, usually of about .090 inches in diameter, was pressed down through the hole and into the mouth of the percussion cap to hold it in place. Then a charge of black powder, generally of about 60 grains, was measured and poured into the shotshell surrounding the firing pin and percussion cap. Very tight-fitting fiber wads were pressed into the mouth of the case and down on top of the powder charge leaving no air space (100% loading density). The next step was to measure the shot charge, pour it in the case and retain the shot with a top wad.

The two French 20-gauge pinfire cartridges shown in Figure 4-10 are the cartridges from which the drawings were made. The lower case has become somewhat worm-eaten with time—the top wad is tilted and one side of the paper tube

has been nibbled or worn away. Nevertheless this lower illustration shows one important aspect of finishing the cartridges. In many cases a decorative thin paper wrapper was glued to the outside of the case covering part of the brass head and giving an artistic design to the cylindrical part of the case. It was often folded over the mouth of the shell and glued to the top wad to give some additional protection against weather or rough handling. The upper shotshell in Figure 4-10 is similar in construction but has weathered the passage of time relatively intact.

A drawing showing the details of construction of a 20-gauge pinfire shotshell is shown in Figure 4-11. The dimensions were taken from the upper shotshell in the previous illustration. The head is clearly marked "20" with a "G" below it standing for 20 gauge. The maker's name is in a circular ring around the outside of the head of the shell. Corrosion due to age and the faint stamping of the lettering makes the manufacturer's name illegible. The rim of the case is slight, with a dimension of .726 inches compared to a body diameter of .700. This type of case was extracted from the chamber of the shotgun by pulling on the firing pin rather than the rim of the case. The brass head is small, extending only .208 inches above the base. The firing pins at first appear to be at right angles to the cases but a closer examination shows that they are tilted at a slight angle. The

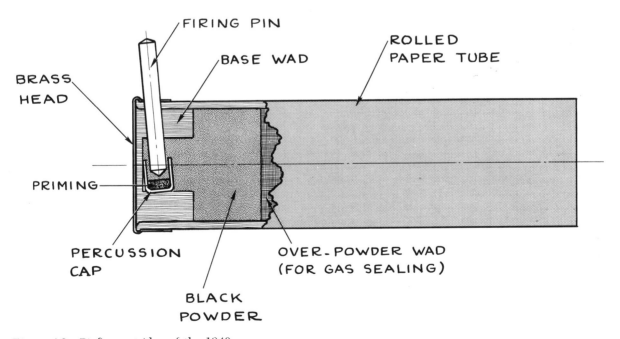

Figure 4-9 Pinfire cartridge of the 1840s.

Figure 4-10   French pinfire shotshells.

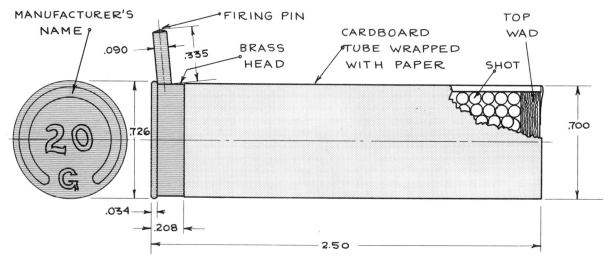

Figure 4-11   Construction details of pinfire shotshell.

schematic drawing of the internal construction shows why this would be necessary. Overall length of the shell was 2½ inches and the firing pin projected .335 inches above the circumference of the head.

The exposed firing pin obviously made these shotshells more dangerous than those of modern design to handle. If a modern shotshell is dropped even from a height of several stories it will not fire, unless a pebble or other projection is in the exact location of a primer at the time of impact—a circumstance rare enough to be considered remote. If it does go off, the smokeless powder will develop sufficient pressure to split the cartridge case and then generally extinguish itself, for smokeless propellant requires high pressure to burn effectively. Black powder is a different proposition: it ignites much more easily and will burn whether confined at high pressure or simply exposed to the open air. In all probability if a pinfire shotshell were dropped and landed on the firing pin with sufficient force to drive the firing pin inwards, the

shell would go off like a firecracker and would probably scatter shot around, although at low velocity.

Pinfire Shotguns

The French gunsmith Lefacheaux brought out a double-barreled breechloading shotgun for pinfire cartridges in 1836. The gun was remarkable in containing many features still incorporated on modern double-barreled shotguns. The barrels were hinged on a horizontal pin and the gun broke open in the same way as a modern double-barreled shotgun. Two shotshells were dropped in the chambers with the firing pins extending upwards through small slots cut into the upper part of the chamber. A lug welded to the underside of the barrel and a swinging lever underneath the breech locked the barrels down in firing position. A very ornate double-barreled pinfire shotgun with many of the characteristics of the Lefacheaux design is shown in Figures 4-12 and 4-13. The

Figure 4-12 French double-barreled pinfire shotgun.

Figure 4-13 Ornate breech of French pinfire shotgun.

46

barrels are locked in the down position by the long lever extending below the breech. When this lever is swung about 90° to one side and the hammers are cocked, the barrels can be pivoted into a loading position. After two shells are slid into the chamber, their pins extending upwards through the slots, the barrels are pivoted again to the closed position and locked in place by swinging the lever into alignment with them.

Although the original Lefacheaux shotgun of 1836 had a wooden forearm this model has only the elaborate receiver to hold on to. The stock is made from finely figured walnut, but is unusual in having no checkering. The metal work is elaborate as shown particularly in the closeup view of Figure 4-13. The lockplate has an extremely elaborate profile carefully set into the wooden stock and ornate designs have been carefully chiseled into the metal surfaces and the background colored grey to highlight the polished figures of dogs and deer. Scrolls, leaves and flowers have also been carefully sculptured and polished. The elaborately formed curls of the trigger guard disrupt the otherwise smooth and flowing lines of the shotgun. The shotgun is also fitted with sling swivels for easy carrying in the field, but both the trigger guard and the blade of the locking lever would tend to dig into the shooter if it were slung over the shoulder.

The full length of this 14-gauge shotgun is 46½ inches and the barrels are 30¹¹⁄₁₆ inches in length. The markings are strange, in that there is no maker's name anywhere—simply the words "ACIER PUDDLE" in large gold letters on the rib between the two barrels. The French words *Acier Puddle* mean steel (*acier*) made by a small reverberatory furnace in which iron was purified to make high-quality steel. Obviously the maker was so proud of the use of this fine-quality steel that this was what he wanted to emphasize on the shotgun. The care and attention to detail in the metal work is so outstanding, however, that it seems strange that the maker omitted his name.

A double-barreled pinfire shotgun of this type would permit the owner to go out in any weather and have an enjoyable day's shooting without the endless steps of muzzle loading and without any gas leakage at the breech to blow back in his face. Pinfire pistols, rifles and shotguns were developed and widely used in Europe and this type of shotgun was imported into the United States but only by wealthier sportsmen who could afford the high cost of the guns and the expensive ammunition.

English and continental gun makers continued to strengthen the breech action and developed many improvements on the original Lefacheaux design. In 1862 Westley Richards patented an extremely strong one, on which there was a steel extension projecting back between the two barrels and fitting into a recess in the standing breech. The upper part of this extension had a circular swelling, which became known as a "doll's head," which fitted into a matching recess in the breech. The result was a very strong longitudinal lock. The barrels were held downward by a horizontal sliding lock which fitted into a slot between the doll's head and the lower section of the barrel extension. The position of the breech lock was controlled by a top lever such as that fitted on modern double-barreled shotguns.

During the 1860s Westley Richards even developed an ingenious design with strikers and hammers that could fire both pinfire and the newer centerfire shotshells.

Sharps Shotguns

By far the most successful—and famous—breechloading firearms for caseless ammunition were invented in the United States by Christian Sharps and patented on September 12, 1848. Sharps was born in 1811 in Washington, New Jersey, where he was educated in the public schools. During his teens he was apprenticed as a machinist and became skilled in the manufacture of firearms. During the 1830s he worked for John H. Hall at the Harpers Ferry armory, learning about the manufacture of the Hall breechloading rifles. Christian Sharps was in an excellent position to benefit from this experience—he had a clever mind and was a fine craftsman—and when the manufacture of the Hall rifles was discontinued at Harpers Ferry about 1844 he was well aware of the principles of interchangeable manufacture of gun components and knew all about the gas leakage problems that had led to the failure of the Hall rifles in Army service. During the late 1840s Sharps lived in Cincinnati, Ohio, where he continued to experiment with developing the basic principles of his firearms. He proposed to solve the problem of sealing the breech by making a rectangular breech block which slid vertically on tracks within a short rigid receiver. The Sharps were sealed by having carefully machined flat surfaces on the rear of the cast-steel barrel and on the face of the breech block. This allowed the machining of more accurate surfaces than the slightly curved sealing surfaces required on the Hall rifles. By 1848 Sharps had received his basic patent covering the design in crude form and by 1850 had secured a test by the Army Ordnance Board. A highly favorable official test report was issued on November 27, 1850. During the 1850s Sharps brought out a series of rifle and carbine designs incorporating gradual improvements in the mechanism calculated to minimize the gas leakage at the breech and improve its functioning. He even went so far as to install platinum sealing rings in the face of his breechblocks in the 1851 model. By 1853 a moveable ring seal had been invented and the most successful design, the model of 1859, had a moveable plate fitted into the front of the breech block. The design of the model 1859 action is shown in Figure 4-14. This shows the construction details of the Army model rifles and carbines, the same basic action of which was used for the Sharps shotguns.

The Sharps was a lever action mechanism. As the lever was thrown down it rotated about a pivot at the lower front corner of the receiver. The rotary motion pivoted a link attached to the breech block and as the motion was continued the breech block was drawn downwards in a fully opened position exposing the entire chamber of the firearm. Sharps used paper cartridges for both rifle and shotgun ammunition. Using his finger, the shooter pushed a fresh cartridge through the loading trough and into the chamber. The breech block had a knife edge at the upper surface of the gas sealing plate, and as the lever was pushed back up, the breech block rose and sliced off the rear section of the paper cartridge, exposing the raw powder to the breech face. In the fully upward position the linkage was arranged so that the breech block could not be driven down by any external force—any pressure tending to push the breech block down merely rotated the locking linkage towards a more horizontal position, thereby wedging the breech bolt more tightly in place.

The final step in loading was to place a percussion cap on the nipple projecting above the breech block and cock the hammer. Pulling the trigger caused the hammer to fall, igniting the percussion cap and sending a jet of flame down through the nipple and into a cross hole drilled through the

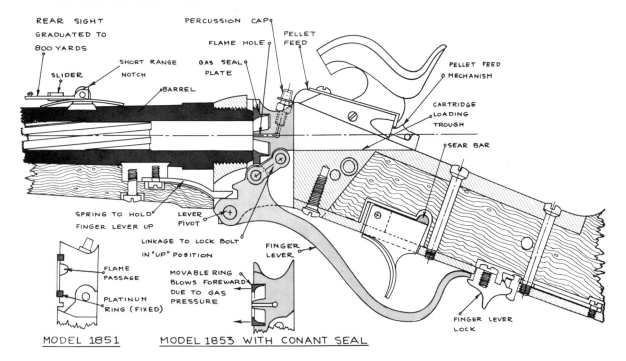

Figure 4-14   Percussion action of the Sharps Model 1859.

breech block. The flame then had to go around a right-angle turn and come out through a second small hole extending through the center of the breech block at which point it struck the raw powder and ignited the main charge.

The design of the breech seal was so ingenious it is still used today on some of the most modern experimental caseless firearms for the Army and Air Force. It was designed so that the gas pressure within the breech block tended to drive the sealing ring forward with great force against the rear surface of the barrel. As long as the face of the barrel and the gas sealing plate were kept clean and smooth this sealing system resulted in very little gas leakage, but when the seal got dirty or scartched it was a different matter and gas leakage from the 60-grain powder charge could be severe.

The Sharps rifle company was careful to use the latest and best materials although some of the descriptions sound strange a century later. The description in the 1864 catalog states:

> The Receiver is of the best wrought iron case hardened. After the barrel has been screwed into the Receiver and the slide fitted it should not be unscrewed, except in case of necessity, and by a competent mechanic. The Slide, which closes the rear end of the barrel, is cast steel, hardened. In its face a steel ring attached to a face-plate is inserted, around the circumference of a concavity, in the center of which the vent enters. The ring and plate is called a "gas-check", the action of the charge when fired, against its inner surface, forcing it out an imperceptible distance, against the rear of the bouching (barrel), so as to close the joint and prevent the escape of any portion of the force of the fired charge.

Model 1853 Sharps Shotgun

The breech of a Model 1853 Sharps shotgun is shown in Figure 4-15. The overall appearance is virtually identical to other Sharps carbines of the period except for the ornate engraving on the receiver and lock. This shotgun is light and handy, with an overall length of only 37¾ inches and a weight of 6¾ pounds. It was fitted with a 21¾ inch barrel cylindrically bored to a diameter of .570 inches from the muzzle to the chamber. The chamber has a diameter of .626 of an inch with a fairly abrupt forcing cone at the front. The receiver and lock plate are ornately engraved with

scrollwork, showing great care and attention. The shotgun is fitted with an engraved steel butt plate and there is also slight engraving at the muzzle of the barrel. The sighting system consists of a very shallow U-shaped notch cut into the receiver with the bead front sight on the barrel.

The outside diameter of the barrel at the muzzle is .832 inches giving it an extremely heavy wall thickness of .130 inches. It appears as if the shotgun was fitted with a standard carbine barrel which had simply been machined smooth on the inside surface. The wooden stocks are of deluxe walnut with a close grain and finely figured pattern. The forearm is tiny, only 6¾ inches in length with a pewter or German silver forearm cap.

The Sharps models of the early 1850s had a sloping breech block with the rear of the barrel cut off at an angle. During the late 1850s Sharps found this an unnecessary complication and switched to a vertical breech block and a more elaborate sealing system, as shown in Figure 4-14. The Model 1853 shotgun is fitted with a perfectly plain breech block with neither the Conant seal nor the platinum ring. A recess was cut into the bolt face similar to that shown in Figure 4-14, but it was all solid-steel construction with no movable ring. Sharps may have had the idea that this recess would provide some balancing gas force driving forward, but as long as the breech block was solid one-piece construction this was not true. The only way a dynamic seal could be achieved with a recess was if a movable ring could be driven forward relative to the breech block by the gas pressure. The top of the breech block was machined to provide a fairly sharp cutting edge on its upper surface, to trim off the rear of the paper cartridge. With the sloping breech design a triangular section was cut out of each cartridge which probably meant a loss of 5 to 10 grains of propellant.

The shotgun is, however, beautifully machined with close fits and fine surface finishes. The engraving is carefully done and it has every hallmark of high quality manufacture. It was fitted with the Lawrence pellet priming mechanism which was installed on all Civil War Sharps rifles and carbines. This mechanism was contained in the extension of the lock plate which may be seen above the receiver. It has a vertical hole, extending from the top to the bottom of the lock plate, which contained a stack of shallow copper cups containing fulminate priming compound. A spring-

Figure 4-15 Closeup of the Sharps Model 1853 action.

driven follower at the bottom of the hole pressed the stack upwards. A horizontal slide with an arm extended into a cam track in the hammer; as the hammer was cocked the slide was drawn to the rear allowing the uppermost primer to jump upwards into the path of the slide. As the shotgunner pulled the trigger and the hammer fell, the slide was driven quickly forward projecting the priming cup out of the front of the slot and onto the top of the nipple. The mechanism was so carefully timed that the cap arrived over the nipple just as the hammer struck, thus providing an automatic means of ignition. Believe it or not, this "Rube Goldberg" arrangement was very successful and saw wide usage during the Civil War. If a soldier did not have the requisite special shallow cups, the Sharps could be primed with regular percussion caps which were manually placed on the nipple for each shot.

Handling this Sharps shotgun gives a drastically different feel than most of the shotguns of the midcentury. Percussion and flintlock single-barreled shotguns were almost all fitted with very long barrels with thin side walls. Even if the guns were light they were unwieldy to handle. The Sharps, with its extremely short overall length and its weight concentrated well to the rear in the receiver area was a nimble gun in the hands and one that would be excellent for upland game shooting.

AMERICAN CARTRIDGE SHOTGUNS

At the end of the Civil War there were two giant companies in the American firearms industry. The Colt's Patent Firearms Company, founded in 1836 and famous for its revolvers, was the larger of the two. The older giant was E. Remington and Sons of Ilion, New York, founded in 1816. Originally rated as the largest manufacturer of high quality percussion rifles in the United States, Remington in 1857 had begun to manufacture percussion revolvers based on designs by Fordyce Beals, and by the time the Civil War broke out in 1861, the Remington-Beals revolvers in .44 Army and .36 Navy caliber were ready for large-scale production. Their rugged, solid frames and long-sighting radius made these very popular in the Federal service, and over 100,000 of the .44 Army models alone were produced during the Civil War years. Remington also had extensive war contracts for its famous Model 1862 percussion, muzzle-loading "Zouave" rifle. This was the most handsome firearm of the Civil War, with brown walnut stock, blued barrel, case-hardened lock plate and hammer, and shiny brass barrel bands, butt plate and trigger guard. They also produced the standard U.S. Model 1863 rifle-musket in .58 caliber.

Remington Rolling Block Shotguns

Though at the end of the Civil War Remington was set up to manufacture percussion rifles and revolvers of the highest quality in large quantities, they were abundantly aware that future business lay in breechloading cartridge firearms and had laid the groundwork during the late 1850s and early 1860s. To their skilled designers, Fordyce Beals and William Elliott, they added two other very important men: Leonard Geiger and Joseph Rider. In 1863 Geiger had patented a new type of breech action in which most of the mechanism was located below the centerline of the barrel. Philo Remington became aware of Geiger's breech mechanism and brought him into the design team to start intensive work to perfect this approach. Joseph Rider added some innovations

and received patent No. 45,123 in November, 1864, for a rimfire design with a breech block which rotated about the pivot. Rider's breech block was slotted in its upper surface to allow a heavy hammer to rotate into the slot striking the exposed upper edge of the rimfire cartridge. Although the breech block could be easily rotated when the hammer was cocked, the falling hammer locked it firmly shut. Geiger's design, and Rider's improvement, defined what came to be known as the "split breech Remington rolling block." This split-breech action was offered to the Ordnance Department, resulting in a contract for some 20,000 rifles. The time needed to prepare production, however, delayed delivery until after the Civil War.

Further design improvements were incorporated and patents issued in April, 1866, August, 1867, and in 1871. A contract for 5,000 single-shot 50 caliber pistols was issued in November, 1866, one for 5,000 carbines in 1867. Design improvements in the mid-1860s led to the elimination of the split-breech design and the use of a solid breech block, which greatly added to the strength. In 1867 Remington brought out a model known as the Remington-Rider shotgun No. 1, which is shown in Figure 4-16. The shotgun was produced until 1892 and approximately 100,000 were manufactured.

SHOTGUN BARRELS

The barrel was an extremely expensive part of any shotgun. The manufacturing technique used for producing Civil War musket and shotgun barrels was to take a long strip of carefully prepared iron, roll it into a tube and forge weld the seam. This technique was highly developed in both government arsenals and private industry and pro-

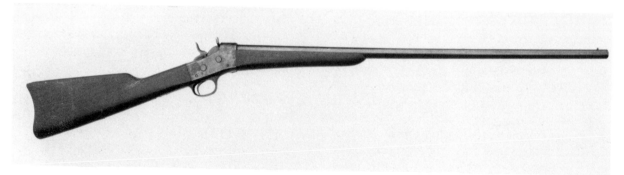

Figure 4-16   Remington-Rider No. 1 rolling block shotgun.

duced strong, reliable barrels. However, as better machinery became available in the second half of the nineteenth century, there was a gradual changeover to barrels drilled and machined out of solid cast-steel bars. The Remington catalogue of 1877 lists the rolling-block shotgun as "Remington's breech-loading shot-gun," in 16 gauge with a plain barrel. The price was $18.00. If a Damascus twist barrel was desired the price jumped to $55.00. An engraved shotgun was $70.00 and one that is extra engraved is listed at $80.00. The tremendous cost in labor of manufacturing a Damascus twist barrel can be seen from this enormous price differential. The barrels were offered in 30- and 32-inch lengths with the overall length of the shotgun 48 inches. The weight was approximately 6½ pounds.

The rolling-block action shown in the 1877 catalog is similar to the Remington Navy rifle action shown in Figure 4-17. The upper illustration shows the position of parts at the instant of firing. The hammer has struck the firing pin buried in the breech block and it in turn has fired the centerfire primer in the shotshell. The thrust of the cartridge to the rear is taken on the face of the breech block (B) which tried to rotate upon its pivot (b). However, its motion is prevented by the cylindrical surface on the hammer (C) which transmits the force of rotation down to the hammer pivot (b). As weakness in the cross pins could cause a serious failure they were made of solid steel .455 of an inch in diameter. The receiver walls were rugged and the components carefully manufactured to make it an extremely strong, sturdy action. The hammer was driven by a powerful leaf spring (a) which had a small roller on the working end to reduce friction between hammer and spring. On the Navy rifles there was a safety interlock (D) which rode in a slot in the breech block and prevented the trigger from being pulled unless the breech block was closed. The action is shown in the open position in the lower illustration. When the hammer was drawn back into the fully cocked position the support from under the breech block was withdrawn and it could be easily opened. An extractor drew the fired shotshell or cartridge to the rear where it could be picked out by the fingers and thrown away. If the breech block were snapped open smartly, the shell would be spun clear of the chamber. The action was then easily reloaded with a fresh shell and a light pressure of the finger would snap the breech block into the closed position again. It was held in a closed position by a light spring action.

The Remington rolling-block action was one of the most successful single-shot designs, manufactured in many sporting and military models. A Navy model was standardized in 1870 and an Army model in 1871. Many state militias used them and they were sold to foreign nations around the world. Over 1,000,000 Remington rolling-block rifles were manufactured during the second half of the nineteenth century.

AMERICAN DOUBLE-BARRELED SHOTGUNS

During the second half of the nineteenth century, American shooters began to use double-barreled shotguns in such large numbers that from 1880 until the early twentieth century this style of shotgun dominated American shotgunnery, usually in a 10-gauge size, used with black-powder paper or brass shotshells. These shotguns incorporated three enormous improvements over the traditional American muzzle-loading flintlock or percussion-style breechloaders. One was that they allowed much faster, safer reloading while hunting. The second was the use of two barrels, which gave a fast second shot at game. And the third was the use of chokes to control and improve patterns, thereby greatly increasing effective range.

Shotgun chokes had been invented, forgotten and reinvented many times during the eighteenth and early nineteenth centuries. Fred Kimble in the United States and W. W. Greener in England were responsible for finally bringing the advantages of choke to the attention of sportsmen on both sides of the Atlantic. Kimble developed a long-range choke-bored muzzle-loading shotgun while doing some experiments in the 1870s. His first design was choked much too tight and the patterns were poor. He cut off the barrel to remove the choked section, but did not quite remove it all and accidentally had a choke close to optimum for his shotgun. Since Kimble had a muzzle-loading shotgun, the shot charge did not have to pass through a forcing cone or pass the end of the mouth of the shell. Kimble claimed that his shotgun would put 100% of the shot in a 30-inch circle at 40 yards. Even though he was a skilled market hunter, however, he found that the pattern was so tight that he kept missing birds until he finally mastered the difficult shotgun and

FIG. 2.

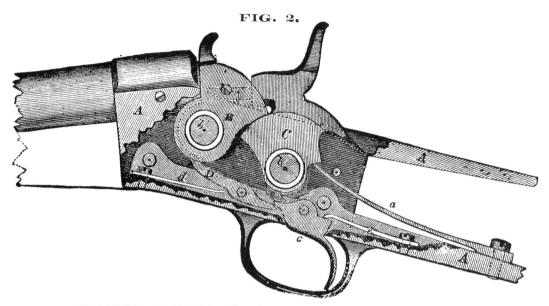

BREECH SYSTEM.—Sectional View with Breech Closed.

FIG. 3.

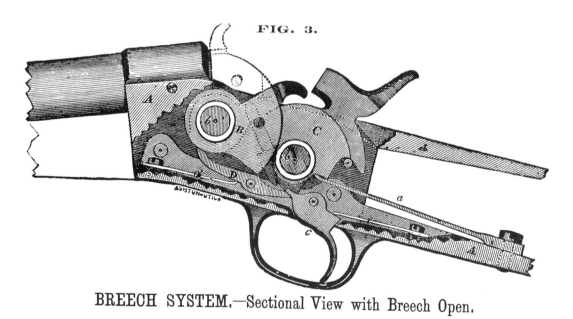

BREECH SYSTEM.—Sectional View with Breech Open.

Figure 4-17 Remington model 1870 rolling block action.

then claimed to down birds regularly at ranges of 70 to 80 yards along the Illinois flyway.

While few shooters could use such tight chokes the advantages of choke boring were widely discussed in the sporting press, and the practice came into wide use during the 1880s.

The relatively complex double-barreled shotgun design became practical in the United States because of the development of sophisticated precision machinery in the North to meet the manufacturing needs of the Civil War. Sharps carbines required precision seals to prevent the leakage of powder gas at the breech; the Henry and Spencer lever-action repeating rifles, and the Colt and Remington revolvers all required a precision in manufacture which would have been impossible during the 1830s. When the Civil War was over, this manufacturing skill became available for other products.

Parker Shotguns

Typical of these developments were the Parker shotguns. Charles Parker was born on January 9, 1809. His early experience was in casting and with manufacture of coffee mills. By 1860 he was president of Parker, Snow Brooks and Company, manufacturing many hardware products. The company was awarded a contract for 15,000 muzzle-loading muskets during the Civil War.

There is some indication that the time required to learn about this new field of manufacture so delayed full production that only 10,000 were completed by the end of the war, but it was a great learning period. Parker also proposed two styles of repeating rifles to the government during the war. Although neither went into production, Parker continued his experiments, and the first models of a commercial double-barreled shotgun were completed and marketed in 1868. It was a breech-loading 14-gauge shotgun with 29-inch barrels using "outside primed" ammunition. This was a transitional ammunition with the powder charge, wads and shot contained in a brass case with a small hole in the base. Ignition was provided by conventional percussion caps, which were fitted on nipples similar to those on muzzle-loading shotguns. The flame from the caps was directed through a small passage and passed through a hole in the head of the shell, igniting the main charge. This type of ammunition was quite similar to the Maynard rifle cartridge widely used during the Civil War.

The locking mechanism on the first Parker was both crude and ungainly in appearance, but it was strong and sturdy and consequently remained in use for more than thirty years. It was operated by a lever under the breech mechanism.

The Parker became known as an extremely reliable high-quality shotgun but the rapid design changes of the 1870s required improvements and a skilled gun craftsman. Charles A. King joined the Parker Brothers Company in 1874, and headed up the gun design and development efforts. During the next decades other lifter-type actions were developed, and early hammerless shotguns were designed where the hammers were hidden inside the lock mechanism, but the cocking was accomplished by levers outside the lock plates. Later, true hammerless designs were developed in which the internal hammers were cocked by the opening motion of the barrels. When C. A. King started to redesign the bolting system he worked closely with Charles Parker himself. At this time Parker was 71, but he had retained a keen interest in the development of improved models, especially as competition in the field was growing rapidly with Remington, Baker, L. C. Smith, Colt, and Lefever all active.

The new bolting system developed by King used a doll's head extension to the top rib of the barrel, and a hardened, tapered wedge set into the vertical lug below the barrels. This hardened block was known as a combination bolt plate. A sliding bolt, operated by a top lever extended from the breech face, had a matching beveled surface which was angled at 12½°, which slid over the bolt plate and locked it firmly in a down position. This basic locking system was so satisfactory that it remained an integral part of the Parker design for the next half century. Minor improvements were incorporated until the final design was achieved in 1910.

Although Parker is considered an American shotgun, the barrels were manufactured in Belgium. The production of laminated-twist barrels had become a highly skilled art in Europe, where centuries of gun-making skills had been developed by long apprenticeship in the art of barrel making. Parker and other American manufacturers found it best to import the "rough tubes" and finish them themselves. The Damascus barrels were beautiful examples of the gun maker's art. Wrought-iron rods were twisted to form a spiral pattern, then hammered into a square cross section. These rods, sometimes alternating with twisted steel, were heated cherry-red hot, and wrapped around a mandril slightly smaller than the interior bore of the barrel. During the process the rods were hammered, forging them into a continuously welded barrel with a spiral pattern around the mandril. After final machining, the barrels were etched with acid, and a beautiful fine pattern of light and dark colors emerged.

The Damascus barrels were of high quality and were offered in the following grades on the early Parkers:

PH—A plain-twist standard barrel.
GH—A fancier barrel with two bars of iron wrapped around the mandril side by side.
DH—A three-bar (known as three-blade) design.
CH—The fanciest-twist barrels with extremely fine figure.

The process of improvement of the basic Parker design continued. In 1882 the lifter bar, in front of the trigger guard, was dropped in favor of a swinging top lever. In 1889 a hammerless shotgun design was introduced, and in 1902 automatic ejectors were offered.

A closeup view of the breech of a very high quality Parker, the BHE grade, is shown in Figure 4-18, in which the attention to fitting and detail is apparent. The engraving on the receiver is fine and carefully executed, including a hunting scene with two dogs. The walnut butt stock and forearm have been extensively checkered to a complex pattern which required a lot of time to lay out and execute. The butt stock adjacent to the receiver is carved with a panel and fleur-de-lis, and then the panel checkered. These details are possible only on shotguns costing several thousand dollars today.

An even more elaborate Parker, the A-1 Special grade, shown in Figure 4-19, also gives an overall view of the Parker at the peak of its reputation. The ornamentation is even more extensive than on the BHE Model with the engraving extending forward onto the barrels. The receiver is

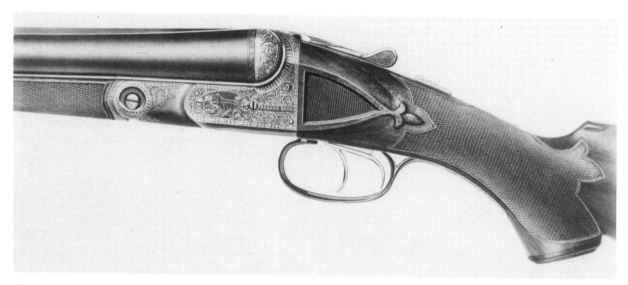

Figure 4-18 Breech of the Parker BHE grade double-barreled shotgun.

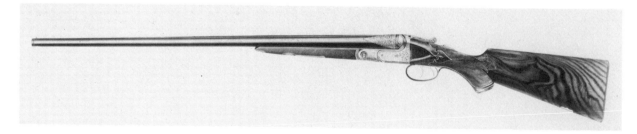

Figure 4-19 The Parker A-1 Special shotgun.

completely engraved, and the forearm is checkered all over. The butt stock is more extensively carved and checkered, and a silver-on-gold nameplate is set into the butt stock near the butt plate. Such elaborate shotguns were made in extremely small numbers. Total production reached 200,000 shotguns by 1930, an average of slightly over 3,000 guns a year from the first model in 1868.

The development of Parker shotguns continued in the twentieth century. In 1905 the first 28 model was developed and in 1910 the top-lever and bolting action reached its final form. In 1917 the cocking mechanism was redesigned to reduce the number of components. The models shown in Figures 4-18 and 4-19 probably incorporated all these improvements. In 1922 a single-trigger mechanism was put in production, and in 1923 the first beaver-tail forearm was developed and introduced.

A late model, more modest-grade Parker is shown in Figure 4-20. This is a VHE, which incorporates the beavertail forearm and single trigger. Although the earlier models were both pistol-grip designs, this particular late VHE was of the optional straight-grip design. The checkering of the stocks is much plainer and the receiver has only modest decoration around the borders. High costs were forcing severe pressures on profits, and in 1934 the company was sold to Remington. Production remained at the Meriden plant until 1937, when the business, including tools and skilled craftsmen, was transferred to the Remington factory at Ilion, New York. Production continued at Ilion, with very low production during the war years, until high costs forced termination of production in 1947.

Remington Double-Barreled Shotguns

Development of American double-barreled shot-

gun design can be traced through the models designed by E. Remington and Sons, for Remington participated in this market from 1874 until the rapid sales growth of the slide-action and semi-automatic Remington shotguns made double barrels unprofitable in the Remington line just before World War I.

During the late nineteenth century, while companies such as Baker, Ithaca, L. C. Smith, and Lefever were founded to manufacture double-barreled shotguns, other companies such as Remington, Stevens, and Winchester were bringing out shotguns to diversify their lines of rifles. Winchester double-barreled shotguns were entirely manufactured abroad, and remained in the product line for only a few years, but the Remington models were designed and produced in the United States with the probable exception of the Damascus twist barrels.

Remington Model 1874

In 1874 E. Remington and Sons introduced their first double-barreled shotgun, which became known as the "Remington-Whittmore 1874 Model." The standard model with plain walnut stock and a decarbonized-steel barrel is shown in Figure 4-21. The price in 1877 was $45.00. With a checkered selected walnut stock and twist barrels the price was $60.00. With checkered selected walnut stock and Damascus barrels and some engraving on the receiver the cost was $75.00. With an English walnut stock and extra-fine engraving the price ranged from $85.00 to $100.00. A number of special optional features were offered to satisfy customers. For example, a pistol grip could be ordered for an extra $5.00 to $8.00. Rebounding locks, in which the hammer rebounded to a safety position after striking the firing pin, cost an extra $5.00. The 1874 model could also be ordered as a

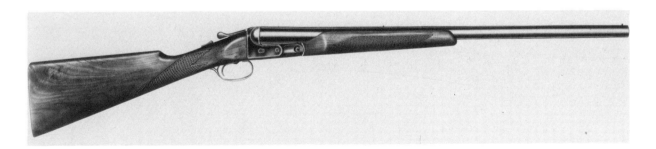

Figure 4-20   A late Parker shotgun, Model VHE.

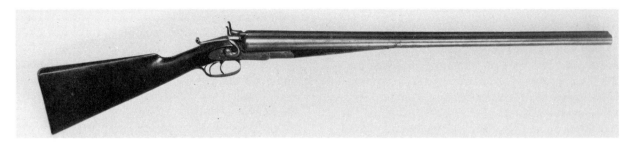

Figure 4-21 Remington Model 1874.

double-barreled rifle with decarbonized-steel barrels for $65.00 or as a combination rifle and shotgun for the same price. However it came, it was a deluxe shotgun with sidelocks rather than the less expensive back-action locks used on more moderate quality firearms. The barrels were fitted with extractors, and locking was accomplished by a lump welded to the underside of the barrel and a locking bolt, which extended from the standing breech of the receiver into a recess cut into the barrel lump. The action was opened by lifting the top lever, which withdrew the locking lug and permitted the barrels to be pivoted open. The shotguns weighed 8 to 8¾ pounds and were offered in 10 and 12 gauge with 28- and 30-inch barrels. Although this model was manufactured only from 1874 to 1878, production has been estimated at more than 50,000 shotguns.

The catalogue illustration of this shotgun also shows a Remington brass shotshell which had an unusual tubular anvil. During the 1870s and 1880s most sportsmen purchased empty brass or paper shells and reloaded their own ammunition. With the modest pressures of a black-powder shotgun, brass shotshells would last almost indefinitely if they were cleaned carefully after shooting. Prices of brass shotshells were quite high, for some of these early lists showed 10 to 11 cents for each empty brass shell. Considering the wages of the

1870s this would be equivalent to $.50 to $1.00 in contemporary currency.

Remington steadily improved their double-barreled shotguns. In later years the Model 1874 became known as the "hammer-lifter action." An improved model known simply as the "lifter action" was brought out, and additional new models reflecting design improvements were introduced in 1882, 1885, 1887 and 1889.

Remington Model 1889

The Remington Model 1889 double-barreled shotgun was one of the finest hammer-type shotguns manufactured in the United States. Listed in the catalogue as the "Remington New Model," it was available with a wide variety of options. (The design is shown in Figure 4-22.) The basic model, with "decarbonized steel" barrels, was available in 10, 12, and 16 gauge at a price of $30.00. With fine-twist barrels the price was $35.00 and with Damascus-steel barrels $40.00. An extra set of barrels could be purchased for half the price of the gun.

The action was updated to use the swinging top lever, and the locking system continued to be a locking bar operated by the top lever, which wedged into a recess in a lump welded underneath the barrels. In addition a "doll's head" ex-

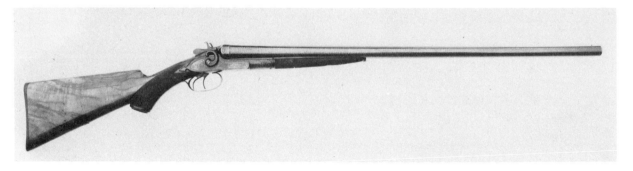

Figure 4-22 Remington Model 1889.

tension was fitted to the top of the barrels with a second locking surface, thus giving additional strength to the locking system. The hammer profiles were very low and curved, probably to minimize the danger of an accidental discharge when carrying the shotgun through brush. This was a common hazard with hammer-style shotguns, for if a branch drew back one of the hammers only part way, so that it did not engage the safety notch, the hammer could fly forward when the branch released it and fire the shotgun.

The shotguns were available in 10, 12, and 16 gauge. Ten-gauge shotguns have gone out of style in the United States with modern improvements in ammunition, but they were an extremely popular design in the late 19th century. The large-bore diameter of .775 inches gave plenty of room for a husky charge of shot and a large black-powder charge. The Remington models were available with 30- and 32-inch barrels, and weighed 8½ to 10¼ pounds. The 12-gauge models were available with 28-, 30-, and 32-inch barrels and weighed 7 to 9 pounds. The 16-gauge models were available with the 28-, 30-, and 32-inch barrels and weighed 6¾ to 7½ pounds.

Deluxe models of the shotgun were also available. For example, the "style No. 4" was listed with Damascus-steel barrels, better-quality engraving and a curly walnut stock at $60.00. The "style No. 7," with superior quality Damascus-steel barrels, extra fine roll engraving, and an elegant curly walnut stock was sold at a price of $125.00. These deluxe models were made only on special order, to the customer's specifications.

Hammerless Remington Shotguns

Although hammerless double-barreled shotguns had been designed in Europe in the 1860s and 1870s, American sportsmen tended to be more conservative than Europeans in adopting them. Most of the American companies whose business was specifically to manufacture shotguns—such as Parker, Ithaca, Fox and Lefever—made their reputation on hammer-styled double-barreled shotguns. Lefever and Fox introduced hammerless models in the 1880s, Parker only in 1889. When the Winchester Repeating Arms Company decided to enter the shotgun field they introduced a line of imported English hammer-style shotguns from 1880 to 1884. Remington introduced their double-barreled hammer-style shotguns in the 1870s, as described earlier. American sportsmen relied upon

these designs until well after the turn of the century.

When it was time to introduce a new Remington shotgun in 1889, it was a hammer-style double barrel, which was manufactured until 1908. The popularity of hammer-style shotguns can be judged from the fact that 133,800 Remington Model 1889s were produced in that twenty year period. It was not until 1894 that Remington introduced their first hammerless double-barreled shotgun, then in 1900 brought out an improved model which was virtually identical in appearance. The Model 1894 is shown in the upper illustration of Figure 4-23 and a trap version of the Model 1900 in the lower illustration. Both models were manufactured until 1910. A total of 41,200 of the Model 1894 and 98,485 of the Model 1900 were produced.

The Remington hammerless shotguns were available with an enormous number of options. The catalog of 1902 lists the basic model, the grade K, at $35.00, and the top of the line, the Remington Special at $750.00. The Model K was available in 12 and 16 gauge with barrels of 28- to 32-inch length. This shotgun was similar to the upper illustration in Figure 4-23, with a semi-pistol grip stock, rubber butt plate, case hardened frame and mountings, and a flat matted rib. The gun had plain extractors and double triggers. The design featured an automatic safety which was operated by the top lever.

The catalog stated:

> To open the gun, push the top lever to the right; this retracts the main bolt and throws the safety plunger into position, thereby locking the triggers securely. This action being positive, the gun cannot be opened without operating the safety mechanism. Any person desiring to use the gun without the automatic safety, can, by removing the stock, take out the safety plunger, thereby removing the automatic attachment, which will, however, allow the safety being operated by the thumb.

As the barrels were pivoted open around the hinge pin, a cocking bar (which was also pivoted on the hinge pin) lifted the toe of the hammer and forced it backwards. When the hammers reached their fully cocked position the sears dropped into notches in the hammers and held them securely. The sears in turn were locked by the safety so that the action was quite safe.

For a mere $10.00 extra the shooter of 1902

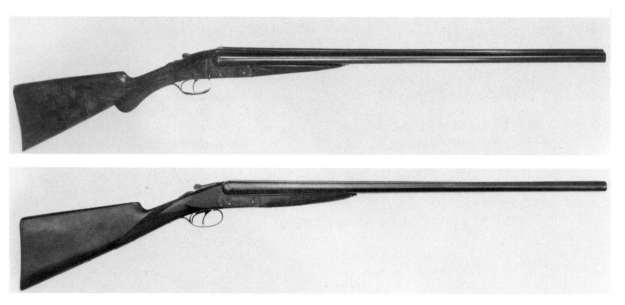

Figure 4-23 Remington hammerless shotguns: above, Model 1894; below, Model 1900.

could purchase the Model KED which featured a Damascus barrel, a selected walnut stock, and automatic ejectors. The other specifications were the same. Automatic ejectors have always been a complex feature for double-barreled shotguns. Ideally they should be designed to sense whether the shell has been fired in each of the barrels. If the shells are unfired then the extractor should merely lift the rim of the shell a slight distance to allow the shooter to *easily* remove it from the action. Only if the shell has been fired should the automatic ejector come completely into play and kick it clear of the barrel. The catalog describes the construction:

The automatic ejector is composed of hammer, sear, center sear, main and sear springs, and is cocked by the action of the extractor when closing the gun. It is operated when the gun is fired by the mainspring moving forward and lifting the ejector sear out of the ejector hammer notch. This allows the ejector hammer to fall on the center sear where it remains until the gun is nearly open, when the joint check engages with the center sear and raises it out of the ejector hammer notch. Then the ejector hammer, moving forward, strikes the ejector stem causing the fired shell to be expelled from the gun.

Needless to say, automatic ejectors required—then as now—both careful machining and meticulous hand fitting for proper operation. Most inexpensive shotguns will feature plain extractors for

the cost of the extra parts and fitting required for good automatic ejectors is significant.

Some hunters preferred plain extractors, so that the higher-priced Remington Model hammerless shotguns were offered that way, with automatic ejectors $5.00 more. The grade EE automatic ejector had a base price of $225 with plain extractors, or $230 with automatic ejectors. It was available in 10, 12, and 16 gauge. The 10-gauge models were manufactured with 30- and 32-inch barrels and weighed from 8½ to 10 pounds. The 12-gauge models were available with 26-, 28-, 30-, and 32-inch barrels and weighed from 6¾ to 8¾ pounds. The 16-gauge models were available with the same barrel lengths and weighed from 6½ to 7½ pounds. The other features were listed in the catalog as:

Finest Damascus barrels, choked-bored, best English walnut stock, straight, half or full pistol grip, horn or skeleton butt plate, checkered foreend, case-hardened frame and mountings, Purdy foreend snap, flat-matted rib, automatic safety, top snap, triple locked action.

The triple-locked action referred to the Remington design that included two locking bolts extending into ribs beneath the barrel plus a third locking surface on a top rib, which extended from in between the top of the chambers and fitted into a slot in the top of the frame. The gun was also available with a hollow rib or the standard flat matted rib. The receiver was engraved with "finest quality bird and game engraving," and the butt stock was fitted with a gold nameplate.

There was also an interesting but oblique comment on the strength of Damascus barrels. Remington offered to fit the shotguns with "Ordnance" steel barrels at no additional charge:

> Ordnance steel is of the highest grade, and is especially recommended for heavy charges of nitro powder (smokeless powder). The tensile strength of the steel is 110,000 pounds, and the elastic limits 60,000 pounds, this being greatly in excess of any strain to which shotgun barrels are subjected with reasonable loads of nitro powders.

Thus, even by 1902 the limited strength of Damascus barrels was becoming of concern to responsible American manufacturers. There was no question that a high-quality Damascus barrel made a shotgun which had the appearance of a work of art, but it was also true that the hundreds of welded seams within the Damascus design made for points of weakness, which could cause trouble if excessive pressures were encountered. The trend to homogeneous steel barrels grew rapidly, and very few Damascus barrels were fitted to American shotguns after World War I.

Imported Double-Barreled Shotguns

In addition to those made in America, many double-barreled shotguns were imported from Europe. A medium-quality double-barreled shotgun from the author's collection is shown in Figures 4-24 and 4-25. It is unusually short with an overall length of only 40 inches, and the 12-gauge

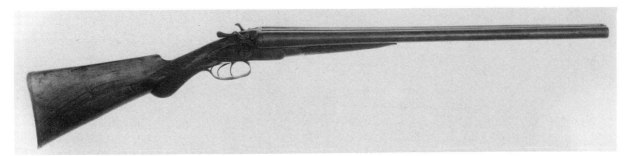

Figure 4-24 "W. Richards" shotgun—either a mediocre Westley Richards or an imitation.

Figure 4-25 Closeup of the breech of the W. Richards shotgun.

60

barrels are only 24 inches in length. The basic features are similar to the Remington model of 1889 with very curved, low hammers and a doll's head extension on the top of the barrels which fits into a matching recess in the standing breech. The locking cut in the barrel, barely visible, is a square ledge cut into the lump welded to the underside of the barrel. The locking bolt, actuated by the top lever, fits over the ledge locking the barrel downwards when the gun is fully closed. With the action closed, the "doll's head" fitting into the recess in the standing breech provides additional locking, preventing the barrel from springing away from the breech in a longitudinal direction.

The shotgun is marked "W. Richards" on the locks and "Laminated Steel" on the rib. The serial number, 49,665, is marked on the underside of the barrel and on the frame. It is not known whether this is a medium-quality Westley Richards shotgun manufactured for the export trade or an imitation manufactured in England or on the conti-

nent to sell on the Westley Richards reputation for superb firearms. Careful examination of Figure 4-25 will show a rather mediocre quality of cross checkering on the hammers and top lever, but the gun is carefully engraved and the action is quite tight even after three quarters of a century. The stock and forearms are carefully manufactured and checkered. Some documented Westley Richards shotguns in the Winchester Gun Museum are of similar quality, but Westley Richards firearms were usually manufactured with superb attention to detail.

Winchester Double-Barreled Shotguns

In 1880 Winchester announced a line of double-barreled hammer-style shotguns manufactured in England, and the examples remaining in the Winchester Gun Museum are all of extremely high quality. One of them, shown in Figures 4-26 and 4-27, is similar in construction to the Rem-

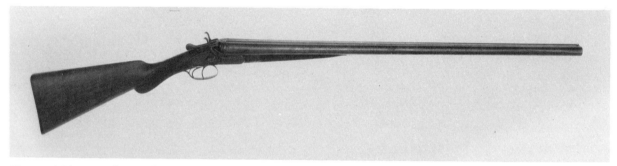

Figure 4-26 Winchester double-barreled shotgun of 1880.

Figure 4-27 Closeup of the breech of the 1880 Winchester shotgun.

ington Model 1889 and the Westley Richards shotgun. A block of metal has been welded to the underside of the barrel and a square recess cut into it. A locking member, which slides horizontally in the breech, is positioned by the top lever and when the barrels are down and the shotgun fully locked, slides into a recess in the lump, thus holding the barrels solidly against the standing breech. A doll's head extension, extending rearward from the top of the barrels, fits a matching recess in the standing breech, thus providing additional control of headspace under firing loads. A plain extractor lifts the shells about half an inch out from the chambers after firing. The hammers, shown in the fully cocked position, are gracefully curved and ornately engraved. The lock is arranged so that the hammer strikes the firing pin and then rebounds into a safety position. This feature was incorporated in many later shotguns, for it meant not only that the gun could be carried with greater safety (by leaving the hammers in the rebound position) but aided the easy opening of the gun. If the hammers were resting on the firing pins they tended to hold the firing-pin tips into primer indents locking the action closed. Opening the gun, then, could only be accomplished by applying sufficient force to cam the firing pins rearward out of the primer recesses against the hammer force.

This Winchester double-barreled shotgun weighs 7 pounds and has an overall length of 46 inches. The 12-gauge barrels are 29½ inches long. Both locks are marked "Winchester Repeating Arms Co." and also "Match Gun." The barrel rib is marked "Winchester Repeating Arms Co. (Match Gun) New Haven, Conn. U.S.A." The trigger guard is marked with a very ornate trademark used by Winchester in that period. Basically it consists of an ornate "A" with a "W R & Co." intertwined around the A. The underside of the barrel is marked with a series of English proof marks with a notation "Not for Ball," indicating that the barrels had been proven for shot charges but were not designed for solid bullets. This shotgun was the top of the line and listed at $85.00. Other models were available, listed as Class A at $70.00, Class B at $60.00, Class C at $50.00, and Class D at $40.00. Some lower-grade shotguns were also sold at prices as low as $20.00.

Baker and L. C. Smith Double-Barreled Shotguns

In the turmoil of the post-Civil War period, an inventive designer, William H. Baker, was involved in founding three gun companies. First he produced 10- and 12-gauge double-barreled shotguns with long massive Damascus barrels of London steel marked W. H. Baker and Co. They were opened by pushing the front trigger *forward,* thus withdrawing the locking bolt, and were patented in August 1875. These were sturdy and successful guns.

In the late 1870s Lyman C. Smith bought out two of the four partners of W. H. Baker thereby controlling 75% of its business. The guns continued in production but were marked "L. C. Smith and Co., Maker of the Baker Gun." This marked the founding of the L. C. Smith Company. In 1883 the reference to the Baker shotgun was dropped, and in 1888 the business was sold to the four Hunter brothers who owned the Hunter Arms Company.

William H. Baker left the company about 1880 causing something of a crisis, for his original design was becoming obsolete in the rapidly changing market of the period. Fortunately a gifted gun designer, Alexander T. Brown, had joined the company in 1878 as a machinist. In 1883 Brown applied for a patent to cover a modernized design including a rotary locking system, which was operated by a top lever similar to those used on double barrel shotguns today. The lock was a vertical cylinder with a cam cut that locked the barrel lug in a down position. In addition the cam was rotated by a spring that drove the lock into a fully engaged position, thus compensating for wear in the lock mechanism.

Brown's patent also included lugs on the locking cylinder, which withdrew the firing pins when the top lever was rotated. Upon introduction of the new gun, all reference to the Baker shotgun was dropped and in 1888 the business was sold to the Hunter Arms Company. Hunter continued manufacture of L. C. Smith shotguns until 1945 when the business was sold to the Marlin Firearms Company. L. C. Smith himself had meanwhile become interested in the typewriter and went on to found the L. C. Smith and Brothers Typewriter Company, now Smith-Corona Marchant (SCM), a leader in the office machine field.

Marlin continued to manufacture L. C. Smith shotguns at its Fulton, New York, plant until 1951, when decline in interest in double-barreled shotguns together with rising costs, forced L. C. Smith off the market. However, more than 60,000 shotguns had been manufactured. After the Ful-

62

ton plant was shut down, the tooling, machinery and all the work in process inventory that could be salvaged was moved to the Marlin plant in New Haven, Connecticut. It was obvious that trying to manufacture the L. C. Smith in New Haven using the same techniques that were used at the Fulton plant was doomed to failure, and that a revised approach was required. Marlin's answer was an extensive manufacturing study which lasted two years. In effect the gun was "value engineered," and every operation scrutinized to see what changes could be made in production techniques without compromising quality.

The redesigned L. C. Smith Field Grade Double Barrel Shotgun, shown in Figure 4-28, is an unusual hammerless shotgun, for it is a sidelock design whereas almost all American double-barreled shotguns have been "box lock" designs with the hammer mechanisms held within the receiver. In this case, the hammer mechanism is contained in side plates which bolt to each side of the action. The technique for disassembling the side locks, for cleaning and adjustment, is shown in the lower section of Figure 4-28. However, the

basic features of the L. C. Smith design have been retained, including the rotary lock, and the side lock mechanism. The design is fitted with a safety, which automatically goes into the "on" position as the gun is opened. The weight of the shotgun is about 6¾ pounds. The appearance is quite colorful, with the hand-checkered American walnut butt stock and forearm. The barrels are blued and frame and side plates are color case hardened. It is offered with 28-inch barrels in modified and full choke, and 26-inch barrels in the more open chokes of improved cylinder and modified. The new L. C. Smith shotgun reflects sturdy, long-lasting construction. With its plain extractor and double triggers, it is a simple basic design which will give long hard service. With the renewed interest in double-barreled shotguns by American hunters, the L. C. Smith shotguns may well enter their second century of production.

Ithaca Double-Barreled Shotguns

The Ithaca Gun Company was founded by the

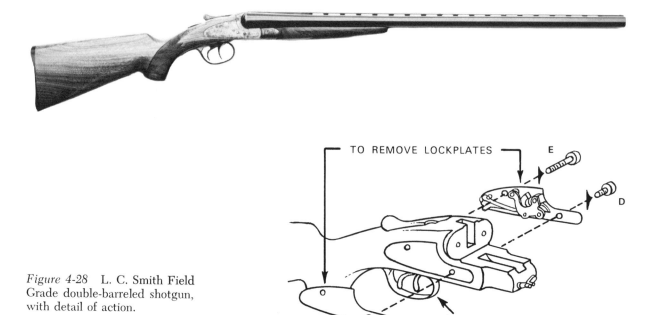

Figure 4-28 L. C. Smith Field Grade double-barreled shotgun, with detail of action.

ever-active and energetic William H. Baker and several partners, including L. H. Smith, brother of Lyman C. Smith. George Livermore, who was L. H. Smith's brother-in-law, and Lou Smith, a son, joined the firm, and the Smith family continued to manage the company for many years.

The first Ithaca shotgun was produced in 1883 in a small wood frame building. At first the company was known as W. H. Baker & Co., Gun Works, but the name was changed about the time of Baker's death in October, 1889. The company's first gun incorporated all the knowledge that Baker had developed in his years of gun design and production. Early advertisements modestly stated: "Strongest, simplest and best American gun manufactured"; "Baker's latest and best invention." Early illustrations show a sturdy shotgun with Damascus barrels, and an unusual box-lock action, with the hammers mounted on the extreme rear of the receiver (most hammer shotguns were side-lock designs with the hammer mechanism mounted on long lock plates fastened to the receiver at the front and set into the wood butt stock at the rear). The Ithaca shotgun had a doll's head extension on the barrel rib, and the locking arrangement was generally similar to the British shotguns shown in Figures 4-26 and 4-27. During the late nineteenth century Ithaca achieved a reputation for manufacturing sturdy double-barreled shotguns of excellent quality, well suited to the needs of American sportsmen.

In 1893 Ithaca introduced a hammerless shotgun known as the Crass Model. Production started at serial number 17,235, and was discontinued in 1903 at serial number 94,108, for a total production of almost 77,000 shotguns.

In 1904 the Lewis model Ithaca double barrel was introduced, and this was discontinued in 1906 at serial number 123,677. Another improved model, the Marien double, was introduced that year and discontinued in 1908 at serial number 151,770. Next came a longer-lasting model, the Flues Ithaca, introduced in 1908 at serial number 175,000 and produced until 1926, serial number 398,365. The early shotguns all had Damascus-twist barrels, in 10 and 12 gauge, but the trend to a homogeneous steel barrel became strong in the early twentieth century, and most models were offered with both types of barrel.

In 1904, 16- and 20-gauge shotguns were introduced. In 1911 28-gauge models were added and in 1926 the 410 bore.

The most important Ithaca double-barreled shotgun of the twentieth century was the New Ithaca Double, introduced in 1926 at serial number 425,000. Before discontinuation in 1948, a total of approximately 47,000 was manufactured. The New Ithaca Double is shown in Figure 4-29. It was a sturdy hammerless box-lock action design with a checkered pistol-grip butt stock. The early models were fitted with a relatively small checkered forearm, the later ones with the large, checkered beavertail forearm shown in the illustration. The New Ithaca Double was manufactured with both plain extractors and selective ejectors. Locking was by means of a sturdy barrel extension which extended rearwards in between the barrels and fitted into a slot in the receiver. A rotary lock in the receiver passed through a hole in the barrel extension. Rotary locks are strong, but if not carefully fitted will bounce open when the first barrel is fired. The internal parts of the mechanism reflected Ithaca's extensive experience in manufacturing double-barreled shotguns plus the knowledge that advanced manufacturing techniques had to be used wherever possible to keep manufacturing costs reasonable. Double-barreled shotguns inherently require a tremendous amount of hand labor. Barrels are tapered from breech to muzzle, and if

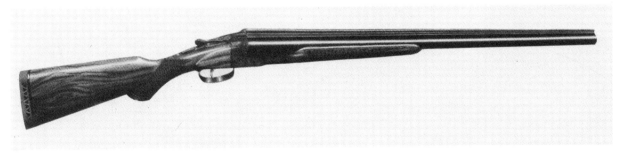

Figure 4-29 New Ithaca Double shotgun.

they were simply finished individually and soldered together the bores would not be parallel and the shot patterns would cross-fire badly. The traditional solution to this difficulty is to machine flats on the barrels at the breech end to bring the chambers closer together and then to literally bend the barrels into a slightly curved shape so that the front half of the barrels have parallel bores. In effect the shot charge in the right-hand barrel starts off aimed slightly to the left, then travels a very slight arc ending up in the front half of the barrel going parallel to the line of sight. This process requires tremendous skill on the part of the manufacturing craftsmen. If the barrel bending is not done with extreme care, pattern locations can vary widely from one barrel to the other. The situation is most crucial, of course, in double-barreled rifles, and this is one reason for the high price of these firearms. Often the assembly, testing, disassembly, resoldering and retesting involved in getting both barrels of a double-barreled rifle to shoot to the same aiming point requires literally days of patient experimentation and adjustment. To a lesser extent this is true with double-barreled shotguns. In general the cheaper the shotgun the less time that can be given to this effort, and the less chance that the two barrels will deliver their shot pattern in the same location.

The New Ithaca Double continued the Ithaca tradition for sturdy construction, high quality and long wear until rising costs finally forced it off the market in 1948.

Lefever Double-Barreled Shotguns

The D. M. Lefever Co. was founded by another pioneer in breechloading firearms, Dan Lefever, who learned his trade as an apprentice to the famous muzzle-loading rifle maker William Billinghurst. During the Civil War Lefever furnished accurate muzzle-loading rifles to Northern sharpshooters. He also made a number of muzzle-loading three-barreled guns with two shot barrels and one rifle barrel.

In 1867 Lefever began experimenting with breech-loading break-open actions, but his first models were not strong enough and shot loose. Still, by 1872 Lefever and his partner, F. S. Dangerfield, had patented a strong locking system and in 1878 introduced the first hammerless break-open shotgun to be manufactured in the United States. It was a side-lever model. A shaft extending through the pivot of both hammers and out the left side of the action had a long lever attached to it. When this lever was depressed it recocked the hammers and opened the action. In 1884, after a number of partnerships, Lefever founded the Lefever Arms Company which he served as president, becoming known as "Uncle Dan" within the industry. He continuously incorporated improvements in his designs, developing an "automatic hammerless" in the late 1880s. The outside lever was replaced by an internal mechanism, and the motion of the shooter's thumb on a button located on the tang served to open the gun. He also developed a "compensated action," which allowed easy adjustment to take up for wear. Instead of the barrels pivoting on a cross shaft, Lefever used a ball-and-socket joint which could also be adjusted to take up wear.

Lefever added double-barreled rifles to his product line near the end of the century, and even offered three-barreled weapons on special order.

Dan Lefever was eventually forced out of his company in 1901, and the next year organized the D. M. Lefever, Sons and Company in Syracuse, New York. "Uncle" Dan's five sons joined him in this venture and the shotguns were marketed as "The New Lefever." The Lefever Arms Company continued to make sidelock double-barreled shotguns, while the new company switched over to a box-lock design. In 1906 "Uncle" Dan Lefever died, and his new company ceased operations. The Lefever Arms Company was sold to the Ithaca Gun Company, with a new model "The New Lefever Nitro Special" being introduced in 1921.

The mechanism for "The New Lefever Nitro Special" is shown in Figure 4-30. This was a hammerless box-lock shotgun which was introduced at the incredible price of $29.00. Every attempt was made to design it with every modern production technique that would eliminate as much hand work as possible and yet still provide reliable, rugged functioning. It was offered in 12, 16, and 20 gauge with 28-inch barrels in all three gauges and a 30-inch barrel in 12 gauge. The 20-gauge model was quite light at 6¼ pounds. The 16-gauge model weighed half a pound more and the 12-gauge models ranged from 7¼ pounds with 28-inch barrels and 7 pounds 10 ounces with the 30-inch barrels. It was claimed that the new lock was snapped over

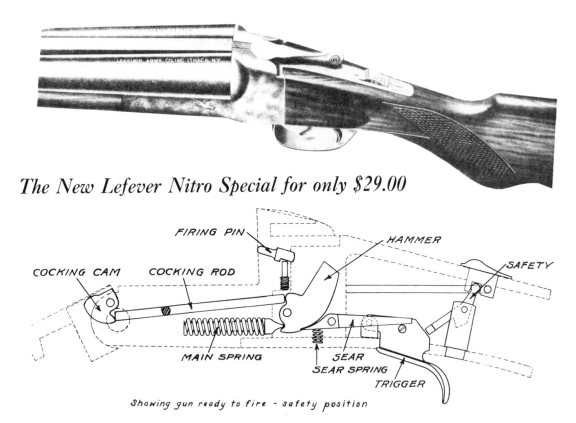

The New Lefever Nitro Special for only $29.00

Figure 4-30   New Lefever Nitro Special, and drawing of mechanism.

77,000 times and that the first test gun fired about 10,000 times without a break. The shotgun had a floating firing pin that was held in position by a vertical screw. The outline of the box-lock frame is shown in dotted lines. The hammers were located deep within the frame and were driven by powerful mainsprings, located low in the frame and pressing on plungers which tended to rotate the hammer counterclockwise. After the gun was fired the hammers were recocked by a long cocking rod which bore on a cam surface located above the hammer pivot. The cocking rod, in turn, was driven by a cocking cam attached to the barrels. As the gun was broken open, the cocking cam rotated around the pivot and drove the cocking rod to the rear, rotating the hammer clockwise. When the fully cocked position was reached, the sear was snapped into the sear notch by the sear spring. The triggers, pivoted at their extreme forward end, had a lateral extension which is shown as a screw head in the illustration. Pulling the trigger lifted the rear end of the sear, rotating it around the sear pivot and releasing the hammer. This linkage

gave a high mechanical advantage and could be arranged to give a very low trigger pull, but would have to be carefully adjusted or the pull would tend to be long and creepy. The shotgun was also fitted with a tang safety. In the "on" position, as shown in the illustration, the safety would block the motion of the trigger. This design was basically quite safe although it would be preferable for the safety to operate on the sear (but much more difficult to incorporate into the design). The gun was also fitted with an automatic safety which can be seen as the long slender rod extending forward from the safety in the direction of the cocking cam. With this design the safety would automatically be put in an "on" position each time the gun was opened. The Lefever Nitro Special was introduced at serial number 100,000 by Ithaca and continued in production until 1947, with a total of nearly a quarter of a million manufactured. Another model, the double-barreled "Lefever A Grade," was produced from 1934 to 1939; Lefever also produced thousands of moderately priced single-barreled shotguns of both hammer and hammerless styles.

Eventually, like most of the other double-barreled shotguns, the Lefever was forced off the market by rising costs.

Fox Double-Barreled Shotguns

One of the few companies manufacturing double-barreled shotguns today in the United States is the Savage Arms Company of Westfield, Massachusetts. The company was founded by Arthur W. Savage in 1894 with help from John Marlin, founder of the Marlin Firearms Company, who manufactured the first Savage lever-action rifles with a rotary magazine. This famous rifle was patented in 1893, and evolved into the Savage Model 99, still the backbone of Savage Arms production. In 1930 the Fox Arms Company was purchased by the Stevens Arms Company, founded in 1864, for their fine line of double-barreled shotguns.

Both the Stevens and the Fox double-barreled shotguns are manufactured today in the modernized Savage factory in Westfield, Massachusetts. Both are solid shotguns in the medium-priced field, offering modern design and rugged construction.

A Savage Fox Model B shotgun is shown in Figure 4-31. It is fitted with a ventilated rib barrel and beavertail forearm. Both forearm and butt stock are manufactured with an elaborate pattern of impressed checkering. The shotgun has double triggers and a tang safety to give the shooter good solid service without expensive features.

Winchester Model 21

During the 1920s the Winchester Repeating Arms Company was going through an extremely difficult period, which finally led to bankruptcy in 1930. The company had increased the size of its manufacturing plant enormously to meet the demands of the First World War. Because of the tremendous urgency of production contracts, new buildings were not integrated into an efficient overall manufacturing operation, but were separated from each other depending on where space was available. The company was also caught in large fixed-price contracts which became unprofitable as spiraling wage costs between 1914 and 1918 rendered their cost estimates unrealistic. A further problem was the wave of isolation and anti-war feeling that swept the United States in the 1920s. Congress, particularly under the Nye Committee, generated great publicity against manufacturers who had contributed to the war effort, labeling them "merchants of death." Winchester, in common with most of the other arms manufacturers, was caught with excess plant capacity and a desperate need to diversify in order to build sufficient sales to support their enormous fixed overhead. Unfortunately the ventures into such areas as refrigerators, washing machines, roller skates and general hardware did not achieve the desired financial results and the value of the common stock declined from an unrealistic high of more than $2,500 per share during the war years to no value at all by the time the company was in receivership in 1931.

Despite the financial disaster which took the company into bankruptcy during the 1920s, the company maintained an excellent gun-design department under the leadership of Thomas Crossley Johnson. Variations of lever-action rifles were brought out, especially the model 53, a modernized version of the Model 1892. A modernized version of the Model 94 rifle was brought out with a 24-inch barrel and half magazine. Winchester also introduced a new heavy-caliber bolt-

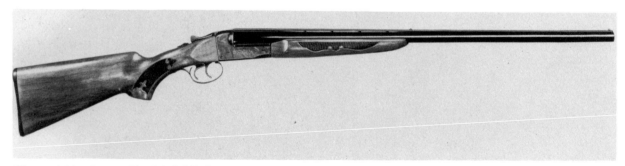

Figure 4-31   Savage Fox Model B shotgun.

action rifle, the Model 54, in 1925. This eventually became the famous Model 70 in the 1930s. In addition a number of rimfire rifle bolt-action designs were introduced.

During the late 1920s the technical staff started the design of the finest double-barreled shotgun that American ingenuity could create. It was a strange objective in the face of corporate financial chaos, but it also reflected the rising conservation movement of the 1920s with its emphasis on hunting as a sport rather than a means for large-scale harvesting of game. The Model 21 shotgun, finally introduced in 1930, incorporated many innovations in double-barreled shotgun design. One of its most unique design features was the use of barrels of chrome molybdenum steel, which could be finished, heat treated and then joined together by a special vertical dovetail method at the breech which mechanically interlocked the assembly.

The internal mechanism of a modern Model 21 shotgun is shown in Figure 4-32. It is a box-lock mechanism with a single trigger and selective ejectors. The Model 21 is designed with a very long distance between the breech face and the barrel pivot. The barrel has a heavy lug machined integrally with the barrel forgings, its rear end having a large undercut surface. When the barrels are in the fully closed position the locking bolt extends forward from the breech face, fitting over the undercut in the barrel thus locking the barrels in a downward position. This

locking system is extremely strong. When several thousand proof loads were fired through a Model 21 shotgun in an extended torture test to prove the strength of the locking system, the guns passed the test with no problem.

The hammers are powered by coil springs which surround the connecting bars. The rear end of the bar is hooked into a slot in the hammer, the front with a curved toe bears against the cocking cam which is attached to the barrels. The gun is opened by swinging the top lever to the right which draws the locking bolt into the face of the standing breech. The barrels can then be rotated around the hinge, which carries the cocking cam counterclockwise. This drives the connecting rod to the rear, compressing the mainspring and rotating the hammer clockwise. When the hammer reaches a fully cocked position as shown in the illustration a sear (the triangular white bar below the hammer) jumps up into the sear notch cut into the lower surface of the hammer. When the barrels are closed there is a gap between the cocking cam and the connecting rod. As the trigger is pulled it lifts the back end of the sear, rotating it around its pivot and dropping the front of the sear out of the notch in the hammer. This allows the mainspring to drag the connecting rod forward, rotating the hammer counterclockwise and slamming the integral firing pin into the primer of the shotshell.

The selective ejector mechanism senses whether the shotshell has been fired. If unfired, the

Figure 4-32   Cutaway of breech mechanism of Winchester Model 21 shotgun.

ejector merely lifts it a short distance out of its chamber so that the shooter can remove it. If it has been fired the powerful ejector spring shown in the forearm is released, driving the ejector hammer to the rear which, in turn, strikes the ejector rod a sharp blow kicking the empty shells at high velocity clear of the gun.

The Model 21 shotgun was placed in production in 1929, the first deliveries to the warehouse being made in March, 1930. They were double-trigger models with a fairly slender forearm. The gun was announced in the price list of January 1931 and the single-trigger model was available in April of that year. Both styles could be purchased with plain extractors or selective ejectors. It is surprising this was the first double-barreled shotgun manufactured at the Winchester plant. Initial reception of the Model 21 was pretty modest because there just wasn't much of an advertising budget for a company in bankruptcy. When Winchester was purchased by the Western Cartridge Company, John Olin came to New Haven to head Winchester. Mr. Olin always had a strong interest in firearms and he encouraged more active sales-promotion efforts which led to increasing acceptance of the Model 21. During the 1930s most of the shotguns were manufactured with raised matted-rib barrels of 26-, 28-, 30- and 31-inch lengths. Ventilated-rib barrels were gradually added during the 1930s, finally being made available with the 28-inch barrel in 1947. The Model 21 was originally introduced in 12, 16 and 20 gauge with a 28-gauge model added in 1936. The few special-order 410 model shotguns manufactured are truly a collector's delight. The slender lightweight barrels give a delicate appearance to the shotgun and shifts the center of balance well to the rear, making it an extremely fast shotgun for pointing.

During the 1940s there was a gradual shift from plain extractors and double triggers so that by the 1950s all models were single trigger with selective ejectors. In 1959 rising costs forced the discontinuation of regular manufacture. Since that time Model 21 shotguns have been manufactured in the Custom Shop in three grades, Custom, Pigeon and Grand American. A Pigeon grade Model 21 shotgun is shown in Figure 4-33. These shotguns involve an enormous amount of hand labor, making them extremely expensive, but many shooters consider that there is no finer double-barreled shotgun manufactured anywhere in the world. The Pigeon grade has carefully selected deluxe-walnut stocks with a fine grain to the wood. Butt stocks and forearms are extensively checkered with carefully carved borders. The receiver and chamber end of the barrel are engraved with scrolls and hunting scenes making the shotgun a beautiful work of art. Such a shotgun will easily withstand a lifetime of hard use and can be passed on for generations.

SINGLE-BARRELED BREAK-OPEN SHOTGUNS

Break-open breech-loading single-shot shotguns were offered by most American manufacturers during the late nineteenth century but the design variations were staggering. The Stevens Arms Company introduced this type in the 1870s and literally dozens of other manufacturers offered their own particular styles and models. By 1900 the single-barreled shotgun had evolved into two general classes. The lowest-priced shotguns offered by most manufacturers were break-open hammer-style shotguns. At a slightly higher price were the hammerless break-open shotguns such as that shown in Figure 4-34. This is the single-

Figure 4-33   Winchester Model 21, Pigeon grade.

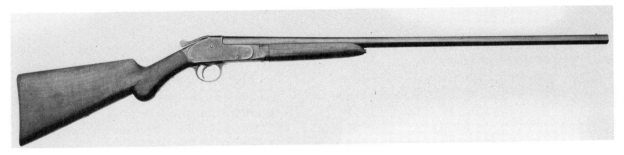

Figure 4-34 Remington Model 1893 hammerless break-open shotgun.

barreled Remington Model 1893 advertised as "The most popular low-priced gun on the market." It was offered in 12, 16 and 20 gauge at the modest price of $10 and in 10, 24 and 28 gauge at $11. The 10-gauge models were available with 32- and 34-inch barrels. The smaller gauges were available with barrel lengths ranging all the way from 28 to 34 inches. All of the shotguns weighed between 5¾ and 6½ pounds.

The Remington Model 1893 was manufactured until 1902 and a total of 86,805 was produced. In 1902 a slightly modernized similar in appearance version was introduced in 12 and 16 gauge with an automatic ejector. A total of 65,698 was manufactured before discontinuation in 1910. The Remington shotguns were fitted with plain walnut stocks, blued barrels and case-hardened receivers. They had a side cocking lever installed on the left-hand side of the action which could be used to cock the internal hammer.

Single-barreled hammerless shotguns were offered by many other manufacturers. The Lefever "Long Range Single Barreled Field and Trap Gun" was a more modern design manufactured into the 1930s. It had an oil-finished black walnut butt stock and forearm which were hand checkered. The gun featured an automatic safety device and an automatic ejector which kicked the fired shell clear as the gun was opened. The guns were offered in 12, 16 and 20 gauge and 410-bore weighing from 5½ to 6½ pounds. Retail prices were quite reasonable at $16.

Single-Barreled Hammer-Style Shotguns

The least expensive shotguns offered by most manufacturers were the hammer-style break-open designs. Over the years almost every major manufacturer has offered this type of model. An early twentieth century design is the Marlin Model 60 shown in Figure 4-35. The number of design variations with this type of shotgun simply staggers the imagination. Some had top levers or levers under the receiver; most were fitted with rebounding hammers, as shown in the illustration. The hammer has rebounded to a neutral position where it is not in contact with the firing pin—on most good designs it could be struck a heavy blow in this position and would still not contact the firing pin. This was accomplished by cutting a deep safety notch in the hammer which engaged the trigger in the rebound position. When the gun was fully cocked and the trigger pulled, the hammer spring drove forward through the neutral position and struck the firing pin, igniting the cartridge. Springs were arranged to return the hammer to the neutral position and as soon as the trigger was released the hammer was locked firmly in that position.

Stocks of walnut and other hard woods were fitted in straight- and pistol-grip designs. Frames were often case hardened.

Since these shotguns were often the lowest-priced models available the competition was intense, leading some manufacturers to make such

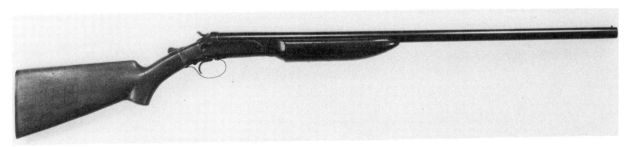

Figure 4-35 Marlin Model 60 hammer-style break-open shotgun.

shortcuts that many marginally safe shotguns of this style were manufactured. In general these old-time economy shotguns should be relegated to the attic rather than dragged out into the hunting field.

As a boy I was always pretty cautious with my new purchases, and fired every new rifle or shotgun remotely with a lanyard before firing from the shoulder. I picked up a used break-open shotgun which appeared to be in excellent condition for about $7.00. I tested it by tying it to an old rubber tire lying on the ground and firing several heavy magnum shotshells through the action. It functioned well when it was tied down, but on every shot fired from the shoulder the top lever would rotate, the action would pop open and the fired shotshell would be ejected half way out of the chamber. I pointed this defect out to the store where it was purchased. They informed me that it was strictly my problem. As it was the type of malfunction I didn't care to fool with, eventually I sold the shotgun at a loss to an acquaintance with access to a machine shop who figured he could fix it.

Modern single-shot break-open shotguns put out by the major manufacturers are all proof tested before leaving the factory. This type of test assures the owner that the shotgun can withstand a substantial overload and is safe with normal factory ammunition. These shotguns are still extremely competitively priced. Winchester introduced their Model 37 single-barrel hammer-style shotgun in the early 1930s, but by the 1950s were losing substantial amounts of money on this model. We performed design study after design study seeking concepts which would add features of value to the shooter but manufacturing costs were too high to justify the purchase of new tooling and return a profit. Many ingenious designs were tried, including shotguns in which the barrel slid forward within a cylindrical receiver, and one in which the barrel twisted open around a shaft located low in the forearm. Die-cast receivers with steel inserts and other modern manufacturing approaches were investigated but there was no way that we could find that would yield an adequate return on the investment required. Eventually the problem was solved by marketing a break-open hammer-style shotgun manufactured by Winchester of Canada. Many other manufacturers have dropped this kind of shotgun because of the severe cost problems.

Ithaca Single-Barreled Trap Shotguns

The Ithaca Gun Company is an example of a fine old American firm who made the difficult transition from double-barreled to repeating shotguns. Ithaca introduced their first double-barreled shotgun in 1880. In addition to an excellent reputation for double-barreled shotguns, Ithaca also developed a reputation for trap shotguns, especially single shot. In 1914 they introduced their first single-barreled trap shotgun which has been manufactured in limited production since that time. Originally introduced at prices of $100 to $310, these have always been expensive shotguns—probably the finest single-barreled trap guns made in the United States. A premium model known as the Sousa grade was introduced at $500 in 1916. Prices have changed drastically over the years. By 1955 the original $100 model was $400 and the Sousa grade was $2,000. At present the SE model is $1,750 and the last quoted price on the Sousa was over $4,000. Two deluxe models of the Ithaca Shotgun are shown in Figure 4-36. All models are hammerless single-barreled shotguns with ventilated ribs. The lock mechanism is designed and manufactured with extreme care to give smooth action and crisp trigger pulls. Since these are specialty shotguns appealing to experienced trap shooters, they are ornately engraved and finished with the greatest attention to detail. A closeup of the Sousa in the lower illustration of Figure 4-36 shows the ornately carved checkering patterns and how the receiver and barrel are extensively engraved. Gold pheasants have been inlaid into the side of the stock and the background stippled to give relief. Shotguns of this type make excellent presentation pieces for a special occasion or for use by an extremely skilled trap shooter who can afford such luxury.

Savage-Stevens Single-Barreled Shotguns

The Savage Arms Company has been active in the manufacture of single-shot shotguns for many years. The J. Stevens and Company Arms catalog of 1877 lists a variety of rimfire and centerfire rifles, and single- and double-barreled hammer-style shotguns. The single-barreled shotguns were sold at $15.00 for the plain barrel, $19.50 for a twist barrel, and $21.50 for laminated steel.

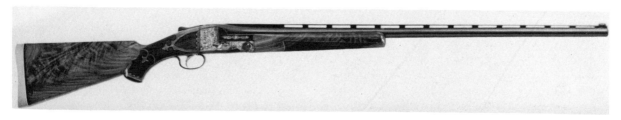

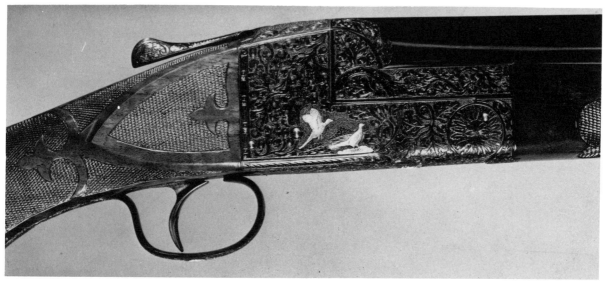

Figure 4-36 Two Ithaca single-barreled trap shotguns. The one shown in closeup has gold pheasants inlaid in the breech.

By the 1960s Savage Arms was marketing five distinct models of single-barreled single-shot shotguns under the Savage and Stevens trademark. The most expensive offering was the Savage Model 220, a hammerless single-barreled shotgun offered in 12, 16, 20 gauge and 410 bore. Instead of a top lever this shotgun was opened by a lever located on the right side of the action. Weight was about six pounds.

The most important single-barreled shotgun was the Model 94 offered under the Stevens trademark. This model is shown in Figure 4-37. The Model 94 is a popular one with more than 1,000,000 manufactured. It is representative of a fully modern American hammer-style shotgun design. It is fitted with a checkered pistol-grip butt stock and forearm. The action is opened with a top lever and is fitted with an ejector which kicks out the shell when the action is open. The hammer is a rebounding design which rebounds to a safety locked position as shown in the illustration. This model is offered in 12, 16, 20, and 28 gauge and 410 bore with barrel lengths of 26 to 32 inches. In 12 gauge a special "long Tom" barrel is offered which is a full 36 inches long. Weight of the shotgun is about 6¼ pounds and overall length is 52 inches with the 36-inch barrel.

In addition to these models Stevens offers two other hammer-style models. One is a modern design with long sweeping curves and a grooved cylindrical forearm similar to that fitted to many slide-action shotguns. The receiver is manufac-

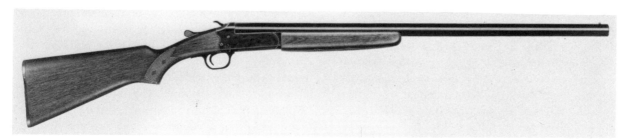

Figure 4-37 Stevens Model 94 single-barreled hammer-style shotgun.

tured with raised curved side panels, and the trigger guard has a long sweeping extension to complete its modernistic appearance. The Savage-Stevens line also includes a series of bolt-action shotguns in single-shot, box-magazine, and tubular-magazine designs.

OVER-UNDER SHOTGUNS

Over-under firearms have been used for centuries as a means of providing two fast-aimed shots. Even in the early days of the United States some native gunsmiths manufactured over-under flintlock firearms—often with one rifle and one shotgun barrel. The general arrangement with these flintlocks was to have two barrels, two pans and two frizzens. The barrel assembly was pivoted on a long iron shaft which extended from the front of the receiver. A latch held the barrels in a vertical position. After the first shot was fired the hunter released the latch and rotated the barrel assembly 180° bringing the bottom barrel on top. When the hammer was recocked the gun was ready for a relatively fast second shot.

Europeans also used over-under designs but with their more sophisticated manufacturing techniques developed more in the direction of side by side double-barreled shotguns. The advantage of the side by side design was that no motion of the barrels was required and the shooter could simply shift from the front trigger to the rear and get his second shot off much faster. The disadvantage was that a great deal of high-quality labor was required. For example the barrels had to be bent, carefully adjusted and soldered together to give patterns which would be located at the same point of aim. If tapered shotgun barrels were fastened together without bending, the centerlines of the barrels would be further apart at the breech than at the muzzle and the shotgun would crossfire badly. American over-under flintlocks usually were of small caliber and used heavy octagonal barrels which were of uniform shape from breech to muzzle. These guns often weighed 10 to 11 pounds with .32- to .40-caliber barrels.

Among the many contributions of John M. Browning to firearms design was an outstanding over-under shotgun. John Browning started work on this shotgun after developing the military Browning Automatic Rifle (BAR) for the United States Government during the First World War. He also developed the caliber .30 and caliber .50

Browning short-recoil machine guns which were standard for use in the United States Army during World War II, as well as other military automatic weapons, including the caliber .45 automatic pistol (Model of 1911) and automatic cannon up to 37mm.

After World War I was over, the Browning brothers went back to their primary interest—sporting firearms. John M. Browning was President of the Browning Arms Company and his brother Matthew was Vice President in charge of the business side until his death in 1923. The Browning sons had also joined the firm by the early 1920s. Design work on the new over-under shotgun was completed in 1926. John Browning went to Belgium that year to be present when the first over-unders were manufactured at the Fabrique Nationale plant in the town of Herstal, and he died there of a heart attack.

The over-under shotgun was put on the market in Belgium with automatic selective ejectors and double triggers in 1927. It was imported into the United States and added to the Browning Arms Company product line in 1928. Later John's son Val A. Browning designed a selective single trigger which was added to the shotgun and is standard today.

The Browning "superposed" trap model shotgun is shown in Figure 4-38. It is offered in 12, 20, and 28 gauge and 410 bore. Magnum models are offered in 12 gauge, chambered for the three-inch shells. Weight of the magnums is slightly over eight pounds, while the standard field guns vary from 6¼ to 7¾ pounds. Special skeet and trap models are manufactured, and a special ⅝ inch wide rib is available on the trap models. Special "super light" models are available, weighing 6 pounds in 20 gauge and only 6½ pounds in 12 gauge. Both straight grip and pistol grip options are offered on the stocks.

Remington Model 32

In 1932 the Remington Arms Company introduced their Model 32 over-under shotgun in 12 gauge. The appearance of the shotgun is shown in Figure 4-39. It was a high-quality shotgun and the large amount of hand work inherent in it made it one of the most expensive firearms in the Remington line. A total of 5,053 shotguns were produced prior to discontinuation in 1942. An average yearly production of just over 500 shotguns poses extremely difficult problems in manu-

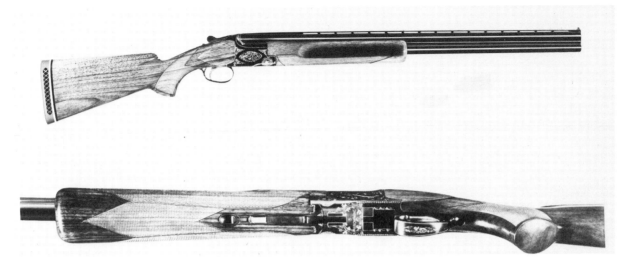

Figure 4-38 Browning superposed shotgun in 12 gauge, side and bottom view.

Figure 4-39 Remington Model 32 over-under shotgun.

facture and management. Complex tooling must be bought, set up and run to manufacture the components and yet the production runs are so short that enormous amounts of time are used in setting up and adjusting the tooling compared to the length of the production run. The alternative is to leave the machines set up for each of the cuts involved in the complex design and only run the machinery for a few weeks each year. The first approach involves high costs for setting up and tearing down the tooling at the end of each short production run, the second involves paying high interest and amortization charges on machinery which is sitting idle for $9/10$ of a year. Production of over-under shotguns was further complicated by the need for a great deal of skilled hand labor to finish and adjust the components to make a smooth-working long-lasting shotgun.

These factors combined to make the Remington Model 32 a high-priced and highly prized shotgun for its lucky owners. It rapidly achieved a reputation for durability and excellent performance.

The Remington Model 32 was offered in only 12 gauge with 26-, 28- and 30-inch barrels. The standard model is shown in Figure 4-39 but it was also available with a solid rib or ventilated rib on special order. The barrels were usually bored with modified choke on the lower barrel and full choke on the upper. Other combinations of full, modified, improved cylinder or cylinder bore were optional on special order. In over-under shotguns the lower barrel was almost invariably bored in a more-open choke than the upper. Since the lower barrel is more directly in line with the shooter's shoulder this is almost always fired first giving minimum disturbance to the aim. The shooter can then recover quickly and fire his second shot at game which is at a greater distance. The exception to this is an over-under shotgun used at skeet, for which both barrels will be bored very close to an improved cylinder choke, or at trap where both barrels are bored full choke.

The Remington Model 32 was fitted with stocks made of selected figured American walnut. The butt stock and forearm were hand checkered with fine 22-pitch checkering—meaning that there were 22 lines of checkering per inch of width.

Normal checkering is 20 lines per inch and less expensive shotguns were often checkered in 18 or less lines per inch. The stock was given three coats of varnish. The single selective trigger was adjusted to give a pull of 3½ to 5 pounds. The weight of the shotgun with 30-inch barrels was approximately 7¾ pounds and the overall length was 47 inches.

The Model 32 trap shotgun was normally manufactured with a 30-inch ventilated-rib barrel. A 32-inch ventilated-rib barrel was optional. Standard boring was full choke on both barrels but other choke combinations were offered as no-cost options. The skeet shotgun, another special design, was normally fitted with a plain 26-inch barrel. The 28-inch barrel and solid or ventilated rib were available on special order. Normal special skeet boring was a choke with a .005 inch constriction in the upper barrel and a .008 inch constriction in the lower. Other combinations were available on special order. Overall length was 43 inches. Special deluxe models such as the Tournament High Grade, the Expert Grade and the Premier Grade, available on special order, featured increasing levels of engraving on the frame and barrel.

Marlin Model 90

In 1937 the Marlin Firearms Company introduced their Model 90 over-under shotgun which they manufactured until 1942 and again from 1946 until 1958. The early models were introduced with a double-trigger mechanism and were available in 12, 16 and 20 gauges. Later Marlin added a non-selective single trigger, designed to fire the bottom barrel first, the top second. A Marlin Model 90ST is shown in Figure 4-40. The shotguns were fitted with checkered walnut butt stocks and forearms. A pistol-grip cap and rubber

recoil pad were standard on late models. Barrel lengths of 26, 28 and 30 inch were available in 12 gauge, and 26 and 28 inch in 16 and 20 gauge. The 26-inch barrels were normally bored with the bottom improved cylinder and the upper modified. The 28- and 30-inch barrels were normally bored with a modified-choke lower barrel and a full-choke upper barrel. Weight of the shotguns was about 7½ pounds in 12 gauge and 6¼ pounds in 16 and 20 gauge.

The action of a Marlin Model 90 shotgun is shown in Figure 4-41. As the top lever was pushed, it cammed the upper surface of the vertical link forward. The bottom surface of the link moved to the rear drawing the locking block out of the V-shaped cut in the barrel. This allowed the barrels to be broken open. As the barrels were tipped upwards, the cocking rod (shown lying along the bottom of the receiver) was driven to the rear. The cocking rod was in contact with the cocking lever which was so designed that a small motion of the cocking rod provided a much greater motion of the firing pins, which were forced to the rear until the mainsprings were fully compressed and the firing pins caught in the sear notches. As the barrels were closed, cocking lever and rod moved forward under the urging of a torsion spring wrapped around the lower pivot of the lever. Movement of the cocking lever to a fully forward position allowed the firing pins to fly forward with no restraint when the triggers were pulled. The sears were designed as levers which were pivoted at their center. The triggers were both pivoted at the extreme forward surface. As the trigger was pulled it lifted the forward surface of the sear rotating it clockwise. This motion withdrew it from the notch in the firing pin, allowing the firing pin to fly free and fire the cartridge.

The Marlin Model 90 was also fitted with a

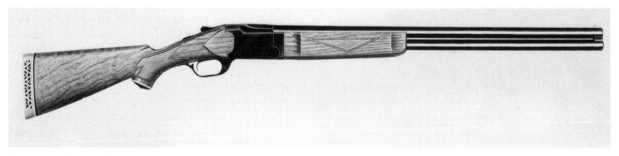

Figure 4-40   Marlin Model 90-ST over-under shotgun.

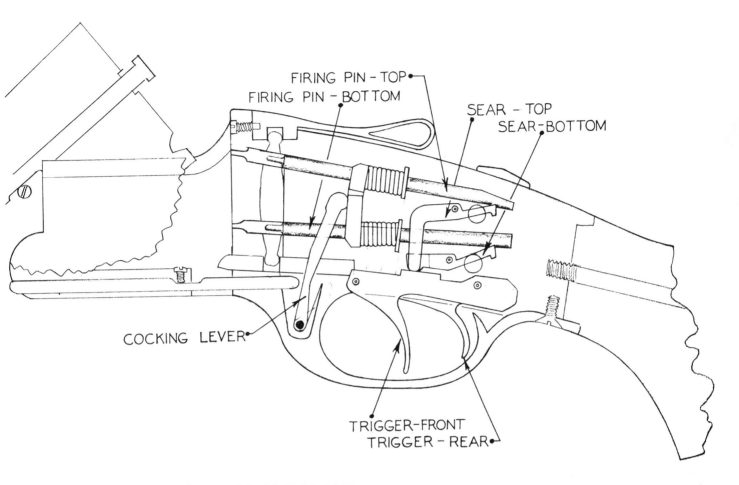

FIRING PIN - TOP
FIRING PIN - BOTTOM
SEAR - TOP
SEAR - BOTTOM
COCKING LEVER
TRIGGER - FRONT
TRIGGER - REAR

Figure 4-41 Firing mechanism of the Marlin Model 90.

tang safety. As the safety was moved to the rear to an "ON" position it moved the upper arm of a belt crank, pivoted near the rear of the receiver, which was rotated clockwise moving its lower surface over to block the rear surfaces of both triggers, thereby preventing any trigger motion.

The Marlin Model 90 was carefully designed to take advantage of modern American manufacturing techniques. The original models were fitted with double triggers and plain extractors. The use of striker mechanisms rather than internal hammers simplified the design of the action. On the later models a "non-selective" single trigger was offered, meaning that the trigger mechanism was designed to fire the lower barrel first and then the upper. Even with this careful effort to simplify the design as far as possible, manufacturing costs rose steadily in the post World War II years, finally forcing discontinuation of this fine model in 1957.

Savage Over-Under Rifle/Shotgun

There is an interesting over-under design that has been manufactured by the Savage Arms Company for many years—their combination rifle and shotgun shown in Figure 4-42. This modestly priced firearm gives the hunter the instant choice of rifle or shotgun depending on the hunting circumstances. Normally these guns have a .22-caliber rimfire barrel on top and a 20-gauge or .410-bore shotgun barrel below. In recent years the models have been expanded so that the upper barrel can be chambered for .22 rimfire, .22 Winchester magnum rimfire, caliber .222 Remington or 30-30 Winchester centerfire cartridges. The lower barrels are chambered for 20-gauge 2¾- or 3-inch shells or for .410 bore 2½- or 3-inch shells. Both shotgun barrels are designed with full choke. Pistol grip stocks are made of walnut and are plain on the modest-priced models and with checkering patterns on the deluxe grades.

Figure 4-42 Savage Model 24V rifle/shotgun, and closeup of breech.

Length of pull is 14 inches and a pistol grip cap is fitted to the deluxe models. Weights are about 6¾ pounds for any of the models. Barrel length is 24 inches and overall length is 40 inches, making it a light and compact firearm. Special models are offered with telescopic sights for the shooter who is primarily interested in varmint hunting, using the shotgun barrel as a backup for occasional short shots at moving game.

Selection of the barrel to be fired is accomplished by a small pivoted lever mounted on top of the hammer. The shooter can easily move the selector to choose the barrel as he cocks the hammer for his shot. The Savage rifle/shotgun combination is a rather unique American adaptation of the extremely expensive German "drilling" rifle/shotgun combination firearms.

Winchester Model 101

During the 1960s American shooters became increasingly interested in hammerless over-under shotguns. This posed a difficult problem to American manufacturers for the high amount of hand labor this style of shotgun needs makes them prohibitive to produce in the United States. Many approaches were investigated. Some major manufacturers tried designing an over-and-under shotgun specifically for American manufacturing techniques, with the hope that sophisticated tooling would reduce the amount of hand labor sufficiently so that the shotgun could be sold at a competitive price. Unfortunately this sort of tooling costs several million dollars and can only be justified if a great many shotguns will be manufactured to the design. Over-and-under shotguns have traditionally been expensive, relatively low-volume models. The one American over-and-under shotgun design that has been on the market continuously during the past 50 years has been manufactured at Fabrique Nationale in Herstal, Belgium, and marketed in the United States through the Browning Arms Company. Both Marlin and Remington have had to give up manufacture in the United States.

During the 1960s most American manufacturers came to the conclusion that production in the United States was not economically practical.

Winchester initiated an intensive study of manufacturers in France, Germany, Spain, Italy and Japan and after years of study established a joint manufacturing company in Japan—Olin-Kodensha Limited. Winchester Product Engineering and Research personnel worked closely with the Japanese engineers to refine designs and develop the best steels and heat treatments for use on internal components. Tooling was manufactured in the United States and shipped to Japan. Winchester resident engineers and managers lived in Japan at the factory to assist in the complex start-up problems and to provide continuous supervision of quality control. Experimental models manufactured in Japan and shipped to the Winchester Research facility in New Haven were given extended endurance tests to evaluate their performance. Some of the tricky problems that were faced included the conversion of American steels of known performance into their exact Japanese equivalents.

To many shooters a shotgun is simply made of steel, but to the design engineer this is a great oversimplification. Some components perform well if made from a medium carbon steel, properly heat treated. Others require a chromium-molybdenum-carbon alloy, which is very difficult to machine but provides great strength and toughness after heat treatment. Still others are manufactured of chromium-vanadium-carbon alloys providing great toughness and wearing quality. Basically the chromium, molybdenum and vanadium make the steels extremely tough, while the addition of carbon means that the steels can be heat treated to various hardness levels to provide the best overall combination of toughness, strength, and wearing qualities.

Finally in 1963 Winchester announced the Model 101 field gun with ventilated rib in 12 gauge. This shotgun is shown in Figure 4-43. In 1966 a 20 gauge model was introduced. All model 101 shotguns are manufactured with single-trigger mechanism, ventilated rib and selective ejectors. A combined safety and barrel selector is fitted to the tang. This device allows the shooter to fire the upper or lower barrel first and provides a manual safety when moved to the fully rearward position. During the past decade additional models have been offered, such as the trap gun available with a standard or Monte Carlo stock, a skeet model and a 12-gauge magnum field gun designed for use with three-inch shells. Barrel lengths of 26 to 30 inches are offered and the weights range from 7½ to 7¾ pounds.

During the late 1960s and early 1970s many other American manufacturers have followed a similar course. Gun manufacturers in Belgium, France, Germany, Italy, Spain and Japan have been investigated and one American manufacturer after another has introduced over-and-under and double-barreled models manufactured abroad but marketed through the American companies. These studies must be very carefully performed for Americans are demanding shooters, being, in general, bigger and stronger than their European and Asian counterparts and demanding considerably more powerful ammunition. Designs which may be perfectly adequate for the normal European 2½ inch, 12-gauge shotshells loaded with one ounce of shot may rapidly fall apart when subjected to the enormous pounding of American 12-gauge magnum shotshells packed with 1½ ounces of shot (at peak pressures close to 13,000 pounds per square inch). The enormous difference in power levels between light European field loads and heavy American magnum loads has caused all kinds of problems for manufacturers on both sides of the Atlantic. I remember when Winchester was shipping Model 50 automatic shotguns to Europe during the 1950s and receiving complaints that the shotguns would not function properly. We ran

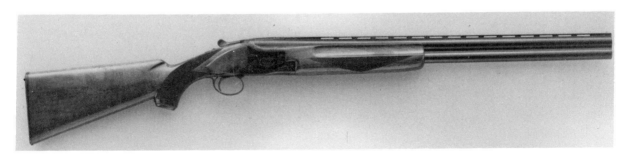

Figure 4-43 Winchester Model 101 over-under shotgun.

an extensive series of tests on European ammunition and found that some of the more popular European loads had a slow pressure rise to a peak of only 8,500 pounds per square inch and then a fairly gradual decline until muzzle exit. The Winchester Model 50 required a fairly sharp pressure rise to its peak to accelerate the floating chamber. The European loads simply rose too slow for the shotgun to function properly. It was finally necessary to modify all of the shotguns being shipped to Europe to give them a longer power stroke. The problem works the other way around, too. European double-barreled, over-under and automatic shotguns which will last indefinitely with the medium-powered European shotshells often get in trouble with American loads. The problem was most crucial with European semiautomatic designs that had not been tested with American ammunition. These types of problems meant that American manufacturers had to be extremely careful in their survey and analysis of overseas manufacturers to be sure that the guns would be strong and tough before marketing them in this country. These problems have been largely overcome and more and more American manufacturers are offering over-and-under and double-barreled designs which are manufactured abroad to meet American requirements.

Chapter 5

EARLY REPEATING SHOTGUNS

REVOLVING SHOTGUNS

The idea of a firearm with a single barrel and a revolving cylinder holding many shots dates back to the Middle Ages. There are examples of matchlock snaphance and wheel-lock revolving firearms in European museums and around 1810 an English inventor named Collier developed a flintlock revolving carbine. It had a large fluted cylinder and individual pans for the chambers. The powder was held in the pans by a band encircling the cylinder. The frizzen mechanism was mounted at the top, and when the hammer fell sparks would fall into the pan aligned with the barrel.

The Collier mechanism required that the chambers be revolved by hand. In an attempt to provide good breech sealing Collier incorporated a conical seat between the chamber and the end of the barrel. The cylinder had to be withdrawn to the rear, rotated to the new position, then snapped forward under a spiral spring, which surrounded the central pivot on which the cylinders rotated. The cylinder was held forward during firing by a small pivoted lock which was operated by the trigger mechanism. Collier firearms were not very successful but were manufactured in both flintlock and percussion designs.

The most successful revolving firearms were the ingenious designs of Samuel Colt. Even as early as the late 1830s Sam Colt envisioned the manufacture of pistols, rifles and shotguns. Three superb examples of his early firearms are shown in Figure 5-1, part of the extensive Colt collection at

the Wadsworth Atheneum in Hartford, Conn. The upper illustration shows a rifle with a full-length stock and octagonal barrel. The forearm is held to the barrel with four wedges that pass through lugs welded to its underside. A conventional wooden ramrod was held in a groove below the stock by two brass ramrod pipes plus a brass ferrule where the ramrod entered the forearm. This is apparently an experimental design made in the mid-1830s. The rear of the cylinder is shrouded within a metal housing so that all of the nipples are hidden. The trigger guard contains two levers, the longer of which, extending below the guard, was used to rotate the cylinder and lock the hammer.

The middle illustration shows another experimental rifle, ornately decorated with an elaborate brass patch box and extensive engraving. The construction is similar to the one above it except that the lever for cocking the hammer and rotating the cylinder is to the rear of the trigger.

The lowest illustration shows another experimental design from about the same time fitted with a half-length forearm. (The wooden ramrods are missing on the middle and lower illustrations.) This bottom illustration has many points of similarity to some of the experimental pistols made at Colt's Paterson, New Jersey, factory around 1836. The rear half of the cylinder is still shrouded within a metal framework and the cocking lever is hidden or missing. By 1837, production models had been developed similar in general to the lowest illustration but the cylinder was fully exposed

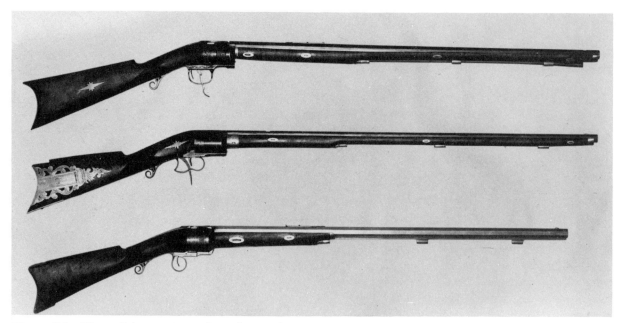

Figure 5-1 Three Colt experimental revolving rifles.

and a ring had been added under the fore part of the frame. When the ring was swung it cocked the hammerless mechanism and rotated the cylinder. On most production models the wooden forearm was eliminated.

Rifles and shotguns used much heavier powder charges than pistols increasing the forces acting on the joint between the revolving cylinder and the barrel with the result that early Colt rifles and shotguns tended to spring open, leaking substantial quantities of gas. It was not until the "Root side-hammer" designs had been developed in 1855 that revolving rifles, carbines and shotguns became really practical.

Elisha K. Root was Sam Colt's top technical man and factory superintendent during the 1850s. An illustration of a Model 1855 Colt shotgun is shown in Figure 5-2. Root designed an entirely new revolver mechanism with a solid boxlike frame into which the shotgun barrel was screwed. Instead of having the hammer on the centerline, as on all earlier Colt mechanisms, the hammer layout was similar to that on conventional firearms— pivoted low to the right of the lock. For this reason these became known as the "Root side-hammer" firearms. They had substantial advantages for a powerful weapon such as a shotgun since the solid frame gave a rigid connection between barrel, frame and butt stock.

A closeup of the gun mechanism with the ham-

Figure 5-2 Colt Model 1855 revolving shotgun.

mer cocked and ready to fire is shown in Figure 5-3. The cylinder position was controlled by the shaft on which the cylinder rotated. Just forward of the hammer there is a cylindrical plate with slots cut into the outer edge. The internal lock mechanism worked on these slots to rotate the shaft and cylinder. Although this particular shotgun, from the Winchester Gun Museum collection, is in excellent condition the cylinder can be wobbled out of alignment with the barrel by twisting it with the fingers. The amount of motion is estimated as about .035 of an inch on each side of the center line. There are no locking cuts in the external surface of the cylinder as on all previous and later Colt models. The use of cylinder locking cuts and a cylinder latch provided much closer alignment between the cylinder and barrel.

The dimensions and weights of this shotgun are highlighted on the table below:

Colt Model 1855 Revolving Shotgun
(Second design manufactured after 1859)

Weight	8¾ pounds
Length Over All	48¼ inches
Barrel Length	30 inches
Gauge	11
Bore Diameter at Muzzle	.746 inches
Diameter of Chambers	.755 inches

The outside diameter of the barrel at the muzzle is .860 inches which gave a wall thickness of .057 inches—fairly heavy for a shotgun barrel. The cylinder on this 11-gauge shotgun is also fairly massive—2.85 inches long with 5 chambers. The maximum width across two chambers is 2.215 inches so that the true diameter of the cylinder is approximately 2.25 inches. The chambers average .753 to .755 inches in diameter at the mouth and are 2.20 inches deep. The wall thickness of the metal in the chambers is slightly more than .080 inches.

The shotgun is marked "Col. Colt, Hartford, Ct. USA" on the top strap. The cylinder is marked "Patented Sept. 10, 1850." The receiver and barrel under the forearm bear the serial number 723.

Colt catalogues of the period show that shotguns could be purchased with barrels of 27, 30, 33 or 36 inches. These styles of firearms were actually manufactured from 1857 to 1872 in relatively small quantities. In 1860 the price list stated that the shotgun was available with a 27 inch barrel at a weight of 8 lbs. 12 oz. and a price of $40.00. This was a fairly high price but the prices previously had been higher for the flyer is marked

Colt's Patent Firearms Manufacturing Company
Col. Sam Colt, President
Reduced Prices for 1860

The .36 caliber Navy revolver was priced at $18.00 and the large .44 caliber Army (the old style Dragoon revolver) was priced at $20.00. Revolving rifles were priced at $32.00 to $43.00.

The price list for 1865 lists the shotguns as having a "caliber or size of bore 75-100ths of an inch diameter" at the following prices:

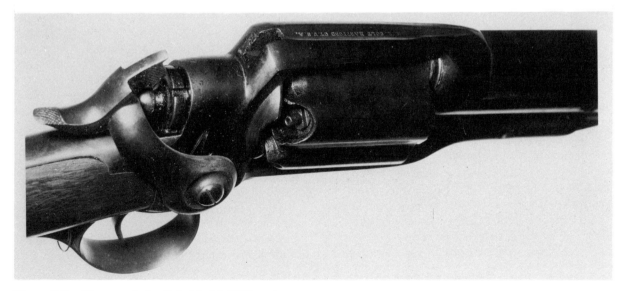

Figure 5-3 Closeup of the Colt Model 1855 action.

Price List, 1865

SHOT GUNS Calibre or Size of Bore, 75-100ths of an inch diameter

27 inch Barrel, Five Shots	Weight	9 lbs.	9 oz.	....	$47.25
30 " " " "	"	9 "	13 "	....	$48.75
33 " " " "	"	10 "	0 "	....	$50.25
36 " " " "	"	10 "	4 "	....	$51.75

The catalogue list of prices also notes that all shotguns were furnished with wad cutter, screwdriver and nipple wrench free of charge.

The price list for 1867 was more diversified containing prices for the shotguns of 75-100ths of an inch (or 11 gauge) and adding a footnote for smaller shotguns of slightly under 20 gauge, or 60-100ths of an inch bore. This price list also added the cost of ammunition. Otherwise prices were the same:

Price List, 1867

SHOTGUNS Calibre or Size of Bore 75-100ths of an inch diameter

27 inch Barrel, Five Shots	Weight	9 lbs.	9 oz.	....	$47.25
30 " " " "	"	9 "	13 "	....	$48.75
33 " " " "	"	10 "		....	$50.25
36 " " " "	"	10 "	4 "	....	$51.75

*Shot-Guns of 60 calibre are also made. Lengths of Barrels 27, 30 and 33 inches. Prices $9 less than corresponding lengths of 75 calibre.

CARTRIDGES—SHOT-GUNS

60-100ths of an inch calibre, in packages of 1,000 per thousand $27.50
75-100ths of an inch calibre, in packages of 1,000 per thousand $32.50

The ammunition for the Colt shotguns was quite ingenious. Sam Colt was well aware that the success of his revolving firearms depended on their having the proper ammunition. If bullets were too small there was a serious danger that the hot gas escaping in the joint between the cylinder and barrel would flash into the adjacent cylinders and fire those charges simultaneously. Carefully designed bullets which fitted snugly in the chamber prevented this hazard. Modern shooters of percussion revolvers often add a little extra insurance by filling the mouth of the chambers with lubricant, which tends to keep the barrel cleaner and provide an additional flame barrier. This danger was even more acute with the Colt rifles and shotguns, for the powder charges were much heavier so the gas pressure was much higher.

Sam Colt solved this problem by arranging for the manufacture of high-quality ammunition that would function properly in his firearms. A wooden block containing five shot cartridges is shown in Figure 5-4. Two wooden blocks have been carefully machined with half a cavity in each block. After the cartridges were loaded into the lower block the upper one was fitted over the top and the assembly sealed with a printed paper wrapper glued in place. The wrapper states that it contains "five combustible envelope cartridges" of No. 3 buckshot. It notes the use of Hazard's powder and states that these are 75-100ths-inch caliber designed for Col. Colt's patent revolving shotgun. It also states "Address Colt Cartridge Works, Hartford, Connecticut, U.S. America."

There are several interesting things about this ammunition, which is contained in the Winchester Gun Museum collection. At some time the powder containers were turned around, for the large end should be adjacent to the shot container. Also the right-hand cartridge in the illustration does not match the others, for it contains a charge of No. 3 shot which is .140 inches in diameter. The shot charge weighs 615.4 grains or 1.4 ounces. The shot charge contains about 153 pellets.

A drawing of the No. 3 buckshot cartridge is shown in Figure 5-5. The ammunition consists of two independent assemblies, one for powder, one for shot. The powder charge consists of 70 grains of black powder manufactured by the Hazard Powder Company, of Hazardville, Connecticut. Microscopic examination of it shows some free

Figure 5-4   Ammunition for Colt revolving shotgun.

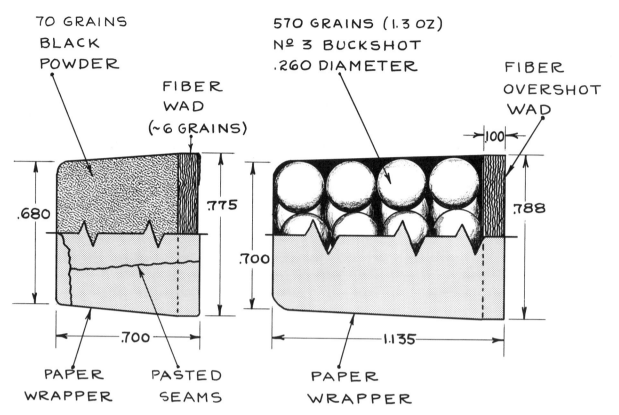

70 GRAINS
BLACK
POWDER

570 GRAINS (1.3 OZ)
Nº 3 BUCKSHOT
.260 DIAMETER

FIBER
WAD
(~6 GRAINS)

FIBER
OVERSHOT
WAD

.680   .775   .788

.100

.700   .700

.700   1.135

PAPER   PASTED   PAPER
WRAPPER   SEAMS   WRAPPER

Figure 5-5 Construction of Colt buckshot cartridge.

sulphur particles in the powder grains, probably indicating a lack of sufficient mixing, wetting and corning in the manufacturing process. The powder cavity was made up by forming a slightly tapered paper cup with pasted seams. After the 70-grain powder charge was measured into the cup, a fiber wad .775 inches in diameter and approximately .100 inches thick was inserted into the top of the cup. The assembly was completed by folding the upper edges of the paper cup over the wad and pasting them in position. A blue disk of paper was then pasted over the exposed edges.

The shot cavity was made in a similar manner. A deep paper cup with a slight taper was folded and pasted and a charge of 1.3 ounces of No. 3 buckshot was poured into it. The charge consisted of 24 buckshot. A fiber pad .100 inches thick and .788 inches in diameter was then inserted into the mouth of the paper cup on top of the buckshot. The edges of the paper cup were folded over and pasted to the wad. A blue disk of paper was then pasted over the exposed edges to make a neat surface. The shot cavity was reinforced by an outer band of blue paper which was pasted over the cylindrical portion of the cavity.

The paper in the powder cavity was nitrated so that the flame from the percussion cap could easily

ignite it and blast through to the powder charge. It is not known whether the paper in the shot container was also nitrated but it is very possible that it was, for residual bits of burning paper in the chamber could be hazardous to the shooter, particularly if ignition occurred as a fresh powder charge was being rammed into the cylinder.

The loading procedure was fairly simple. The hammer was placed in a half-cocked position as shown in Figure 5-6. A powder container was taken from the cartridge pack and dropped into a chamber, which was lined up with loading lever and the lever depressed as shown. The loading lever was mushroom shaped with a large head of .740 inches in diameter. Firm pressure on the lever would ram the powder cavity to the rear of the chamber and provide a good gas-tight seal between fiber wad and the chamber walls. The most convenient procedure was probably to load all five powder cavities first, then add the shot containers on top. These would be rammed a second time to provide a good tight seal between the fiber over shot wad and the cylinder wall.

It is surprising that one thin over-shot wad was adequate. Each time the shotgun was fired the gun recoiled. The heavy shot charges would tend to stay still in space and as the gun recoiled spill

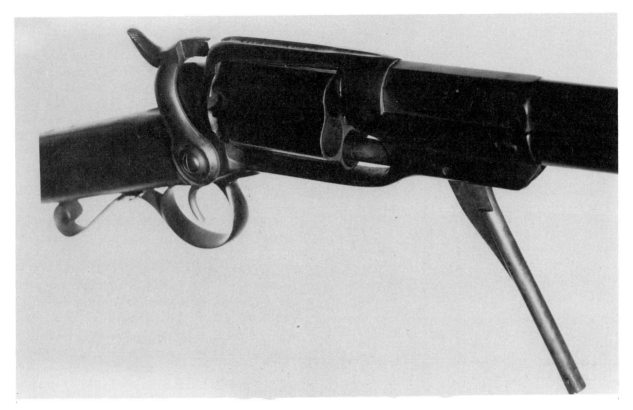

Figure 5-6   Action of Colt revolving shotgun in loading position.

out the front of the cylinder. Only the fiber over-shot wad provided the force to accelerate the shot to the rear as the gun recoiled.

The paper cartridges used with Colt revolvers were developed during the middle 1850s. The paper cartridges for the rifles and shotguns were probably developed slightly later. The cartridges were made at the Colt factory, but in a special building some distance from the main manufacturing area. Sam Colt and Colonel Hazard, the manufacturer of the powder, worked in conjunction with each other. Colt cartridges were also manufactured by Ely Brothers in London, D. C. Sage of Middletown, Connecticut, and Robert Chadwick of Hartford, Connecticut.

An article about Colt's shotgun dated 1859 by a technical writer who signed himself "Spirit of the Times," New York, described tests with the revolving shotgun and stated ". . . Now we are again in a position to communicate directly with thousands of our old sporting friends, who we know will be pleased to learn that the inventive genius of the Colonel has been directed especially to their wants, and that he is now ready to furnish them with the very article they need in the shape of Colt's revolving shot-gun. It is a shot-gun on

the revolving principle. Upon a late trial of this valuable gun, at a distance of 30 yards, it put 175 pellets in a circle of 12 inches diameter, penetrating 75 sheets of ordinary brown paper; the charge used being 1¼ ounces of No. 6 shot, and two drams of powder [one dram = 27.34 grains] to each charge. The gun is a five shooter, and is finished in fine style. The cartridges are manufactured to suit the gun and are impervious to the effects of water, or dampness. It is well worthy the attention of our sportsmen and if in general use will create quite a revolution among fowling pieces."

There is some question as to whether this test was reported accurately for that is an extremely tight pattern. Putting all of the shot in a 12 inch circle at 30 yards is impossible even with a modern shotgun. A second article describes an aerial test by a Mr. Amos Colt who hit 40 champagne bottles in a row thrown in the air, with a Colt revolving shotgun.

Rifle Shotgun Combinations

A deluxe Colt revolving combination rifle and shotgun is shown in Figure 5-7. The rifle is shown

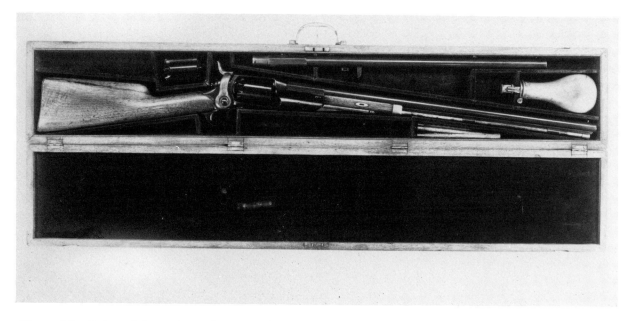

Figure 5-7   Deluxe Colt revolving shotgun with convertible rifle barrel.

assembled in a hardwood case which is 4 feet long, 8 inches wide and 2½ inches deep. The interior has been divided into partitioned areas and is lined with green felt. The rifle is fitted with a wooden forearm and a wooden ramrod. Its cylinder is smooth whereas the shotgun cylinder, in the compartment just to the rear of the hammer, is fluted. The shotgun barrel is at the upper end of the case, just below the handle. The rifle barrel, 24 inches long and of .56 caliber, is rifled with seven grooves. The shotgun barrel is 26¾ inches long and of 20 gauge (60-100ths of an inch caliber). Full length of the shotgun is 45½ inches. The barrel has been browned, the trigger guard and loading lever are case hardened in mottled colors and all of the other metal components are blued. The stock is carefully finished, the mountings made of German silver. The side of the rifle cylinder is marked "Patented September 10, 1850." The top of the shotgun barrel is marked "Colt's PT 1856, Address Col. Colt, Hartford, Ct., USA."

A plain brass powder flask has been included, marked James Dickson and Sons. This Scottish flask has variable graduations to throw powder charges of 2½ to 3 drams (68.4 to 82 grains). This is also a second model shotgun, manufactured after 1859.

Roper Repeating Shotguns

During the Civil War an American inventor, Sylvester H. Roper, who founded the Roper Repeating Rifle Company in Amherst, Massachusetts, to develop and manufacture rifle and shotgun models, developed a repeating rifle and shotgun action which was patented on April 10, 1866. An overall view of a Roper repeating shotgun is shown in Figure 5-8. This is a 12-gauge model with an overall length of 48 inches and a 29-inch barrel. The weight with the gun unloaded was 7 pounds 11 ounces and the length of pull was 14½ inches. Roper had included an ingenious removable choke device which may be seen on the muzzle of the shotgun. The barrel had an inside diameter of .742 inches at the muzzle. The small removable choke was designed to screw onto external threads on the barrel. The inlet side of the choke section had a diameter of .740 inches and it rapidly tapered down to .716 inches at the forward end. This is a very short fast choke with a reduction comparable to a modified improved choke of the modern day. The main difference is that the Roper choke was very abrupt, while modern chokes are designed for a much more gradual forcing of the shot column to minimize pellet de-

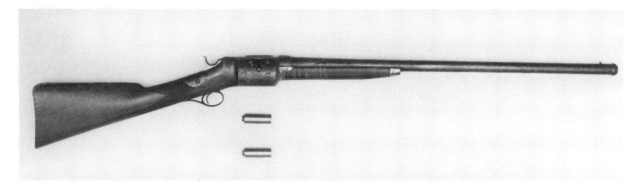

Figure 5-8   Roper repeating shotgun.

formation and give better patterns. The Roper choke was an ingenious concept, for the shooter could carry two or three rings in his pocket and shift the choke pattern in the field by a simple substitution taking less than 30 seconds.

A close up of the Roper shotgun with the action open is shown in Figure 5-9. A spring-loaded trap door is in the top of the action, into which four steel cartridges were dropped and pushed counterclockwise to load the magazine. With the gun fully loaded the last cartridge remained in line with the chamber, held in place by closing the trap door. When the trigger was pulled the hammer and bolt mechanisms slammed forward chambering the cartridge, locking the bolt, and activat-

ing the firing pin to fire the shotshell. An extractor on the front surface of the bolt retracted the fired cartridge case when the hammer was recocked. The magazine spring then fed a fresh cartridge into alignment with the chamber and pulling the trigger chambered and fired the fresh round.

The ammunition was of two-piece steel construction and may best be described by referring to Chapter 8, specifically the lower illustration in Figure 8-3. In the Roper cartridge the outer body was machined entirely from one piece of steel. The center anvil, threaded in from the inside of the cartridge case, projected into a very deep primer cavity the same diameter as that of the Maynard shotshell but about twice as deep. The

Figure 5-9   Roper repeating shotgun with action open.

88

hardened-steel anvil was somewhat similar to that in the Maynard cartridge but was designed to take a pistol-style percussion cap rather than a primer as with the Maynard ammunition. The outside diameter of the steel body was .836 inches at the breech end with a rebated rim of .562 inches outside diameter. The body tapered from .836 inches at the breech to .817 inches at the muzzle. The inside cavity was 2.11 inches long and tapered from .746 inches at the mouth to .716 inches in diameter at the breech end.

The cartridges were hand loaded and the finished assembly probably looked very much like Maynard ammunition in the lower illustration of Figure 8-3. A heavy charge of black powder was measured and dropped into the cavity and held in place by an over-powder wad. The charge of shot was then measured and dropped in and retained in place by a top wad. From the standpoint of patterns it would have been much better to have two heavy wads over the powder and one very light wad over the shot, but most shooters of this early era were not too clear on the problems of gas leakage and many figured that for the ease of loading one wad over the powder and a similar wad over the shot was plenty good enough. The loading procedure was finished by pressing a pistol-style percussion cap onto the anvil until it was flush with the surface of the head of the cartridge.

The Roper shotgun had several serious drawbacks. Steel cartridge cases with a thickness of .035 inches at the case mouth couldn't have expanded and sealed the chamber particularly well. Because the Maynard brass case, for example, had a mouth thickness of only .018 inches it would expand radially providing a good sealing surface. The .035-inch thickness is typical of paper shotshell construction, but steel of this thickness could not be expected to expand significantly under the low pressures of black-powder ammunition. Another major problem of the Roper action was that it fired from an open bolt. When the shooter pressed the trigger, the mainspring had to accelerate the hammer and the bolt assembly forward, chambering a fresh round of ammunition, then activating the firing pin to fire the cartridge. This meant that a lot of machinery was lumbering around after the trigger was pulled which would tend to disturb the aim, particularly when wing shooting. Just moving all the bolt machinery under the urging of the hammer spring took a long time causing a significant delay between pulling the trigger and the shot going off.

The Roper was an interesting and important link in the development of American repeating shotguns, but it was not a very satisfactory shotgun. Within a few years double-barreled break-open shotguns firing brass-cased ammunition were available which were far superior for the sportsmen's needs.

THE SPENCER SLIDE-ACTION SHOTGUN

Christopher M. Spencer invented the finest repeating rifle used in the Civil War, and over 100,000 were manufactured during the war years. But the Spencer Company suffered from its own success, for the Government sold surplus Spencer carbines for as low as $7.00 each, ruining the chances for the company to sell new guns at $35.00 to $50.00. The introduction of the Winchester Model 1866 with many superior features finished the Spencer company off, and by 1869 they were bankrupt.

In the early 1880s Spencer and Sylvester Roper worked out a slide-action shotgun, the patent for which was originally issued on April 21, 1885, to Sylvester H. Roper, who was Spencer's partner in his firearms-manufacturing ventures. This shotgun was the first really successful slide-action shotgun and an important milestone in American firearms development. The patent, #316,401, was extremely broad, covering: "Any magazine firearm having a piston breech, suitably connected to and in combination with an actuating sliding handle situated forward of the receiver, and serving as a means for supporting the barrel, and providing with a path of reciprocation, in a line parallel with the axial line of the barrel."

Spencer started a new Spencer Arms Company in Windsor, Connecticut, and started manufacturing the slide-action shotguns in the late 1880s with tooling purchased from Pratt & Whitney of Hartford, Connecticut, and Brown & Sharpe of Providence, Rhode Island. They were excellent shotguns and functioned well when carefully manufactured and adjusted. Due to financial difficulties, Spencer was forced to mortgage his property to Pratt & Whitney in 1889 and when Pratt & Whitney foreclosed the mortgage, rights to the patents, machinery and an inventory of some 3,000 guns were sold to Francis Bannerman and Sons who had a very prosperous business in military goods, with their main showrooms at 501 Broadway in New York. Bannermans moved the factory to a

Brooklyn location into a tiny brick building only thirty feet wide.

In the 1907 Bannerman catalogue the plant was offered for sale with the following comment:

In 1884 we became interested in C. M. Spencer's new repeating shotgun, believing then that the slide action, or pump gun, would mark an epoch in the history of firearms of the future, as did the old lever Spencer rifle of the Civil War period. It is now a well established fact, in [sic] our judgement of 1884 was correct, that repeating shotguns are the guns of the present and the future. Sportsmen appreciating these merits over the now fast becoming obsolete double guns. There is good money to be made in manufacturing guns. The Spencer Gun Plant is complete, ready to begin work. The machine tools and fixtures were made by the well known firms of Pratt and Whitney of Hartford, Connecticut, and Brown and Sharpe of Providence, Rhode Island, under the supervision of the inventor, Christopher M. Spencer. The plant was used in making 20,000 Spencer guns. It is for sale, either with or without the brick factory building and steam power. The factory is in the borough of Brooklyn, City of New York where all classes of skilled workmen can readily be obtained. The plant is for sale as a whole. The Spencer gun is an up to date gun with original slide lever. The purchase of this slide lever repeating shotgun machinery at a genuine bargain affords an opportunity to a good mechanic with money to enter into a business in which men have made vast fortunes. Mr. Hartley, proprietor of the Remington Arms Company, left an estate of $11,000,000. Hotchkiss, the gun man, left an estate of millions. When his company offered four million stock to the public it was subscribed for over three times the amount offered. The Colt and Winchester Arms Companies plants cover many acres. It will be sold at a great bargain simply because our old established business of buying and selling military goods in which our whole life has been spent, has now grown so large as to require all our time. The Spencer plant machinery tools and models represent an outlay of over $100,000. A quick buyer can purchase this plant at a bargain. Were it not for our military goods business this plant would not be for sale.

Comments are also included on the patent litigation between Bannerman and Winchester:

In 1893 when returns were beginning to come in the Winchester Arms Company brought out a repeating shotgun which infringed our patents, and not heeding our protest, we brought suit for infringement. They tried to prove by a number of old patents and models of guns made up from old paper patents that they had the right to make our sliding lever guns. The court ignored their model guns but decided that owing to our own first invention it seems as if the WRA Co. had the right to make our gun. [This doesn't make sense.] We carried the case to the U. S. Court of Appeals who also ignored the model gun submitted by the defense, but treated our patent as if it had become public property on the grounds that Spencer and Roper, joint inventors of the gun were two and distinct inventors instead of one and in this way our own prior patents and inventions were made to afford a legal right to our competitors to make our gun. The court decided the case substantially on a *mere technicality* as both the Spencer and Roper guns belong to us. We withdrew from making Spencer guns in order to give more attention to our military goods business, which was always profitable and more to our liking and *on which there is no patent.* Before stopping our machinery, we made up a quantity of extra parts in order to supply repairs to sportsmen who are using Spencer guns.

There is an interesting comment on the pricing in 1907, a little note saying "CLUBS—to any party who will send us an order for a case of 10 Spencer guns, accompanied with $139.50, we will include one extra Spencer gun free. We can afford to do this by being saved the expense of packing ten guns in separate cases. If guns are for different parties we will place tags on each gun with name etcetera all packed in one case. A saving of one third in transportation can be made by sending full cases by freight." Thus orders of 10 guns were given a 9 percent discount.

The Spencer plant in Brooklyn had a capacity of manufacturing six thousand guns a year. It was a two story brick building and the guns were targeted in the basement. It is probable that the real reason for selling the Spencer plant was that the Winchester Model of 1893, designed by John Browning, was such an improved shotgun that manufacture of the Spencer was no longer economically practical.

Design of the Spencer Shotguns

The Spencer slide-action shotguns established the basic configuration of this type of design, which has been continued to the present day. The overall appearance of the shotgun is shown in Figure 5-10. The solid-steel barrel was given a surface finish to make it look like the more expensive but weaker Damascus barrel. Fresh ammunition was contained in a magazine tube hung below the barrel, which was also given the simulated Damascus finish. The solid-steel receiver held both of these elements and had long upper and lower tangs extending to the rear, which clamped and held the butt stock. The well-designed stock was made of American walnut carefully checkered

and fitted to the receiver. The shotgun was fitted with an extremely small slide handle also of American walnut carefully checkered. The force from the slide handle was transmitted to the action through a single action slide bar, which contained the extractor. The shotgun has the appearance of being fitted with two triggers. The rear trigger was used to fire the gun. Because ammunition of the 1880s was not completely reliable, an extra device allowed the shooter to recock the hammer by pushing forward on the front trigger letting him try to refire the cartridge with a second hammer blow.

A partial cross-section view of the Spencer shotgun in the firing position is shown in Figure 5-11. The key to the design was the breech block, which

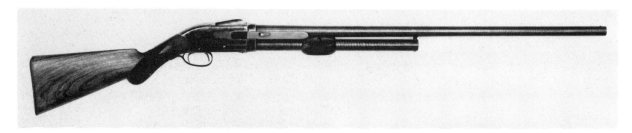

Figure 5-10   Spencer slide-action shotgun.

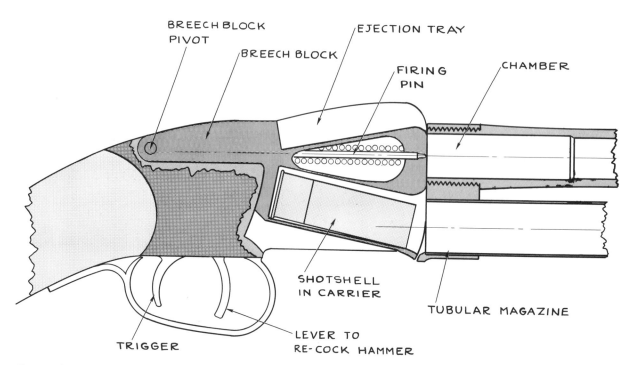

Figure 5-11   Partial cross section of Spencer action.

could rest in three separate positions. In the cross section view a fresh shotshell has been fed out of the magazine by a spiral magazine spring and follower and has been pushed upwards into the carrier. The firing pin is in position to fire a fresh cartridge in the chamber. A closeup of the action in this same firing position is shown in Figure 5-12. The small triangular steel part extending as a bulge from the action slide bar was the extractor which pivoted on the small pin, seen extending downwards vertically through the action slide bar. The metal insert on the lower surface of the re-

ceiver was a spring cutoff to control positioning of the fresh shell in the magazine.

As the action slide handle was drawn to the rear the breech block dropped down into the position shown in Figure 5-13. The small pivoted extractor was cammed inwards by the plate on the outside of the receiver. In the inward position it picked up the rim of the fired shell and drew it into the ejection tray machined into the top of the breech block. As the action slide handle approached a fully rearward position the motion of the breech block was abruptly reversed and it

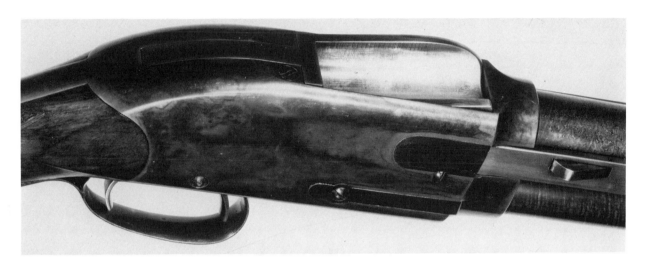

Figure 5-12 Closeup of Spencer action, ready to fire.

Figure 5-13 Spencer action, partially open.

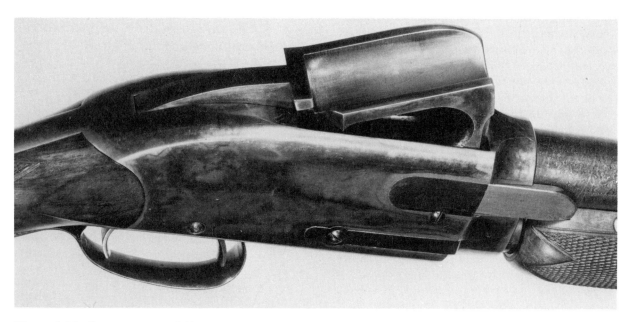

Figure 5-14 Spencer action, fully open.

snapped up into the position shown in Figure 5-14. This quick motion threw the fired shell out of the tray on top of the breech bolt and lined the fresh shell in the carrier up with the chamber. As the slide handle was pushed forward the extractor now became the feeding mechanism and the small right angle tail (shown in the previous illustration) pushed on the head of the shell driving it into the chamber. As the slide action reached a fully forward position the breech block moved down to the central position shown in the cross-section illustration. The total stroke of the action slide arm was slightly over 4 inches.

The barrel was a fairly heavy construction with a basic bore diameter of .730 inches (12 gauge) and a modified-improved choke with a muzzle diameter of .704 inches. The choke was about 2 inches in length and the outside diameter of the barrel was .838 inches—fairly husky for a shotgun. The overall length of the Spencer shotgun in the Winchester Gun Museum is 51½ inches with a 32¼ inch barrel. Overall weight of the shotgun is 8 pounds 2 ounces and the length of pull is 13⅞ inches. (The length of pull is the distance from the center of the butt stock to the trigger.) The serial number, 1029, is marked on the carrier; the barrel is marked "Spencer Arms Co., Windsor, CT U.S.A. Pat. Apr. 1882."

Despite the creative genius of Christopher Spencer and the enormous war orders which totaled over 100,000 Spencer rifles and carbines his plant was in business for less than ten years and was finally purchased by Winchester in the late 1860s. Spencer again came up with a remarkable new design in his slide-action shotgun invented in conjunction with S. M. Roper. Again his invention was obsoleted within ten years, this time by the Model 1893 Winchester slide action shotgun, which was designed by John Browning. Christopher Spencer was one of the American inventors whose impact on firearms technology was enormous, and his creative genius has not been adequately recognized.

WINCHESTER LEVER-ACTION SHOTGUNS

The most famous American firearms designer, John Moses Browning, was born in 1855 in Ogden, Utah. His father, Jonathan, was a firearms designer and manufacturer in the 1850s and fathered a family of 22 children by his three wives. When the father died in 1879, three brothers, John, Matthew and Ed, took over the business. They worked together as an excellent team with Matthew handling the financial and business aspects, John creating new firearms designs and inventions and Ed providing much of the skill to translate these ideas into workable models. On October 7, 1879, John Browning was granted U. S. Patent No. 220,271 for a lever-action single-shot rifle that could be adopted to any of the sporting cartridges manufactured in the United States at that time.

The brothers started putting together a manufacturing lot of 600 single-shot rifles to be sold from their store. In the early 1880s the excellence of these rifles came to the attention of the Winchester management and Thomas G. Bennett, President of the company, immediately took a train to Utah to negotiate with the Brownings. Bennett purchased the patent and the supply of guns that had been made up for $8,000.

At that time John Browning was already working on ideas which led to the Model 1886 Winchester lever-action rifle and Thomas Bennett brought back a wooden model of the action. Many people consider the Model 1886 the finest large lever-action rifle ever designed; its manufacture was continued through a series of model changes into the 1950s. In comparison with the $8,000 paid for the patent on the single-shot rifle (and a quantity of rifles) the best indications are that Browning was paid about $50,000 for the Model 1886 design.

Winchester Model 1887

John Browning next turned his attention to the complex problems of designing a lever-action shotgun. Winchester purchased the patent for the completed design in 1885. The gun was first introduced in the June 1887 catalogue as the "Winchester Repeating Shotgun Model 1887" in 12 gauge. A 10-gauge model was added later that year. The outside appearance of the lever-action shotgun is shown in Figure 5-15.

The design posed many difficult problems, for shotshells are extremely bulky compared to centerfire ammunition. The design of the action in a closed and locked position is shown in Figure 5-16. The breech block basically consisted of a quarter of a circle and was integral with the lever. It pivoted on the small pin just in front of the trigger guard. The purpose of the slot was to allow the block to slide slightly forward out of its locking recess on the opening stroke. The locking surface is shown as the white triangle which breaks the smooth arc of the upper surface of the breech bolt. The hammer also pivoted at the front of the action; it consisted of a V-shaped member pivoted on one arm of the V. Searing notches were cut into the other end of the V and the safety and firing notch may be seen in this illustration. The trigger was a long bar pivoted on the upper tang. A small leaf spring forced the trigger into a forward position. The sear was the projection just in front of a U-shaped slot half way up the trigger length. A hook fitted to the lower surface of the trigger locked the finger lever in an "up" position as the shot was fired. Spare shotshells, kept in the tubular magazine below the barrel, were pushed to the rear by a spiral spring and magazine follower. Figure 5-16 shows a fresh shell partially fed into the carrier. The position of the components with the action open is shown in Figure 5-17. As the lever was moved downwards the breech bolt moved to the rear, extracting the fired shell and moving over the top of the fresh shell which, after the breech face passed its rim, was allowed to feed fully into carrier. With the lever in the fully open position the fired shell has been ejected, the carrier has been lifted to an upward position and the fresh shell is in a position to be pushed by the bolt face into the chamber of the gun.

The main spring driving the hammer is the V-shaped spring immediately above the trigger guard in both illustrations. The trigger, urged forward by the upper spring, rode along the upper surface of the hammer until the trigger notch engaged the sear on the hammer preventing further rotation of the hammer. As the breech block was moved further forward the mainspring was compressed and the gun was ready to fire as soon as it reached the closed position shown in Figure 5-16.

A photograph of the action of the fully open

Figure 5-15 Winchester Model 1887 lever-action shotgun.

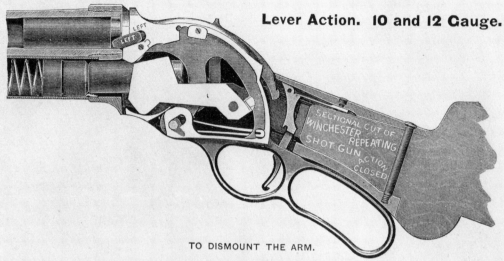

THE WINCHESTER REPEATING SHOT GUN,

Lever Action. 10 and 12 Gauge.

TO DISMOUNT THE ARM.

Take out the mainspring. To do this it will be necessary to use a pair of pliers. Compress the mainspring, and draw it backwards through the hammer slot in the breech-block. Remove the right and left carrier screws. Lift the carrier out through the top of the gun. Push out the breech-block pin, and remove breech-block and hammer. To take out the extractor, push the extractor against the lower side of its slot. Push back the extractor spring pin with the point of a knife, and push the extractor hook towards the breech-block stud. The firing-pin is removed by taking out the firing-pin stop screw. To remove the sear, unscrew the sear spring screw. Drive out the sear pin.

Figure 5-16 Cutaway of the Winchester Model 1887 action, closed and locked.

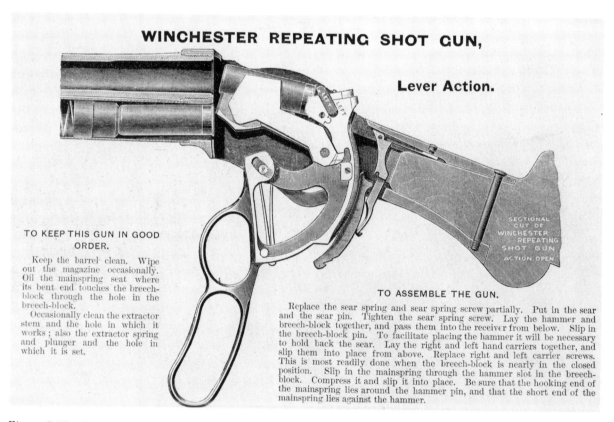

WINCHESTER REPEATING SHOT GUN,

Lever Action.

TO KEEP THIS GUN IN GOOD ORDER.

Keep the barrel clean. Wipe out the magazine occasionally. Oil the mainspring seat where its bent end touches the breech-block through the hole in the breech-block.

Occasionally clean the extractor stem and the hole in which it works ; also the extractor spring and plunger and the hole in which it is set.

TO ASSEMBLE THE GUN.

Replace the sear spring and sear spring screw partially. Put in the sear and the sear pin. Tighten the sear spring screw. Lay the hammer and breech-block together, and pass them into the receiver from below. Slip in the breech-block pin. To facilitate placing the hammer it will be necessary to hold back the sear. Lay the right and left hand carriers together, and slip them into place from above. Replace right and left carrier screws. This is most readily done when the breech-block is nearly in the closed position. Slip in the mainspring through the hammer slot in the breech-block. Compress it and slip it into place. Be sure that the hooking end of the mainspring lies around the hammer pin, and that the short end of the mainspring lies against the hammer.

Figure 5-17 Cutaway of the Winchester Model 1887 action, open.

position is shown in Figure 5-18. As the carrier moved to a fully upward position, the left hand feed guide (the white bar) moved inwards to control the vertical position of the fresh shell to be fed in the chamber. The twin extractors fitted to the lower edge of the breech face picked up the rim of the new shell on the feeding cycle. Note the large conical firing pin which was typical with low-pressure black-powder shotshells.

The basic action components in the lever-action shotgun are shown in Figure 5-19. Both the receiver and breech block were expensive to manufacture, since they were relatively large forgings machined all over. The hammer is shown with its basic V shape. It was fitted with a roller just to the rear of the pivot point to reduce the friction between mainspring and hammer, thus increasing the amount of mainspring energy that went into driving the hammer forward. The searing and safety notches are just barely visible at the end of the hammer tail. The cocking surface for the thumb was small, but is visible just to the rear of the hammer face.

The Model 1887 was manufactured with both single and double extractors. Components of both types are shown in the illustration. The carrier consisted of a right-hand and left-hand member plus a cartridge lifter that lifted the shell more or less parallel to the barrel center line. The upper edge of the left-hand carrier had a projection that prevented the shell from feeding up too far and

being flipped out of the top of the action. This projection is visible in Figure 5-18.

The standard models of lever-action shotguns are shown in Figure 5-20, a page from the 1894 Winchester catalogue. The standard 12-gauge model was fitted with a 30-inch solid-steel barrel and sold for a price of $25.00. The standard 10-gauge model had a two inch longer barrel, weighed about 9 pounds and sold for the same price. The extremely high cost of manufacturing a high-quality Damascus barrel is shown in the lowest illustration. The addition of the fancy walnut stocks and checkering would add a modest amount to the cost of the gun, but the substitution of a Damascus barrel made by laborious hand techniques for the solid-steel barrel which could be machined from a solid bar almost doubled the price. The "good (three blade) Damascus barrel" refers to the use of three iron strips which were twisted and welded together around the mandrel in a spiral pattern to make the barrel. The "fine (four blade) Damascus barrel" was made using four twisted iron bars and added an additional $5.00 to the cost of the shotgun.

The 1894 catalogue describes the lever-action shotgun:

> Sportsmen will find this a strong, serviceable arm. The system contains but sixteen parts in all, and can be readily understood from the sectional cuts.

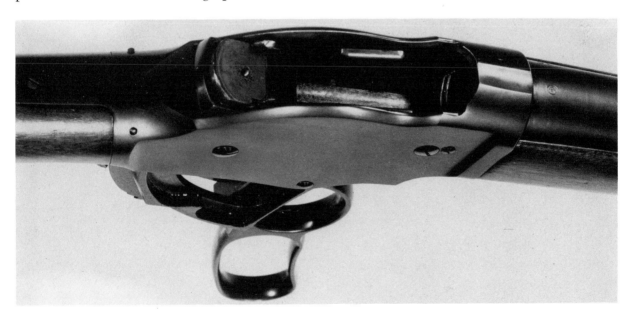

Figure 5-18 Winchester Model 1887 action, fully open.

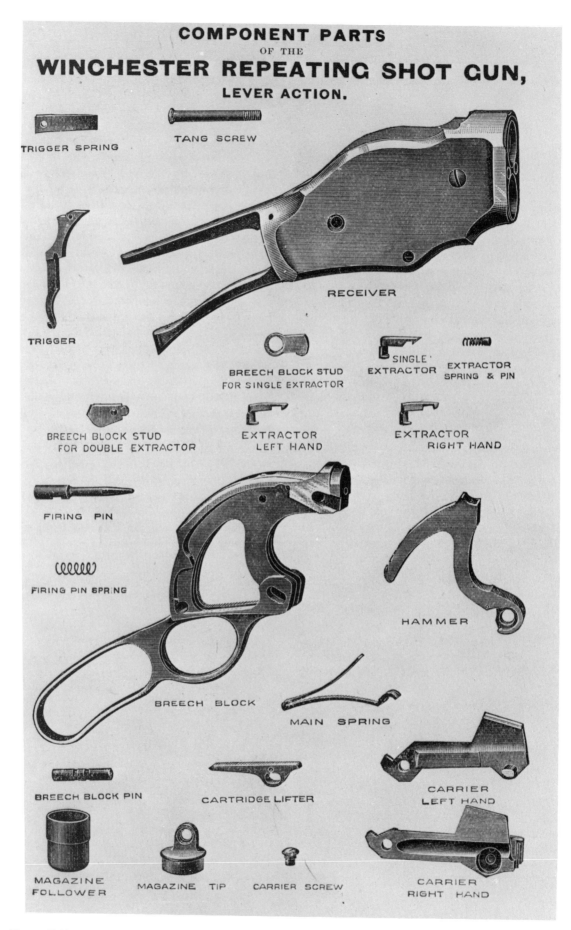

Figure 5-19 Components of the Winchester lever action.

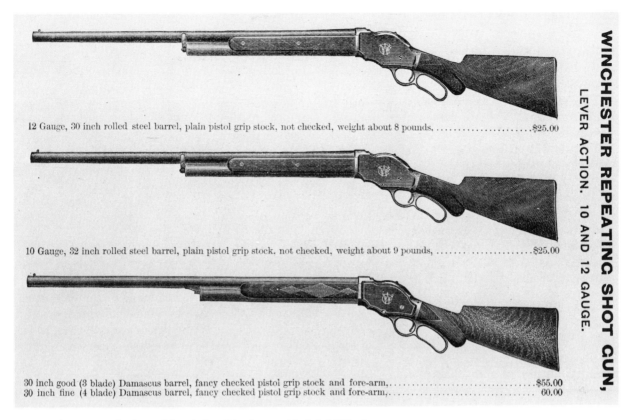

12 Gauge, 30 inch rolled steel barrel, plain pistol grip stock, not checked, weight about 8 pounds,.....................$25.00

10 Gauge, 32 inch rolled steel barrel, plain pistol grip stock, not checked, weight about 9 pounds,.....................$25.00

30 inch good (3 blade) Damascus barrel, fancy checked pistol grip stock and fore-arm,..............................$55.00
30 inch fine (4 blade) Damascus barrel, fancy checked pistol grip stock and fore-arm,..............................60.00

Figure 5-20   Standard models of the Winchester Model 1887 shotgun.

The breech-block and finger lever form one piece, and move together in opening and closing. The hammer, placed in the breech-block, is automatically cocked during the closing motion; but it can also be cocked or set at half-cock by hand.

The trigger and finger lever are so adjusted that the trigger cannot be pulled prematurely, and the gun cannot be discharged until closed.

The barrel can be examined and cleaned from the breech.

The magazine and carrier hold 5 cartridges, which, with one in the chamber, makes 6 at the command of the shooter. Anyone accustomed to shooting can readily shoot double birds with this gun.

This gun is made in both 10 and 12 gauges; the 12 gauge gun will handle shells 2⅝ inches long or less, and the 10 gauge will handle shells 2⅞ inches long or less.

To fill the magazine, throw down the lever and push four cartridges through the carrier into the magazine, placing the fifth in the carrier. The forward and backward motion of the finger lever, which can be executed while the gun is at the shoulder, throws out the empty shell, raises a new cartridge from the magazine, and puts it into the barrel. The gun is then ready to be fired.

The standard gun will be made up with rolled steel barrel, case hardened frame, and pistol grip stock of plain wood, not checked. All guns will be full choked, and no guns will be sent out which will not make a good target. Guns with cylinder bore or modified choke will be furnished to order.

The standard length of barrel will be 30 or 32 inches, as may be desired. But unless otherwise ordered, 12 gauge guns with 30 inch barrels and 10 gauge with 32 inch barrels will in all cases be sent.

Two kinds of damascus barrels will be furnished when desired, at prices given below.

The standard gun will have a stock 12¾ inches in length and 2⅝ inches drop; and any variation from standard length or drop will be charged for extra.

In the detailed price list that followed, options included a fancy walnut stock and forearm, not checkered, for $10.00 extra and a $5.00 charge for checking stock and forearm. A rubber buttplate could be ordered for $2.00 and the substitution of the good (three-blade) Damascus barrel was an incremental charge of $15.00, the fine Damascus barrel $20.00. Since the plain-steel barrel probably represented about $8.00 of the total retail price, either of the Damascus barrels cost as much as all of the other gun components together.

The Model 1887 became a popular shotgun in its day and many hunters used it to bag enormous quantities of game along the Mississippi flyway and the coasts, where tens of millions of birds migrated annually. The late 19th century was the golden age of wild-fowl hunting, for the bird population was enormous and the development of choked shotguns, breech-loading ammunition, and repeating actions allowed hunters to extend their range and rapidity of fire. A skilled hunter with good equipment could bag as many as a hundred birds in a single day. Trap shooters even used the lever action in competition with double guns. The Model 1887 tied for first place in a trap-shooting contest in Plainfield, New Jersey, in February 1887.

Sales of the Model 1887 shotgun were fairly modest, at 7300 guns in its year of introduction. In 1888 the total jumped to 18,400 guns, and then dropped to 5100 guns in 1889. A total of 64,885 were manufactured until 1901, when the design was modified and reissued with a new model designation.

Winchester Model 1901

By the turn of the century the Winchester slide-action shotgun models of 1893 and 1897, described below, were becoming extremely popular in 12 gauge. The development of new smokeless-powder shotshells allowed more powerful ammunition within the 12-gauge shell, and the rugged reliability and high speed reloading of the slide-action design made these guns popular. As a result of these trends, Winchester management decided to redesign the Model 1887 to handle the more powerful smokeless-powder loads and to limit the manufacture to 10 gauge. The new model was first marketed in January 1902. Major changes were the strengthening of the action and a change in the frame from case hardened to a blued finish. Specifications remained basically the same: the standard barrel remained 32 inches in length, and was available in full choke, modified and cylinder bore. The three-blade and four-blade Damascus steel barrels were continued at a high extra charge until they were discontinued in 1914. Since the model change was minor, the serial numbers of the Model 1887 were continued starting with number 64,856. A total of approximately 13,500 Model 1901 shotguns were manufactured before discontinuation in 1920. The lever-action was the only repeating 10-gauge shotgun ever manufactured by Winchester.

WINCHESTER SLIDE-ACTION SHOTGUNS

John Browning had invented three superb lever-action models that were manufactured by Winchester in the 1880s: the Model 1884 single-shot rifle, the Model 1886 lever-action repeater and the Model 1887 lever-action shotgun. In the late 1880s he turned to slide-action designs, and the first model produced was the Model 1890 slide-action, .22-caliber rimfire repeater. He also developed the Model 1893 Winchester, an enormous improvement over any slide-action shotgun then available.

Winchester Model 1893

The overall appearance of the Model 1893 shotgun is shown in Figure 5-21, and a close up of the action in the locked position in Figure 5-22. The patent of this Browning design was purchased in 1890 and it was first announced in the June 1893 catalogue with the following comments:

> This gun is operated by a sliding forearm below the barrel. It is locked by the closing motion and can be unlocked only by pushing forward the firing pin, which may be done by the hammer or by the finger. When the hammer is down, the backward and forward motion of the sliding forearm unlocks and opens

Figure 5-21   Winchester Model 1893 slide-action shotgun.

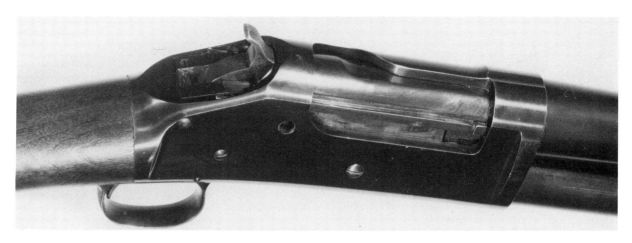

Figure 5-22 Closeup of Winchester Model 1893 action, closed.

the breech lock, ejects the cartridge or fired shell and replaces it with a fresh cartridge. The construction of the arm is such that the hammer cannot fall or the firing pin strike the cartridge until the breech block is in place and locked fast. The trigger touches the sear only when the gun is closed—that is, the hammer cannot be let down except when the gun is locked. Having closed the gun and set the hammer at half-cock, it is locked both against the opening and pulling of the trigger. While the hammer stands at the full cock notch, the gun is locked against opening.

To open the gun, lift the hammer to full cock and push forward the firing pin, pulling back the action-slide.

The 1894 catalogue states that the gun could be furnished in 12 gauge only. Weight was given at about 7¾ pounds.

The standard gun will be made up with rolled steel barrel, blued frame, and pistol grip stock of plain wood, not checked. All guns will be full choke, and no gun will be sent out which will not make a good target. Guns with cylinder bore or modified choke will be furnished to order.

The standard length of barrel will be 30 or 32 inches, as may be desired; but, unless otherwise ordered, guns with 30 inch barrels will in all cases be sent.

Two kinds of Damascus barrels (three-blade, and four-blade) will be furnished when desired.

The standard gun will have a stock 13 inches in length and 2¾ inches drop; and any variation from standard length or drop will be charged for extra.

The barrel of this gun has been proved with 9½ drams of powder, #5, and 2½ ounces of shot. The gun, assembled, has been proved

with two shots, 4 drams of powder (special bursting), 1¼ ounces of shot. It has been shot for pattern three shots, and to prove manipulation, eight to fifteen tests are shot.

With our regular trap cartridge, containing 3¾ grams FFg powder; one card and two black-edge wads on the powder (this means three over-powder wads for good gas sealing) loaded with 1½ ounces of #8 shot and one thin card wad over the shot, the guns will be found to pattern above 325 pellets in a 30 inch ring at 40 yards.

Winchester had no sooner introduced the shotgun than they became involved in a violent patent fight with Bannerman, the military goods dealer. On October 2, 1894, Bannerman filed suit against Winchester's New York Agent Philip G. Sanford and the Company, sending out circulars stating that all persons, firms or corporations using or selling the Model 1893 shotguns or Model 1890 rifles were infringers of the Spencer patent and would be held responsible for such infringement. Winchester vigorously defended the suit and a classic patent battle occurred. A search was made of American patent records and a Winchester patent attorney was sent to Europe to examine European patent records. He found that three significant British patents had been issued: to Alexander Bain in 1854, Joseph Curtis in 1866 and William Krutzsch in 1866. In addition a significant French patent by M. M. Magot had been issued in 1880. The Bannerman lawyers claimed that all of these patents covered unworkable firearms and the high point of the trial was when the Winchester lawyers introduced into evidence actual French-made Magot shotguns and working models of the Curtis and the Krutzsch inventions which Winchester model makers had constructed from the patent drawings.

The decision on June 5, 1897, was in favor of Winchester, but curiously was based on a technicality rather than on the abundant evidence which had been introduced at the trial. The technicality was that Bannerman had brought suit claiming infringement against Patent 316,401 whereas the judge found that the actual infringement was against an earlier patent issued to Roper in 1885. The result was to make Bannerman apoplectic, leaving a bitterness that extended into the twentieth century. It is the author's opinion that the decision based on issues would have been the same. Winchester immediately notified all its agents and customers of the favorable decision and the sales volume for the Model 1893 shotgun increased enormously. The cross-section view with the action closed is shown in Figure 5-23, with the action open in Figure 5-24. The two primary moving action elements were the breech block and the large, heavy, machined carrier. The first motion of the action slide arm, operating in a cam track on the side of the carrier, moved the carrier downward. The breech block was locked against an abutment in the heavy carrier and once the carrier moved downward,

the breech block was free to move to the rear in a straight line. The carrier continued to move downward in the position shown in Figure 5-24 where it picked up a fresh shell from the magazine. On the closing stroke, the carrier motion was reversed and it lifted upward, lining the fresh shell up with the chamber into which it was rammed by the bolt. A view of the action in the full open position is shown in Figure 5-25. Note how the breech block has moved straight to the rear on the tracks machined into the receiver and breech block. The carrier has dropped down into the feeding position ready to pick up a fresh shell from the magazine.

The appearance, prices and description of "The New Winchester Repeating Shotgun, Model 1893," shown in Figure 5-26, is taken from the 1894 catalogue. The standard model was offered at exactly the same price as the lever-action Model 1887 shotgun—$25.00. The deluxe shotgun had all the elaborate features which could be offered including the finest-quality "four-blade" Damascus barrel, fancy walnut stock and a rubber butt plate. Since this sturdy and serviceable model could be purchased for a mere $25.00, the

THE WINCHESTER REPEATING SHOT GUN, MODEL 1893.

12 Gauge only.

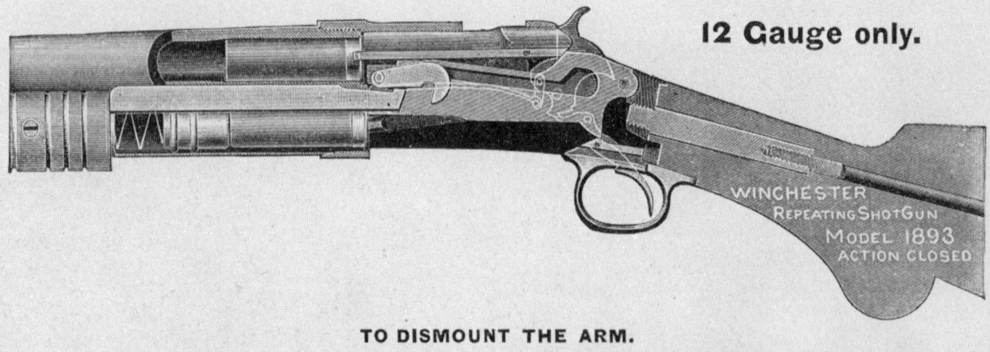

TO DISMOUNT THE ARM.

Open the gun. Drive out the action slide stop pin found in the forward end of the carrier block when the block is down. Unhook the action slide from the carrier by pushing it forward. Press in the firing pin and drop the carrier down. Drive out the carrier pin (which is found just back of the hammer) from the right side. Take out the carrier block. Draw back the breech-block and take out the action hook screw through the hole left in the right side of the receiver for this purpose. Remove the action hook. Withdraw the breech-block.

TO DISMOUNT THE PIECES CONNECTED WITH THE CARRIER.

Let down the hammer. Unscrew the sear spring screw. Take off the sear spring. Drive out the sear pin. Drive out the hammer pin and withdraw the hammer. Remove the mainspring strain screw.

TO DISMOUNT THE PARTS ATTACHED TO THE BREECH-BLOCK.

Hold back the extractor spring and pin and lift out the extractor. Remove the extractor spring from the hole which contains it. Drive out the firing pin stop pin. Remove the firing pin stop. Drop out the firing pin.

Figure 5-23 Cutaway of Winchester Model 1893 action, closed.

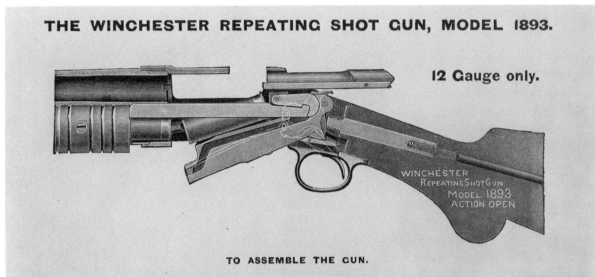

THE WINCHESTER REPEATING SHOT GUN, MODEL 1893.

12 Gauge only.

WINCHESTER
RepeatingShotGun
MODEL 1893
ACTION OPEN

TO ASSEMBLE THE GUN.

Put in the breech-block and replace the hook. Put in the action hook screw. A hole is left on the right hand side of the frame through which this screw may be placed. Cock the hammer, push the bolt and firing pin forward and insert the carrier from below. Put in the carrier pin. Let down the hammer. Drive in the slide bar stop pin with the beveled side of head to the rear.

Figure 5-24   Cutaway of Winchester Model 1893 action, open.

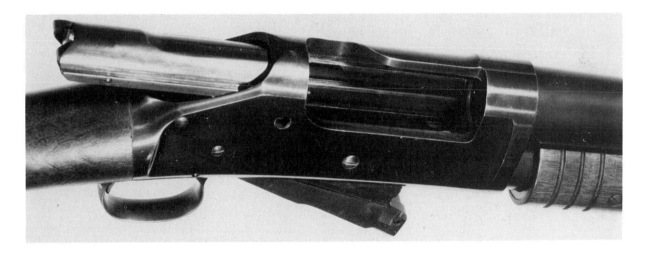

Figure 5-25   Closeup of Winchester Model 1893 action, open.

For Price List see page 61.

Figure 5-26 Winchester catalog page announcing the Model 1893.

price differentials for additional features were substantial. For example, fancy walnut stocks and forearms were $10.00 additional and checkering was $5.00 more. The three-blade Damascus barrel was available for a premium of $15.00, the four-blade Damascus barrel for $20.00.

The Model 1893 became a popular model with about 34,050 being manufactured until its redesign in 1897. There were mechanical weaknesses in the design that were aggravated by the use of the new higher-pressure smokeless-powder cartridges.

Winchester Model 1897

The new model of 1897 was virtually identical in appearance to the 1893 model but had substantial mechanical improvements. The frame was strengthened and made longer to handle 12-gauge 2¾-inch shells as well as the older 2⅝-inch ones. Metal was added to the top of the receiver so that the ejected shell was kicked out to one side. Another important change was the addition of an action slide lock. While the 1893 model could be opened if the firing pin was depressed into a forward position, the 1897 model required a slight forward motion of the slide handle before the action would unlock. The difference seems trivial but was a significant safety feature. For example, the shooter trying to reload extremely fast could hold rearward pressure against the action-slide arm. As soon as the hammer hit the firing pin the action lock on the 1893 model was released and the slide handle could start moving to the rear. Thus the shooter was discharging the cartridge and opening the action at the same time. In most cases the speed of ignition was fast enough so that no safety hazard existed, but a slight hang fire could cause serious problems. With the 1897 model the gun would remain locked even with this rearward pressure. If the gun fired and recoiled to the rear, there was an involuntary forward motion due to the shooter's hand remaining relatively stationary and the gun recoiling to the rear, thus releasing the action only after the shot had been discharged.

The addition of the action slide lock was an important safety feature and its use has been continued on all good-quality slide-action shotguns to the present day.

The Model 1897 was originally introduced in 12 gauge with a solid frame only. A takedown model was added in October, 1898, and a 16-gauge takedown model in February, 1900. The gun remained in production for almost half a century. In addition to the standard field guns, special models such as Trap Guns and Pigeon models were introduced. The Pigeon model, for example, was first listed in November, 1897, and continued in production until 1939. Brush guns and Riot models were all introduced before the turn of the century. Trench guns were developed for the First World War and were continued in production until 1945. The Trench and Riot guns were fitted with 20-inch barrels. The Riot gun weighed 7 pounds, 2 ounces; while the Trench model weighed 7 pounds, 14 ounces, mainly due to the special bayonet stud and perforated hand guard that went around the barrel at the forward end. The purpose of the hand guard was to protect the soldier's left hand from a hot barrel if the shotgun was used with the bayonet.

The Model 1897 shotgun had a five-shot magazine in both 12 and 16 gauge. Barrel lengths of 26 to 32 inches were available in 12 gauge and 26 and 28 inches in 16 gauge. The gun was offered in cylinder bore, modified and full choke. A 30-inch barrel and intermediate chokes, such as improved modified and improved cylinder, were added in 1930 and 1931. Skeet chokes were added in 1940. Approximately 1,024,700 model 1897s were manufactured before they were discontinued in 1957.

MARLIN SHOTGUNS

The Marlin firearms company was founded by a vigorous Connecticut man, John Mahlon Marlin, who, age twenty five when the Civil War broke out, went to work as a tool-and-die maker at the Colt factory in Hartford. Colt in 1861 was using the most-advanced tools and machinery available in the United States. Special equipment had been designed to manufacture revolver components in mass production to identical dimensions. Since revolvers must rotate and align the cylinder very accurately, the manufacturing tolerances were extremely small.

Many smart young men got their early training at Colt's, and some, such as John Marlin and Christopher Spencer, went on to found their own companies. In 1863 Marlin left Colt and opened a gun shop on St. James Street in New Haven. He moved several times in the next few years and not much is known about his work. The earliest known Marlin firearm is a small .22-caliber single-shot pistol (derringer), about 4 inches long.

In 1867 Marlin moved back to Hartford, then returned to New Haven in 1870 to manufacture his small derringer containing a new patented cartridge extractor. During the 1870s and 1880s the company manufactured a series of revolvers and single-shot pistols, marketing them at prices considerably below Colt and Smith and Wesson.

By 1875 John Marlin was ready for bigger things, and began manufacturing the .44 caliber Ballard "Hunters' Rifle." Marlin had patented a double-ended firing pin, one end for rimfire, the other for centerfire. With this addition the Ballard rifle could handle either the .44 long rimfire, or the .44-40 centerfire cartridges! Other styles were added in the calibers popular in the 1870s and 1880s. In 1881 Marlin launched his first repeating rifle, a large lever-action rifle capable of handling the long black-powder cartridges such as .32-40, .38-55, .40-60, .45-70 government, and a special Marlin high-velocity cartridge—the .45-85.

In 1888 Marlin brought out a light-weight, lever-action rifle with a short lever motion chambered for the .32-20, .38-40 and .44-40 cartridges. Within a year he had replaced the Model 1888 with the first Marlin solid-topped receiver—the Model 1889. New models followed rapidly. In 1891 a .22 caliber lever action was introduced, and a solid-topped centerfire rifle for longer cartridges was introduced in 1893. This was chambered for the .32-40, .38-55, and later for the new smokeless .30-30 cartridge. The Model 1895 Marlin rounded out the rifle line. It was a large lever-action rifle, replacing the Model 1881, and was eventually chambered for the .38-56, .40-65, .40-82, .45-70 Government, .45-90 and .33 Winchester Smokeless.

By the late 1890s Marlin had a strong position in lever-action repeating rifles. With his tool-and-die background Marlin put emphasis on high-quality steels and workmanship. The Marlin reputation for centerfire rifles was well deserved, and the company was ready to diversify into the large American shotgun market.

Marlin Model 1898

Marlin launched its entry into the shotgun field with the Model 1898, a 12-gauge slide-action shotgun with a visible hammer competing directly with the Winchester Models 1893 and 1897 slide-action shotguns which had proven enormously popular on the American market. A close-up of the deluxe version of the Marlin Model of 1898 is shown in Figure 5-27. Marlin continued its tradition of a solid-topped receiver and designed a shotgun for side ejection. This was the only shotgun in which John Marlin was directly involved, for he died in 1901 in his middle 60s. The shotgun, offered only in 12 gauge, was manufactured from 1898 to 1905. The design was then modernized and over the years the offerings were expanded. By 1915 it was available as the Model 24 in 12 gauge, the Model 26 in 16 gauge, and the Model 30 in 20 gauge. Over a million shotguns of this basic action were manufactured before final discontinuation in 1935. The Marlin catalogue of 1915 states:

Our first model of repeating shotgun, with visible hammer, was brought out in 1898; we have had 17 years experience with this form of gun and have put out over 150,000 of them. Every point that has shown by this practical experience a possibility of improvement has been refined, improved, perfected; and such features as the improved take-down construction, the shapely, comfortable forearm, the double extractors, and the improved automatic recoil safety lock, add greatly to the efficiency and value of the gun and the safety and convenience of the shooter.

Our aim has been to produce shotguns that should combine the elegance of outline, perfection of balance, ease of taking apart and quality of finish of the best double guns with the superiority in sighting and shooting of the

single-barrel, and give five or six shots quickly instead of only two.

The arguments for the visible-hammer and solid-topped construction were quite persuasive for the early 20th century shooter:

Our solid topped, side-ejecting construction acts both ways, protecting the head of the shooter from the exploding cartridge and the ejected shell, while at the same time protecting the action of the gun from rain, snow and all foreign substances.

The breech bolt of this gun, when closed, fills the opening in the frame completely, adding to the neat and pleasing appearance and keeping out sand, dirt, twigs, pine needles, etc.

The visible hammer, always in sight tells instantly, day or night, whether the gun is cocked or not cocked; you can cock or uncock it at will; everybody understands this type of gun. You can carry the gun with hammer in half-cock safety notch and raise hammer instantly with your thumb as you throw the gun to your shoulder.

The Model 1898 shotgun was generally fitted with a full-choked barrel. By the early 20th century its price was $24 in the standard grade and it was available with 28-, 30- or 32-inch barrels. Weight was 7 to 7¼ pounds. A special model known as the "Marlin Brush or Riot Gun" was available with a 26-inch barrel and cylinder bore weighing approximately 6¾ pounds, and at the same price. The comment was made that "this is an excellent arm for bird shooting in thickly wooded sections and also for shooting with buck-

Figure 5-27   Marlin Model 1898 repeating shotgun.

shot. It is also the best arm made for home protection and for the use of express messengers, prison guards, bank watchmen, etc."

Deluxe models of the 1898 shotgun were available with a special high-alloy steel used in the barrels. The steel used for standard barrels had a tensile strength of 66,000 pounds per square inch and the "special smokeless steel" used in the deluxe model guns was advertised with a tensile strength of 100,000 pounds per square inch. The grade C deluxe shotgun was assembled with the special steel barrel and a stock and forearm of specially selected fancy grained walnut which was carefully hand checkered. The action was hand engraved.

The top of the line was the grade D, which was sold at the very high price of $95.00 early in the 20th century. The quality of this shotgun was described in the following lyrical prose:

This great gun has a high quality Damascus barrel, specially bored and finished. The stock and forend are of the finest imported "Circassian walnut" finished by the London process of filling, giving a rich dull surface that does not glisten nor shine and does not show scratches as plainly as the highly polished wood. The stock and forearm are checkered with the finest possible hand work. The frame is elaborately engraved with fine quality handwork. Screws and trigger are of tooled steel, heavily gold plated. This is the finest repeating shotgun built.

It is believed that the shotgun illustrated in Figure 5-27 is a Model D.

By 1915 the design had been slightly modified to reflect improvements based on 17 years of manufacturing experience. Prices had declined slightly, with the standard or A model offered at $21.60. The B model incorporated the high-strength barrel and matting along the entire top of the barrel to minimize glare. The butt stock and forearm were hand checkered and the price of $33.25 reflected the additional effort. The model C was slightly more expensive at $43.25 and the price on the Model D remained the same at $95.00. A special trap model had been offered which was available at $35.00 with pistol grip stock and $37.50 with a special straight stock. The specifications were otherwise very similar to the Model B. A brush gun was offered at the same price for the 26-inch cylinder bore barrel and a riot gun was offered with a 20-inch barrel at the same price.

By 1915 a special economy model of the basic 1898 shotgun was offered as the Model 26. This was a solid-frame shotgun with a straight-grip stock. The catalog says:

The change allows of considerable economy and manufacturing, so that we can offer the gun at a much lower price than any good repeating shotgun has ever been regularly sold. The omission of the take-down feature saves a number of pieces, making the gun extremely clean, simple and light. The gun has two independent and positive extractors, also the improved automatic safety lock that waits for the cartridge to go off, and is operated automatically by the recoil. It is entirely satisfactory and will work with light or heavy loads.

Three models were offered. A standard shotgun with 30- or 32-inch full-choked barrel weighing about 7⅛ pounds at $19.50. A brush gun was offered with a 26-inch cylinder-bore barrel weighing about 7 pounds at the same price. In addition an extra-short light shotgun known as the Model 26 riot gun was offered with a 20-inch barrel weighing 6⅞ pounds at the same price. All of the hammer-style Marlin shotguns had a magazine capacity of 5 shots which, with one shot in the chamber, gave an overall capacity of 6.

Cross-section views of the basic model 1898 action are shown in Figure 5-28. This rather unusual action was strong enough for the moderate-powered shotshells of the early 20th century. When properly adjusted, the action should have been considerably smoother to operate than the Winchester models of 1893 and 1897 but careful workmanship would be required to keep the headspace within reasonable limits. The bolt slid back and forth in a rectangular slot in the receiver. Locking was accomplished by a long pivoted bar which is shown in the upper illustration filling the lower section of the bolt, below the firing pin. The locking block was pivoted near its center. As the bolt reached a fully forward position the front end of the lock was cammed upwards by a lateral extension on the action slide arm. This rotating motion dropped the rear of the locking block into a machined recess in the receiver. The action is described as follows:

The breech mechanism consists of a large and strong breech bolt, a straight locking bolt lying inside of said breech bolt, and pivoted near its center so that its end moved through

Many people will appreciate a gun that can be taken apart by a man who is not an expert. *Taking out one screw allows the entire breech mechanism to be removed from the frame in the Marlin Repeating Shotgun visible hammer models.*

To Take Apart—With *the action open* take out the carrier screw E (see cut on page 84), then holding the gun in the ordinary position, move the forearm forward slowly about an inch and the carrier will drop out through the opening in the bottom of the frame. The breech bolt containing the locking bolt can then be drawn out to the rear.

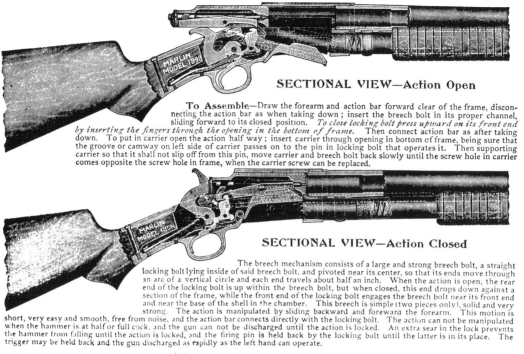

SECTIONAL VIEW—Action Open

To Assemble—Draw the forearm and action bar forward clear of the frame, disconnecting the action bar as when taking down ; insert the breech bolt in its proper channel, sliding forward to its closed position. *To close locking bolt press upward on its front end by inserting the fingers through the opening in the bottom of frame.* Then connect action bar as after taking down. To put in carrier open the action half way ; insert carrier through opening in bottom of frame, being sure that the groove or camway on left side of carrier passes on to the pin in locking bolt that operates it. Then supporting carrier so that it shall not slip off from this pin, move carrier and breech bolt back slowly until the screw hole in carrier comes opposite the screw hole in frame, when the carrier screw can be replaced.

SECTIONAL VIEW—Action Closed

The breech mechanism consists of a large and strong breech bolt, a straight locking bolt lying inside of said breech bolt, and pivoted near its center, so that its ends move through an arc of a vertical circle and each end travels about half an inch. When the action is open, the rear end of the locking bolt is up within the breech bolt, but when closed, this end drops down against a section of the frame, while the front end of the locking bolt engages the breech bolt near its front end and near the base of the shell in the chamber. This breech is simple (two pieces only), solid and very strong. The action is manipulated by sliding backward and forward the forearm. This motion is short, very easy and smooth, free from noise, and the action bar connects directly with the locking bolt. The action can not be manipulated when the hammer is at half or full cock, and the gun can not be discharged until the action is locked. An extra sear in the lock prevents the hammer from falling until the action is locked, and the firing pin is held back by the locking bolt until the latter is in its place. The trigger may be held back and the gun discharged as rapidly as the left hand can operate.

Figure 5-28   Cutaway views of the Marlin Model 1898 action.

an arc of a vertical circle and each end traveled about half an inch. When the action is open the rear end of the locking bolt is up within the breech bolt, but when closed this end drops down against a section of the frame, while the front end of the locking bolt engages a breech bolt near its front end and near the base of the shell in the chamber. This breech is simple (two pieces only), solid and very strong. The action is manipulated by sliding backward and forward the forearm. This motion is short, very easy and smooth, free from noise, and the action bar (slide arm) connects directly with the locking bolt.

This design would appear to reflect John Marlin's background as a tool-and-die maker. So many tolerances entered into the head space that it would be difficult to manufacture this design with interchangeable parts to the tight tolerances required for today's shotshells. The problem was solved in Marlin's day by extreme attention to detail and careful hand adjustments on final assembly. The design was amply strong for blackpowder shotshells and low-pressure smokeless shells. Some locking failures occurred with higher powered smokeless shotshells.

As the action slide handle was moved to the rear the first motion pushed the front of the locking bar downwards, lifting it out of the recess in the receiver. The breech bolt then slid to the rear cocking the hammer and extracting the fired cartridge case from the chamber. As the bolt neared a fully rearward position, as shown in the upper illustration, the fired shell was ejected laterally through the open port. The carrier dropped and the cutoffs operated, releasing a fresh shell from the magazine which slid into the position shown in the upper illustration. As the motion was reversed the carrier rose rapidly to the position shown in the lower illustration, bringing the rim of the shell in front of the breech bolt and lining the front of the shell up with the chamber. The carrier remained in the up position with the action closed, so that reloading the magazine could easily be accomplished by pushing fresh shells in through the bottom of the action past the cartridge cut offs. There was an intermediate or safety position for the hammer, which was a type of safety system well known and understood by American shooters of the nineteenth and early twentieth century. Additional safety devices had been added which prevented the firing pin from striking the shotshell until the action was fully locked. The redesigns of the Model 1898 incorporated a hang-fire device which delayed opening the action even with pressure on the forearm until shotshell recoil had released the internal safety member.

John Mahlon Marlin died in 1901 but the Model 1898 shotgun lived on another 30 years. The business was taken over by two sons. Mahlon H. Marlin became president, and J. Howard Marlin vice president. During the next 15 years they made many additions to the product line. A 16-gauge version of the Model 1898 shotgun was brought out in 1906 with the designation "Model 16." An economy version, solid-frame 12-gauge shotgun was also introduced in 1906 as the Model 17, but this only lasted two years. In 1906 a 12-gauges were introduced in 1911 as the Model 30. also introduced and dropped. A Trap model, known as the Model 21, was introduced with a straight grip and remained in production for 3 years. In 1908 an improved Model 1898 trap shotgun was introduced as the Model 24. This remained in production until the hammerless shotgun was introduced in 1915. Lighter-weight versions of the Model 1898 shotgun in 16 and 20 gauges were introduced in 1911 as the Model 30. These remained in production until 1915.

In 1915 the Marlin sons sold the business to a New York syndicate headed by industrialist A. F. Rockwell for $1,500,000. The company was renamed the Marlin-Rockwell Corporation and commercial production was severely curtailed, company business being focused on the manufacture of light machine guns for the military. Marlin-Rockwell purchased the Hopkins and Allen plant in Norwich, Connecticut in 1916 and manufactured Browning light machine guns at that location. Marlin also manufactured a light-weight air-cooled machine gun of their own design for both ground and aircraft use. They also manu-

factured the Colt light machine gun, a gas-operated air-cooled machine gun designed in the 1890s, which had the nickname of the "Potato Digger" or "Hedgeclipper" because of the long swinging lever underneath the forearm.

When military production was curtailed in 1920 the company turned again to commercial production. The chief engineer and plant superintendent, Carl Swebilius, was an extremely skillful designer, engineer and manufacturing man. He later left Marlin to found his own corporation, the High Standard Manufacturing Company. The Model 1898 hammer-style shotgun was revamped again and offered in 12 gauge as the Model 42, remaining in production until 1934.

By 1924 the Marlin Firearms Company had gone bankrupt and was sold by the New Haven County Sheriff to the highest bidder. It wasn't much of an auction, the highest bidder being an enterprising New Haven businessman, Frank Kenna, who paid an even $100 for the entire factory and inventory. Of course, there was one slight hitch in the form of a $100,000 mortgage which he also assumed. Kenna's efforts to get the Marlin Company back on its feet led to one final variation of the Model 1898 shotgun. This less-expensive version of the Model 42, available with 26-, 28- or 30-inch barrel, was manufactured from 1925 to 1928. Mr. Kenna offered a Model 49 shotgun as a free bonus to stockholders who purchased a certain amount of preferred stock. Over 3,000 of these economy-model shotguns were manufactured and were ornamented with one of the early applications of "rolled" checkering on the pistol grip and forearm. Over the years the one basic Model 1898 model with improvements was listed as Model 1898, the Model 16, the Model 17, the Model 19, the Model 21, the Model 24, the Model 30, the Model 42 and the Model 49. For the firearms historian this situation is to say the least a little confusing.

Chapter 6

20TH-CENTURY REPEATING SHOTGUNS

Stevens Hammerless Slide-Action Shotgun

By the turn of the century the J. Stevens Arms Company had a diversified line of shotguns, rifles and pistols, including compact, lightweight firearms designed by bicyclists. In 1904 Stevens introduced the first American slide-action hammerless shotgun, the Model 520, which was manufactured until 1930. This design was a result of John Browning's preoccupation with repeating shotgun designs. After the Winchester Model 1897 he experimented with hammerless designs in which all of the mechanism was enclosed within a solid-steel receiver. The design was quite distinctive, for the receiver had a stepped top surface—higher in the front over the ejection port than it was for the rear half of the length. The back of the receiver had a modified square back, as on the autoloading designs. The Stevens Model 520 was a landmark, doing much to start the trend towards hammerless slide-action shotguns.

REMINGTON REPEATERS

Remington Model 10

In 1907 Remington introduced its first slide-action hammerless shotgun. The design is shown in Figure 6-1. These were well-made, relatively expensive shotguns. For example, the price of the standard shotgun was $52.50 in 1922, back in the days when a complete Model T Ford could be purchased for under $500 and most workmen

were earning about $20.00 a week. A total of 275,000 Remington Model 10 shotguns was manufactured from 1907 to 1929. They were offered only in 12 gauge with 26-, 28-, 30- and 32-inch barrels. Chokes include cylinder, modified and full. Overall weight of the standard shotgun was 7½ pounds. A variety of models was offered including the riot model with a 20-inch barrel at the standard price, and special-grade and trap-grade models at $71.75. Ventilated-rib models known as the Model 10T started at $123.50 and went up to the Premier grade at $324.00.

The Remington Model 10 was designed with features that early-twentieth century shooters really liked, including a half pistol-grip stock and a take-down design that allowed the entire barrel, magazine tube and forearm assembly to be detached from the receiver. This was important, for many shooters traveled by bike and train and the take-down feature allowed the shotgun to be put in a compact "leg of mutton" type of gun case. The Remington shotgun had another feature which was continued on some of the later models and is still available in the Ithaca Model 37. This was a construction which allowed the shells to be loaded into the magazine tube through a loading port in the bottom of the receiver and the fired shells were also ejected out of the bottom of the receiver. The Model 10 had a special carrier design—a tray pivoted in one side of the receiver. The Model 10 carrier can be visualized as a paddle with a shaft along one side so that it formed a tray in the down position, but would

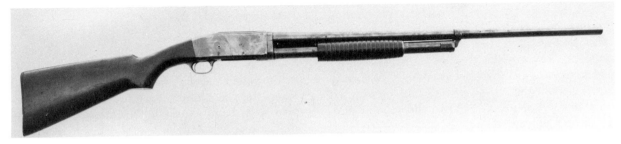

Figure 6-1 Remington Model 10 slide-action shotgun.

vanish into a recess in the wall of the receiver when rotated upwards. As the bolt reached the rear position, the shell was ejected downwards and the carrier recessed into the wall of the receiver. After ejection the carrier rotated downwards. Cutoffs were timed so that a fresh shell from the magazine was released into the carrier just as it reached a fully rotated position. When the forearm motion was reversed, the carrier rotated again, pushing the shell upwards. The trick was to get the rim of the shell up in front of the bolt rather than underneath it. Obviously the carrier cannot be a solid tray, as fitted to the Winchester Model 12, or the fired shell could never be ejected out of the bottom of the receiver.

The rugged, solid-topped Remington Model 10 was well liked by sportsmen for it kept out rain and snow and was equally good for a right- or left-handed shooter. This type of design must be carefully manufactured to close tolerances, particularly in the carrier system for if parts were out of tolerance or worn, there was a tendency for the fresh shell from the magazine not to feed properly into the chamber. Sales of a quarter of a million units show that the American sportsmen found this a thoroughly reliable, rugged shotgun.

Remington Model 17

In 1921 Remington brought out a new lightweight shotgun in 20 gauge which is shown in

Figure 6-2. The Model 17, manufactured for 12 years for a total of 72,644, continued many of the features of the 12-gauge Model 10 action, including the solid-topped receiver, semi-pistol grip, and grooved cylindrical forearm. But basic changes were made in the action and in the takedown construction.

The Remington Model 17 was designed by John Browning, and represented a substantial design improvement over the Model 10. Instead of a flipper, the shotgun was designed with a long U-shaped carrier, with the bottom of the U pivoted in the rear of the receiver. The two arms of the U lay in recesses high up in the receiver walls. As the bolt neared a fully rearward position the carrier suddenly moved downwards, sweeping the fired shell off the bolt face and throwing it out the bottom of the action. When the bolt reached a fully rearward position the carrier cutoffs operated, sending a fresh shell from the magazine rearwards into the carrier. When the shooter started moving the slide handle forward, the carrier moved rapidly upwards carrying the shell up in line with the chamber. The bolt moving forward carried the shell into the chamber, then pushed the arms of the carrier outwards into recesses machined into the walls of the receiver.

The take-down system of the gun was quite changed. The magazine tube and forend assembly remained permanently attached to the receiv-

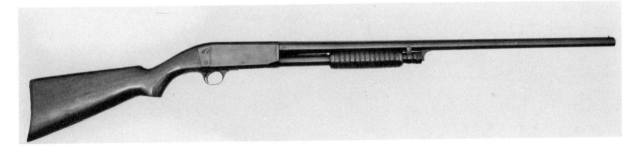

Figure 6-2 Remington Model 17 slide-action shotgun.

er and the barrel was easily removed by screwing the magazine plug back towards the receiver, then rotating the barrel a quarter of a turn and removing it from the receiver. This take-down construction gave two subassemblies of nearly equal length and is the type of take down used on almost all of today's modern slide-action shotguns.

Standard Model 17 shotguns were available in 26-, 28-, 30- or 32-inch barrels in cylinder, modified and full choke. The magazine held four shells which, with one in the chamber, gave a capacity of five shots without reloading. Weight was about 5¾ pounds; overall length about 47 inches. The Model 17 was available in a series of grades including standard, special, tournament, expert and premier grade, the latter being ornately engraved over all the receiver and parts of the action slide and barrel. There was an interesting catalogue comment offering a solid-ribbed barrel for the Model 17 repeating shotgun: "The solid ribbed barrel prevents reflection of light on the top of the barrel from interfering with the shooter's line of sight. This feature is particularly appreciated by shooters who have used a double gun. The barrel and rib are made in one solid piece, consequently we cannot fit a rib on a plain barrel."

The cost of machining a barrel and rib in one solid piece would be prohibitively expensive today, for the barrel blank would have to be forged with a lump of metal to form the rib. After drilling and reaming operations the rib must be milled to shape and then all of the curved contours on the remainder of the barrel profile milled in with contour-formed milling cutters, rather than simply being turned on a high-speed lathe.

The design features of the Remington Model 17 were excellent and many of these qualities have been continued today in the Ithaca Model 37 shotgun.

Remington Model 29

In 1929 Remington redesigned the 12-gauge Model 10 shotgun. In addition to internal changes in the action the shotgun was given a modernized full pistol-grip stock and both the stock and forearm were hand checkered. In other respects the appearance was similar to that shown in Figure 6-2. The Model 29 was sold at just below $50.00 in the standard grade. The options were continued with barrels of 26, 28, 30 and 32 inches with cylinder, modified and full choke. Deluxe models were available with straight grips, plain and ventilated rib barrels in a series of grades leading up to the premier grade, which sold for $304.00. A total of 37,933 Model 29 shotguns was sold before it was superseded in 1933 by the Model 31.

Remington Model 31

In 1931 Remington introduced an all-new slide-action shotgun that was eventually offered in 12, 16, and 20 gauge. A standard Model 31 is shown in Figure 6-3. The take-down system was somewhat similar to that on the Model 17. The magazine tube, permanently attached to the receiver, had a barrel-support guide and a movable nut at its front. When the knurled nut was turned rearwards, moving it towards the receiver, it released a latching surface on the barrel bracket allowing the barrel to be rotated a quarter turn and removed from the receiver. This gave a take down of two units of more or less equal length, which was quite handy for carrying in a gun case on public transportation. This type of take down had a second advantage for the shooter who wanted to use the same gun for both skeet and hunting conditions in that he could simply buy a second barrel rather than the entire barrel, magazine

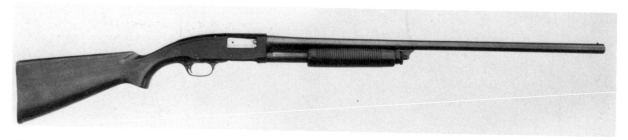

Figure 6-3 Remington Model 31 slide-action shotgun.

tube and forearm assembly as required on the Model 10 or Model 29.

Remington offered a wide range of options on the Model 31; 12-gauge barrels were available with cylinder, improved cylinder, skeet, modified, full, and long-range chokes. In addition Poly chokes and Cutt's compensators were offered as options. While the standard shotgun as shown in Figure 6-3 was not checkered, deluxe models were available with hand-carved 20-line checkering on butt stock and forearm. The 12-gauge models weighed approximately 7½ pounds, the 16-gauge models 6¾ pounds and the 20-gauge models 6½ pounds. The metal parts were given a highly polished and blued finish and the wood received no less than three coats of lacquer, even on the standard model. Magazine capacity was four shots in the magazine and one in the chamber. The trigger pull was specified at between 4 and 6 pounds. In addition to the standard model a riot grade with 20-inch barrel, police special with 18½-inch barrel and deluxe models such as the skeet, trap and hunter's special models were offered. The deluxe models went up in range to the premier grade, which was heavily engraved with game-scene panels on each side of the receiver and a background of fine scroll design extending onto the barrel and trigger plate.

The Model 31 was a highly successful shotgun design, remaining in production until 1949. A total of 189,243 shotguns was produced.

WINCHESTER MODEL 12

Until the turn of the century Winchester relied on John Browning for all of their repeating-shotgun designs. With the collapse of negotiations for the manufacture of the Browning semi-automatic shotgun in 1900, a new approach had to be taken. Fortunately Winchester had an experienced design team, headed by Thomas Crossley Johnson, who were experts in converting John Browning's hand-made models of new gun mechanisms into manufactured products. Thomas C. Johnson joined Winchester on November 30, 1885, and had over 25 years experience when the Model 12 shotgun design was created. There are many stories about "Tommy" Johnson, ranging from an acceptance of his many firearms patents as prima-facie evidence of true gun-design genius to those who take a more modest view of his contributions. It was regular practice in many organizations of the late-nineteenth and early-twentieth centuries for the head of the design department to patent all inventions of the department in his own name. Some old timers at Winchester remember these early-twentieth century practices and claim that Tommy Johnson was an excellent superviser who could find "bugs" in almost any mechanism designed by his staff but state that he did very little creative design work himself.

Whatever the true situation in the design department, the Model 12 shotgun was a happy result, for it has been considered the finest slide-action shotgun ever designed. It was originally designed in 20 gauge with a 25-inch, round nickel-steel barrel and was extremely compact and light-weight. First deliveries to the warehouse were made in August 1912 and it was announced in the 1913 Winchester catalogue. Both 12- and 16-gauge models were added in 1914. A 12-gauge riot gun was added in 1918, and a 28-gauge version manufactured in 1934.

The Model 12 shotgun has remained in the Winchester line for over 50 years. Early models had long sloping pistol grips and very slender forearms, typical of the style of the early 1900s. In 1934 butt stocks were redesigned to a more modern shape as shown in Figure 6-4. The standard field guns were fitted with plain stocks and barrels but the deluxe models had checkering. In 1944 a new-style slide handle was designed with

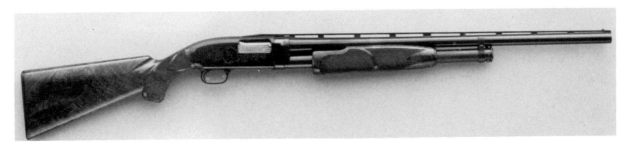

Figure 6-4 Winchester Model 12 slide-action shotgun, post-1934.

much larger cross section and circular grooves to aid the grip. The large-size slide handle shown in the figure is a semi-beavertail shape for deluxe shotguns designed about 1934.

The Model 12 Action

A cross-section illustration of the Model 12 action in the locked position is shown in Figure 6-5. The receiver was a solid steel forging with many intricate machine cuts on the interior. The bolt tilted upwards on closing, locking into the recess cut on the inside upper surface of the receiver. A safety interlock held the firing pin in a rearward position unless the gun was fully locked. The operation of this interlock may be seen in the illustration. A semi-circular "tail" has been cammed downwards by contact with the receiver thus releasing the firing pin to go for-

ward. The hammer is shown in a fully forward position at the instant of striking the firing pin and igniting the cartridge.

The carrier is shown in a fully downward position ready to receive a new cartridge. The fresh cartridge, partially out of the magazine, is prevented from moving to the rear by a projection on the bottom of the bolt known as the "beard." After firing, the first motion of the slide handle to the rear unlocked the bolt by rotating it counterclockwise until the locking surface cleared the receiver abutment, and then moved to the rear. As the bolt moved to the rear it recocked the hammer, and extracted the fired shell from the chamber. The fresh shell in the magazine followed the bolt to the rear, sliding into a proper feeding position in the carrier.

The action is shown in a fully unlocked position in Figure 6-6. The fresh cartridge is fully in

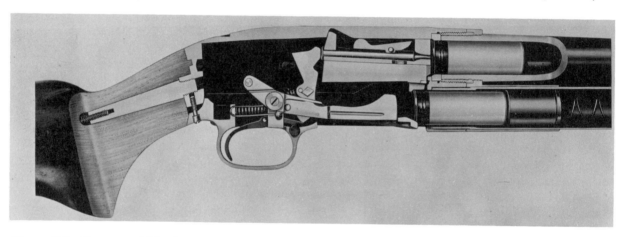

Figure 6-5   Cutaway of Winchester Model 12 action, closed.

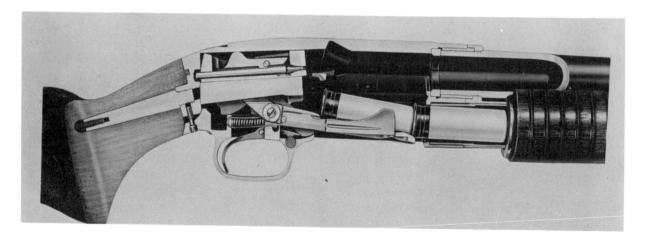

Figure 6-6   Cutaway of Winchester Model 12 action, open.

the carrier and the old cartridge has been extracted from the chamber and ejected from the gun. A camming surface on the bolt has engaged the angled extension to the carrier and as soon as the bolt is moved forward by the slide handle the linkage rapidly raised the carrier so that the fresh shell was in front of the bolt and in a position to be fed into the chamber. A pivoted shield on the side of the carrier prevented the shell from jumping sideways and jamming in the ejection port.

The Model 12 shotgun was extremely expensive to manufacture. Some of the reasons for this can be seen in Figures 6-5 and 6-6. Notice the number of complex cuts inside the receiver—all of which had to be made with relatively small cutters working from within the solid-steel forging. The locking recess, for example, was so difficult that a two-piece machining setup had to be used. An extension drive was pushed in from the front of the receiver at an angle to engage a separate cutter assembly which was inserted from the bottom to machine the locking recess. Another reason for the high expense can be seen in the chamber construction. The shotgun was designed with a "take-down" system which allowed removal of the entire barrel assembly. In order to keep head space within tolerance, a separate ring was fitted to form the rear section of the chamber. Special machining operations were required to assure concentricity between this separate ring and the remainder of the chamber. The illustration also shows the extra threaded sleeves and collars required for the take-down construction.

Model 12 shotguns were designed almost without regard to cost. Nickel-steel barrels were fitted and chrome-molybdenum alloys were used in receivers and interior components. This meant that the gun was always very high-priced in relation to other slide-action shotguns. It also meant that the guns were virtually indestructible and if given adequate care and cleaning would last several lifetimes.

The Model 12 in 20 gauge was originally introduced at the price of $20 and became extremely popular. Over 100,000 were sold in the first two years. Sales continued strong for many years and the one millionth Model 12 shotgun was presented to Lt. General Henry H. Arnold, Chief of the Army Air Forces, in August 1943.

During the 50 years of standard production many different models were manufactured. The vast majority were "field" models with plain barrels and stocks. The standard 12-gauge model with a 30-inch barrel weighed about 7¼ pounds. The 20-gauge model as originally designed was extremely light and compact at only 6¼ pounds. The 28-gauge was heavier at about 7¼ pounds and the 16-gauge fell between these models at 6½ pounds. Heavy duck guns chambered for the 3-inch magnum were generally quite heavy, at about 8½ pounds. Special skeet and trap models were manufactured with solid and ventilated-rib barrels.

The Model 12 shotgun earned such an enviable reputation for reliability in the field that it was often called "The Perfect Repeater." Attempts to simplify the design and reduce manufacturing costs were almost continuous during the period following World War II, for the competition from other shotguns at considerably lower prices cut heavily into the Model 12 sales volume. Attempts to achieve lower costs through the use of solid frame construction, such as on the Winchester Model 25, and simplifying redesigns, as with the Model 12 "Featherweight," simply did not provide sufficient manufacturing economies to maintain a necessary minimum sales volume. By the late 1950s it became apparent that the shooting public was no longer willing to pay the premium for such a shotgun and with great reluctance the Model 12 was dropped from regular production during the early 1960s.

The New Winchester Model 12

During the late 1960s the Model 12 shotgun was manufactured in a special custom shop together with the Model 21 double-barreled shotgun. With the extremely limited volume manufactured, the selling price hovered around $800.

Since demand for the Model 12 continued, the Winchester product engineering and manufacturing engineering departments studied ways to put it back into limited production. A special project engineer was assigned to follow all the production aspects of re-introduction. The cost of replacing all of the tooling would have been prohibitive, but techniques were worked out to use investment castings made of chrome-molybdenum alloy steel for components such as the receiver, bolt, carrier, trigger, hammer, barrel band and receiver extension. Some new machinery was purchased and a production area prepared. In the summer of 1972 three basic models of the Model 12 were announced, all under $400 in price. The basic model is the "field gun" which is certainly a deluxe shotgun to drag through the brambles. It features selected walnut stocks, hand-cut checkering, high-gloss finish, and a ventilated rib. It is offered with a 26-inch cylinder bore barrel, 28-inch modified choke and 30-inch full choke barrel.

Skeet and trap models are also offered. The trap model is fitted with a full-choke 30-inch barrel, ventilated rib and standard or monte-carlo butt stock. Forearm and butt stock are hand checkered and of extra-fancy walnut. The specifications for the skeet shotgun are similar, except that it is fitted with a 26-inch open-choke barrel.

When customers heard that the Model 12 was going back into production at a more moderate price, some 8,000 orders accumulated even before any formal announcement was made. With nearly 2,000,000 Model 12 shotguns in the field over a 60-year history it remains one of the best and most successful of all slide-action shotgun designs. The Model 12 is virtually indestructible—for many years they were the standard shotgun used for testing ammunition in ballistic ranges. Every year the guns would be withdrawn from service on a rotating basis, sent over to the Product Service Department for minor adjustments and occasional replacement of a worn part and then returned to the daily grind of ammunition testing for another 12 months.

When commercial ammunition production was terminated in New Haven during the 1960s some of the old Model 12s came to research. From the obvious amount of wear on the outside of the wood and metal parts it seemed impossible that the mechanism inside could still function properly. In a majority of cases the guns were perfectly fine, requiring only minor adjustments to put them back in first-class functioning order.

We often searched out old Model 12 shotguns to use for some of our wilder ammunition experiments. One research department modification actually converted a Model 12 into a crank operated Gatling gun, with shells being fed from detachable box magazines. This shotgun mounted on a tripod and loaded with modern buckshot would spew out a deadly hail as fast as the crank could be turned. The idea was to place these shotguns in strategic positions around air fields for night-time defense against enemy soldiers attempting to penetrate the base perimeter. Model 12 shotguns actually did see combat in both world wars. In war and peace it has proven to be one of the finest slide-action shotguns of all time.

BOLT-ACTION REPEATERS

After the First World War the German firearms industry was forbidden by the Versailles Treaty from manufacturing military firearms. At the same time there were millions of Mauser bolt-action military rifles left over. Ingenious manufacturers struck on the idea of converting surplus Mauser rifles into inexpensive bolt-action shotguns to be sold around the world at low prices. Since shotshells are much bigger than the 7.9mm German army cartridge (a 12-gauge shotshell is 18.5mm in diameter), it was necessary to machine out the entire locking surface at the front of the receiver. This meant that the bolt action was locked only on the rear safety lug which experience showed was strong enough to do the job with moderate-powered shotshells. Early in the 1920s some American manufacturers, such as Mossburg, Marlin, and Savage-Stevens, started making bolt-action shotguns specifically designed for this purpose. The designs were successful and have been offered over the past fifty years. A modern Mossberg Model 395K bolt-action repeater with a box magazine is shown in Figure 6-7. This shotgun is designed with a one-piece hardwood stock which has been given a walnut finish and is fitted with a rubber recoil pad and a variable choke device at the muzzle. Twisting the knurled collar allows fast adjustment of the choke from improved cylinder to full choke. The action consists of a rugged, tubular-steel receiver in which the bolt assembly slides. The shotgun is locked by two rear-locking lugs which fit into matching recesses in the receiver. One of the locking lugs is at the base of the bolt handle, the other on the opposite side. This arrangement keeps the front of the receiver a smooth inner profile which helps feeding blunt shotshells and yet gives adequate strength in the locking system. The barrel is permanently screwed to the receiver and a combined recoil plate and rear sight are clamped between barrel and receiver. The recoil plate can be seen as the double line at the front end of the receiver. A square lower surface transmits the rearward firing force of the shotshell from the receiver to the wooden stock.

Two shotshells are contained in the detachable box magazine. If a shell is slipped into the chamber before the magazine is inserted, the overall capacity of the shotgun is three shots. The magazine is shown disassembled in the lower center section of Figure 6-8. The firing system consists

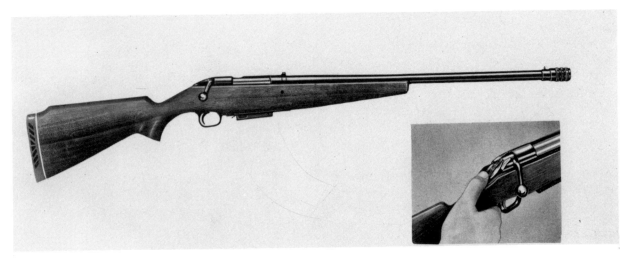

Figure 6-7 Mossberg Model 395K bolt-action repeating shotgun.

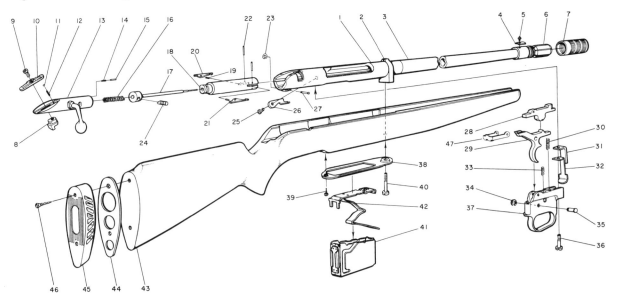

Figure 6-8 Exploded view of Mossberg Model 395K shotgun.

of a cylindrical striker (part 17) which is driven by a powerful striker spring (16). The striker is held in a cocked position by the sear (28) which is in turn controlled by the trigger mechanism which is shown on the right side of the illustration. All of the trigger-mechanism components are contained in a molded trigger-guard housing which is aligned with the receiver by a retaining pin. The shotgun is fitted with twin extractors which carry the fired shotshell to the rear until it is struck by the ejector (26) which kicks the fired shell diagonally up and to the right and out the ejection port. Construction of variable choke device is shown in the uper right corner of the illustration. The forward section of the barrel is slotted (6) and then covered with a knurled tube which has a tapered inner surface. As the knurled tube is screwed to the rear the tapered surface drives the slotted fingers inwards, thus constrict-

ing the muzzle and giving a larger degree of choke. Mossberg bolt-action repeating shotguns are available in 12, 16 and 20 gauge and 410 bore. The 12-gauge and 410-bore shotguns weigh about 6¾ pounds while the 20-gauge model weighs only 6¼ pounds. Overall length of the 28-inch barrel is 47½ inches.

Other manufacturers make bolt-action shotguns of basically similar construction in box-magazine and tubular-magazine configuration. The tubular-magazine designs have a feeding system quite similar to that of a slide-action shotgun with a large magazine tube buried in the wooden forearm of the shotgun. The bolt-action shotgun designs provide sturdy, low-cost repeating shotguns. The main problem with this type of design is that bolt action is inherently a rather slow action to operate. The average shooter must bring the shotgun down from the shoulder to operate

116

the bolt which makes it difficult to get a fast second shot at the rapidly retreating game.

MARLIN HAMMERLESS SHOTGUNS

The announcement of the Remington Model 10 slide-action shotgun in 1907 and the announcement of the Winchester Model 1912 hammerless shotgun clearly showed a trend. Marlin responded with a new 12-gauge hammerless shotgun, the Model 28, in 1913. A slightly improved model in 16 and 20 gauge, the Model 31, was introduced in 1914. The new shotguns had a relatively short production life, for they were discontinued with the shift to military machine-gun production in 1915. After the War was over, new hammerless shotguns with minor design improvements were brought out as the Model 43 in 12 gauge and the Model 44 in 20 gauge. All of the shotguns were similar in appearance. Two Model 43 shotguns

are shown in Figure 6-9. The upper illustration shows a deluxe trap shotgun fitted with a nice pistol-grip stock, monte-carlo cheek piece and an early style rubber recoil pad. The forearm is large and designed to slide over the front part of the receiver in a fully rearward position. This is the reason why the front of the forearm is cylindrical, while the rear has high square edges so that the receiver can fit inside. Both butt stock and forearm were extensively checkered and the barrel has a matted top surface to reduce glare. The lower shotgun is also a deluxe model with a checkered semi-pistol-grip stock. Both deluxe and standard models were fitted with hard-rubber butt plates.

By the late 1920s the models had been redesignated Model 43A in 12 gauge, and 44A in 20 gauge, to reflect additional small design improvements. The catalog copy was written by an enthusiastic salesman:

Figure 6-9 Two Marlin Model 43 shotguns: upper, Trap; lower, Deluxe.

Model No. 43A, 12-gauge hammerless, the gun that won the world's championship at the Olympic Games. The safest breech loading shotgun ever built. Solid steel breech, solid top, side ejection, barrel matted on top entire length . . . press-button cartridge release, automatic safety device for protection against hang fire; double extractors that pull any shell; the most practical and convenient take down; quick acting trigger safety. This Marlin has better lines and more style than any other similar construction and is a wonderful gun for ducks, geese, foxes, trap-shooting and all long range shooting. Retails at $45.00.

The Marlin line of hammer-style and hammerless shotguns continued the company's long tradition of carefully manufactured firearms. Mechanical construction of the hammerless shotguns was more complex than on the Winchester Model 12 and it appears that this design required careful machining and fitting of internal components to get good functioning. The addition of these hammerless slide-action models provided Marlin with modern designs to compete in the important hammerless repeating-shotgun market.

The 20-gauge shotgun known as the Model 44A had basically the same features and was chambered for the new powerful 2¾-inch 20-gauge shells, which were just making their appearance in the 1920s, replacing the 2½-inch loads from the nineteenth century. The selling price for the Model 44A was also $45.00. At the same time the old Model 1898 shotgun, redesignated the Model 42A, was sold at $38.00.

A cutaway view of the Marlin hammerless action is shown in Figure 6-10. The receiver had an unusual design with a flat top and angled rear section joined by a small radius curve of transition. This design gave Marlin shotguns a distinctive look, but reduced the volume within the receiver. Operation of the mechanism was somewhat complex which may have been necessary due to the strong patent positions that Winchester and Remington had secured on their hammerless slide-action shotguns. The "action bar" was a long bar of steel which passed through the

Left side of receiver and trigger plate cut away to show the repeating mechanism.

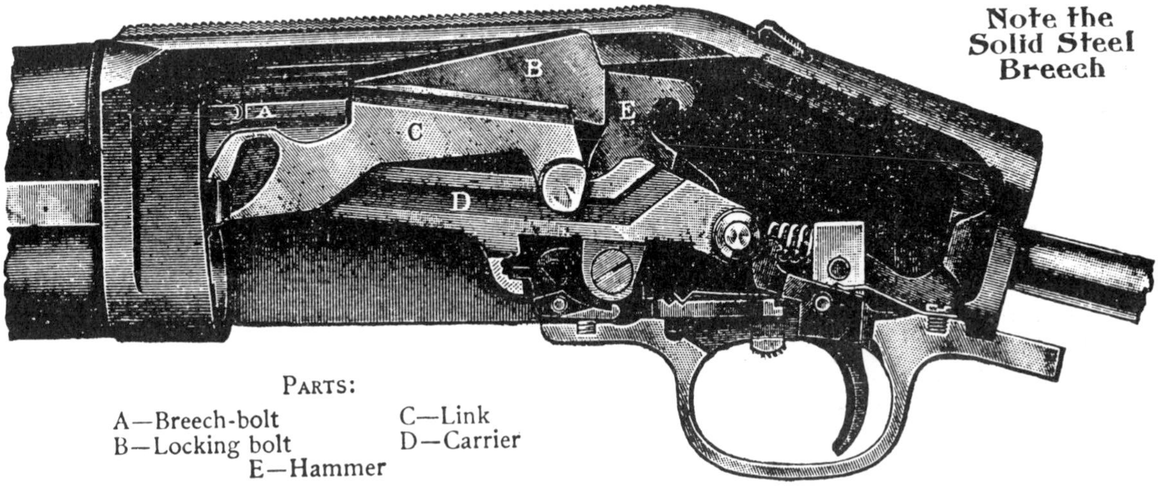

PARTS:

A—Breech-bolt
B—Locking bolt
C—Link
D—Carrier
E—Hammer

Operation. The large stud at the rear end of link "C" operates in a straight slot in the left side of frame. A stud at the rear end of the action bar connects with the front end of link; a corresponding stud on the link operates the carrier "D." Drawing back the action bar first depresses the front end of link and unlocks the gun by drawing down the locking bolt "B," then opens the action, ejects empty shell, cocks the hammer and allows a new cartridge to enter upon the carrier. The forward motion raises carrier, inserts the new cartridge into the chamber, closes and locks action, leaving the gun ready to fire.

Figure 6-10 Cutaway of Marlin hammerless action.

front of the receiver and attached to the wooden action-slide handle surrounding the magazine tube. The bar may be seen extending forward of the receiver between the barrel and magazine tube, its rear end just barely shown in the illustration. The rear section of the bar had a lateral stud which rode in a cam slot in the link C. The rear end of the link contained another stud, shown in the illustration, which rode in a horizontal slot machined into the inside of the receiver wall.

As the shooter pulled the wooden slide handle to the rear, the action bar moved rearward. It tried to ride up the curved cam slot in the front of the link C. Since the action bar could not move upwards (since it was restrained by the receiver) the effect was to drag the front end of the link downwards. The link had another stud, which was connected to the locking bolt B. As the front end of the link moved down it cammed the locking block downwards out of the locking recess machined into the top of the receiver. Once the locking bolt was disengaged from the recess the bolt, link and action bar moved together towards the rear of the receiver. Another stud on the link rode in track D, machined into the side of the carrier. As the link approached a fully rearward position it struck the sloping cam surface in the carrier causing it to rotate rapidly downwards around its rear pivot (which is shown in the illustration). When the carrier reached a fully downward position the cutoffs were operated, feeding a fresh shell from the magazine into the carrier.

On the forward stroke the early motion would cause the carrier to rise rapidly with a fresh shell in the tray. This brought the rim of the shell up in front of the bolt and lined up the front of the shell with the chamber. Further motion forward chambered the shell. The final forward motion of the action bar caused the link to rise, lifting the locking block back into the locking recess and making the gun ready for the next shot.

The firing system had several safety features. As soon as the locking block moved down out of the recess and towards the rear, it recocked the hammer. The hammer E is shown against the rear of the locking bolt. The hook-shaped sear is clearly visible. As the hammer reached a fully cocked position an extra sear in the lock mechanism engaged this hook and held the hammer fully depressed until the action was closed and locked. At that point the hammer was released

from this primary notch and allowed to jump up to the sear notch on the trigger. This insured that even if the trigger was held fully to the rear, the gun would not fire until the action was closed and locked. This was important, preventing a "follow down," where the hammer could possibly follow the breech bolt in its forward motion and fire the cartridge before the gun was fully locked. Such a safety feature was also built into the Remington and Winchester hammerless slide-action shotguns. One tricky aspect of this mechanism is that these guns can be fired at an extremely high rate of speed by simply holding the trigger fully to the rear and shucking the slide handle back and forth. The gun will automatically fire as soon as the action is fully forward. A skilled shooter can immediately reverse the motion of the slide arm and actually operate the slide-action shotgun as fast as most shooters can operate a semi-automatic.

Marlin included another safety feature in their hammerless design by the use of a two-piece firing pin. The two sections of the firing pin aligned only when the gun was fully cocked. At any other time the hammer blow would only move the rear section of the firing pin and not have any effect on the motion of the front half.

Marlin continued its practice of renumbering firearms whenever a minor design change was performed. Thus the Model 28 slide-action shotgun was introduced in 12 gauge in 1913 and discontinued in 1915. The Model 31 was a 20-gauge version of the same shotgun. It was introduced in 1914 and discontinued in 1915. In 1920 a new 12-gauge shotgun was brought out using the design improvements included in the 20-gauge Model 31. The new 12-gauge model became the Model 43 and the 20-gauge model became the Model 44. In 1929, after another minor redesign, the model designation was changed to Model 53. In 1930 the internal mechanism was slightly changed and the designation was changed to Model 63, which was announced in 1931 and continued until 1935.

The 12-gauge models were normally manufactured with 30- or 32-inch full-choke barrels, but the 1915 catalogue states:

"but on special order guns with 26, 28, 30 or 32 inch barrel, full choke, modified choke or cylinder bore, can be furnished at the same price ($22.60). Barrels are chambered for 2¾- or 2⅝-inch shells; specially bored for both black and smokeless powder; fully proved with excessive loads. All full-choke barrels are *guaranteed* to pattern more than 325 pellets in a 30-inch circle at 40 yards, using 1¼ ounces of No. 8 chilled shot. The 30-inch full-choke barrel is sent unless otherwise ordered."

The same practice was followed with the 16- and 20-gauge shotguns. An unidentified order would receive a 28-inch full-choke barrel in 16 gauge, although 26-inch barrels and other chokes were available, if specially ordered, at the same price. Twenty-gauge shotguns were normally shipped with a 25-inch full-choke barrel, which made an extremely light and handy shotgun of 5⅞ pounds. The guns could be specially ordered with 28-inch barrels and with the full choke, modified choke or cylinder bore at the same price ($24.00 in 1915).

Marlin Model 120M

In 1972 Marlin announced a new Model 120 Magnum slide-action shotgun. This re-entry into the slide-action market, after an absence of 37 years, was designed as a premium priced high-quality shotgun. It is shown in Figure 6-11. Butt stock and forearm are made of American walnut with a pressed checking design. White line spacers, pistol-grip cap and rubber recoil pad are fitted to the butt stock. The receiver is milled from a solid block of alloy steel, a steel trigger guard is fitted and the two components are polished as an assembly. Internal parts in the gun mechanism are steel and the action is fitted with twin action slide bars to give smooth functioning. Twin action slide bars are used on most modern shotguns, for it has been found that this minimizes the twisting motion of the bolt mechanism within the receiver thus providing a smoother action.

All Marlin Model 120M shotguns are fitted with ventilated ribs. Barrel lengths of 26, 28 and 30 inches are available with open to full-choke borings. Extra barrels are interchangeable by unscrewing the magazine cap, opening the action slightly to disengage the bolt lock and sliding the barrel off the magazine tube. The bolt locks into a recess machined into the top of the short, hardened barrel extension. The barrel is chambered for 2¾ or 3 inch magnum shells interchangeably. Magazine capacity is four shots with 3-inch shells and five shots with the standard 2¾-inch shells. The steel parts on the shotgun are highly polished, except for a matte top on the receiver and a grooved ventilated rib. This combination gives good appearance to the shotgun and still minimizes glare for fast wing shooting.

The Marlin Firearms Company moved into an all-new manufacturing plant during 1970. Machinery and tooling for the manufacture of the Model 120M was installed in the new factory and production models started rolling down the line in mid-1972.

ITHACA MODEL 37

The Ithaca Gun Company of Ithaca, New York, has a long history in the manufacture of high-quality shotguns, their first double-barreled shotgun being introduced in 1880. Ithaca continued manufacture of this style of shotgun into the twentieth century and in 1926 introduced their most significant model, the New Ithaca Double, which was produced until 1948 with a total production run of approximately 47,000 units.

In 1937 Ithaca introduced its first and only slide-action shotgun. The shotgun is similar to the Remington Model 17, designed by John Browning. The Ithaca Model 37 has the same basic action layout with a receiver with solid sides and top. The shells are both loaded and ejected out of the bottom of the action. Ithaca production utilizes both old and new processes.

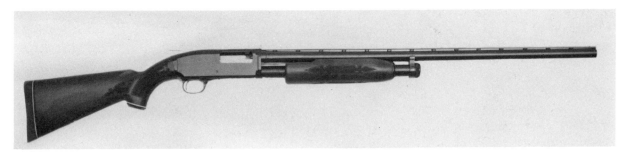

Figure 6-11   Marlin Model 120 Magnum hammerless shotgun.

120

The receivers are milled out of a 7-pound block of steel—one of the old and traditional techniques. The barrels, on the other hand, are made by the newest of manufacturing processes. They start out as 15-inch long, heavy-walled tubes of alloy steel which are slid a mandrel and rotary-forged by a series of hammer blows into a thin-walled barrel contour with a length of more than 30 inches. The barrel is then removed and finished on traditional barrel-making machinery. This type of barrel-manufacturing process, also used by Remington and Winchester, leads to strong, tough barrels. The Ithaca Model 37 shotguns have always been known for their light weight. Even though the original receiver blank weighs 7 pounds, the great majority of this weight is removed in the machining process. The standard 12-gauge Ithaca Model 37 shotgun weighs only 6½ pounds with all the components assembled. The 20-gauge weighs only 5¾ pounds. Shotguns are offered with 20-inch cylinder-bore barrels on the special "Deerslayer" specifically designed for rifled slugs, and with 26-, 28- and 30-inch barrels in the standard shotgun models. Sixteen and 20-gauge models are available with 26- and 28-inch barrels. Chokes from improved cylinder to full are offered.

A wide variety of models are available. The standard-grade repeater is competitively priced with the Winchester and Remington models. Deluxe models, with a ventilated rib, are premium priced by about $20.00. A supreme-grade repeater premium, priced at $100.00 above the basic model, features extra-fancy walnut, hand-cut

checkering and extra care in the metal finishing operations. Ithaca also offers a number of special models, such as the skeet and trap models. The skeet shotgun has similar stock dimensions to the standard gun, with a 1⅝-inch drop at the comb and a 2⅝-inch drop at the heel. The trap models have a higher line of sight with a 1½-inch drop at the comb and a 1⅞-inch drop at the heel. All models have a 14-inch length of pull. Two models are offered for rifled slugs, the Model 37 Deerslayer and the Model 37 Super Deluxe Deerslayer. They are fitted with rifle-type sights and are offered in 12 and 16 gauge with 20- or 26-inch barrels. Provision is made for mounting a telescopic sight for increased accuracy with rifled slugs.

A modern Ithaca Model 37 deluxe-grade shotgun is shown in the upper illustration of Figure 6-12. The Ithaca Model includes many minor design improvements and is an excellent, smooth-functioning shotgun which has been manufactured for the past 35 years. The steel receiver is machine engraved with hunting scenes on both side panels. The walnut butt stock and forearm are checkered to improve appearance and give better hand grip. The shotguns are fitted with rubber recoil pads which significantly reduce the recoil sensation.

The top of the line Ithaca Supreme Model 37 shotgun is shown in the lower illustration of Figure 6-12. This is a deluxe shotgun with dense, highly figured walnut in the butt stock and forearm. Hand checkering patterns have been added to finish off the design. There is so much extra

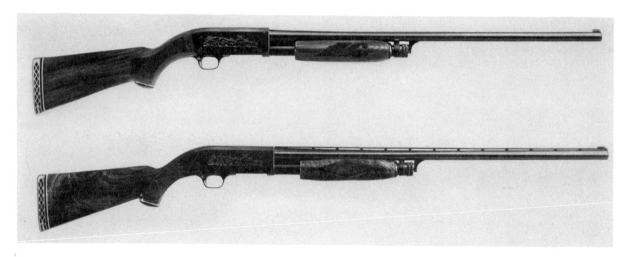

Figure 6-12 Two Ithaca Model 37 slide-action shotguns.

handwork in the Supreme model that it is priced almost $100 above the standard Model 37 repeater.

The Ithaca Model 37 functions the same as the Remington Model 17. There is no ejection port cut into the side of the receiver, shells are loaded in through the bottom of the receiver into the magazine tube. On the rearward stroke of the action slide handle, the bolt is cammed out of the locking recess cut into the top of the receiver. The bolt then moves to the rear, extracting the fired shell from the chamber. As the bolt reaches a nearly fully rearward position the carrier arms, which have remained high in the receiver, sweep downward, picking the fired shell off the bolt face and throwing it out the open bottom of the action. As the carrier reaches a fully downward position the cartridge cutoff releases a fresh shell, which slides out of the magazine on to the carrier arms. When the action slide handle is moved forward the carrier rises rapidly, bringing the fresh shell up in front of the bolt face and in line with the chamber. The carrier remains in the up position. The bolt slides through the carrier arms, ramming the fresh shell into the chamber and pushing the carrier arms outwards into the recesses machined into the receiver wall.

An Ithaca Model 37 was the first repeating shotgun I owned. It was a modified-choke model and I carried it for several seasons. My shooting skill was not up to the close patterns of a modified-choke shotgun and I was amazed at the number of rabbits I missed. The dense pattern would chew up the ground on one side or the other of the darting rabbit and would seldom connect with the fast-moving target.

However, I found the Ithaca 37 to be a high-quality, smooth-functioning shotgun. There were occasional malfunctions if I did not operate the slide handle a full stroke—for it was likely that the fresh shell be dropped on to the ground rather than to be fed into the action. This was a rare and minor problem and the shotgun gave excellent service.

After 35 years of production the Ithaca Model 37 remains a competitive shotgun. In addition to the hundreds of thousands manufactured for the commercial market, military models have been produced for both the Army and Navy. The action has proven to be rugged and long lasting, reflecting careful manufacturing and assembly in the Ithaca tradition.

MODERN SAVAGE SLIDE-ACTION SHOTGUNS

The Savage Model 520, introduced in 1904, started the trend to hammerless shotgun designs. After its discontinuation in 1930, Savage and Stevens continued introduction of new models. The current Savage slide-action design is the Model 30-T, shown in Figure 6-13. The design features monte-carlo butt stock, roll-engraved receiver and ventilated-rib barrel. All of the models are built on the same basic action. The steel receiver is machined with internal tracks on which the bolt slide reciprocates. The rear of the receiver is open. The trigger mechanism assembly is contained in a die-cast alloy-metal housing. This is a complex assembly, which contains the trigger mechanism, the carrier mechanism and the closure for the rear of the receiver. The upper portion of the closure may be seen as a triangular section extending to the rear of the receiver and containing a tang safety. The die-cast housing also includes the socket, to which the butt stock is attached by means of a butt-stock bolt. The trigger mechanism is modern in design, with safety interlocks that hold the hammer cocked until the action is fully locked. Safety control in the trigger mechanism is provided both by the spring-loaded sear mechanism and also by an ac-

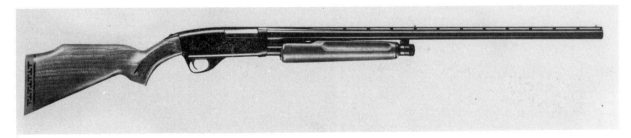

Figure 6-13 Savage Model 30-T slide-action shotgun.

tion slide lock which senses the position of the bolt slide and will not permit the gun to fire until fully locked. The bolt is basically a cylindrical member which rides on top of a flat slide assembly (bolt slide). Camming surfaces are designed into both the bolt slide and bolt. As the bolt slide goes to a fully forward position, these cams lift the rear end of the bolt into a locking recess cut in the top surface of the receiver. On the rearward stroke other camming surfaces drag the bolt down out of the locking recess until it rests flat on top of the bolt slide and then the two units move together to the rear of the receiver. The bolt slide is moved by a single-action bar which lies on the left side of the receiver and connects to the wood forearm.

Interchangeable barrels are fitted to the Model 30 shotguns. For take-down, the nut at the front of the magazine tube is unscrewed several turns to remove a conical surface which engages a recess in the end of the magazine tube. This allows the barrel to be rotated one-quarter turn, releasing the interrupted threads on the barrel and receiver. The barrel is then slid forward and removed from the shotgun. It is perfectly practical to own a short, open-choked barrel with sights for use with rifled slugs, a long full-choked barrel for duck hunting and an open-choked barrel with ventilated rib for skeet shooting.

The 410-bore Model 30 shotgun has the same design features and some common parts with the 12- and 20-gauge models. Most of the components are miniaturized to reflect the much smaller size and longer length of the 410-bore 3-inch shotshells.

The various models of the Savage Model 30 shotguns all reflect careful attention to the needs of the modern sportsman. Use of a large-size forearm with a cutout groove for easy gripping, convenient take-down system, and a tang safety located where it may be flicked on and off easily with the thumb, all reflect modern design practice. Savage-Stevens has a long reputation of providing sturdy, moderate-priced shotguns for the American sportsman.

HIGH STANDARD SLIDE-ACTION SHOTGUNS

Since World War II the High Standard Manufacturing Company of Hamden, Connecticut, has produced slide-action shotguns marketed both under their own trademark and through Sears, Roebuck and Company. The latest shotguns are the Flite King models, available in 12, 20 and 28 gauge and 410 bore. All are designed with beavertail forearms which have checkering patterns. Walnut butt stocks are also checkered and fitted with rubber recoil pads. The Flite King shotguns are available with plain and ventilated rib barrels and adjustable choke devices. Barrel lengths of 26 to 30 inches are available and weights vary from 6¼ pounds in the 410-bore to 7¾ pounds in the 12-gauge models. A special skeet model is offered in 12, 20 and 28 gauge and 410 bore. It is fitted with a 26-inch ventilated-rib barrel bored with a skeet choke. Overall length of the shotgun is 45¾ inches and the weight is 7½ pounds in 12 gauge. The checkered walnut butt stock is fitted with a plain butt plate rather than the rubber recoil pad which is fitted to the other High Standard models. A special trap model is manufactured in 12 gauge with a 30-inch full-choked ventilated-rib barrel. Weight of the shotgun is 8¼ pounds and overall length 49⅝ inches.

The trap shotgun is similar to the skeet gun, with the exception of a monte carlo butt stock, which gives a higher line of sight to compensate for the rising targets that occur in trap shooting. High Standard offers a third special model, the 12-gauge Pump Brush Gun, which is fitted with a 20-inch cylinder-bore barrel, bringing the overall length down to 39¾ inches and the weight to 7¼ pounds. This shotgun, specially designed for use with rifled slugs, is fitted with open rifle-type sights.

REMINGTON MODEL 870

During the 1940s the Remington Research and Engineering Departments were developing designs for a new line of postwar rifles and shotguns. In 1950 one of their most famous and successful shotguns was introduced—the slide action Model 870, introduced in 12, 16 and 20 gauge. The standard 12-gauge Model 870 is shown in Figure 6-14. The enormous investment in research-and-development expense led to a design that was so successful it has been manufactured with only minor changes for the past 22 years. What is even more interesting, from a manufacturing standpoint, is that the Model 870 was designed not for compatibility with the Remington auto-loading shotgun of 1950 (the Model 11-48), but instead designed to have a common design

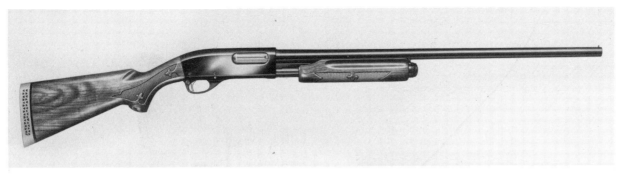

Figure 6-14 Remington Model 870 slide-action shotgun.

with the later generation of gas-operated shot-guns including the Models 58, 878 and 1100. Careful examination of the receivers shows that almost all the design features are the same, except where special modifications must be made in the auto-loading design, such as the cocking-hand slot which extends rearward from the ejection port, or the lengthened barrel-extension and return spring assembly in the butt stock in the Model 1100 design.

Over the years Remington has purchased large numbers of tape-controlled manufacturing machinery on which much of its production is performed. Normally tape-controlled machines are used for the production of limited runs of extremely accurate components, such as those used in aircraft engines and helicopters. Its advantage is that the machines will automatically follow instructions punched into a tape and the dimensions of the component can be changed simply by inserting a new tape. All the parts manufactured from that single tape will be identical in dimensions within the accuracy capabilities of the machine. The disadvantage is the high capital investment required, but this is somewhat offset by the advantage in manufacturing flexibility.

In 1969 Remington introduced 28-gauge and 410-bore Model 870 shotguns. In 1971 they added a left-hand version of the shotgun in 12 and 20 gauges. The total number of variations available at the present time is staggering. A recent Remington catalogue lists 84 variations of gauge, barrel length, choke and barrel and butt-stock styles for this one model. The basic features include a five-shot capacity with four shells in the magazine and one in the chamber. Overall length of the shotgun is 48½ inches with a 28-inch barrel. Average weight of the 12-gauge shotgun is 7 pounds and the 20-gauge weighs only 6½ pounds. The light-weight Model 870 is the 28-gauge, which weighs only 5½ pounds. Normal barrel lengths vary from 18 to 30 inches and chokes from skeet to full. Special 34-inch extra barrels are available for the trap, duck and goose models.

Skeet and trap models are designed with special features for those sports, such as special stocks and ventilated-rib barrels. Other specialized models are available, such as the Brushmaster, which is designed specifically for use with rifled slugs, including a short 20-inch barrel and rifle sights.

A slide-action shotgun is a relatively complex firearm. The components which make up a Remington Model 870 are shown in Figure 6-15. The bolt lock (37) fits inside the breech bolt (4) and the slide (57). The motion of the slide is controlled by the action bars (28) which are rigidly fastened to the forearm (27). The entire cycle of operation of the Model 870 is described by Remington, as follows:

FIRING

With the cross bolt safety pushed to "OFF" position (red band showing), the gun is fired by pulling trigger. The top section of trigger rotates forward carrying the connector, in ready position, forward against sear. This movement pivots sear out of engagement with hammer. The released hammer then rotates forward, urged by hammer plunger atop recessed hammer spring, and strikes firing pin, which is spring-retracted and pinned within breech bolt. The firing pin in turn strikes the primer and ignites powder charge. Just before firing pin is struck, hammer plunger in its upward motion engages action bar lock. Movement of front of action bar lock downward is restrained if fore-end is being held tightly rearward until pressure against it is briefly and involuntarily released by the shooter as arm recoils rearward. When action bar lock is freed either by a light fore-end grasp or by involuntary release under recoil, forward end of action bar lock is lowered from its position at rear of left action bar and rear section rises and lifts connector from contact with sear. This completes the "lock" or firing mechanism firing cycle. The two-fold guardian performance of the action bar lock is a safety feature that disconnects trigger assembly and sear until a shell is fully sealed

REMINGTON 870

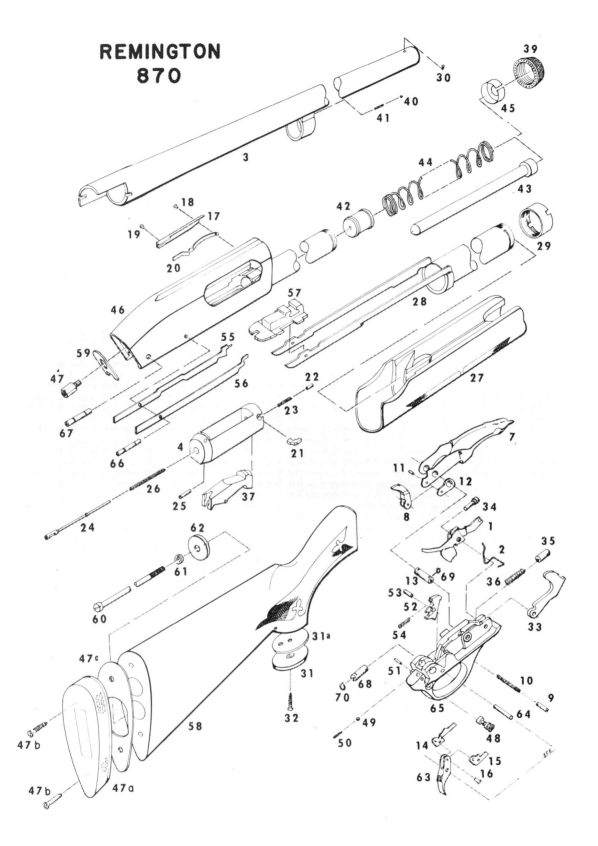

Figure 6-15 Exploded view of Remington Model 870 action.

in chamber and breech mechanism again is ready for firing.

After pulling trigger, the rearward movement of fore-end will open action and accomplish the Unlock, Extract, Eject, Cock, and Feed cycles. In detail they are as follows:

UNLOCK

The *initial* rearward movement of fore-end, after shell is fired, carries slide to rear of breech bolt. In passing to rear of breech bolt, the slide cams locking block from recoil shoulder of barrel, thereby unlocking action and camming firing pin to rear—locking the firing pin and preventing protrusion through bolt face.

EXTRACT

Further movement of fore-end rearward opens action. The breech bolt is moved back and the fired shell is extracted or withdrawn from chamber. The extractor claw, which overhangs bolt face, grips rim of shell tightly as extraction progresses. Pivot pressure is exerted on rear of extractor by extractor plunger and its recessed spring.

EJECT

As fired shell clears chamber, its base engages shoulder on rear of ejector spring, which is located on left side of receiver. This causes shell to pivot so that the front is ejected first through ejection port.

COCKING

Before ejection occurs, the rearward travel of breech bolt forces hammer downward against coiled hammer spring to engage sear. Pressure of sear spring locks sear in a notched position against cocked hammer.

FEEDING

The completion of the rearward motion of fore-end carries slide, breech bolt assembly, and locking block to rear of receiver. Termination of this rearward stroke also permits left action bar to cam left shell latch, thereby releasing first shell from magazine. The released shell is urged from tubular magazine by pressure from a spring loaded follower. The carrier in its extended bottom position receives released shell. Meanwhile, the right shell latch, which was cammed into magazine way by the right action bar during extraction cycle, intercepts base of second shell.

With loaded shell resting on down thrust carrier, the forward or return movement of fore-end will close action and complete Load and Lock cycles. In detail they are as follows:

LOADING

The *initial* return movement of fore-end will carry slide, breech bolt, and locking block forward. A carrier dog attached to rear of carrier is engaged by returning slide and pivots shell loaded carrier upward, placing shell in path of breech bolt. The advancing bolt depresses ejector spring into its channel in ejector and the shell is picked up and loaded into chamber. The carrier dog, released from pressure of passing slide, is forced upward by the carrier dog follower and its recessed spring, and pivots the carrier from path of loading shell. The oncoming second shell from magazine, being retained by right shell latch, is released by camming action of returning right action bar. This shell is then intercepted and held by left shell latch until next feeding cycle.

LOCKING

As shell is loaded fully into chamber, action closes and the breech bolt is 'home' against shell. Travel of slide within bolt continues and cams locking block into recoil shoulder of barrel extension. The locking block secures breech bolt firmly against chambered shell and in turn is supported fully in barrel by slide as its forward travel is completed. With locking block fully seated in recoil shoulder of barrel, the passage-way through locking block then allows for proper protrusion of firing pin through bolt face to fire gun. The fore-end return motion is completed as slide comes to rest within and against front section of breech bolt. This fully locked action enables action bar lock to clear end of left action bar. The suspended spring actuated connector will then be released and dropped to a ready position before sear and pivot action bar lock to a similar position with end of action bar.

The modern slide-action shotgun must not only perform all of these functions, but also do the neat trick of locking up so securely that it can stand the 5,000 pound thrust of a magnum shotshell, and then glide open easily as the hunter reloads for a fast second shot.

The Remington Model 870 has proven to be one of the most successful slide-action shotgun designs. It remains in high volume production two decades after its introduction.

WINCHESTER MODEL 1200

The rugged and reliable Model 12 shotgun had served millions of American sportsmen during the first half of the twentieth century. While this was a superb, long-lasting shotgun, it was extremely expensive to manufacture and American sportsmen were unwilling to pay $20.00 to $30.00 above competitive shotguns for it.

By 1957, it was clear that a radically new slide-action shotgun would be required if Winchester was to recapture an adequate share of the market. Design layouts for the Model 1200 slide-action were started in early 1957, at the same time as the semi-automatic Model 1400. Basic studies of sub-systems of the firearms, such as the locking system, the trigger mechanism and the receiver construction, were performed, carried out by design teams who developed recommendatioins of the optimum design approach to be used in each area of the gun. These recommendations were coordinated with the basic specifications established by Arms Research and Development and Marketing departments. Large-scale layouts of both the slide-action and semi-automatic gun mechanisms were prepared and great attention was paid to the design configurations that would be compatible with both requirements. Since the semi-automatic mechanism operates with high forces and in short time intervals, the forces and stresses are much higher than in a slide-action shotgun. The final results of these design studies was to make the action of the two guns almost identical, and to use a different forearm assembly for the slide-action shotgun. This meant that many components within the Model 1200 were stronger than they had to be for a slide-action shotgun, but the design team felt that these decisions would result in a smooth-working, long-lived shotgun.

Designers and research engineers get pretty attached to their particular design concepts and many long meetings were held to hammer out the combination of features that would best meet the program's objectives. It was exciting to be part of this team, for we were all aware of the vital importance of new design programs to Winchester's future. The cost of manufacturing the fine traditional old models was so high that the gun division was losing several million dollars a year, and serious consideration was being given to completely dropping gun manufacture. Most of the designers were gun enthusiasts and none of us wanted to see this happen.

When the design approach was finally frozen in large-scale layouts the team made detailed drawings of each component in the gun mechanism. During this phase, seven or eight designers were working on detail drawings specifying the exact shape, dimensions, tolerances, materials, heat treatment and surface finish for every component in the mechanism. The result was a stack of about 120 drawings. When sufficient time was available the drawings were sent out for competitive bids. Toolmaking shops near New Haven quoted for the fabrication of one or two sets of the experimental components. Often time was so tight that the components were fabricated in the Winchester Arms Research Model Shop. It was not unusual for a single model of the shotgun to cost $8,000, when all of the components were fabricated to accurate dimensions by skilled toolmakers or jig borers, milling machines, lathes and grinders.

During this design phase, research engineers worked with manufacturers all over the United States to develop production techniques for economical manufacture. The process men worked with the designers, pointing out ways in which designs could be modified for improved manufacturing techniques. Fabrication of an experimental model normally took about two months. The senior designer visited the vendors and when fabrication was complete he assembled the components into a complete mechanism with all the parts still soft. Inevitably some dimensions would be slightly in error, due to drawing mistakes or small errors in fabrication. Wherever possible the parts were modified to bring them into tolerance, but occasionally entirely new parts had to be made. Components were then given heat treatment and surface finish and reassembled into the finished mechanism.

Preliminary firing tests were performed by the senior designers with assistance from the Arms Test Section personnel. At first the gun was clamped into a mechanical test fixture and loaded with standard ammunition for a preliminary function test. The next step was to fire with a proof load to test the strength of the action, and then the experimental shotgun was disassembled to inspect the components. With the early models the designers always found things that they wanted to change and improve. New components were designed, fabricated, heat treated and assembled into the mechanism until the gun performed to the designer's satisfaction. It was then turned over to the Arms Test Section which gave it a carefully programmed 1,000-, 5,000- or 10,000-shot endurance test. The Arms Test Section was organized as an independent test group, since experience showed that we gun designers tend to give our "brainchild" more tender loving care than shotguns receive in the field. The use of an independent test group more closely simulates the rugged handling that guns receive under field conditions.

Endurance tests inevitably point out weak parts in the design. After the tests were completed and analyzed, there were suggestions for detail changes to improve functioning and performance and the whole cycle was repeated again and again until the mechanism had been so refined that it could stand long endurance tests without breakage.

By the early 1960s the design shown in Figure 6-16 had been established. The rotary bolt had four lugs which locked securely into the barrel extension. The barrel extension was permanently screwed to the barrel and rested against the front face of the receiver. This construction permitted careful balancing of materials. For example, the bolt and barrel extension were made of high-alloy steel, heat treated to very hard surfaces and high tensile strength. The barrel was made of a softer steel alloy to minimize the chance of its shattering if the bore was plugged with mud, or if a 20-gauge shell was accidentally dropped in the chamber ahead of a 12-gauge shell. The receiver was made of an aircraft-grade high-tensile aluminum alloy to minimize weight. The slide arms were fabricated from alloy-steel strip which could be formed in large presses nearly to the finished shape. After heat treatment to make the

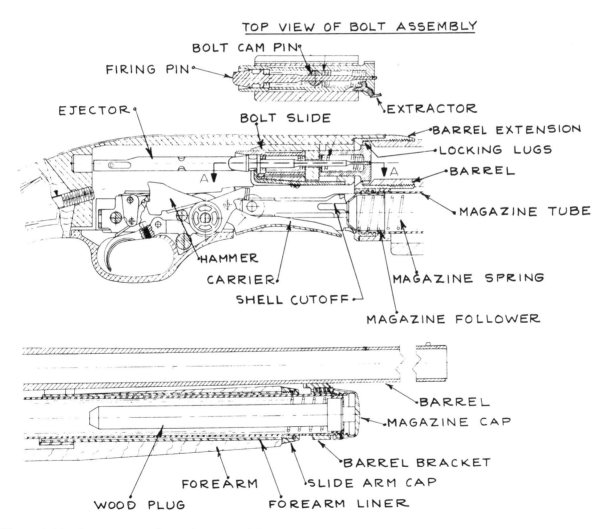

Figure 6-16 Cross section of Winchester Model 1200 action.

Figure 6-17   Winchester Model 1200 slide-action shotgun.

parts tough, the critical surfaces were ground to the finished dimensions. Tubular parts, such as the magazine and forearm liner, were made of alloy-steel seamless tubing, and machined in large automatic six-spindle lathes to finished dimensions.

The bolt and trigger mechanisms shared many components with the Model 1400 shotguns. The major differences between the two were in the receiver and magazine assembly. Market surveys had established that hunters preferred a long "beaver-tailed" forearm which was comfortable under field conditions. This was designed and assembled to a thin steel liner, which provided a smooth-sliding surface over the magazine tube and a good connection to the action slide arms.

Take down was simply by removing the cap on the end of the magazine tube and sliding the barrel assembly forward, out of the action. The magazine capacity was four rounds and an additional round could be loaded in the chamber.

The Model 1200 shotgun was announced in January 1964 with deliveries to customers starting in the summer of 1964. Production built up rapidly and soon the volume of Model 1200 shotguns manufactured each year was more than ten times the annual production of Model 12s during the 1950s. The outside appearance of the Model 1200 shotgun is shown in Figure 6-17. This illustration shows the basic field-grade gun, but a tremendous number of variations were available as shown in the table below:

Winchester Model 1200 Shotgun

Gauges Available	12, 16 and 20
Barrels Available	22″ Deer Model 26″, 28″, 30″, for Shotshells Plain and Ventilated Rib
Chokes Available	Skeet, Modified, Improved Modified, Full. (Also Winchoke with Interchangeable Tubes)
Stocks	Field, Skeet, Trap, Monte-Carlo
Weights	Deer Gun — 6½ Pounds Field — 6¾ Pounds Trap — 8½ Pounds Skeet — 7¼ Pounds

From a customer's standpoint these variations are most worthwhile, but for the production and marketing departments they are a big problem. It is difficult to balance production so that the correct number of each style is available to meet the market needs. This is one of the areas where computers have proven to be very valuable. Field sales information flows to the marketing department and is run through a computer which calculates the proper number of each style of shotgun to be manufactured in the months ahead. This was a particularly acute problem on the Model 1200 shotgun, for it was the largest selling shotgun in the Winchester line all during the 1960s, and it continues to sell in high volume in the 1970s.

Chapter 7

AUTOMATIC SHOTGUNS

The late nineteenth century was a period when American and European inventors became deeply involved with automatic weapons. When an American, Hiram Maxim, invented a fully automatic, self-powered machine gun in 1885, his success started an enormous competition to re-equip the world's armies with automatic machine guns and rifles, a conversion which was only completed in the 1950s. During the 1890s inventors began designing automatic sporting weapons, although there was little demand for them. In America most shotgunners were equipped with double-barreled designs, and the changeover to repeaters was just beginning. There were also some important shifts in the American firearms industry reflecting the financial strength of companies with strong products in the repeating-rifle field.

By the 1890s, the Winchester Repeating Arms Company was in an extremely strong position. In February 1888, Winchester had purchased the Whitney Arms Company, which had been manufacturing a competitive line of repeating centerfire rifles. The Whitney Armory was located about two miles away from the Winchester plant, below a dam on Lake Whitney in New Haven, Connecticut. Whitney had manufactured revolvers for Colt as far back as 1847, and had been continuously active in repeating-firearms manufacture since that date, using profits from the Civil War to build a better dam and water supply for the City of New Haven—still an important part of the New Haven water supply.

Winchester operated the Whitney Armory to manufacture Winchester products until 1903, when the land and buildings were sold to the New Haven Water Company and Winchester moved the machinery and tools into its main plant. Winchester withdrew the Whitney firearms from the market shortly after purchasing the plant.

In the late 1880s the Remington Arms Company of Ilion, New York, had gone bankrupt and in March 1888, Remington was purchased jointly by Hartley and Graham (a large sporting-goods distributor in New York City) and Winchester for $200,000. The plant was operated jointly by the two companies with Marcellus Hartley as the president and Thomas G. Bennett, president of Winchester, as vice president.

By the 1880s Winchester had a working agreement with John Browning to purchase all the rifles and shotguns he designed. Browning developed new models each year, and Winchester purchased them whether they were placed into production or not. Examination of the inventor's models in the Winchester Gun Museum shows many interesting designs which were never produced for manufacturing or marketing reasons. Although Browning sold his pistol patents under royalty agreements to Colt in Hartford, Connecticut, and to Fabrique Nationale in Herstal, Belgium, all sales to Winchester were purchased outright. Usually much of the purchase price was paid in Winchester products which, in turn, Browning marketed through his sporting-goods store in Ogden, Utah.

In the 1890s, Browning became interested in

automatic gun mechanisms. One of his earliest attempts was conversion of a Winchester Model 1873 lever-action into a semi-automatic rifle! This strange conversion was successfully accomplished by placing a perforated cup over the muzzle of the barrel with a small hole for the bullet to pass through, and an annular surface for the gas to impinge against. The gas imparted a forward motion to the cup which was translated through linkages to operate the lever action of the gun!

Browning developed a gas-operated light machine gun somewhat on this principle which was introduced in limited United States service use in the 1890s. This was the machine gun known as the "Potato Digger," since the linkages swung down below the action during the operating cycle, as if someone were digging up the ground. Browning also became interested in semi-automatic pistols, designing a line of blowback and short-recoil automatics which were manufactured by both Colt and Fabrique National. This effort culminated in the U.S. pistol caliber .45, Model 1911, still the United States standard military hand gun.

In the late 1890s, Browning turned his attention to automatic-shotgun designs. ("Automatic" is actually not the correct term, but since even manufacturers often use it rather than "auto-loading," I will use it here interchangeably.) This was about the most difficult firearms design in the world. Shotshells were relatively weak compared to centerfire cartridges, and were loaded with black powder which rapidly fouled the action. They were available in a wide range of power level in any single gauge. Browning's solution was to use a "long recoil" action, which is shown schematically in Figure 7-1. In the upper illustration the gun is ready to fire. The bolt is locked securely to the barrel extension and barrel, through a vertically sliding lock. The barrel has a barrel ring which encircles the magazine tube and drives a friction brake rearwards against the return spring. When the gun was fired, the gas pressure inside the case accelerated the shot and wads forward at about 1,100 feet per second and sent the entire barrel, barrel extension and bolt assembly to the rear at about 23 feet per second with a light load or 34 feet per second and with a heavy magnum load. The barrel, barrel extension, bolt and fired shell all recoiled together to the extreme rear of the receiver, as shown in the middle illustration. At this point the bolt assembly was latched to the rear by a linkage connected to the carrier mechanism.

After rebounding off the rear of the receiver, the barrel and barrel extension started to move forward. Since the barrel extension was moving forward under the urging of the recoil spring, and the bolt assembly was latched to the rear, *something* had to give. Browning arranged for an ingenious sub-mechanism within the bolt assembly so that as the bolt was moved forward with the bolt carrier latched to its rear, linkages unlocked it from the barrel extension, as shown in the lowest illustration of Figure 7-1. The fired shell, bolt and bolt carrier remained latched to the rear and the barrel and the barrel extension slid forward moving the chamber forward off the fixed shell.

As the barrel got to a fully forward position a fixed stud on the side of the barrel extension struck the left side of the fired shell. Since the shell was held against the bolt face by an extractor on the right side, this blow caused the shell to pivot, spinning out of the ejection port and flying clear of the gun.

The magazine system was important and is not shown in these illustrations. When the barrel extension was fully to the rear, a fresh shell could move rearward from the magazine all the way into the carrier. As it reached a rearward position in the carrier, it automatically unlatched the bolt assembly. The bolt assembly was driven forward by a second spring, located in the butt stock of the shotgun. As it moved forward it raised the carrier, placing the fresh shell in front of the bolt which then shoved it forward into the chamber and locked the gun in the position shown in the upper illustration.

Browning's design was a significant milestone in American firearms He recognized the enormous sales potential of the gun and worked closely with Winchester in developing the design so that no patent infringement occurred. The original design, developed in 1899, conflicted with a patent of Hugo Borchardt of November 1896. Winchester designers were unable to figure a way around this infringement, but Browning worked out a different series of linkages, which avoided a patent problem. On August 1, 1900 Browning sent an improved model gun with the following letter:

Winchester Repeating Arms Company
New Haven, Connecticut
Gentlemen:
We are in receipt of yours of the 23rd, and the gun which I have put in good order and returned today by express. Have made a few changes which experiments in auto. guns

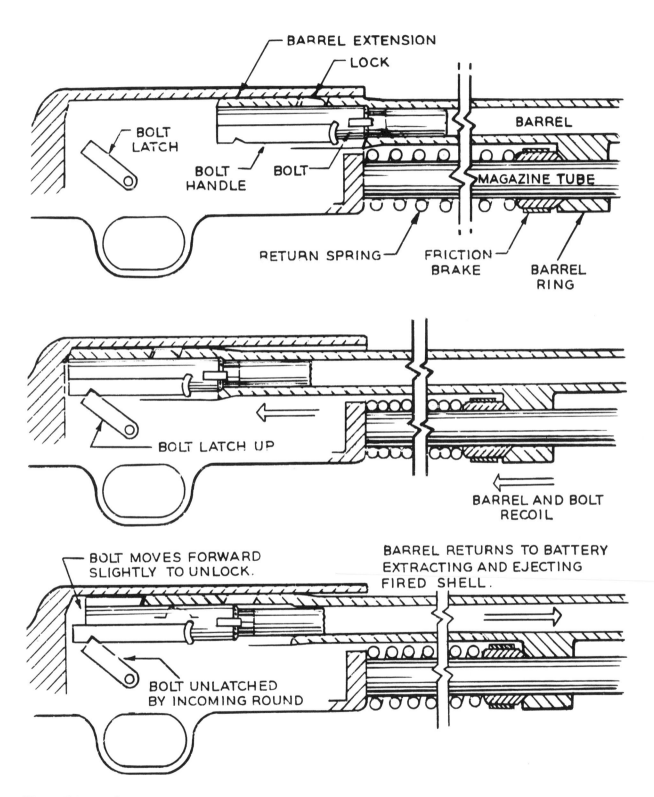

Figure 7-1 Mechanism of a long-recoil shotgun.

132

since that was made, have shown to be for the better. I see the gun has been worked with considerably by parties who did not understand the system. The reason it jarred off was on account of the sear having been bent. You will see I have made an easier and shorter pull than it was before, yet, it will not jar off. We have had no mis-fires and think this fault is with the cartridges . . . . The changes I have made are in the carrier latch, the ejector and ejector lever and the end of the sear. Have also straightened the trigger which was bent. Think the way the trigger and sear got bent was by jerking the trigger plate out, unhooking the trigger from the sear; before pulling the trigger plate out, the link should be drawn back. Our experience has been that a gun gets worse treatment in a draughtsman's office than in a duck hunter's camp. Another thing, the gun requires no oil at all and if you should oil it, it is not necessary to fill it full. Did you ever put oil on the end of a Winchester breech block and snap it; if not, just try it. We have fired a lot of cartridges in the shop and in the field at ducks and have had no failures whatever and we hope you will have better luck with it. We have always considered the standard load for the gun is 31 grains of DuPont, one ounce of shot, $2\frac{9}{16}$ inch shell, which is what we generally use, but the gun will work all right with 31 grains, $\frac{7}{8}$ oz., 34 grains, $\frac{7}{8}$ or 1 oz., $3\frac{1}{2}$ or $2\frac{3}{4}$ drs. black powder, $\frac{7}{8}$ or 1 oz. shot. The gun will operate with smaller loads than above if held reasonably firm against the shoulder, but 31 grs. DuPont smokeless, 1 oz. in repeater or leader shells is a good load in our regular 16-gauge cartridge . . . .

The various mechanical problems with the gun were carefully designed out between 1899 and the end of 1901 so that the gun was ready to put into production early in 1902.

Winchester recognized the enormous importance of this model and put Thomas C. Johnson, the head of their design department, in charge of the technical end of the patent application. He worked with the New Haven law firm of Seymour and Earl and three patent applications were made and granted. The design of the gun in early 1900 is shown in Figure 7-2. The patent is complex, with four pages of illustrations and nine pages of description. It was an extraordinarily strong patent. Normally an inventor claims everything that might wildly be considered patentable under his invention in a series of specific statements. The patent examiner usually knocks out all but a few

claims, particularly in a field as well patented as firearms technology. In modern practice six to ten claims would be excellent. Browning had done so much pioneering work and the patent was so carefully drawn that 36 claims were considered novel and were allowed. Browning's basic statement was:

My invention relates to an improvement in automatic portable firearms of the class in which the recoil following the explosion of a cartridge in the gun-barrel is utilized to operate the breech mechanism of the gun, the object of my present invention being to produce an improved arm of this class in which the recoiling parts are housed for their protection, as well as the protection of the user of the arm and in which the parts are constructed with particular reference to simplicity of construction, strength, durability, and reliability of operation.

The upper illustration in the patent showed basic layouts of the gun. The barrel spring surrounding the magazine tube was used to return the barrel assembly forward. The second return spring in the butt stock is connected to the bolt mechanism. Swinging lever K in the butt stock of the shotgun was used to manually recock the mechanism. When this lever was drawn to the rear it pulled on the bolt return spring and drew the linkage H shown in the lower illustration to the rear. The linkage H rotated the cam G, which pulled down the vertical lock F thus unlocking the bolt from the barrel extension as shown in small view "Fig. 5" in between the two main views on the patent.

Once the bolt was unlocked from the barrel extension, further motion of the pivoted lever drew the bolt assembly to the rear, where it was latched up by the carrier mechanism. The swinging lever which did the actual latching is not shown in the illustration. When the shooter dropped a fresh shell in the action and pressed the release button, the action would slam shut, chambering the shell. After this an additional four shells could be loaded into the magazine tube, giving a total capacity of 5.

During the operating cycle the bolt and barrel extension remained locked together until both parts had struck the rear of the receiver. The carrier latch then locked up bar H. As the spring surrounding the magazine tube pushed the barrel forward, the cam G was rotated around pivot G pulling the locking block F downward and disengaging the bolt from the barrel extension.

No. 659,507.

Patented Oct. 9, 1900.

J. M. BROWNING.
RECOIL OPERATED FIREARM
(Application filed Feb. 8, 1900.)

(No Model.)

5 Sheets—Sheet 2.

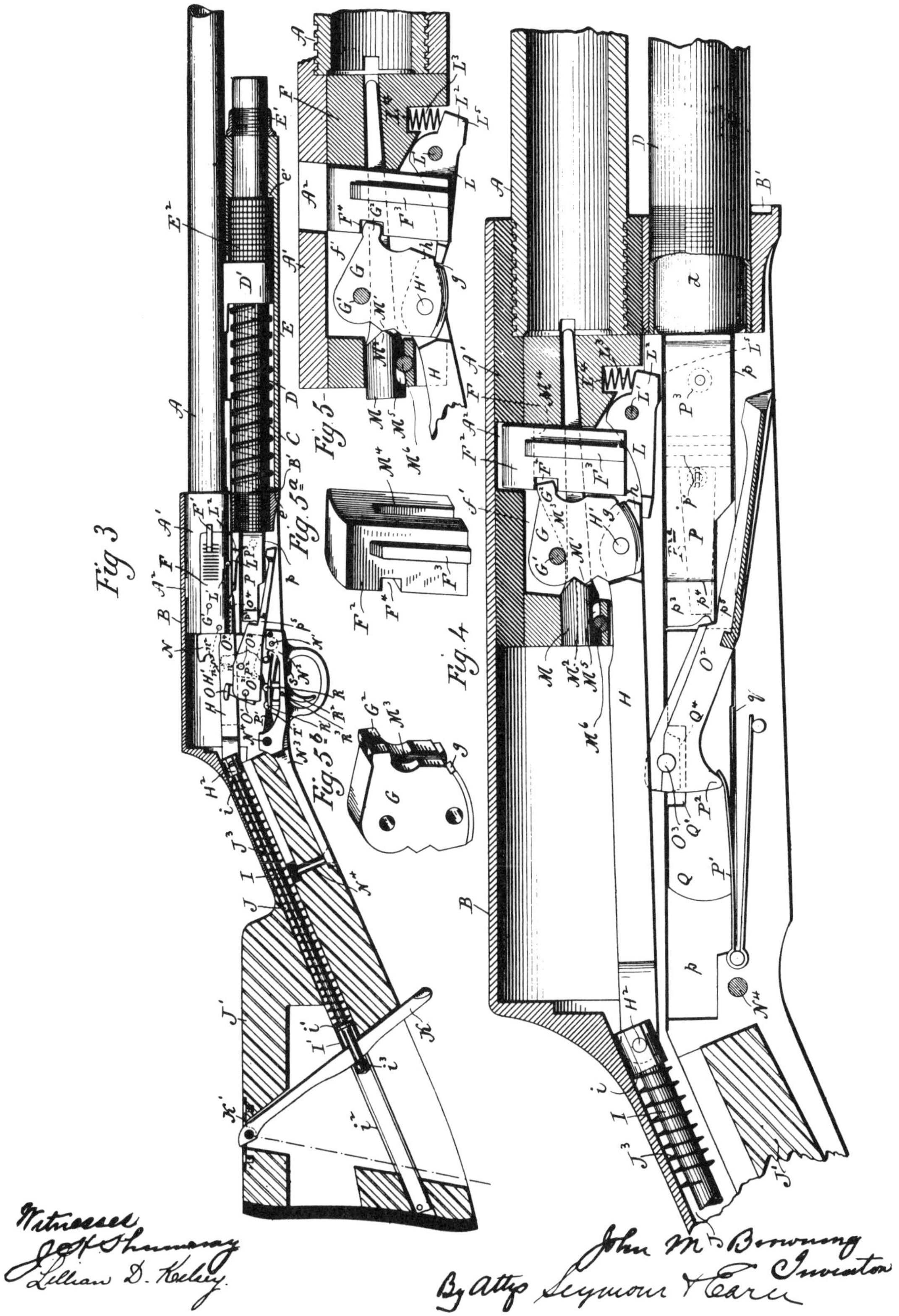

Figure 7-2   The Browning recoil-operated action of 1900.

Some of the claims were extremely broad. For example, Claim No. 1 was, "In a magazine-fire-arm, the combination with a recoiling barrel and barrel extension, of a breech-bolt, a vertically-movable locking-block mounted in said bolt, and adopted to be entered into a locking opening formed in the barrel extension, and a means mounted in said bolt for operating said block in locking and unlocking the bolt to and from the barrel extension." This would be considered so broad it would block any competitor from using a vertically sliding lock in a long-recoil action.

A second patent application was filed on March 18, 1901 covering modifications to simplify and improve the action. The swinging lever in the butt stock had been eliminated, and a conventional cocking handle had been added to the right side of the mechanism. Many small design refinements were made in the internal construction as shown in Figure 7-3. The construction of the carrier mechanism and the breech-bolt assembly and the vertically sliding lock remained substantially the same. The designs included an interlock, which prevented the firing pin from striking the primer unless the gun was fully locked.

Browning included the variable friction device to compensate for light and heavy loads. The design is shown in the middle illustration in Figure 7-3, listed as "Fig 4, Fig 5 and Fig 6." The split ring surrounded the magazine tube and provided a frictional drag along the surface. In the configuration shown in the illustration, a conical surface in the barrel ring mated with conical surface in the friction ring driving it inward, causing a heavy frictional drag on the rearward stroke. The higher the acceleration, the greater the inward force so that this provided a heavy frictional drag on the forward stroke. This type of friction ring has been included on all long recoil shotguns since Browning's invention. On most designs, the ring is designed so that it can be reversed, giving a heavier frictional drag in one position for magnum shotshells and a lighter frictional drag in the other position for field loads. In the late 1890s, Browning had negotiated a number of royalty arrangements with pistol manufacturers, and this brought in a steady income as his designs were manufactured. Browning clearly recognized the importance of the automatic shotgun, so he tried to negotiate a royalty arrangement with Winchester. The Winchester Company had had a firm policy of purchasing all inventions outright and were extremely reluctant to change this

policy, even for Mr. Browning. To refuse meant the loss of John Browning's services for this gun and probably for the future. T. G. Bennett made the decision to refuse Browning's royalty request, a decision that has cost Winchester many millions of dollars in lost profits during the past seventy years. When negotiations broke down, John Browning made an appointment to see Marcellus Hartley, who was then president of the Remington Arms Company, in New York. Winchester had sold out their half interest in Remington under a verbal agreement with Hartley that Remington would not manufacture competitive repeating firearms. While John Browning was waiting for his appointment, word came that Marcellus Hartley had died of a heart attack at a board of directors meeting. Blocked in the United States, Browning took the boat for Belgium and negotiated a royalty agreement with Fabrique Nationale of Herstal, Belgium, who manufactured his pistol designs. F. N. was glad to execute a royalty agreement and placed the gun in production about 1904. The agreement with F. N. covered the marketing of the semi-automatic shotguns under the Browning name in the United States and under the Fabrique Nationale name in Europe.

Remington Auto-Loading Shotguns

When Remington went bankrupt in the late 1880s, the company had been purchased by Marcellus Hartley, and the Winchester Repeating Arms Company. Hartley was a partner of Schuyler, Hartley, and Graham of New York City and one of the founders of the Union Metallic Cartridge Company of Bridgeport, Connecticut. A dynamic businessman, he became president of Remington and under his guidance the Company regained its financial strength. He eventually purchased Winchester's interest in the Company. When he died in 1902, he was succeeded by his grandson, Marcellus Hartley Dodge who, as soon as the business situation had settled down, executed agreements with the Browning brothers to manufacture their new auto-loading shotgun on a royalty basis. There had been no written agreement between Remington and Winchester to prevent this action, and John and Matthew Browning went to work at the Remington plant in Ilion, helping to set up machinery for the manufacture of the new guns. The Browning brothers got into violent arguments which amazed the Remington workmen. Apparently this was just

No. 689,283.

J. M. BROWNING.
AUTOMATIC FIREARM.
(Application filed Mar. 18, 1901.)

Patented Dec. 17, 1901.

(No Model.)

5 Sheets—Sheet 2.

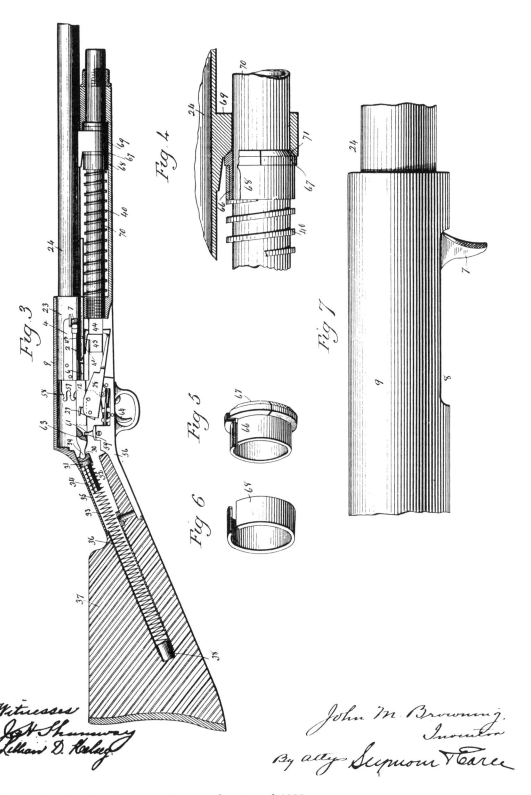

Fig 3

Fig 4

Fig 5

Fig 6

Fig 7

Witnesses

John M. Browning,
Inventor
By atty Seymour & Earle

Figure 7-3 The Browning recoil-operated action of 1901.

their way of relieving tension, so when the work day was over the Brownings would pull out their banjos and entertain everyone with popular songs of the day.

By 1905 the production problems had been overcome and the Remington Model 11 auto-loading shotgun was introduced. The appearance of a relatively late Model 11 shotgun with a ventilated rib is shown in Figure 7-4. The design was similar to that shown in the Browning patent, but included minor manufacturing modifications developed to ease production and improve functioning on a mass-produced basis. Note that the ventilated rib starts about 3 inches forward of the receiver; this distance is necessary, for the barrel slides this distance into the receiver during the long recoil stroke. The late-model shotguns were fitted with hand checkering on the pistol grip and forearm and an engraved pheasant on the side of the receiver.

The internal construction of the Remington Model 11 is shown in Figure 7-5. In this illustration the barrel and bolt have recoiled all the way to the rear, the bolt has been latched up and the barrel has returned to a forward position. A fresh shell has moved out of the magazine onto the carrier and in the position shown has just tripped

the bolt release. Immediately after this the force of the bolt-return spring will lift the carrier, placing the shell in front of the bolt face, and the bolt will ram it into the chamber and lock up. One significant change can be seen in the locking arrangement; the vertically sliding lock with rotating cam has been replaced by a rotating lock. The pivot may be seen in the upper-rear surface of the bolt. The locking surface is the triangular element above the firing-pin spring. The center line of the lock is cut away to make room for the firing pin, but it extends downward and is pinned to the link, which connects with the bolt-return spring in the butt stock.

The 12-gauge model auto-loading shotgun was introduced in 1905 and remained in production until 1948. A 20-gauge model was added in 1930, and a 16-gauge model in 1931. A total of 913,000 Remington Model 11 shotguns were produced in all 3 gauges. The 12-gauge models were offered with barrel lengths of 26 to 32 inches, in plain barrel styles or with ventilated ribs. The butt stock and forearm were made of American walnut and checkered with 20-pitch checkering. The length of pull was 14 inches and the drop from line of sight to comb was 1⅝ inches. The 12-gauge model weighed approximately 8 pounds

Figure 7-4   Remington Model 11 semi-automatic shotgun.

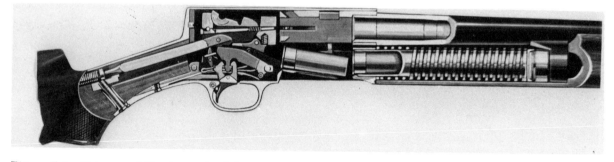

Figure 7-5   Cutaway of Remington Model 11 action, barrel forward.

and had an overall length of 49¼ inches with a 30-inch barrel. The 16-gauge model weighed 7 pounds, and the 20-gauge standard shotgun 6¾ pounds. The magazine capacity was four shots with one in the chamber, giving a five-shot capacity. The barrel marking was "Remington Arms Co. Inc., Ilion, N.Y., Made in USA, Browning US PATS. 689, 283-710,094-730,870-812,326." The guns were chambered for 2¾ inch or shorter shells.

By 1940 the commercial shotguns were offered with long-range choke, full, modified skeet, cylinder or cylinder improved, polychoke and Cutts compensators. In addition to the standard models, a special riot model with a 20-inch plain barrel was available in 12, 16 or 20 gauge. A police special was made in 12 gauge only, with an 18½-inch barrel. Special or quality models were made such as the "Model D Tournament-High Grade" with hand-engraved, simple scroll designs on the panel on top of receivers. The "Model 11-E Expert High-Grade" was offered with additional hand polishing and engraving. The top of the line was the "Model 11-F Premier High-Grade," specially figured American walnut with a gold nameplate and initials optional. In addition two-piece game-scene panels were engraved on each side of the receiver and scroll designs were extended out into the barrel and trigger plate.

The Model 11 established Remington as a leader in automatic shotguns in the United States with total sales of 913,000 prior to their redesign in 1948. It was a successful and profitable shotgun. The association with Browning proved valuable and Remington continued to introduce new Browning designs in the early 1900s. The auto-loading shotgun was followed by the Model 8 auto-loading centerfire rifle, which operated on the same long-recoil principle. Construction details of the rifle were different however, since it utilized a box magazine and the barrel was contained within a stationary barrel jacket.

BROWNING AUTO-LOADING SHOTGUNS

The Browning Arms Company has marketed auto-loading shotguns made to John Browning's patent in the United States continuously since their introduction about 1904. The standard Browning automatic shotgun manufactured in the early 1960s is shown in Figure 7-6. Mechanical construction details were similar to the Remington shotgun, but there were differences in styling, particularly in the pistol-grip area, reflecting European design practice. The Browning shotguns tend to have more hand engraving on the receiver and different checkering patterns on the stock. The forearm on the Browning design of the 1960s was somewhat slimmer than that shown in Figure 7-4. This was accomplished by making the wood very thin and reinforcing it with an inside metal liner. Later Remington shotguns utilized a slimmer forearm profile by the same technique.

In the period since World War II, Fabrique Nationale has manufactured special lightweight models utilizing steel-and-aluminum receivers in addition to the standard-weight models as shown in Figure 7-6. The Browning shotguns have remained popular and are noted for their rugged reliability and long endurance life.

WINCHESTER MODEL 1911

The breakdown of negotiations with Browning posed a serious problem to the Winchester management. The design staff, headed by Thomas Crossly Johnson, was instructed to design an auto-loading shotgun that would circumvent the Browning patent. This proved a formidable task, requiring almost 10 years before the new model

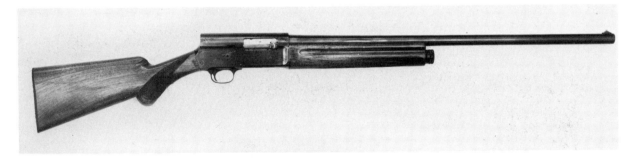

Figure 7-6 Browning automatic shotgun of the 1960s.

was introduced in 1911. Its patent specifications had been drawn with great care and the many claims covered broad features as well as specific concepts, which were important to the successful design of the long-recoil auto-loading shotgun.

The Model 1911 was the first Winchester firearm in which the hammer was concealed inside the mechanism. It is shown in Figure 7-7. The design reflected ingenuity, but it had two major problems. One was that no way had been found to circumvent Browning's patent of the cocking handle on the bolt, so the only way to operate the action manually was by pulling back on a knurled section of the barrel, thus compressing both the barrel spring surrounding the magazine tube and the bolt spring in the butt stock. This meant that the loading operations were much more cumbersome than on the Browning design. Another problem was that the "M-11 Winchester self loading shotgun" was an expensive gun to manufacture, and was the highest-priced firearm in the Winchester line at $38.00. It was introduced with 26- and 28-inch barrels, full and modified choke and cylinder bore. Standard and matted barrels were offered. Neither solid nor ventilated ribs were provided.

Four styles of shotguns were manufactured, known as plain, fancy, trap and pidgeon. The trap and pidgeon models were introduced in 1913. An interesting design feature was the use of laminated-birch butt stocks. The forearm was also made of birch with an insert of rock elm. Standard shotguns weighed about seven and one half pounds with a 26-inch barrel. The guns were announced to the trade in early 1911 but factory records indicate that the first ones went into warehouse inventory only in October of that year. The shotgun remained in production until 1925, a total of 82,774 being manufactured. Because of the strength of the Browning patent, the Model 11 Winchester was never fully competitive. The total sales of 82,000 represented substantial business in the early 1900s, but this was far overshadowed by the number of Remington and Browning shotguns sold under the Browning patents.

WINCHESTER MODEL 40

In the late 1930s, Winchester started the design of an all-new auto-loading shotgun based on the long-recoil principle. Great attention was paid to style, with the result being a smooth profile completely eliminating the abrupt squareback of traditional long-recoil designs. The Winchester Model 40 is shown in Figure 7-8. The Browning patents had all expired by this time and designers were free to incorporate his cocking handle in the bolt. Design studies took most of the late 1930s

Figure 7-7   Winchester Model 1911 auto-loading shotgun.

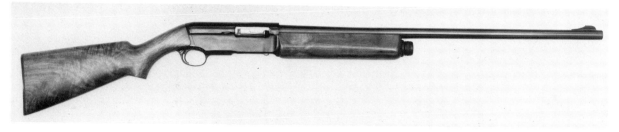

Figure 7-8   Winchester Model 40 auto-loading shotgun.

with production start-up in 1939. The Model 40 was announced in the January 1940 price list and first deliveries to the Winchester warehouse were made that same month.

The Model 40 was offered in 12 guage in standard and skeet models. Standard guns were offered in 28- and 30-inch barrel lengths with plain or matted ribs and any Winchester choke. The skeet model was offered with a Cutts compensator, the overall length with a skeet tube attached being 24 inches. The magazine capacity was four shells plus one in the chamber, an overall capacity of five.

The stocks on the standard model were made of American walnut and were available with either straight or pistol grip, uncheckered. Skeet models were available in straight or pistol-grip configuration but were checkered. The forearms were semi-beavertail American walnut with a rock-elm insert for strengthening and were plain on the standard model and checkered on the skeet model. The standard shotgun and the skeet model weighed about 8 pounds.

When I first joined Winchester in 1953 thousands of museum guns were stored in open wooden racks on the second floor of the Research building. The storage area was actually the stage of a theater which had been built during World War II as part of the employee-morale program. Many fascinating firearms were on these dusty racks and some of us young designers were particularly intrigued by the row after row of Model 40 shotguns. Discussions with the oldtimers turned up that the Model 40 shotgun had a weakness in the bolt-spring housing, which extended from the receiver into the butt stock. When the shotguns got out in the field some were found to be rugged, reliable and virtually indestructible. Others had mechanical failures at the juncture between tube and receiver. Styling considerations made it difficult to overcome this fault, and the model was withdrawn from the market in 1941 after some 12,000 had been produced.

The Model 40 was an expensive gun to manufacture. It was designed with a philosophy of forged parts, which were then milled all over to finished dimensions. Close fits and excellent finishes were characteristic of the design which led to expensive manufacture and relatively high prices. There is no firearm more difficult to manufacture than an automatic shotgun. The design must handle the large, bulky, square-ended shells which are difficult to handle in a magazine and even more difficult to feed. The overall size of the mechanism must be kept to a minimum and the weight held down to no more than 8 pounds. These constraints add up to a designer's nightmare, and when you add the additional restriction that the shotgun must handle *all* commercially available American shotshells from the light trap-loads to magnum loads, the design and engineering problems become enormous. The Model 40 was pushed into production against a fairly tight deadline and as the War came along, Winchester management had to choose between a large investment of engineering talent to refine and perfect the mechanism for large-scale manufacture and the urgent need for this same staff to develop military firearms. During this period, Winchester was the first commercial manufacturer to go into production on the M-1 Garand rifle, and the design staff was also deeply involved in a Winchester semi-automatic military rifle chambered for the .30-06 cartridge for the Marines and on the Winchester M-1 carbine, which was accepted by the Government for production in 1941. In the face of these demands, Winchester management decided to withdraw the Model 40 from the market and shift the design teams to the solution of the urgent military problems.

SAVAGE AUTOMATIC SHOTGUNS

The Savage Arms Company introduced their first automatic shotgun, the Model 720, in 1930. It was based on the Browning long-recoil design and was similar in appearance to the Remington Model 11 shown in Figure 7-4. Savage continued to manufacture this shotgun through the 1930s and the early post-war years. By 1949 they had introduced the new streamlined shotgun shown in Figure 7-9. This was eventually produced in two versions, the Model 755 standard weight with a steel receiver, and the Model 775 light weight with an aluminum-alloy receiver. The standard-weight shotgun was manufactured in 12 and 16 gauge. The 12-gauge models were available with 28-inch modified and full-choked barrel and 30-inch full-choke barrel. Average weight was about 8¼ pounds. The 16-gauge models were slightly lighter at 8 pounds and were fitted with 28-inch modified or full-choke barrels.

The Savage Model 775 lightweight automatic shotgun was virtually identical in appearance to the heavier standard-weight model. It was introduced later in the design cycle and remained in

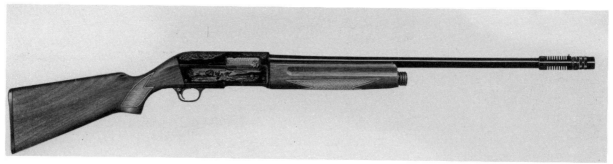

Figure 7-9 Savage Model 775-SC auto-loading shotgun.

production until 1961. Receivers on both shotguns were engraved with hunting scenes. For a long time Savage used a chemical etching process, by which process the main subjects on the panel are kept as highly polished surfaces while the background is etched into a dull matte finish, thus giving a contrast of both color and texture in the side panels of the receiver. The top of the receiver was etched with a pattern of branches and leaves. The shotguns were fitted with walnut butt stocks and forearms and were checkered with small patterns.

Savage shotguns were available with plain barrels and different muzzle devices, such as Poly-Choke, ventilated sleeve Poly-Choke, or Cutts Compensator. The shotgun in Figure 7-9 is fitted with a most unusual muzzle device that combines a Cutts Compensator with a variable-choke device fitted forward of the compensator. Normally the Cutts Compensator was fitted with short-choke tubes that were unscrewed and replaced with a different short tube to change the style of choke. The idea of combining a Cutts Compensator with a variable-choke device would provide significant recoil reduction, as well as an easy change of choke.

These Savage semi-automatic shotguns were carefully designed and manufactured and usually sold at slightly lower prices than the Remington and Browning long-recoil shotguns. Rising manufacturing costs and declining sales however forced their discontinuation.

REMINGTON MODEL 11-48

During the 1940s the Remington design staff in Ilion, New York, started on a complete redesign of the Model 11 shotgun with the objective of creating a completely modern, streamlined new design. The secondary objective was to use many common parts between the auto-loading and the new Model 870 slide-action shotgun. The redesigned shotgun is shown in Figure 7-10 and a

cross-section drawing of the action in Figure 7-11. A comparison of this cross section with the earlier Model 11 shotgun shown in Figure 7-5 shows an amazing transformation. The key elements to make the redesign successful were the configuration of the receiver, barrel extension and bolt. The smooth profile was achieved by shortening the barrel extension and sloping its upper surface to match a sloping contour on the inside of the receiver. The bolt extended beyond the rear barrel extension and it too was sloped on its upper rear corner. A hole was machined into the rear of the receiver to form a pocket for the firing pin.

Endless hours of layout, redesign, test and modification were required to achieve the balanced design that would provide good parts' life with the smooth streamlined profile that was desired by the Marketing Department. The bolt assembly consisted of three major components: breech bolt, slide and locking block, the latter a rotating member that pivoted within the breech bolt. A hook-shaped projection at its forward surface locked into a mating cut in the barrel extension and withstood the heavy force as the cartridge fired. Relative motion between the breech bolt and the slide moved the locking block to the "locked" and "unlocked" position. The slide was driven forward by twin links which were stamped from heavy sheet metal and straddled the hammer, and extended to the rear and connected to the action spring in the butt stock. The spring was contained in the action-spring tube, which was brazed to the receiver at the rear end and provided a line of strength from the receiver through the butt stock. At the lower end of the butt stock was a threaded connection. Screwing up on the action-spring tube nut solidly clamped the butt stock to the receiver, providing a strong, rigid assembly.

The trigger mechanism had many parts in common with the Remington Model 870 slide-action shotgun. Trigger mechanism components were made of steel and were contained in a die-cast

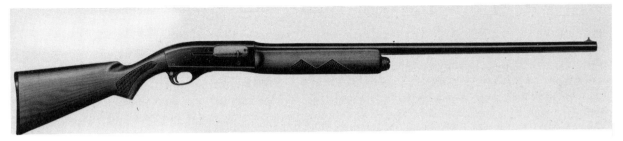

Figure 7-10   Remington Model 11-48 auto-loading shotgun.

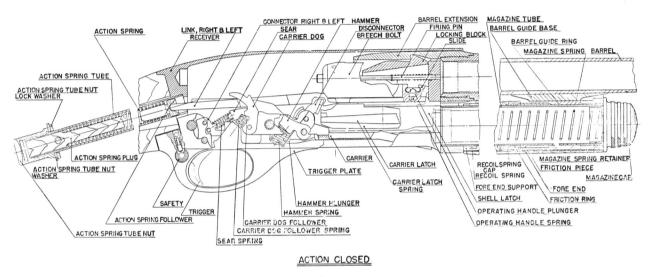

Figure 7-11   Mechanism of Remington Model 11-48 shotgun.

aluminum-alloy housing. A cross-bolt safety was fitted immediately behind the trigger guard, firmly held in either the "safe" or "off" position by a small spring and detent arrangement shown in Figure 7-11. The"carrier dog" was an important element in the design. As the barrel and bolt assembly moved fully to the rear, the carrier dog rotated counterclockwise against the "carrier dog follower spring." A cut in the bottom of the slide engaged the notch in the carrier dog, and as the bolt assembly rebounded from the rear impact against the receiver, the carrier dog latched the bolt assembly solidly to the rear. The barrel meanwhile was free to move forward under the urging of the recoil spring, which was very similar to that shown in Figure 7-5. For compactness the recoil spring was wound up of rectangular rather than round wire, which gives more force and a smaller outside diameter. As the barrel extension reached a fully forward position, a fresh shell slid fully into the carrier, and the rim of the shell drove the "carrier latch" to one side unlocking the carrier mechanism. The action spring in the butt stock continued to try to drive the bolt assembly forward. The only way it could move

was to rotate the carrier dog sharply and as it did this the linkage was arranged to drive the carrier dog pivot downward, rotating the carrier to an upward position. In the up position the shell was placed in front of the bolt face ready to be rammed into the chamber.

The Remington Model 11-48 shotgun was introduced in 12, 16 and 20 gauges in 1949. All three models were similar to Figure 7-10. The 28-gauge model was introduced in 1952 and a 410 bore in 1954. The 28-gauge and 410 models remained in production until 1969. The 12-, 16- and 20-gauge models were discontinued in 1962, when they were replaced by the Remington's first gas-operated shotgun, the Model 58.

Catalogue listings of the Model 11-48 show a five-shot magazine capacity, 12, 16 and 20 gauge, and a four-shot capacity in 28 and 410 bore. The standard-grade models weighed about seven and one-half pounds in 12 gauge, six and three-fourths pounds in 16 gauge and six and one-half pounds in 20 gauge. The 28-gauge and 410-bore models weighed about six and one-fourth pounds with a 25-inch barrel. The smaller models were available with plain and ventilated rib barrels in full, modified and improved cylinder choke, and all with the same barrel length. The larger gauges were available with 26-inch barrels and improved cylinder suitable for skeet, 28-inch barrels with modified and full choke, and the 12-gauge models were available with a 30-inch full-choke barrel.

In addition to the standard 11-48 model, Remington listed a "Sportsman 48" model which differed in three details. The forearm was grooved, a decorative pistol-grip cap was fitted and the overall magazine capacity was cut to three shots. The Sportsman 48 was also offered as a skeet gun with a 26-inch barrel and special skeet boring. The addition of the ventilated-rib barrel added about 4 ounces to the weight of each gun.

The Remington Model 11-48 and Sportsman-48 models became enormously popular and were manufactured in large volume. Their smooth profile and the use of the tried and true Browning long-recoil action appealed to many American sportsmen who used these guns under all kinds of hunting conditions.

INERTIA-OPERATED SHOTGUNS

The early twentieth century was a golden age of automatic-shotgun design. John Browning had proved the practicality of auto-loading shotgun design. Many inventors tried to invent alternate designs or improvements which would lead them to fame and riches. Yet few of the designs were reduced to successful working models and extremely few placed into production and marketed. One of the most unusual was the Sjögren inertia-operated automatic shotgun which received U. S. patent #954,546 on April 12, 1910. The inventor was C. A. T. Sjögren of Stockholm, Sweden. Axel Sjögren was a Swedish engineer with a remarkable imagination who developed an inertia-operated automatic shotgun which retary rifle applications. Shotguns were offered to the public as the "Normal" automatic shotgun and were apparently manufactured by the Swedish Arms and Ammunition Company, Ltd., of Stockholm. The model contained in the Winchester Gun Museum is marked "Kjobnhavn" on the right side of the receiver indicating that the gun had some connection with Copenhagen, Denmark. To further confuse the picture there are English proofmarks on the breech end of the barrel. There is reason to believe that many of the Sjögren shotguns were fabricated in Denmark for the Swedish firm and many of them were

marketed in England by the Normal Powder and Ammunition Company of England. This may account for the British proofmarks.

The method of operation is shown in Figure 7-12. The receiver on the Sjögren shotgun consists of only the lower half and an L-shaped extension on the front, into which the barrel is screwed. The inertia weight rides on top of the receiver like a saddle, extending over the sides and being guided by tracks machined in the upper surface of the receiver. A heavy "accumulator spring" is interposed between the inertia slide block and the bolt. The gun in the ready-to-fire position is shown in the upper illustration with the L-shaped lock hooked into a locking recess in the receiver.

As the gun fires the heavy inertia weight tends to remain fixed in space. The remainder of the gun is accelerated rearward at nearly 1,000 Gs acceleration due to the 6,000-pound thrust of the shotshell at peak pressure. As the gun moves to the rear, the powerful accumulator spring is compressed, as shown in the middle illustration.

The gun moves only a short distance before it begins to decelerate against the shooter's shoulder. At the same time the accumulator spring is rebounding from its compressed position, accelerating the inertia slide block to the rear. This combination of forces catapults the inertia slide to the rear as shown in the lower illustration. This motion unlocks the action, and compresses a bolt-return spring in the butt stock. It also withdraws the fired shell from the chamber and ejects it. A tubular magazine is located below the barrel, and as the slide moves to the rear a fresh shell feeds into the carrier mechanism. As soon as the fresh shell is fully into the carrier, the carrier lock releases allowing the bolt-return spring to lift the carrier and ram the fresh shell into the chamber.

The Sjögren inertia-operated shotgun is an ingenious design. A test-and-analysis program performed in Winchester Group Research in the mid-1960s under the leadership of E. Raleigh Hodil indicated that the forward motion of the slide relative to the frame is very short, no more than .200 inches. The accumulator spring has to be very powerful and because of the construction of the gun, it can have no pre-load. This combination of circumstances demands that the spring have a very high "rate." The relative motion between the inertia block and the receiver provides an excellent time delay before unlocking. Tests

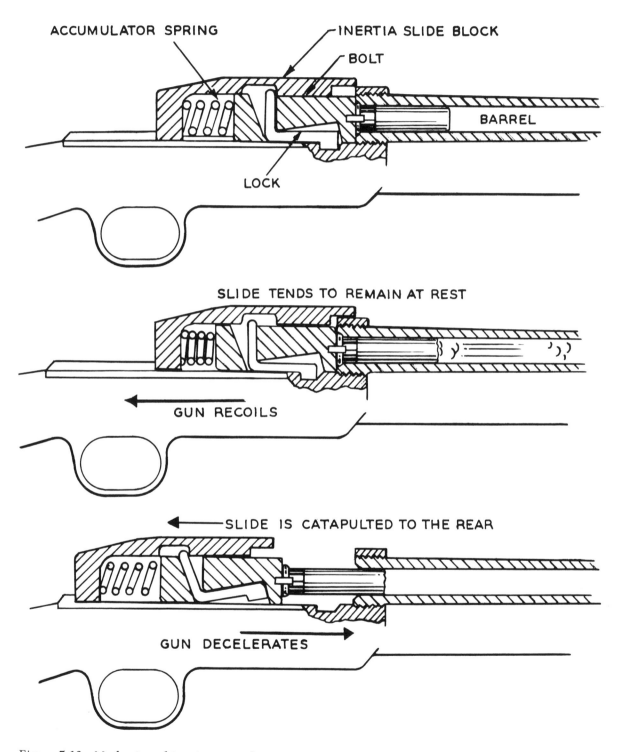

ACCUMULATOR SPRING

INERTIA SLIDE BLOCK

BOLT

BARREL

LOCK

SLIDE TENDS TO REMAIN AT REST

GUN RECOILS

SLIDE IS CATAPULTED TO THE REAR

GUN DECELERATES

Figure 7-12 Mechanism of inertia-operated action.

indicated that the time delay with magnum shot-shells was 4½ milliseconds and the delay with light 12-gauge field loads, such as the Winchester Ranger, was 5½ milliseconds. This delay before unlocking compares to about a 12-millisecond delay in the Browning type of long-recoil action firing magnum loads, or a delay of 4 milliseconds in a typical modern gas-operated shotgun.

While the Sjögren design contained many novel features, there were also serious disadvantages. The distance the gun travels to the rear before reaching its peak velocity is relatively short, about .200 inches, which does not give much distance to develop the operating energy for the action. If the guns were operated under favorable conditions the performance was good. Under adverse conditions the operating energy became marginal and performance suffered. From the shooter's standpoint the Sjögren is a disconcerting gun. The large inertia block is immediately in front of the shooter's face and as the gun is fired rapidly moves to the rear, giving the impression that it is going to fly off and hit you in the face. Although the stopping surfaces inside the receiver are adequate in size, they are not readily visible and you must take it on faith that adequate thought has been given to prevent the weight from flying off.

Sjögren shotguns were available in the United States, marketed by the Normal Powder and Ammunition Company. In England the Sjögren had a difficult time. British shotgunners have been partial to double-barreled, hammerless shotguns in the twentieth century and British dislike of repeating firearms went so far that Burrard does not even mention automatic shotguns in his classic two-volume treatise on shotgun technology, published in the early twentieth century. British shotgunners who showed up with repeating or automatic shotguns at weekend shoots held by wealthy aristocrats were likely never to be in-vited again. In the face of this antipathy the career of the Sjögren in England was short and relatively unsuccessful. Browning designs were more reliable and received wider market acceptance in the United States and on the Continent. A limited number of Sjögren shotguns were marketed in Europe, but not enough to keep the company going.

SHORT-RECOIL AUTOMATIC SHOTGUNS

In the period following World War II, the Browning Arms Company developed an automatic shotgun utilizing the "short-recoil" principle. It was introduced as the Browning "double-automatic" in 1958. The standard model was offered with a steel receiver and the "12F Twelve" and "20 weight" models were offered with aluminum receivers. In 1958 the gun specifications were as follows: The standard-weight shotgun weighed 7¾ pounds and the price, with a ventilated rib, was $147.75. The "12F Twelve" weighed 7 pounds and sold at $159.50 with ventilated rib. The "20 Weight" weighed 6.5 pounds and sold for $167.50 with ventilated rib.

The appearance of the Browning double automatic is shown in Figure 7-13. The shotguns are manufactured by Fabrique Nationale d'Armes de Guerre (FN) in Herstal, Belgium. The receivers have a hand engraved zig-zag border. Slight un-evenness of the upper and lower lines are visible in the illustration, showing it was not done by machine. The center panel of the receiver has an elaborate scroll pattern. Both areas of engraving are filled with a gold paint making a strong contrast with the dark receiver. Both stock and fore-arm are made of close-grained European walnut and are hand checkered with a fine pattern. The ventilated rib starts about two inches forward of the receiver and extends to the muzzle. Take down is accomplished by moving a small catch at

Figure 7-13 Browning double automatic shotgun.

the rear of the forearm and pivoting the forearm downward and releasing the barrel.

A schematic illustration of the Browning short-recoil action is shown in Figure 7-14. The position of the components when the gun is ready to fire is shown in the uppermost illustration. The bolt assembly is locked to the barrel extension. A bar connects the bolt assembly with an inertia

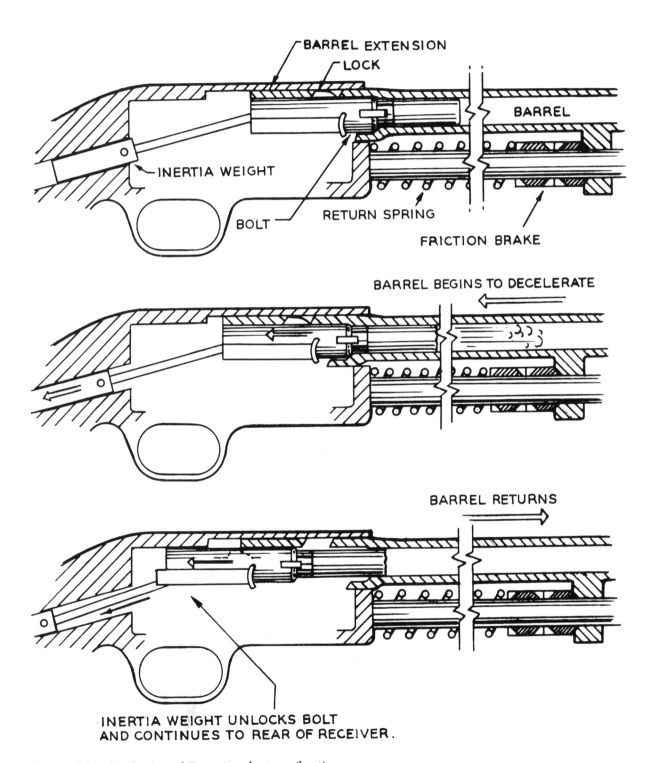

Figure 7-14 Mechanism of Browning short-recoil action.

weight and return spring in the butt stock. The action holds two shells, one in the chamber and a second in a carrier within the receiver space. The tube extends forward from the receiver but it is too small in diameter to hold any shells. The tube is surrounded by a return spring which is wound with a variable distance between coils. A powerful friction brake surrounds the tube and rests against the return spring. A band, rigidly fastened to the barrel, surrounds the return spring tube and rests against the friction rings.

As a shot is fired the parts move into position shown in the middle illustration. The barrel, barrel extension, barrel ring and friction brake all move to the rear, reaching a maximum velocity of 29 feet per second with a magnum load. The friction brake and variable-wound return spring put a heavy frictional drag on the barrel motion, decelerating it to a stop at the end of about two inches of travel.

The rapid acceleration of the barrel assembly to the rear also accelerates the bolt assembly and inertia weight. As the friction assembly slows the barrel down, the inertia weight keeps moving and unlocks the bolt from the barrel extension. The bolt assembly continues to accelerate to the rear, reaching a maximum velocity with a magnum load of over 35 feet per second relative to the gun two milliseconds after the shot is fired. The barrel is decelerated to a stop after 7 milliseconds and then starts returning to a forward position, slowly accelerating to a forward velocity of slightly over 8 feet per second before impacting on its forward stop surface after 40 milliseconds. The bolt assembly has continued to move to the rear at high velocity, striking the rear of the receiver after 11 milliseconds with a velocity of about 22 feet per second. The separation of the bolt and barrel allow the fired shell to be ejected. The bolt rebounds off the back of the receiver with a maximum velocity of about 6 feet per second and moves forward a short distance before being latched up by the carrier mechanism. The only way the bolt can continue to move forward is by lifting the carrier mechanism and placing the fresh shotshell in position to be fed into chamber. The bolt assembly moves forward under the urging of the return spring in the butt stock and reaches a fully forward and locked position at the end of about 140 milliseconds. The maximum velocity of bolt relative to the gun on the forward stroke is about 8 feet per second.

The gun mechanism automatically adjusts for the difference between magnum and light shotshells. For example, the distance the barrel travels before the bolt unlocks is 1½ inches with a magnum load and about 1.1 inches with a light load. The total distance the barrel travels before reversing its direction and moving forward is 2 inches with a magnum load and about 1.35 inches with a light load. The total distance the bolt travels is 3.5 inches.

The weight of the barrel assembly is 2.08 pounds and during the initial phase of the cycle the bolt assembly and inertia weight bring the total recoiling mass up to 3.3 pounds. After separation the 1.22 pound mass of the bolt assembly continues to the rear slamming into the receiver with a velocity of about 33 feet per second with magnum loads and slightly under 18 feet per second with a Ranger shotshell. The difference in performance can be better understood when it is considered that the powder charge in the magnum shotshells is about 34 grains of ball propellant and only 19 grains are in the light load. The light loads have one ounce of shot compared to 1½ ounces with the magnum load.

During the 1960s, Browning adopted aluminum receivers, dropping the standard model and offering only the "12F" which weighed 6¾ pounds with a standard barrel and the "20 weight" which could weigh as little as 6 pounds. The guns were offered in standard, skeet, and trap models.

FLOATING CHAMBER SHOTGUNS

Winchester Model 50

The Winchester Model 50 shotgun was based on patents for a "floating chamber" developed by "Marsh" Williams, the famous inventor of the short-stroke gas systems used in the Winchester M-1 carbine of World War II. The Model 50 design was developed after World War II as an all-new Winchester automatic shotgun.

The design team was headed by "Marsh" Williams with assistance from Winchester designers and toolmakers. Williams was a real character and very secretive about his work, so the major responsibility of one of the Winchester senior designers was to put on paper everything he did. Williams, like John C. Garand and John Browning, preferred to work in metal rather than on paper. He machined components in the milling machines until he felt they looked right and then carefully fitted them into the mechanism. He kept testing and modifying the mechanism until he was satisfied with the performance. One of the problems with this type of design (which was prevalent in the nineteenth century) is that you do not know the dimensions of the components within the mechanism. This sounds like an easy problem to overcome by simply removing the parts, measuring them up and making drawings. The problem is that after an inventor like Williams had finished whittling away on the components with the milling machine, they might function well but be extremely difficult to manufacture. Winchester designers did however manage to translate the successful models into workable firearms that could be manufactured by mass-production techniques but only by much engineering effort.

The Model 50 production line was set up in the early 1950s and the first production guns went to the warehouse in April 1954. The standard shotgun is shown in Figure 7-15. It was offered as a field gun with a standard barrel, field gun with a special ventilated-rib barrel, and skeet gun with ventilated rib. A trap gun with ventilated rib and monte-carlo stock was offered. Very deluxe models known as the "Pigeon grade" were also offered. Standard guns were available with 26-, 28-, and 30-inch barrels.

The Model 50 shotguns were made with a steel receiver machined out of bar stock. The large internal components, such as the floating chamber, the bolt assembly and carrier were machined from solid steel. Smaller internal components such as the hammer, trigger and carrier pull were fabricated by the "investment casting" technique. The American walnut stocks were hand checkered. The magazine tube held two shells, giving a total capacity of three shots. The 12-gauge model weighed approximately 7¾ pounds.

After production was well established a 20-gauge model with a steel receiver was introduced. This was a beautifully compact shotgun with all the components sized down to 20 gauge. It was similar in appearance to the 12 gauge but weighed only 6¾ pounds. Late in the 1950s an aluminum-receiver Model 50 Featherweight shotgun was introduced. An aircraft-grade 70-75 high-tensile aluminum alloy was selected which could be machined on nearly the same tooling as the steel receiver. The 12-gauge Featherweight model weighed slightly under 7 pounds.

The operation of the Model 50 shotgun could best be explained by referring to Figure 7-14. Visualize the barrel extension being attached to a very small short barrel consisting only of the chamber and forcing cone. This "floating chamber" fitted loosely inside the remainder of the barrel, the barrel itself being fixed rigidly to the receiver. As the gun was fired the floating chamber, bolt assembly and inertia weight moved rapidly to the rear for a distance of .08 to .10 inches. At that point the floating chamber struck an abutment in the receiver and stopped. The inertia weight continued to the rear, unlocking the bolt and carrying it to the back of the receiver. The floating chamber was then returned to a forward position by a small internal spring. The rest of the functioning was conventional.

The Model 50 shotgun was so well liked by shooters that 196,402 were manufactured before discontinuation in 1961. It was replaced by a modernized version known as the Model 59. The author used a Model 50 shotgun with ventilated-rib barrel and bleached-blonde stocks for skeet shooting for many years. The gun was fitted with some experimental components, a very long barrel, and a Cutts compensator. Overall weight was about 8½ pounds and this, combined with the very smooth action, made for a very pleasant skeet shooting gun.

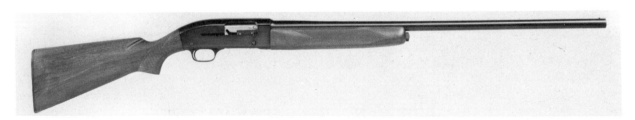

Figure 7-15   Winchester Model 50 shotgun.

Winchester Model 59

The Winchester Model 59 shotgun was based directly on the Model 50 action. The major changes were the use of a roll-engraved aluminum receiver and a *fiberglass* shotgun barrel. The gun is shown in Figure 7-16. A duck-hunting scene was engraved on the right side of the receiver and scrolls were added at the ends. A closeup of the action is shown in Figure 7-17.

The barrel was the development of an extensive research program started in the mid-1950s. A thin steel line was expanded at the rear end and fitted with a machined steel breech. *Five hundred miles* of glass fiber were wound around the thin liner and breech plug and bonded into a unified assembly with a polyester matrix. The outer surface of the barrel was then covered with fiberglas cloth, machined to a smooth outside contour and colored gun blue. Removable choke tubes were developed and made available in 1961. This gave a choice of full, modified or improved cylinder patterns in the same barrel by changing choke tubes. This feature also reduced recoil due to the gas pushing forward on the slots in the choke tube.

The Win-lite fiberglas barrels were extraordinarily strong. The extreme obstruction tests (dropping a 20-gauge shotshell into the chamber and then firing a standard 12-gauge load) would leave these barrels untouched. The same tests would bulge any steel barrel, and usually shattered an aluminum barrel. The Model 59 was discontinued in 1965 due to dropping sales volume.

GAS-OPERATED SHOTGUNS

Winchester Model 1400

At the end of World War II American firearms manufacturers had an enormous job of reconversion to peace-time production. Some had received new tooling and equipment during the war, but many, including Winchester, had been running their commercial machines on a 24-hour-a-day basis through much of the war period. Reconversion was made more complex, for the rapid changes in labor costs during the War years meant that a high percentage of prewar designs were no longer economically practical. Winchester's response was to develop post-War designs reflecting advanced tooling and improved design

Figure 7-16 Winchester Model 59 shotgun.

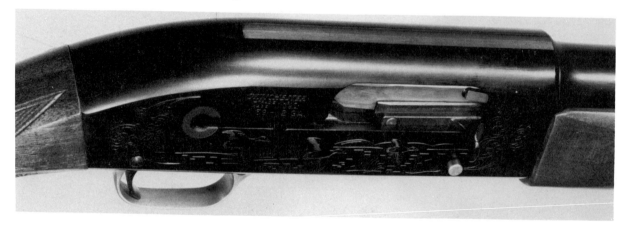

Figure 7-17 Closeup of Winchester Model 59 action.

features which would have greater appeal to the customers and cut manufacturing costs.

The first generation of new designs included the Model 88 lever-action centerfire rifle and the Model 100 semi-automatic centerfire, the Model 77 rimfire semi-automatic in box- and tubular-magazine configuration and a semi-automatic single-shot .22 caliber rifle, the Model 55. In the shotgun field the superb Model 12 shotgun was slightly redesigned into a "feather weight" version and the all new Model 50 semi-automatic shotgun developed.

Increased labor costs and competition from European manufacturers resulted in a second generation of designs in the late 1950s. The Model 94 lever-action centerfire rifle and Model 70 bolt-action rifle were redesigned, keeping the traditional appearance and function but utilizing much more modern manufacturing techniques. A major program was established to design a new line of semi-automatic, slide- and lever-action centerfire rifles, semi-automatic slide-and lever-action rimfire rifles, and slide- and semi-automatic shotguns. The ground rules for these programs were to start with a completely fresh sheet of paper and create designs that would be modern in every respect. The centerfire rifles did not go into production, but the entire line of rimfire rifles became a Winchester mainstay through the 1960s and into the 1970s. The shotgun designs became the Model 1200 slide-action shogtun, and the Model 1400 semi-automatic.

Design layouts for the Model 1200 and Model 1400 were started in early 1957. Basic studies of subsystems of the firearms, such as the bolt-locking system, the gas system, the trigger mechanism and the receiver construction, were performed. Studies of these areas were carried out by design teams who developed recommendations for the optimum design approach to be used in each area of the gun. These design recommendations were coordinated with the basic specifications established by the Marketing Department and Arms Research and Development. Concurrent with the design program was a manufacturing-engineering program to develop the improved processing required for the new designs. Critical to the success of the whole program was the development of an aluminum extrusion for the receiver. This component is made of high-strength aircraft-aluminum alloy and required tolerances which were an advance of the "state of the art" in the late 1950s.

Winchester engineers worked with manufacturers all over the United States to develop the techniques to make this design successful. The final process worked this way: A bar of aircraft-grade high-alloy aluminum was sawn to length and placed in a heavy steel punch-and-die set. An enormous press then cold-forged the aluminum, extruding it into a hollow boxlike member, with the internal configuration of the receiver squeezed into the metal. This approach meant that the aluminum flowed around the male punch in such a way as to give added strength at the attachment points for the barrel, magazine and butt stock. The design included many new features for a shotgun, such as a front-locking rotary bolt, a self-compensating gas system and a trigger-guard assembly which contained all of the trigger mechanism and carrier mechanism, plus side rails which supported the action-slide arms within the receiver and also held the magazine cutoffs.

A semi-automatic shotgun is one of the most difficult of all firearms to design and develop for it must function reliably with the lightest-weight ammunition and yet not batter itself to pieces with heavy magnum ammunition. It must be light in weight, easily disassembled, have attractive styling and yet must be able to be manufactured and sold at a reasonable price. These difficult requirements demand that a great deal of research and development money be spent before a design is locked up for production with its concomitant millions of dollars spent on machinery, tools, gauges and fixtures. The research and development on the Winchester Model 1400 continued through the late 1950s and early 1960s to meet these goals.

The procedure was to have design teams specialize in subassemblies such as the gas system, the locking system, and the trigger mechanism. A senior designer prepared the overall layout incorporating the results of the sub-studies. When the master layout was complete the members of the team worked together to make detailed drawings of every component in the shotgun. Every dimension was defined and, since no part can be manufeatured perfectly, allowable tolerances were established above and below the drawing dimensions. The materials, heat treatments and surface finishes were also specified. An entire semi-automatic shotgun requires approximately 120 separate detail drawings.

Copies of the drawings were transmitted to the

Purchasing Department which secured quotations from skilled modelmakers. It was not unusual for a single model of an experimental shotgun to cost $15,000 for fabrication and require three months' time. The parts were usually received from the vendor without heat-treatment and the senior designer assembled the components to make sure that fits and clearances were correct. Invariably there were mistakes which were easier to correct with soft components. If we were lucky, the parts could be modified by grinding a little additional clearance in tight locations, or reaming holes to slightly different sizes. Occasionally parts were found to be so incorrect that redesign was required and a new part fabricated. After preliminary fitting was satisfactory, all of the components were heat-treated and given a proper surface finish, such as chrome plating or bluing. Then came the satisfying moment when the parts were reassembled into a finished design.

In many cases the shotgun didn't look like a finished shotgun, for the forearm was left off and extensive additions were made for instrumentation. An example of an experimental shotgun is shown in Figure 7-18. A large projection has been added to the barrel at the breech to take a piezoelectric crystal which measured the gas pressure in the chamber as the shot was fired. A second pressure-measuring device has been added to the gas system so that the pressure rise within the gas cylinder could be measured. Windows have been cut in the side of the receiver so that a special high speed motion picture camera, capable of taking 7,000 photographs a second, could monitor the motion of all the internal parts of the gun during the firing cycle. Additional instrumentation was added to the butt stock to measure the force transmitted to the shooter's shoulder.

There is risk attached to any highly experimental new firearm and so safety precautions were carefully maintained. The shotgun was fired from a recoil device with a long cord attached to the trigger. The shooters actually stood outside of a steel door and fired the gun remotely during the early stages of the test program. All experimental guns were fired with special high-pressure-proof cartridges to insure that their safety margins were adequate. Invariably the gun doesn't function very well in early tests. The designers have made the clearances too tight, internal components are misaligned or the vendor has made a part out of specifications. After a great deal of experimental effort requiring modification or redesign and refabrication of components the mechanism is improved until it functions quite reliably. Eventually approval is received to fire the shotgun from the shoulder and an elaborate test procedure is followed to gather a great deal of information about the mechanism performance.

A fairly complex setup showing the author firing a fully instrumented Model 1400 shotgun is shown in Figure 7-19. A gauge to measure the force transmitted from the butt stock to the shoulder is attached to the rear of the butt stock and the electrical connection lies over the shooter's shoulder. Pressure-measurement gauges have been attached to the chamber and the gas cylinder and each is electrically connected to an oscilloscope with a Polaroid camera attached. As the shot is fired the three oscilloscopes individually record the pressure-time relationships for a particular gauge. The photographic records must be carefully calibrated for time and pressure and then can be used for analysis of the performance of the gun mechanism.

In addition to the pressure-measurement devices, a large battery of lamps is shown in the foreground of the picture. The high-speed motion-picture camera is located on the right side of the illustration. The procedure for firing a shot is similar to a small-scale rocket launching. The instrumentation is all hooked and double checked for performance. The shotgun is loaded and the shooter stands in position. The battery of lights

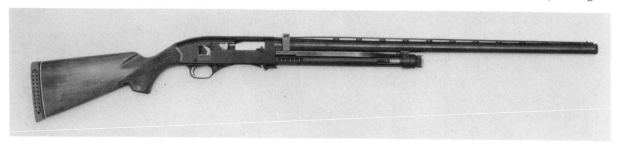

Figure 7-18 Experimental Winchester Model 1400 shotgun.

Figure 7-19 Test-firing setup.

is turned on and the camera focused. The chief instrumentation man calls out "one, two, three," and the shooter fires. As he calls out "two," an extra surge of electricity is thrown into the battery of lights, overstraining them and causing a brilliant flare of light. At the same time the high-speed motion-picture camera is engaged and rapidly accelerates from zero to 7,000 frames per second. Performance of the camera is so rapid that it will run through a 100-foot roll of 16-mm film in less than half a second and the end of the film is literally beaten to pieces inside the camera case by its violent whipping motion as it snaps off the lower reel. The lights are then shut off and the test crew prepares for the next shot.

Analysis of the high-speed movies shows a world that none of us can ever see with the naked eye. The mechanism seems to start motion haltingly and then lazily move to the rear, jiggling and jumping and vibrating as it goes. The fired shell is slowly drawn out of the chamber,

clearly strikes the ejector and then lazily floats out of the ejection port surrounded by a cloud of gas. The incoming shell from the magazine moves with such deliberate care that it appears to take five minutes to get from the magazine into the carrier and then is very slowly picked up by the bolt and fed into the chamber of the gun.

For analysis the motion-picture film is threaded into a special measuring device known as an "optical motion analyzer." This device moves the film frame by frame over a grid, and the use of carefully calibrated scales permits measurement of the parts motion to 1/100 of an inch accuracy. From careful measurements made on the high-speed motion-picture film, graphs can be prepared showing the displacement, acceleration and velocity of the gun mechanism during the entire firing cycle. Another advantage of the high-speed motion pictures is that the gun designer has an opportunity to examine the flow of motion through the mechanism and see if it agrees with

152

his design calculations. Some of the most valuable high-speed motion pictures occur when the gun malfunctions, for this often provides valuable knowledge of weaknesses in the mechanism.

A second technique to analyze the gun mechanism is the use of a "time-displacement" camera, an operation that will be described later. By coordinating the result of the high-speed motion pictures or the time-displacement camera, with the pressure-time information from the chamber, the gas system and the shoulder-force gauge, the gun designer had a good opportunity to understand the intricate working relationships within the mechanism he has designed.

The design-fabrication-test-and-evaluation process was repeated many times in the late 1950s and early 1960s. Twelve gauge-slide and semi-automatic shotguns were the primary designs, although efforts were made to make sure that the 20-gauge models would be compatible. Many radical design approaches were investigated during this program including the use of laminated plywood forearms with plastic and caps, and the use of short stroke gas systems. A very radical design was investigated using a modified "inertia-operated" action, based on the Sjögren principle. Design approaches such as the use of a long carrier pivoted at the rear of the receiver were investigated before decisions were reached on a trigger-mechanism design that would have a high degree of commonality with the new designs of rimfire and centerfire "New Winchester line" firearms then under study.

During the early 1960s the designs solidified; small variations were checked out in experimental models reflecting minor design changes, and investigations of critical dimensional changes, such as the clearance between the gas piston in the cylinder. Larger quantities of models were fabricated for field and marketing tests. The manufacturing-engineering group carried on endless

discussions with machine-tool builders all over the United States, selecting machinery which would be the very best to perform the complex manufacturing functions. Tool designers began to work out the special tools and clamping fixture to hold the components in the machinery during operations, and the gauges to measure dimensions after machining. The plant-layout group organized the manufacturing area in which production would be performed and established the flow of work from one set of machines to the next, so that production would be smooth, orderly, and economical. Areas for final inspection of components, storage of accepted components and gun assembly areas were established and fitted with all the special tools and gauges required for each operation. After final assembly the guns went to proof and function testing, where the strength and performance of each individual gun was carefully checked. One of the crucial problems of modern manufacturing is the long time required to build and equip special machinery. It is not unusual for two years to elapse between the time a machine is specified and the time it has been built, tested at the vendor's plant, shipped to the factory, installed, the tooling assembled and the final adjustments made to manufacture components within the very tight tolerances required for modern gun manufacture.

These steps were performed in the early 1960s and the Model 1200 slide-action and Model 1400 semi-automatic shotguns were placed in production in late 1963. The final shotgun is shown in Figure 7-20—a far better looking product than the experimental shotgun shown previously.

The new Winchester Model 1200 and 1400 shotguns were announced to the trade in January 1964 with availability dates of June of that year. Both were initially announced in 12 gauge only. The close cooperation between research, engineering, marketing and production led to a manu-

Figure 7-20 Winchester Model 1400 shotgun, as finally produced.

facturing cost slightly under the design objectives for both shotguns that had been established by the Marketing and Financial departments. Any multimillion dollar program must return an adequate profit on the investment to be worthwhile, and careful design and manufacturing efforts are required to make a profit under the intense competition of the American market. Pricing of the Model 1200 slide-action shotgun was extremely competitive and sales rapidly built up above the planned productions. The Winchester Model 1400 had a more difficult time.

During the first full year of sales, in 1965, 28,700 Model 1400 shotguns were sold on the domestic market, and 51,600 Model 1200 shotguns. By 1967 sales of the Model 1200 had risen to 61,600 units, while sales of the Model 1400 had declined to 23,400 in the face of the very strong Remington offerings in both long-recoil-action and gas-operated designs. During the early sixties, Remington maintained both long-recoil semi-automatic shotguns, constructed on the Browning approach, and gas-operated models. At one point the Remington Model 11-48 long-recoil shotguns were offered from 12 gauge through 410 bore, and two different gas-operated shotguns, the Model 58 and 878, were in production at the same time.

Winchester's Arms Product Engineering people performed a series of design studies in the mid-sixties to improve the sales features of the Model 1400 shotgun. These led to the introduction of the Winchester Model 1400 Mark II in the spring of 1968. Design changes included a new style action release with an external button mounted on the underside of the receiver. Design changes in the trigger mechanism, and checkering designs were also included to uprate the features.

How a Gas-Operated Shotgun Works

During the past thirty years there has been a definite trend towards gas-operated semi-automatic firearms in both the commercial and military fields. American efforts have been strong in both areas. During World War II the U.S. Rifle M-1 "Garand" military rifle was in wide use, using a "long-stroke" gas system. Another military design was the Winchester M1 carbine which used a "short-stroke" gas system in which the piston moves less than ¼ of an inch to power the mechanism. Early design studies on the

Model 1400 program investigated both styles of gas systems as well as a third variation known as a "cut-off-expansion" type of gas system. Other types of gun actuation were studied on paper, including short-recoil, inertia-operated, and delayed-blowback designs. The final decision was to utilize a long-stroke gas system with modified cut-off-expansion features and a gas-control valve to smooth out the power flow into the mechanism when fired with either light or heavy loads. The gas-operated system uses a ready source of energy and provides a good method of delaying unlocking of the gun mechanism and opening the action until the chamber pressure has fallen to a safe level. Many factors can be controlled to provide the proper timing and energy to operate the gun mechanism.

Semi-automatic firearms pose very difficult problems in the analysis of the forces operating the mechanism. This is because the pressure buildup from the barrel into the gas system occurs in less than 2/1000 of a second. At one instant the gas piston is sitting quietly and two milliseconds later (2/1000 of a second) it is driving to the rear at maximum force level.

The basic arrangement of a shotgun with a long-stroke gas system is shown in Figure 7-21. A gas port, drilled into the barrel, allows gases to escape from the barrel into a gas cylinder in which a piston is located. The size of the gas port determines the quantity of gases entering the gas system and the pressure buildup within the system. Since the power level within the gun mechanism can easily be controlled by varying the gas port size, final balancing of a completed mechanism is usually performed by first drilling a small hole and then firing a series of instrumented tests with small increases in gas-port size between tests until proper mechanism velocities are recorded.

Location of the Gas Port

The location of a gas port is chosen to meet many conflicting requirements. If the port is placed close to the chamber, the gas pressure and temperature will be high and the duration of the pressure pulse relatively long. This also results in an early impulse to the gas system, which is undesirable. In sporting firearms, the gas port is generally located as far down the barrel as external gun styling considerations allow. In most sys-

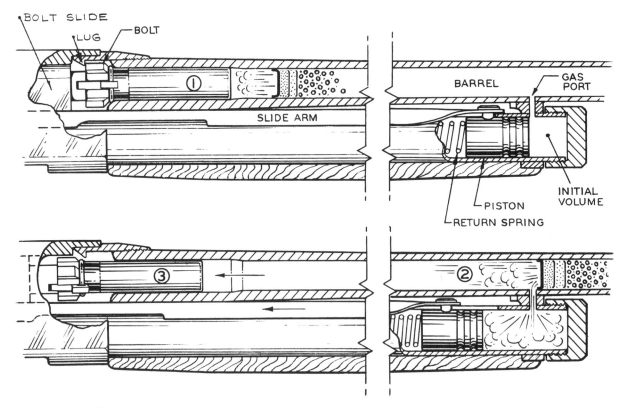

Figure 7-21 The long-stroke gas system.

tems the hole is located between 9 and 12 inches from the bolt face, which gives a delay of about 1 millisecond (.001 second) in the start of pressure buildup within the gas system.

As pressure builds up within the gas system, it acts on the piston shown in Figure 7-21. The piston is connected to a pair of long and relatively slender slide arms. The slide arms in turn are attached to a heavy weight known as the "bolt slide" which is partially shown on the left side of the figure. The bolt slide in turn retains the bolt, which is in contact with the shotshell. In the upper view, the bolt is shown locked to a locking lug on its upper surface. The locking lug in turn is rigidly attached to both the receiver and the barrel. The bolt, locking lug, barrel and receiver form a rigid system to retain the 5,000 pound rearward thrust of the shotshell.

In the lower view the gas system is shown in operation. As the shotshell wads pass the gas port, gases pass down through the port at high velocity and begin to build up pressure within the gas system. The illustration shows considerable motion of the gas piston as the wads pass the port. In actual fact, there is a very appreciable delay because of the large initial volume in the gas system. In the Winchester Model 1400

shotgun, initial volume is about .360 cubic inches and the cross-sectional area of the gas ports is about .020 square inches. A rather large gas piston is used with a cross sectional area of .660 square inches. These dimensions provide a low-pressure gas system that provides a long time delay before the unlocking of the gun mechanism.

Shotshell Characteristics

The shotshells used in today's commercial shotguns vary widely in operating characteristics. The lightest 12-gauge loads project 1 to 1⅛ ounces of shot at a velocity of about 1,200 feet per second at the muzzle. These loads develop a peak pressure in the range of 9,000 pounds per square inch .5 milliseconds after firing (.0005 seconds). At the end of 2½ milliseconds, the pressure has fallen below 500 pounds per square inch. At the time the shot charge passes the gas port, the pressure is about 1,800 pounds per square inch.

The heaviest loads used in standard commercial 12-gauge shotguns are Magnum shotshells projecting 1½ ounces of shot at a velocity of about 1,350 feet per second. The gas impulse to deliver this muzzle energy is, of course, much higher, with a peak pressure of slightly over

12,000 pounds per square inch at .55 milliseconds after firing. At the end of 2½ milliseconds, the pressure is about 1,000 psi (pounds per square inch). The gas pressure with a Magnum shotshell is about 2,200 psi at the time the shot charge passes the gas port.

The widely differing characteristics of the shotshells highlights one of the most difficult problems in developing a satisfactory gas-operated shotgun. The energy into the gun mechanism varies greatly, depending on the load the hunter selects.

The Compensated Gas System

In order to minimize the variation in input energy into the gas system, compensating devices have been developed. The one used on the Winchester Model 1400 semi-automatic shotgun is shown in Figure 7-22 and the patent in Figure 7-23. The gas system has been designed so that the gas flows into the interior of the hollow piston. As the piston moves, the gas flow is cut off and trapped until the end of the piston passes the gas port. This type of gas-system design is known as a "cutoff-expansion" system. The theory is that a certain amount of gas will flow in and fill the initial volume in the gas system and then will be cut off and trapped due to the initial motion of the piston. The timing of the cutoff can be controlled by varying the diameter of the hole in the piston, which is always larger than the hole into the barrel. This type of gas system is also used on the M-14 Army rifle, the M-60 machine gun and the Winchester Model 100 semi-automatic rifle. The second and most important means for controlling the variable impulse of the shotshell loads is the gas-control valve on the front of the gas system. This was designed with a pre-loaded valve-member, which opens only slightly when light shotshell loads are used. When Magnum shotshells are fired, the threshold pressure of the valve is substantially exceeded and it moves off its seat. It rapidly moves into a fully open position as shown in the lower illustration of Figure 7-22. By varying the weight of the valve and the spring force, it is possible to develop a system that will be quite selective, dumping a little gas with light loads, and a great deal of gas with the heavy loads, thus bringing the impulse to the system down close to that with the lighter shotshells.

Shotgun Dynamic System

A schematic drawing of the important moving parts in a semi-automatic shotgun is shown in Figure 7-24. This dynamic model is similar to that used in all gas-operated shotguns. The weight of the various elements differs with particular designs, but it is a generally accepted design criteria that the "primary mass" (the parts tied to the gas piston—piston, slide arms and bolt slide) should be heavy in comparison to the bolt assembly. One of the most efficient systems recently examined is the Soviet AK-54 semi-automatic military rifle, which has been widely manufactured in Soviet Russia and China. The Chinese copy shows a weight tied to the piston of 1.046 pounds, and a bolt assembly of .194 pounds, for a weight ratio of 5.4 to 1.

Analysis of Gun Mechanism Performance

In addition to the high-speed motion pictures a second technique, known as a "time-displacement camera," is used to understand the operation of the automatic mechanism. In this system, bright reference lines are placed on the receiver of the gun and on the bolt and the rest of the mechanism is made dark. A long sheet of photographic film is placed inside a motor-driven drum on the camera. During a test, the motor is started and the drum brought up to speed. A bright light is focused on the gun mechanism and as the shot is fired the camera lens is opened for one turn of the drum. The result is a time-displacement trace such as that shown in Figure 7-25. This trace is for a Magnum shotshell fired by a shooter in a standing position. By analysis of this time-displacement trace, each of the important events in the operation of the gun mechanism can be identified and measured. The initial events include the picking up of the hammer, the beginning of gas flow into the gas system and the closing of the gas ports due to the movement of the piston.

The peak acceleration between the gun and the moving internal parts occurs between 2 milliseconds (.002 seconds) and 3 milliseconds (.003 seconds) after firing. There is a change in velocity of 8 feet per second over this time interval corresponding to an average acceleration of 8,000 feet per second^2. This rate of acceleration requires an average force of 210 pounds over this period.

The force is supplied by gas pressure from the barrel acting on the gas piston. The cross section

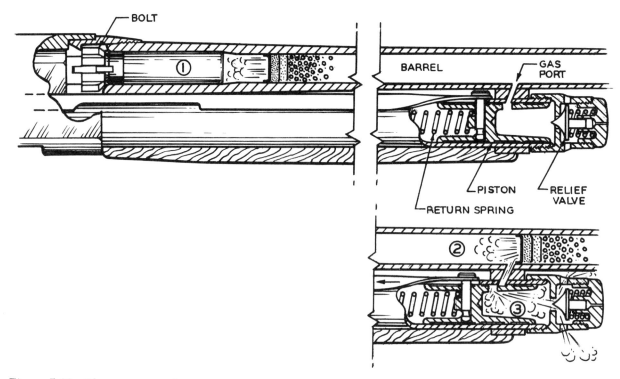

Figure 7-22 The compensated gas system.

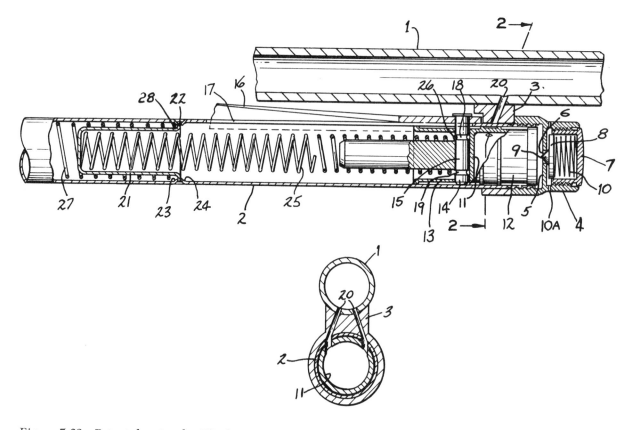

Figure 7-23 Patent drawing for Winchester compensated gas system.

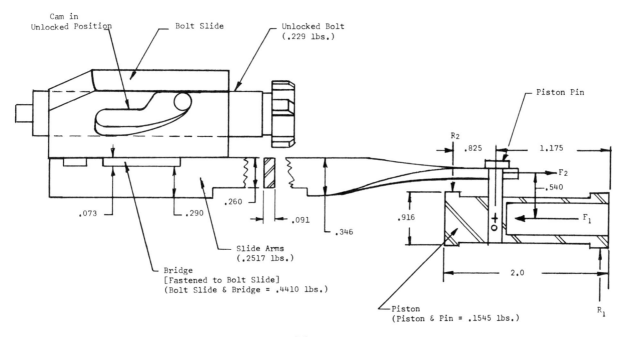

Figure 7-24 Dynamic elements in Winchester Model 1400 action.

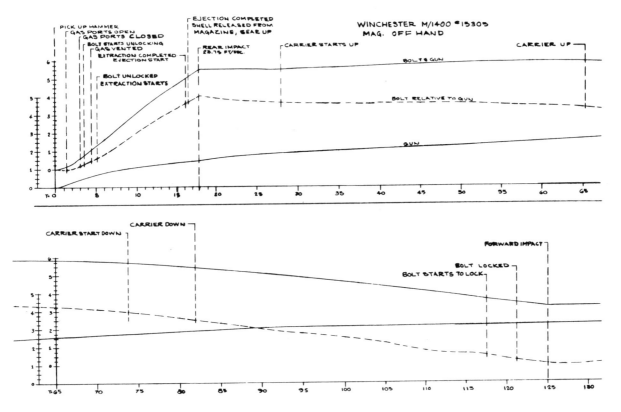

Figure 7-25 Typical time-displacement trace.

158

area of the gas piston is .660 square inches. An average gas pressure of only 324 pounds per square inch would be required over this period to provide 8,000 feet per second^2 acceleration to the primary mass at 100 percent efficiency.

The velocity relationships during the operating cycle are shown in Figure 7-26.[1] The gun velocity is shown in the solid line, and the parts tied to the gas piston (known technically as the "primary mass") are shown in the broken line. The peak acceleration between the primary mass and gun is shown between the events (3) and (4) on the curve, as gas is flowing into the gas system.

The velocity in the primary mass builds up to 17.5 feet per second relative to the gun at the end of 4 milliseconds after firing (.004 seconds). At this point, the primary mass has traveled .150 inches, and starts to unlock the bolt. The velocity

builds up slowly during the next millisecond as energy is transferred from the primary mass to the bolt through the unlocking cam.

Kinematics of the Unlocking System

The locking system of the Winchester Model 1400 shotgun consists of a front locking rotary bolt with four locking lugs. The bolt locks into a barrel extension which is rigidly attached to the barrel and receiver. The rotation of the bolt is controlled by a cam cut in the bolt slide as shown in Figure 7-27. A husky pin fitted to the bolt rides in the cam track in the bolt slide.

The rotary motion during unlocking is very rapid. The rotational velocity at the start of the unlocking is zero. The velocity averages 3,100 revolutions per minute during the 1.6 millisecond unlocking sequence, and returns to zero at the end of the unlocking cycle. Total rotation is only 30°, and this is controlled by an efficient helical cam on the unlocking stroke.

After the bolt is fully rotated it is accelerated

[1]This analysis performed by E. R. Hodil and described in Hodil, E. R. & Butler, D. F., *Fundamental Study of Semi-Automatic Shotgun Functioning* (Winchester Western Technical Report, 1966).

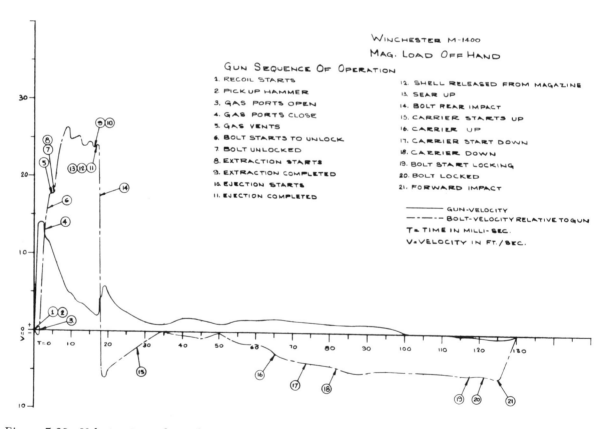

Figure 7-26 Velocity-time relationships in Winchester Model 1400.

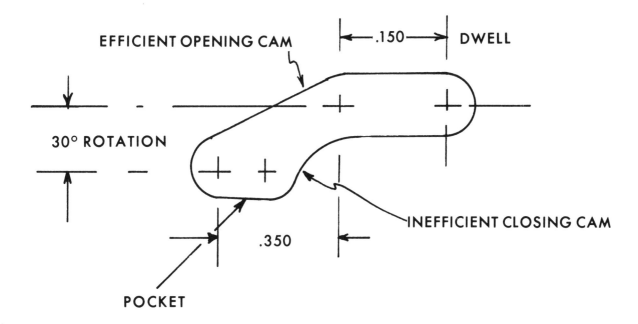

EFFICIENT OPENING CAM

.150 DWELL

30° ROTATION

.350

POCKET

INEFFICIENT CLOSING CAM

Figure 7-27 Locking cam of Winchester Model 1400 action.

rearward by the cam pin in the bolt striking the end of the cam cut in the bolt slide. The vibration between the two assemblies holds the primary mass at a constant velocity relative to the gun until the bolt is fully accelerated. This is shown at point 7 on the velocity curve of Figure 7-26.

The primary mass then builds up to its maximum velocity relative to the gun of 25 feet per second. A series of impacts then occur between the primary mass and the bolt. This results in the velocity changes of the primary mass between the peak velocity and point 11 on the curve. The velocity changes of the secondary mass are greater. The oscillations continue until the primary mass strikes the solid surface at the rear of the receiver. The rear impact shown in the figure results in an average deceleration of the primary mass of 28,500 feet per second² over the period of impact. This acceleration requires a force of over 950 pounds since both the primary and secondary mass are decelerated at the same time.

The conditions shown in Figure 7-26 firing a Magnum shotshell represent the most severe conditions the gun mechanism must endure, and the parts must be stressed to handle these impact loads. With lighter shotshells, such as skeet or trap load, the velocity levels are substantially reduced, with a maximum bolt-slide velocity relative to the gun of about 17.7 feet per second, and a velocity just prior to rear impact in the range of 8 feet per second.

The overall energy loss in the moving parts on

rear impact is high, which is exactly what is desired. The moving parts should reliably reach the rear of the receiver on every shot with all types of ammunition under widely varying conditions of holding and of lubrication, but the parts should never rebound from this impact at high speed. It required many thousands of dollars of research study in the early 1960s to find a design which would achieve these results.

The kinetic energy of the gun parts is rapidly transferred to the receiver during rear impact as shown on event 14 in Figure 7-26. The rebound velocity is shown as the distance *below* the line since it is in a *forward* direction. The gun accelerates to a higher velocity against the shooter's shoulder as a result of the impact. The rebound velocity is much smaller:

	Kinetic energy of gun (ft.-lbs.)	Kinetic energy of moving parts (ft.-lbs.)	Total kinetic energy (ft.-lbs.)
Before impact	.39	11.29	11.68
After impact	3.2	.001	3.20

Thus, the kinetic energy loss in this rear impact amounts to 72 percent. If momentum calculations are performed using the absolute velocities, the momentum prior to impact is 1.256 pound-seconds, and only 1.106 pound-seconds after impact. This loss is because the gun is not a free body in space, but supported by the shooter's shoulder. The peak force between gun and shoulder can reach 400 pounds with a hard butt plate and a Magnum shotshell. This force is reduced by the use of a rubber recoil pad, as fitted on many modern shotguns.

The closing stroke differs radically from the opening stroke as shown in Figure 7-26. The opening stroke is at high speed with a peak velocity of 25 feet per second. The maximum closing velocity is a little over 5 feet per second. The time for the opening stroke is 18 milliseconds (.018 seconds), while the closing stroke requires 110 milliseconds (.110 seconds).

The energy for the closing stroke is provided by a powerful return spring located in the forearm of the shotgun. This spring provides enough energy for gently feeding the new shotshell into the chamber under all conditions. The rebound velocity after rear impact, therefore, represents *excess energy*. A mechanism has been designed to absorb this excess energy and bring the bolt slide to a stop relative to the receiver. This is done by an overriding pawl on the carrier-feed mechanism. The pawl locks the bolt slide fully to the rear until a new shotshell has fed out of the magazine tube and is properly positioned in the carrier. This action is shown in Figure 7-26 at 35 milliseconds after firing. The carrier is not fully released until 50 milliseconds after firing, when the new shotshell is properly positioned and ready to load. At event 16 the carrier has lifted the new shotshell into alignment with the chamber and the bolt has contacted the rear of the shell and started to ram it into the chamber. At event 17 the shell has entered the chamber and the bolt slide has started to knock the carrier downwards out of the way.

The cam in the bolt slide, shown in Figure 7-27 is modified on the closing side in two ways. A "pocket" is cut into the cam to prevent the bolt from vibrating in a rotary direction (torsional oscillation) when the bolt and slide slam into the receiver at the end of the rearward stroke. At the end of the pocket, an "inefficient" closing cam is cut. As the bolt picks up a fresh shell from the carrier it must push the shell forward. The bolt is caught between the shell, which wants to stay still, and the bolt slide, which is moving forward due to the return spring. The bolt tends to slide rearwards into the bolt slide, and this presses the closing cam against the husky pin in the bolt. If the cam were gentle, as on the opening side, the bolt would rotate hard against the guide in the top of the receiver. With an "inefficient," or steep, cam angle the force against the guide is much less, and the bolt chambers the fresh shotshell more easily.

As the shell is fully rammed into the chamber the bolt head rides off the end of a long track extending the length of the receiver, and is free to rotate into a locked position. It is driven into the locked position by the steep cam cut in the bolt slide.

The final motions of the closing cycle are the locking sequence. As the shell reaches a fully forward position in the chamber, the rim contacts the chamber seat. All forward motion of the *bolt* and *shotshell* are stopped by compression of the rim. As the bolt slide continues forward, the cam pin in the bolt strikes the steep locking surface in the cam cut. The bolt rotates into a fully locked position, and the remaining energy in the bolt slide is absorbed in a minor impact between the bolt slide and the forward surfaces of the receiver.

The entire auto-loading sequence takes about ⅛ of a second, with all of the action sequentially timed and interlocked within this time span. It takes considerably longer for the shooter to recover from the recoil and aim the next shot. A good semi-automatic is always ready for the hunter, and eliminates the need for a number of manual operations between shots.

The reliability of the system is dependent on a good source of power and a well-developed mechanism to handle the power flow in the system. A closer look at the source of the power may be of interest.

Dynamics of the Gas Piston

After the shot passes the gas port, the pressure builds up rapidly within the gas system. During the Model 1400 gun-design phase the gas flow into the gas system was calculated by a series of equations, and then checked by instrumented firing tests. In the Model 1400 firing Magnum shotshells, the gas flow starts 1.75 milliseconds after the shot is fired, and by 2.00 milliseconds (0.25 milliseconds later) the pressure *in the gas system* has reached 450 pounds per square inch. The pressure then oscillates, finally reaching slightly more than 500 pounds per square inch as the shot charge leaves the muzzle of the shotgun. Muzzle exit of the shot occurs 2.6 milliseconds after firing. Gas continues to flow into the gas system after the shot charge has left the muzzle for a short time, and then the flow reverses. Pressure in the gas system has dropped back to normal 5.0 milliseconds after firing.

The important dynamic elements in the system

are shown in Figure 7-24. The situation within the mechanism at the end of 2.8 milliseconds after firing is as follows:

Gas pressure within piston ... 500 psi
Rearward thrust on Piston F_1 . 330 pounds
Average velocity of primary
system (piston, slide arms,
bolt slide) .... 8.0 ft/sec.
Average acceleration as measured on bolt slide
(6.5 foot per second gain in
velocity in .0005 seconds) ... 11,000 ft/sec.^{2}
Force required to accelerate
piston assembly at this rate . 52.6 pounds
Force required to accelerate
primary system at this rate . 289 pounds
Net force at piston-pin to slide
arms joint (F_2) .... 236 pounds

A simplified assumption can be made for purposes of this example, that the primary friction loss in the system is due to the clockwise moment on the gas piston, causing heavy rubbing within the gas cylinder. The frictional drag is aggravated by the boundary lubrication conditions due to gas fouling on the piston and cylinder after many shots are fired.

The forces in the system can be solved by writing a series of moment equations. The easiest way is to take the moments about the centerline of the gas piston where it intersects the axis of the piston pin (point "O" on Figure 7-24. Solving the equations shows that the vertical forces on the piston (R_1 and R_2) are equal and:

$$R_1 = R_2 = 63.7 \text{ lbs.}$$

The horizontal forces also may be solved, showing that they balance out if the frictional drag on the piston amounts to 41 lbs. This corresponds to a coefficient of friction of .32.

In actuality, the coefficient of friction is less because the powder gases make a surprisingly good lubricant under most firing conditions.

Winchester Model 1400 Mark II

During the late 1960s design studies were performed to further refine and improve the Model 1400 shotgun. The improvements were focused on a new carrier release mechanism, improvements in the trigger mechanism and revised styling. There were design changes in the checkering patterns, and a redesigned forearm which shrouds more of the gas control valve. A new carrier-release mechanism was included for increased convenience to the shooter.

When the last shot has been fired from an automatic shotgun the mechanism remains locked in an open position. This serves two functions. One is to tell the shooter that the gun is empty, and the second is to make it easy to reload. The shooter merely has to toss a fresh shell into the side of the ejection port and press the carrier-release button forward. The action automatically chambers the fresh cartridge and two more shells can be loaded into the magazine. The carrier-release mechanism on the Mark II shotgun is more convenient to use than that of the original design.

Computer Gun Dynamics

The mathematical analysis of a semi-automatic shotgun mechanism requires a tremendous amount of time and thousands of calculations. During the late 1960s and early 1970s, Winchester started modeling gun mechanisms on the digital computer. The Model 1400 Mark II shotgun was the first gun mechanism so modeled. Skilled programmers went through the gun mechanism writing equations for the motion of every important moving part in the gun. All of the elements discussed in this section were fully described by differential equations and in addition the motion of the shells in the magazine and the hammer mechanism were described. The motion of the gun against the shooter's shoulder was taken into account. The shooter's shoulder is a complex problem, for no two shooters are exactly the same. Many tests were performed and a shooter's shoulder was finally described by the classical techniques of mechanics as a combination of an inertia weight, a spring and a "dash pot" for damping.

All the equations were written into a computer program together with detailed instructions of how the computer was to use the equations to calculate the detailed performance of the shotgun mechanism during each few milliseconds of time. Input data for a particular study included a detailed description of the ammunition characteristics in terms of pressures and weights, and the type of shooter firing the gun. The computer then went into a calculation sequence and printed out thousands of numbers describing the velocity of the key parts such as the receiver, bolt slide and gas piston assembly, bolt, and shells in the magazine. The final phase of the computer program was to plot out a velocity-time curve as shown in Figure 7-26 for the performance of the shotgun cycle.

Thousands of hours of research time were required for the computer programmers, mathematicians and research engineers to develop a program that would accurately reflect the performance of the Model 1400 Mark II shotgun. This was really a first-phase computer modeling of the gun mechanism and was soon supplanted by considerably more advanced programs which were used to analyze the performance of new and highly experimental military rifle mechanisms. In addition, the computer programs were used as a very important tool in the development of an advanced semiautomatic shotgun which is deep in the Product Engineering phase at the time of this writing.

One of the most valuable aspects of computer analysis of gun mechanisms is that many variations in the mechanism design can be studied.

For example, the arms product designer may ask: What happens if I increase the weight of the bolt slide? What happens if I decrease the volume of the gas system? What happens if I increase the area of the piston? What happens if the tolerances allow a lot of gas leakage in the gas system? Instead of having to design, fabricate and test models of every variation, each of which must be studied before a design is locked up for production, many of these questions can be answered by studying the variations on the computer model.

A scale cross-section illustration of the Mark II gun mechanism is shown in Figure 7-28. Major components have been identified with labels, but the actual relationship between the bolt slide, slide arms and gas piston are more clearly shown in Figure 7-24. The firing force is taken by the bolt, which engages the locking lugs on the barrel extension. The barrel extension is screwed to the barrel and presses against the front of the re-

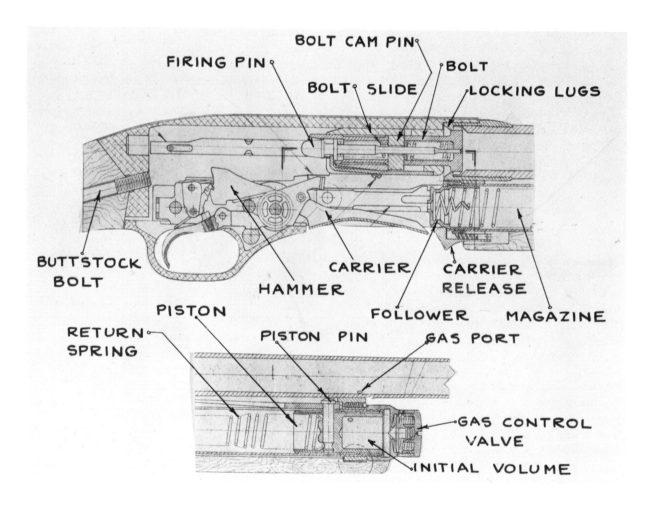

Figure 7-28   The Winchester Model 1400 Mark II action.

ceiver. As the shot is fired the base of the shell presses up against the bolt and the force flows to the locking lugs and from the barrel extension to the front of the receiver, down the length of the receiver through the butt stock and to the shooter's shoulder. The shooter feels less kick with an automatic shotgun such as the Model 1400 shotgun because of the motion of the automatic mechanism.

The husky bolt cam pin which rotates the bolt within the bolt slide is shown in the illustration. Unless the bolt is in a fully locked position the hammer cannot be released by the trigger. This control is provided by a mechanism known as the "action slide lock." The action-slide-lock mechanism lies along the left side of the trigger mechanism and is timed by an angled cut on the rear of the slide arms. A very short motion of the trigger disengages the sear from the hammer notch. A torsion spring, wound around the large drum on the hammer pivot accelerates the hammer in a clockwise direction, slamming it into the firing pin and igniting the cartridge.

Shotshells are placed in the magazine by pushing the carrier upwards out of the way and shoving the follower forward with the nose of the fresh shotshell. Shotshells are retained in the magazine by two "cartridge cutoffs," one on each side of the action. As the mechanism operates, first one cutoff and then the other releases the shell, allowing it to slide rearwards into the carrier. On the forward stroke of the bolt mechanism the carrier is rotated upwards by a carrier pawl mechanism which lies on the right side of the gun and which has been removed from the illustration. The shotshell is stripped from the carrier and rammed into the chamber.

When the last shot is fired, the carrier tries to rise but is blocked by the projection at the center of the follower. This locks the gun mechanism in a fully open position, warning the shooter that the gun is empty.

The configuration of the gas ports, gas piston and gas control valve are shown in the lower illustration. The return spring, which closes the gun mechanism, is a two-diameter spring which is nestled into the rear section of the gas piston. The operation of the gas control valve is shown most clearly in Figure 7-22.

High Standard Gas-Operated Shotguns

The High Standard Company of Hamden, Connecticut, was started by Gus Swebelius who had

been the chief designer at the Marlin Firearms Company designing machine guns during the First World War. Swebelius, a skilled tool maker, started High Standard by manufacturing semi-automatic pistols. Over the years High Standard developed a reputation for sporting and target .22 caliber automatic pistols which were eventually used by the United States teams in the Olympics.

During the 1950s High Standard began developing a semi-automatic shotgun to be marketed through Sears, Roebuck and Company. The J. C. Higgins Model 60 semi-automatic shotgun, announced in 1956, was the first successful shotgun with a concentric gas system. It was somewhat similar to that illustrated for the Remington Model 1100 shotgun. The magazine tube contained four shotshells. A hollow cylindrical piston surrounded the magazine tube and fitted inside a short cylinder, which was brazed to the barrel of the shotgun. As the shot charge passed by the ports in the barrel, gas flowed into the annular space between the cylinder and piston driving the piston sharply to the rear. Force was transmitted through a single slide arm lying on the side of the action which moved the bolt slide to the rear. After a short period of dwell the bolt slide cammed a vertical locking block down vertically within the bolt. As soon as the locking block cleared the recess machined in the top of the receiver, the bolt and slide traveled together for the remainder of the stroke. Feeding was accomplished by a conventional tray type of carrier which was pivoted within the aluminum die-cast trigger guard.

The J. C. Higgins shotgun was sold during the late 1950s and in early 1960s. During the 1960s design improvements were incorporated and the shotgun became the J. C. Higgins Model 66. The basic design has been modernized again and is now sold under the High Standard trademark as the "Supermatic" auto-loading shotgun. It is available in 12 and 20 gauge with 26- to 30-inch shotgun barrels. The 20-gauge shotguns weigh 7 pounds, the 12-gauge models with standard barrel 7½ pounds. Both gauges are available with plain and ventilated-rib barrels in standard and skeet models. In addition, the 12-gauge model is available as a special duck gun, trap gun, or a deer gun designed for use with rifled slugs.

Remington Sportsman-58

The Remington Arms Company has always been the largest manufacturer of auto-loading shotguns in the United States. During the post-World War II period, while Winchester was performing research and development on the radically new Model 50 shotgun with a floating chamber, Remington was performing pioneering research in the field of gas-operated automatic shotguns. This research led to the introduction of the 12-gauge Sportsman-58 model in 1956. A Remington press release at the time of introduction describes some of the new features and the advantage of gas operation for the sportsman.

APRIL 1956
NEW GAS-OPERATED SHOTGUN ANNOUNCED BY REMINGTON

In what is termed to be one of the greatest advances ever made in sporting firearms design, Remington Arms Company, Inc., has announced the development and production of another autoloading shotgun as an addition to its famous line of high quality firearms.

This is the Remington Sportsman-58, a 12 gauge, 3 shot gas-operated autoloader in which is incorporated a number of new and unique features which will gladden the heart of any shotgun fancier.

The action of the Sportsman-58 functions on the "Power-Matic" or gas-operated principle . . . . As gas from the fired shell moves the Power-Matic piston rearward, there is a forward reaction on the gun, opposing and slowing recoil and softening its effect on the shooter's shoulder. This recoil is unusually mild, which allows the production of a fast handling gun of light weight. The Sportsman-58 weighs only about seven pounds.

This model is said to be the fastest loading shotgun ever made. The non-recoiling barrel is easily interchanged, allowing the owner to shift from one type of hunting to another without making adjustments on his barrels. Double action bars add to the gun's sturdiness and dependability of function.

Another unique feature, exclusive to the Remington Model Sportsman-58, is the "Dial-A-Matic" load control, which is designed to insure minimum recoil with all standard length shotgun shells, regular or magnum. A slight twist of the dial makes the proper adjustment and the large letters reveal at a glance just how the gun is set. This adjustment ("L" for light, low base loads, and "H" for heavy, high base loads), coupled with the "Power-Matic" action, assures the shooter of dependable, positive action that allows him to maintain the stability of his pointing alignment while firing at a rapid rate of fire. . . .

The Sportsman-58 will not replace the popular Remington Model 11-48 which will remain in the line.

The deluxe Remington Model 58 ADL is shown in Figure 7-29.

The 12-gauge model remained the only gas-operated Remington shotgun until the introduction of the 16- and 20-gauge models in 1967. The M-58 shotguns were always deluxe models, but were offered with various levels of ornamentation, including hand-engraved versions costing several thousand dollars. Both plain and ventilated-rib barrels were available in lengths of 26 inches in skeet and improved cylinder choke, 28 inches in modified choke and 28 and 30 inches in full choke.

Great care had gone into the design during the decade following World War II and there were many common features with the Model 870 slide-action shotgun, many of the components for both being manufactured on the same tooling. These included such items as the butt-stock assembly and the major components contained within the trigger assembly. Receivers had the same basic dimensions but differed in minor machining operations. The barrel assemblies were very similar and the bolt assembly had many common parts.

A cross-section illustration of the Remington Model 58 is shown in Figure 7-30. A hard-steel

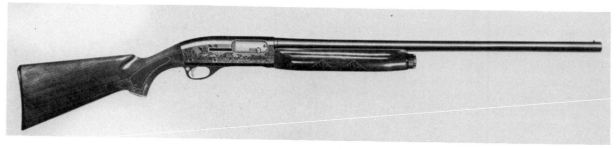

Figure 7-29   Remington Model 58 ADL gas-operated shotgun.

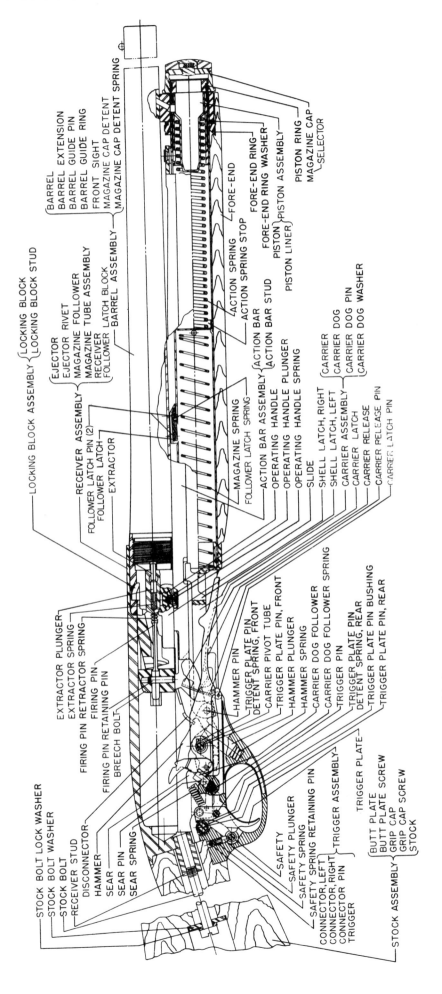

Figure 7-30 Mechanism of Remington Model 58 action.

barrel extension was screwed to the barrel and the locking recess machined into this extension. The bolt-locking system included a hollow breech block into which fitted a locking block which could rotate. The functioning was rather similar to the old Model 11 and the new Model 11-48, but the construction was different. Motion of the locking block was controlled by the slide, which in turn was rigidly fastened to the action-bar assembly. The action-bar assembly was composed of long slender arms that extended from the slide in the receiver all the way up the magazine tube, and were connected to the gas piston at the forward end. The magazine tube was divided into two sections, the rear half containing a two-shot magazine, the front half the gas cylinder, return spring and a hollow piston.

The functioning of the Model 58 was performed in a split second, but each mechanical motion was carefully timed and programmed. Gas flowed from the barrel into the hollow piston. As the gas piston moved to the rear it transmitted the force to the action bars or slide arms through the stud that was riveted to the action bars and interlocked with the upper surface of the piston. The force was transmitted through the action bars to the slide (or bolt carrier). Initial motion of the slide relative to the bolt pivoted the locking block out of engagement with the locking recess cut into the upper surface of the barrel extension. As unlocking was completed the energy contained in the bolt slide, slide arms and gas piston plus the residual gas pressure drove the entire assembly to the rear, compressing the mainspring and ejecting the fired shell.

Remington engineers designed a device to control the power level in the gas system. The cap fitted to the end of the magazine tube consisted of a main assembly which was screwed solidly against the barrel ring and a movable ring which may be seen at the extreme forward end of the magazine tube in Figure 7-30. This ring, marked with a setting for low and high base loads, was known as the "Dial-A-Matic" load control. For firing low base loads the "L" setting was lined up with a guide mark and a small amount of gas was vented through holes in the gas cap. For high base loads the "H" setting was lined up with the guide mark and much larger vent holes were available to reduce the pressure in the gas system by venting larger quantities of gas.

The Remington Model Sportsman-58 was a highly successful shotgun and remained in production until 1962.

Remington Model 878 Automaster

The Remington design staff continued active efforts on gas-operated shotgun technology. The next Remington model was introduced in 1959 and contained an advanced power-compensation system built right into the gas piston. The design was ingenious and several patents were issued covering it. In its most simplified form, the principle was for the gas piston itself to sense the pressure rise between low-base and high-powered magnum shotshells and to provide a variable cut-off of the gas flow. This ingenious concept eliminated the need for hand adjustment of power level and internalized all of the mechanism within the magazine tube.

The official description of the functioning of this new design was:

CYCLE OF OPERATION

The Model 878 Autoloading Shotgun is operated by utilizing the energy of a small portion of the propellant gases, conducted from the bore of a non-recoiling solid chamber barrel to a piston device. The initial recoil of the gun when fired causes the piston to be displaced toward the muzzle due to its inertia. This displacement restricts the amount of gas permitted to flow from the barrel bore to the piston chamber. The amount of restriction is proportional to the recoil and therefore to the power of the type of shell being fired. Thus the energy of rearward push applied to the piston and operating mechanism is controlled to practical limits. The breech bolt assembly is linked to the piston through the action bars and is caused to unlock and open by the rearward "PUSH" of the piston.

The detailed movements of the individual components which react to perform these basic operations are listed as follows:

Firing—With the cross bolt safety pushed to "FIRE" position (red band showing), the gun is fired each time by pulling trigger. The top section of trigger rotates forward carrying connector, in ready position, forward against sear. This movement thus pivots sear out of engagement with hammer. The released hammer then rotates forward urged by hammer plunger and recessed hammer spring, and strikes firing pin, which is spring-retracted and pinned within breech bolt. The firing pin in turn strikes primer and ignites the powder charge. Just before firing pin is struck, the hammer plunger, in its upward motion, engages disconnector. When disconnector is freed, forward end of disconnector is lowered from its position at the rear of left action bar and the rear section rises and lifts connector from contact with sear. The gun cannot be fired again until breech bolt is back in locked up position and trigger released, permitting the disconnector to again seat up behind the left action bar and connector to again make contact with sear, respectively.

After firing, the rearward movement of the gas propelled piston will open action and accomplish the Unlock, Extract, Eject, and Cock cycles. In detail they are as follows:

Unlock—The initial rearward movement of the action bar, after the shell is fired, carries slide to rear of breech bolt. In passing to rear of breech bolt, the slide cams locking block from recoil shoulder of barrel extension, thereby unlocking action and camming firing pin to rear. This blocks firing pin and prevents protrusion through bolt face.

Extract—Further movement of action bar rearward opens action. The breech bolt is moved back and the fired shell is extracted or withdrawn from chamber. The claw of extractor, which overhangs bolt face, grips the rim of shell tightly as extraction progresses. Pivot pressure is exerted on rear of extractor by extractor plunger and its recessed spring.

Eject—As fired shell clears chamber, its base engages shoulder on rear of ejector, which is located on left side of receiver. This causes shell to pivot so that front end is ejected first through ejection port.

Cocking—Before ejection occurs the rearward travel of breech bolt and slide forces the hammer downward against the coiled hammer spring to engage sear. The pressure of sear spring locks sear in a notched position against cocked hammer.

Feeding—The rearward motion of action bar carries the slide, breech bolt assembly, and locking block to rear of receiver. The termination of this rearward stroke also permits left action bar to cam left shell latch, thereby releasing the first shell from magazine. The released shell, urged rearward by pressure from the spring loaded magazine follower is fed back onto the depressed carrier. The piston then travels forward under force of compressed action spring. The slide and breech bolt assembly, being linked to the piston through action bars, also travel forward. A notch in the bottom surface of slide engages carrier dog during this forward travel. Continued travel forces carrier dog downward which by means of its pivoted attachment to rear of carrier, urges carrier upward. The

raised carrier positions the shell for the subsequent "load" phase of the closing cycle.

Loading—As action further closes with carrier pivoted into its loading position, the advancing bolt contacts head of shell, urging it forward and into chamber, the carrier dog, released from pressure of the passing slide, is forced upward by carrier dog follower and its recessed spring, and pivots carrier downward to its normal depressed position. The oncoming next shell from magazine, being retained by right shell latch, is released by camming action of the returning right action bar. This shell is then intercepted and held by left shell latch until the next feeding cycle.

Locking—As the shell is loaded fully into chamber, action closes and the breech bolt is "Home" against shell. The travel of the slide within the bolt continues and cams locking block into recoil shoulder of barrel extension. The locking block secures breech bolt firmly against chambered shell and in turn is supported fully in barrel extension by slide as its forward travel is completed. With locking block fully seated in recoil shoulder of barrel extension, the passageway through locking block then allows for proper protrusion of firing pin through bolt face to fire gun. The return motion is completed as slide comes to rest within and against front section of breech bolt. This fully locked action enables disconnector to clear end of left action bar. The suspended spring actuated connector will then be released and drop to a position to again contact notch on sear. As soon as shooter's finger is released from having compressed trigger, the bottom of trigger moves forward and the top moves rearward, and gun is again ready to fire.

The Model 878 was offered only in 12 gauge, and the design of the gas system limited magazine capacity to two shots. The addition of a shell in the chamber gave an overall capacity of three shots. Weight of the shotgun was about 7 pounds. The Model 878 was available with many options. Plain and ventilated-rib barrels were manufactured in 26-, 28- and 30-inch lengths with choke options of improved cylinder through full. The basic M878 field gun had a plain receiver and plain walnut stocks and was sold at a substantially lower price than the Sportsman-58 shotgun. Deluxe versions, such as the Model 878 SA "Automaster" skeet gun shown in Figure 7-31, were also available: This model, with ventilated rib, roll-engraved receiver and checkered butt stock and forearm, was a premium-priced and rather un-

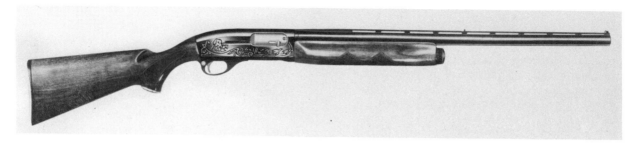

Figure 7-31   Remington Model 878 SA shotgun.

usual variation of the Model 878 design. Although this was an excellent shotgun, its production life was fairly short, as it was soon superseded by the Model 1100.

Remington Model 1100

In 1963 Remington introduced one of the most successful auto-loading shotguns ever designed This was the Model 1100 which continues to prove enormously popular. It was introduced at a price of $150.00, and the Remington long-recoil model 11-48 was continued in the line at a price of $135.00. The basic 12-gauge field-grade Model 1100 shotgun is shown in Figure 7-32. A year after the 12-gauge introduction, the 16- and 20-gauge models were produced. Five years later, in 1969 28-gauge and 410 versions were introduced. A deluxe 410 Model 1100 SA Skeet gun is shown in Figure 7-33.

The full line of Model 1100 shotguns includes a staggering array of options. In addition to the basic 12-, 16- and 20-gauge models, there are three lightweight shotguns, the 20-gauge lightweight, the 28 gauge and the 410. All are offered with plain and ventilated-rib barrels, choke options, and variations in the amount of ornamentation.

The Model 1100 shotgun has a concentric gas system which surrounds the magazine tube and this allows an increase in the magazine capacity to four shots plus a fifth in the chamber for all but the 410 which has an overall capacity of four shells. Barrels are available from 22 inches in length in cylinder bore with rifle sights, for deer hunting, up through the 26-inch length for skeet shooting and up to a maximum of 30-inch in full choke. The average weights of the shotguns are 7½ pounds in 12 gauge, 7¼ pounds in 16 gauge, 7 pounds in 20 gauge, 6½ pounds in 20 gauge lightweight, 6¼ pounds in 28 gauge and 6¾ pounds in the 410. Ventilated-rib barrels add about ¼ of a pound.

Figure 7-32   Remington Model 1100 auto-loading shotgun.

Figure 7-33   Remington Model 1100 skeet shotgun.

A schematic illustration of the Remington Model 1100 gas system is shown in Figure 7-34. The gas system is a ring which surrounds the magazine tube, rather than being housed inside. The gas cylinder is a short large-diameter ring which is brazed to the barrel. Long diagonal gas ports vent gas from the barrel into the very small initial volume between the piston and cylinder. Relatively small gas ports are fitted. On the model that was examined in detail two ports .084 inches in diameter were drilled. The piston area is relatively small and great care must be used in sealing the system since many possible gas-leakage paths exist. The way Remington solved this problem is shown in the lower illustration. As the gas pressure flows into the annular space, it drives both forward and to the rear. As it drives forward it compresses a V-shaped barrel seal inwards against the magazine tube, thus sealing the gas leakage towards the front. Gas driving to the rear contacts

two split piston rings. The front ring is called the piston and is designed so that the gas pressure drives it inwards, sealing the gas-leakage path between the piston and the magazine tube. The rear ring is known as the piston seal, and is designed to be driven outward, sealing off the gas-leakage path between the piston and cylinder. The gas pressure is transmitted through these two rings to the action bar sleeve which is identified with "No. 3" in the lower illustration. The action bar sleeve in turn is connected to the action bars (slide arms) which transmit the force rearward into the slide as in previous Remington designs.

The Model 1100 gas system has no specific design feature that would provide automatic compensation between light and Magnum shotshells. The gas ports are located only 9 inches from the breech face, and this in combination with the small initial volume in the gas system gives relatively high pressure levels. Instrumented tests at

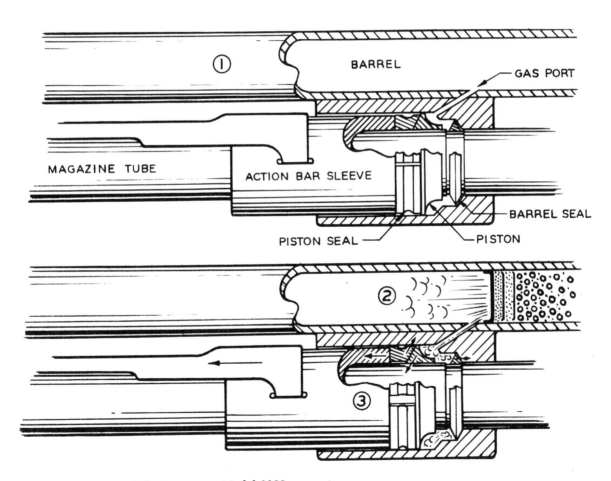

Figure 7-34 Details of the Remington Model 1100 gas system.

the Winchester Research ranges showed pressures of 2,000 psi with Winchester Ranger shotshells, and 2,800 psi maximum with Magnum shotshells. These pressure levels compare to approximately 500 pounds per square inch in gas systems with large initial volumes such as the Winchester Model 1400, the Remington Model 58, and the Remington Model 878. With such high pressure levels in the gas system, Remington engineers have provided compensating factors to bring the operating energy to the correct limits. The compensating factors are the small piston area and the relatively small diameter and long length of the gas ports, which are angled sharply to the rear. (This construction throttles the gas flow, as the gas must turn a very sharp corner, and then travel down a long, slender hole.) In addition, the piston travels only a small distance before the gas pressure is vented to the atmosphere. Since the gas ports are relatively close to the breech face (9 inches away) there would be a tendency to early unlocking, but the Remington designers have compensated for this by a long "free travel" of the action-bar assembly (.675 inches) before the bolt is picked up and unlocked.

The Remington Model 1100 automatic shotgun has become enormously popular and sales have reached very high levels.

Chapter 8

SHOTGUN AMMUNITION

EARLY SHOTGUN AMMUNITION

The ammunition for muzzle-loading shotguns was simple but the loading procedure was tedious. Assuming a double-barreled shotgun, the shotgunner first measured out a charge of powder for each barrel, then took two wads placing one in the muzzle of each barrel, withdrew the ramrod and pressed the wads down hard onto the black powder. The air in the barrel escaped around the wad and out the vent at the breech. The next step was to take a shot bag or shot measure and pour a charge of shot into each barrel. A second wad was placed in the mouth of each barrel and driven home with the ramrod. The final step was to place a percussion cap on the nipple or, in the case of a flintlock, a fresh charge of priming powder in the pans.

This type of ammunition had several advantages. It was relatively cheap and simple and it allowed the gunner to adjust his load for the particular shot he anticipated. The disadvantages were that the procedure was so slow and clumsy, and in the rush of reloading in the field bad accidents occurred when both powder charges were accidentally put into one barrel.

Military shotgun cartridges were usually assembled in paper tubes, like the musket loads. The most common was the buckshot, and often the layers of shot were carefully stacked in the paper tubes and then tied in place by string around the outside of the tube, constricting the paper in between each layer of shot. These paper shotshells had the great advantage of assembling powder, wads, and shot into one premeasured package, but they were rarely used by sportsmen because of cost and tradition.

Early breechloading shotguns, such as the Sharps, could be loaded with loose powder and ball, but the shooter was encouraged to make up paper cartridges.

Ammunition for the Sharps Shotguns

The Sharps catalogue of the early 1860s described the procedure for making shot cartridges, using a double-ended wooden stick, one end of which had a tapered contour and was used for forming the shot container, the other end, of a slightly smaller diameter, being cylindrical and used for forming the powder tube. The description given in the catalogue is:

> The SHOTGUN can be used with loose ammunition, loading at the breech, with one ounce of shot and about 60 grains of powder; and although the powder does not fill the cavity at the breech, no danger need be apprehended. The use of Shot Cartridges has great advantages over any other method, and they are made as follows:
>
> Place the conical part of the Cartridge Stick on the paper as in diagram No. 1, wind the paper and twist and firmly compress the part of it projecting over the end of the stick; withdraw the stick and charge with one ounce of shot, covering with a wad suited to the bore of the barrel.

172

Place the straight end of the stick on the paper as in diagram No. 2, and wind and secure the end of the paper, as before; withdraw the stick and charge with about 60 grains of powder, fold the open end and paste or tie the two parts together.

An assembled Sharps shot cartridge is shown in Figure 8-1. A slightly tapered paper cylinder forming the shot cavity was rolled around the tapered stick and the overhanging end twisted to close the mouth of the tube. One ounce of soft lead shot was poured into the open end and a tight fitting pressed into the tube resting on the shot column. A second paper tube of slightly smaller diameter was rolled up around the cylindrical end of the stick and one end pasted shut. Paste was placed on the outside of the tube which was then slid into the paper shot tube, resting on the wad. The open end of the powder cavity was then filled with 60 grains of black powder and the end folded over to retain the charge.

The cartridge was loaded in the shotgun by simply sliding the entire assembly in through the loading trough with the fingers. A small part of the powder cavity and the folded paper tail extended out the rear of the chamber. As the breech

block was raised the back end was cut off, exposing the fresh powder charge. A percussion cap was placed on the nipple and the loading was finished. As the shotgun was fired, the gas pressure drove the wad forward carrying the shot and part of the paper shot tube up the barrel and ejecting the assembly out of the muzzle. The Sharps shotgun would probably have given a pretty good pattern for there was no top wad to scatter the shot.

Sharps rifles and shotguns were excellent firearms for the rugged conditions in the United States. In an emergency even the shotguns could be loaded with loose powder and shot. This could be done by wadding a small ball of paper and shoving it in the barrel, then pouring in a one-ounce shot charge followed by the wad and then a loose charge of 60 grains of powder. This was similar to the procedure used with muzzle-loading shotguns, but did not require ramming the charge the full length of the barrel. It was fairly easy for the shooter to spend some evenings rolling up paper cartridges using the simple directions enclosed with the Sharps shotguns. Any paper could be used, but a cheap, unsized, coarse-grained paper was the best since it burned easily. This type of paper was also the most readily available on the frontier.

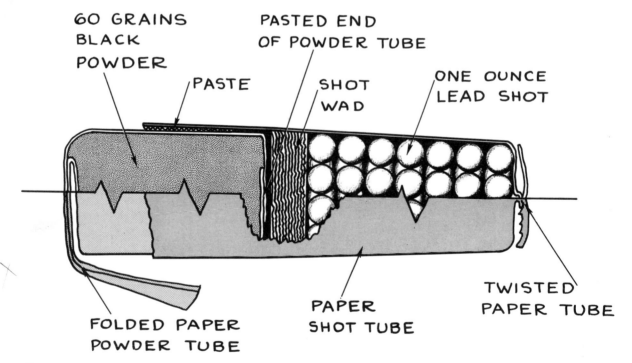

Figure 8-1 Paper shot cartridge for Sharps shotgun.

In the early 1860s improvements were made in the Sharps ammunition for rifles. Cartridges were made both with paper and linen bodies, but instead of a folded tail a flat base of "gold beaters skin" was used. It was not necessary for the breech block to cut off this base for it was so thin the flame could easily penetrate and ignite the powder. It was important that the paper be fully burned and not leave glowing embers in the chamber, for these might ignite the next cartridge as the shooter was loading it in the chamber. One way to solve this problem was to use the coarse grained, unglazed paper and nitrate the paper so that it burned rapidly. This improvement was incorporated in many of the factory cartridges loaded for Colt's and Sharps' firearms during the 1860s.

Lancaster Centerfire Shotshells

An early example of a centerfire shotshell is shown in Figure 8-2. The system, introduced into England by Lancaster in 1852, is an example of the transition firearms and ammunition which incorporated improvements, but in an imperfect form. The Lancaster shell consisted of a tubular body with a copper disk which closed the base in. The copper disk had four flash holes punched through it. Priming material was smeared on the center of this disk and then the entire head assembly was held together by a thin copper reinforcement, much like the brass base used on modern shotshells. The powder charge was then poured in the mouth of the case and a fiber over-powder wad pressed in place. The shot charge was measured and dropped on the wad and an over-shot wad pressed in the mouth of the case. The mouth was slightly crimped over to retain the wad.

The Lancaster shotguns were usually double barreled, with outside hammers. As the trigger was pulled the odd-looking hammer fell, driving a central firing pin forward. The blunt nose of the firing pin crushed the priming between the thin copper outer wrapper and the copper plate. As the priming ignited, it flashed through the four holes igniting the main charge and ejecting the shot up the barrel. These were probably tricky shotshells to manufacture. American experimenters had tried to make rimfire cartridges by pouring a uniform thin layer of priming into the head of the case. They found that when the priming at the rim ignited, the large priming charge developed so much force that it tended to bulge and split the head of the case and drive the bolt to the rear. This same kind of problem could be anticipated with the Lancaster type of ammuni-

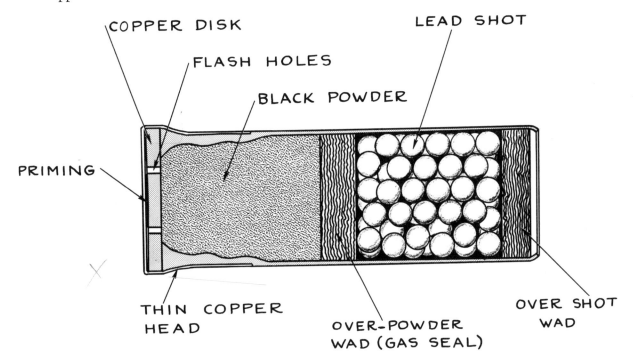

Figure 8-2 Lancaster centerfire shotshell.

174

tion. Priming charges explode violently and in the Lancaster the gas pressure could act across the entire head of the shell, tending to drive the thin copper outer wrapper and the punched copper disk apart. If the priming charge was just right this force could be contained and channeled through the four holes into the main charge. If it was too large it would tend to split the head of the case, causing gas leakage at the breech. If it was too small it would rapidly quench between the two large, cold metal surfaces.

Earliest American Centerfire Shotshells

During the 1850s shotshells using centerfire primers were developed in France. A French designer, M. Pottet, secured a patent in 1855 showing all the essential elements of a successful centerfire shotshell and started manufacture in France. By 1861 the design had been introduced into England by a Mr. Daw who designed a double-barreled shotgun to handle the new and improved ammunition. Daw and Company was the only exhibitor of centerfire shotguns and ammunition at the English International Exhibition in 1862. Although Daw secured a British patent it was based directly on the Pottet patent of 1855 with minor changes in the shape of the anvil inside the primer.[1] Later the patent was broken by Messrs. Ely Brothers of England, and centerfire shotguns and ammunition became widely used in England and on the continent.

The developments in the United States came more slowly. There was no aristocratic clientele willing and able to pay for luxurious new shotgun designs with expensive ammunition. American hunters were very much interested in better shotguns and ammunition, but they were quite used to working with loose powder, wads and shot in their muzzle-loading shotguns and had no intention of paying high prices for "new-fangled" factory-loaded ammunition. What the Americans wanted was rugged reliable cartridge cases that could easily be reloaded during the evening in preparation for the next day's shooting. With the low pressures of black-powder shotguns, good metallic shotshells would last almost indefinitely if they were washed out carefully after each day's shooting. This combination gave the American hunter ammunition that would work in any

weather and allowed quick reloading for fast shooting. Early American shotgun designs were offshoots of the military designs of the 1850s and Civil War. The Sharps shotguns of the 1850s are a good example. The difference between the military carbine models and the shotgun was really limited to the barrel, sights and ornamentation.

Maynard Shotgun and Ammunition

Edward Maynard, a dentist in New York City, was also a successful inventor. During the early 1850s he invented a tape-priming mechanism which was adopted for all United States military small arms in 1855. This consisted of a long tape of paper containing dots of fulminate priming compound spaced at intervals, like a roll of child's caps. A special mechanism inside the lock plate of the rifle or pistol was automatically indexed by the hammer motion and fed a fresh spot of fulminating compound for each shot. Maynard also invented a single-shot breech-loading rifle and carbine which were used during the Civil War. Some 2,157,000 rounds of .50-caliber ammunition for Maynard carbines was purchased during the War. This is not a large quantity of ammunition compared to 21,819,000 rounds for the Burnside carbine or 58,238,924 rounds for the Spencer lever-action firearms.

The Maynard cartridge was made from a deep-drawn brass cup soldered to perforated brass discs. The same base construction was used in the Maynard shotshells shown in Figure 8-3. The Maynard ammunition of the Civil War period was "externally primed." The shotshell contained a black-powder charge, wads and shot and there was a small hole punched in the center of the brass disc. Ignition was provided by a regular percussion cap on a nipple, as in the Sharps percussion shotgun. The flame from the percussion cap passed through small passages and was directed to the small hole punched in the head of the shotshell. It flashed through and ignited the main charge ejecting the shot and wads from the barrel.

Maynard began experimenting with self-primed ammunition and submitted a modification of this cartridge for the Army tests in 1886, consisting of a pellet of priming compound between the bottom of the case and a copper cover.[2]

---

[1]Berkely R. Lewis, Letter January 9, 1972.

[2]Berkely R. Lewis, *Small Arms and Ammunition in the U.S. Service* (Washington, D.C.: Smithsonian, 1956).

The Maynard shotguns were modifications of the Civil War breechloading action—a single-shot design with a movable barrel controlled by an under lever. As the lever was thrown down, the barrel slid forward and then could be tipped upwards at a slight angle for reloading. A fresh shell was placed in the chamber and when the lever was lifted it drew the barrel back and locked it into a firm position against the standing breech.

In the late 1860s Maynard developed self-primed shotshell ammunition and by 1873 had achieved the designs shown in the lower illustration of Figure 8-3. The ammunition consisted of a soldered assembly of a thin deep-drawn brass cup and heavy turned brass head. The empty shotshell itself was very heavy. A 20-gauge shell (illustrated) weighed 409 grains empty or 9/10 of an ounce. The illustration is based on careful measurements of a hand-loaded Maynard shotshell from the Winchester Gun Museum.

The shotshell was primed with a Berdan-type primer, similar to that used today in European ammunition. The primer cavity is quite large at .250 inches in diameter and the anvil is hollow. There are two shallow cuts in the head, so that a sharp pointed tool could be used to dig out primer from the side after firing. The primer could also be removed by punching through the flash hole with a long nail. The cuts in the head of the case really made it easier to remove the fired primer from the outside.

After a fresh primer was pressed into place, a black powder charge of 75 grains (slightly under three drams) was measured and thrown into the case. A single-fiber wad was pressed into the case on top of the powder. Careful examination of this wad shows that it is made of a fibrous material, felted to form an interlocking mass with the appearance of horsehair. Both surfaces of the wad have been covered with a thin layer of paper glued in place. The shot charge weighs 410 grains (.9 oz.) and consists of a miscellaneous assortment of shots ranging in size from .090" to .130" in diameter. Modern shooters are aware that this is a

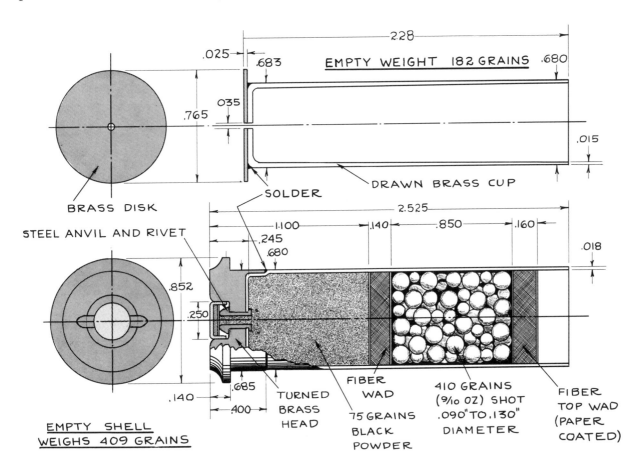

Figure 8-3 Maynard shotshell.

poor way to load the shotshell, since the different sizes of shot will follow varying trajectories and at any reasonable distance the pattern would separate with the heavier shot flying high, and the finer shot flying low. The time of flight would also be different, with the heavier shot reaching the target first. The shot is retained in the shell by a second paper-coated fiber wad. The wads are fairly light at 6 grains each. The wads were probably identical at the time of loading, but the over-powder wad has become slightly more compressed during the past 100 years and is now .020 inch thinner than the top wad. There is room in the case for about 1⅛ ounces of shot.

This is a relatively unscientific shotshell assembly for two reasons. First the shooter would get much better performance if he had put a thick wad over the powder to provide better gas sealing, and only a thin wad to retain the shot. In effect the over-shot wad does nothing to assist in sealing the gas but it is a relatively large wad, tending to spread the shot charge once it leaves the muzzle. The second drawback, of course, is the use of varying sizes of shot, as has already been explained.

The hollow anvil of the Maynard shotshell was a fairly common design of the 1870s. Modern European ammunition using Berdan primers always uses a solid anvil with flash holes drilled through the thin web to the sides of the anvil.

Draper Shotshells

An early shotshell that may show some of the origin of this type of anvil construction is shown in Figure 8-4. This is a 10-gauge Draper shotshell which is marked on the head "Patented Nov. 29, 1864 F.D. & Co." The construction was actually patented by W. H. Wills but manufacture was by Draper and Company. These shotshells must have been extremely expensive, for they consist of three machined elements. The body of the shell was machined as a long thin cylinder with a partition at the base. A special hardened-steel nipple was screwed into a central thread. The nipple was similar in size to those used on percussion revolvers and the shotshell was primed with an ordinary pistol percussion cap. The base flange was provided by a third machined element which screwed into the body. It is not known whether the head had to be removed on each shot to reprime the case. It would appear possible to remove the percussion cap by using a long slender pin pressing through the flash hole and driving the percussion cap off. Repriming would be a simple matter of fitting the fresh percussion cap over the tapered steel nipple and pressing it until it was flush with the head of the case. Although the walls of the shell were machined fairly heavy, they tapered to a thin mouth edge to provide a good gas seal at the front of the chamber. Such a large taper on

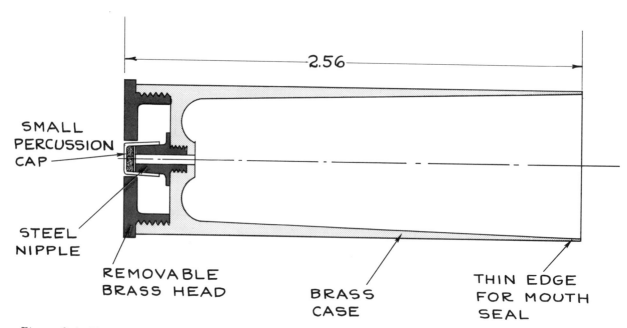

Figure 8-4 Draper centerfire shotshell, 10 gauge.

the inside of the shell had a disadvantage, for the wad fitting over the powder would be squeezed to a smaller diameter than the bore and encourage gas leakage around the wad during its passage in the barrel.

The Draper shotshell of 1864 would be very expensive to manufacture today and would have been even more expensive in terms of the techniques available in the mid-1860s. A small company, the Connecticut Cartridge Company, recently manufactured brass cartridges such as the .50-70 by using automatic screw machines to cut the cases out of solid brass bars, but even with modern automatic machinery these cases sold for $.50 apiece. It is estimated that the Draper cases would cost at least $2.50 apiece if manufactured today on the equipment available in 1864. If the cases were carefully washed after each firing they would last almost indefinitely.

American Shotshell Patents

The most significant early patent for paper shotshell construction was the French Pottet patent of 1855. The Pottet and the English Daw designs were both manufactured in the 1860s. C. D. Leet secured the first United States patent on paper shotshells with a metallic base. He sold his patent to the Union Metallic Cartridge Company which manufactured shotshells on Leet machinery. A man named Chamberlain made the first mass-production shotshell-loading machine.[1] There were many American patents in the late 1860s such as G. H. Daw, No. 89,563 (issued in 1869) for a tube of sheet metal rolled up and soldered at the edges with the rear end crimped into a base cup. An inner wad was made of pulp and pressed into the base of the shotshell. C. W. Lancaster patented a paper shotshell with a paper case, heavy reinforcement at the base with external metal reinforcement and flange. Leet and Hotchkiss patented an important centerfire shotshell design (No. 89,278) on December 28, 1869. This construction included a centerfire primer surrounded by a coiled and compressed paper base wad which was then fitted inside a paper tube and retained by a metallic head.

The Union Metallic Cartridge Company and Remington were early leaders in the manufacture of paper shotshells. The Winchester Repeating

Arms Company manufactured only rimfire cartridges with copper cases until 1873 when the 44-40 centerfire cartridge was introduced. Once the manufacturing techniques were developed for the extensive metalworking required in centerfire ammunition, Winchester began to diversify production, steadily adding new sizes of centerfire and rimfire ammunition.

In 1877 Winchester introduced brass and paper shotshells. The brass shells were introduced in 8, 10, 11, 12, 14, 15, and 16 gauge and were stamped on the head "W. R. A. Co. No. [gauge]." In 1878 the line was simplified to include only 8, 10, 12, 14, 16, and 20 gauge. They were offered in two quality levels and the *premium* or First Quality were stamped on the head "Winchester No. [gauge]." A second line of shells was manufactured and marked on the head "W.R.A. Co. No. [gauge]."

In 1881 the second style of shell was dropped and tin-plated shells in any standard gauge were offered at an additional cost of $1.00 per hundred. In 1882 nickel-plated shells were offered at an additional cost of $2.50 per hundred. The use of tin and nickel plating reduced the corrosion problems with black-powder and early-primer residue.

DRAWN-BRASS SHOTSHELLS

By the mid-1870s American cartridge manufacturing had developed so that the complex shape of the brass head and the body could be formed in one piece by a series of progressive punches and dies. This was a remarkable manufacturing achievement for a century ago. The design of a Remington shotshell manufactured at Ilion, New York, is shown in Figure 8-5. The basic technique was to take a disk of brass which was formed into a cup in a press. Progressive punches and dies were designed which formed the head shape and drew the walls up to an eventual length of 2½ to 3 inches. The head design required a powerful press and a great deal of metalworking to form the complex shapes, including the rim and primer pocket. Accurate die alignment was required to form the thin walls, which tapered from about .020 of an inch thick at the base to .012 at the mouth. This Remington design was introduced in the 1870s and remained in production through the nineteenth century. The primer construction can be seen as an evolutionary design from the Maynard and Draper shotshells, but the Reming-

[1]B. R. Lewis, letter of January 9, 1972.

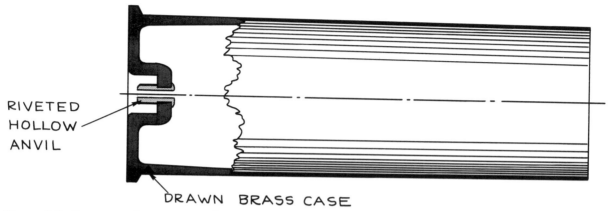

RIVETED
HOLLOW
ANVIL

DRAWN BRASS CASE

Figure 8-5   Remington brass shotshell of the 1880s.

ton shell was far lighter and stronger than the earlier two-piece designs.

Brass has the property of "cold working" as it is drawn through a series of punches and dies. At critical points in the process it became too hard and had to be annealed by being heated to several hundred degrees and quickly quenched in water. The softened brass was then sent back to the manufacturing line for more drawing operations. The result was that the hardness of the brass and grain structure could be controlled to give a very hard surface and high tensile strength at the thin mouth of the case and a softer but tougher metallurgy in the head. The final step in the process was to rivet in the hollow steel anvil or cone. The shells were listed in a Remington catalogue of the 1880s as:

THE REMINGTON
NUMBER ONE,
BRASS SOLID HEAD SHELLS,
STEEL CONE,
uses the
REMINGTON OR BERDAN PRIMER,
Can be reloaded indefinitely.
10, 12, 14, 16 A & 16 B.
Fits any Breech-Loading Gun

Price per 100 . . . .$12.00
Put up in boxes of 20 each, per box 2.40
Put up in boxes of 24 each (with Primer
   Extractor and Reprimer), per box 3.60
Remington No. 1 Primers, for use in Shot-
   Gun Shells, per 1,000 . . . . 2.00
Primer Extractor and Reprimer 1.25

One-Piece Drawn Brass Shotshells

One of the techniques used to advertise ammunition was to make up cartridge display boards which showed a sample of each type of ammunition available in the company's product line. The Winchester cartridge board for 1874 shows all rimfire with the single exception of the 44-40 centerfire cartridge. By 1879 the line had been expanded to include 25 varieties of rimfire cartridges, 24 of centerfire cartridges, four sizes of paper shotshells and eight different brass shotshells. A typical ten-gauge brass shotshell is shown in Figure 8-6. The upper half of the illustration shows an empty shotshell as sold to the customer for loading. Dimensions have been added to emphasize the very thin sections of metal required to hold the low pressure of the black-powder charge. The lower half of the illustration shows a fully loaded shotshell with the large black-powder charge, a tight-fitting wad to provide a gas seal between powder and shot and a second wad to retain the shot in position in the shell. The mouth of the shell was crimped over slightly to retain the upper wad. Dimensions of four sizes of Winchester brass shotshells are compared in the table below:

Head Marking	Length	Rim Diameter	Head Diameter
Winchester No 10	2.875"	.915"	.840"
Winchester No. 12	2.625	.873	.803
Winchester No. 16	2.620	.810	.750
Winchester No. 20	2.500	.750	.690
WRA Co. Rival No. 28	2.500	.670	.615

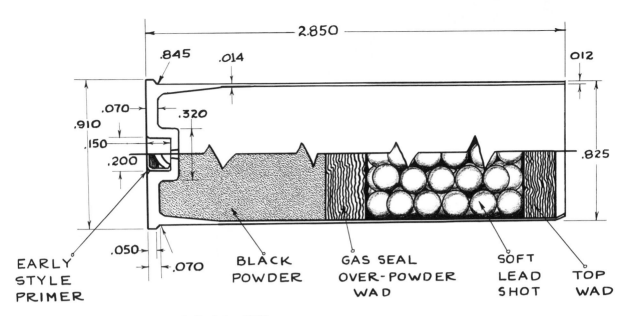

Figure 8-6 Typical brass shotshell of the 1870s.

Similar shells were manufactured by other leading makers such as Remington at Ilion, New York, Union Metallic Cartridge Company at Bridgeport, Connecticut, and by the Government at Frankford Arsenal.

In 1881 the Army issued modified trap-door Springfield rifles fitted with 20-gauge shotgun barrels to units stationed in the West to be used for hunting game to supplement daily food supplies. Empty primed 20-gauge shells were made at Frankford Arsenal and were loaded and reloaded by the units in the field. The boxes were marked "These shells may be fired in the same gun an indefinite number of times without resizing. They should be cleaned as often as possible by steeping in hot water or vinegar and subsequent brushing. Manufactured at Frankford Arsenal." Early shells were made of gilding metal which had the appearance of copper, but by the mid-1880s the design had been shifted over to a tinned brass case.

In 1877 Winchester introduced a line of one-piece drawn-brass shotshells. The Winchester brass shotshell of 1880, shown in Figure 8-6, is typical of the construction of high-quality, one-piece shells. The life of brass shotshells on the American hunting scene was amazingly long. Remington, for example, continued manufacture of these cartridge cases until 1957 and the last shipments were made in 1965.

The Remington one-piece brass shotshells were listed in the same catalogue of the 1880s as the two-piece shells tabulated above. The one-piece shells were sold at the slightly lower price of

$10.00 per hundred compared to $12.00 for the shells with the riveted-in steel anvil. Since the one-piece shotshells required a more complex primer, which contained its own anvil, it could be expected that the primers would be more expensive. They were in fact cheaper at only $1.50 per thousand, compared to $2.00 per thousand for the Berdan primers. The Remington one-piece shells were specified in the catalogue as follows:

REMINGTON NO. 2
uses
Remington Primers, No. 2½,
Winchester Primers, No. 2,
or Wesson Primers, No. 2½.
Can be reloaded indefinitely.
Fits any Breech-Loading Gun.

Price per 100	$10.00
Put up in boxes of 20 each, per box	2.00
Remington No. 2½ Primers, for use in Shot-Gun Shells, per 1,000	1.50
Nickel-Plated Shells, extra, per dozen	.50

Brass Shotshells with Serrated Mouths

With care, brass shotshells lasted almost indefinitely. They could be reloaded with simple tools and many hand loaders simply continued to use much of the equipment they used with muzzle-loading shotguns. After the brass cases were deprimed, washed and dried, a fresh primer could be pushed into the primer pocket with a wooden stick. Good muzzle-loading shotgun powder flasks of the 19th century had graduated charges which allowed the setting for powder charges of 2½ to

4 drams. The charging tube could simply be set to the appropriate volume and the powder charge dropped into the shotshell. Excellent wads were available from English and American manufacturers and the more sophisticated American shooters used these to load their shells. Other shooters simply cut wads from leather or any other handy material and rammed them down on top of the powder with a stick. The shot charge was measured out by volume, often from a standard shot pouch that had been used with a muzzle-loading shotgun. Some hunters didn't even go this far, but merely poured shot into the brass case until there was just room for the top wad. The top wad was pushed in with the fingers and this left only the problem of crimping over the mouth of the case to retain the wad. If no tools were available the hand loader could simply turn the shell upside down and slam it onto a hard surface to slightly close in the case mouth. This was not only a dangerous practice, it also tended to shift everything inside the shell, so that the powder charge was no longer compressed.

An interesting design, developed in the 1880s, is shown in cross section in the lower illustration of Figure 8-7. The shell was standard in all respects except for the teeth cut into the mouth. Eight serrations were spaced about .165 inches apart all the way around the case, and the outer tips had a flat of about .040 inches. Since these were deluxe cases, many were given special corrosion protection such as tinning or nickel plating.

They were also offered as factory-loaded brass shotshells, as shown in the upper figure. A view of the case mouth has been included to show the style of marking, and the way in which the points folded in to securely retain the top wad. Careful examination of the shell shows that the top wad was actually curled over as the points were closed in. After firing, these shells could be reloaded until the tips finally broke off making them useless.

There is good fun in shooting black-powder firearms, either rifles or shotguns. Instead of the sharp crack of modern ammunition it is more like a soft "boom" and a whoosh with a dull sound reverberating across the landscape and an enor-

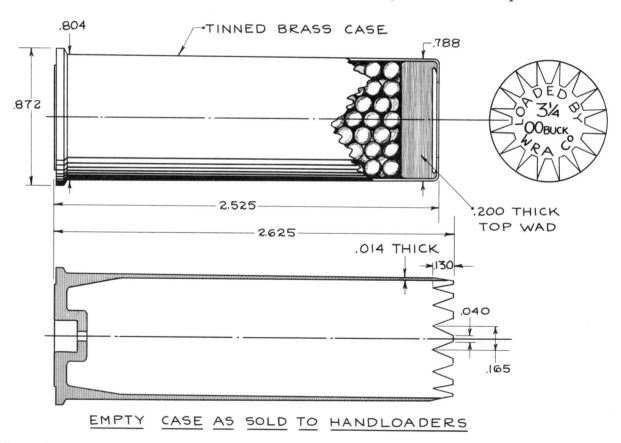

Figure 8-7 Brass shotshell of the 1880s with serrated mouth.

mous cloud of dense grey smoke pouring out the muzzle towards the target. An afternoon of shooting with one of these charcoal burners can really give a feeling of the tremendous changes in shotgun shooting during the past century.

EARLY PAPER SHOTSHELLS

In 1877 Winchester also introduced paper shotshells. These were sold empty for hand-loading purposes until 1886 when the company introduced its first loaded shotshell under the "Rival" trademark. The design evolution of the very early shells is shown in Figure 8-8. A thin sheet of paper was coated with glue and then wound around a mandril until the wall was about .035 of an inch thick. This many-layered tube was extraordinarily strong and resilient. For a 10-gauge shell the tube had an outside diameter of .840 of an inch and a length of about 2½ inches. Early shells had no waterproofing, but in the mid-1880s a wax coating was applied to remedy this defect.

A base wad of a porous gray paper .200 of an inch wide was rolled up into a cylinder .700 of an inch in diameter, with only a small hole in the center for the primer flash to pass through. Three or four layers of ½-inch long paper were coiled around the base wad and the entire assembly pressed into the long paper tube. A brass head, formed of thin metal by cupping and drawing, was placed over the paper tube and base wad and

swaged in place to lock all of the elements into a permanent assembly.

Between 1877 and 1884 the reinforcement on the sides was extended until it was ¾ of an inch above the base of the shell. This head construction was apparently quite satisfactory for it was used for many years.

American hunters must have become more affluent in the 1880s because it became worthwhile for Winchester to offer loaded paper shotshells in 1886. The design of a typical 10-gauge loaded shotshell of the 1880s is shown in Figure 8-9. Ten gauge was the most popular size, for a large internal volume was needed to hold the enormous black-powder charges plus 1 to 1½ ounces of shot. The head construction had changed little in the ten years since manufacture had started, the main difference being the use of a spiral strip of paper for the outermost wrappings of the base wad, which gave a stepped construction of tapering strength. The rolled paper tube was .035 inches thick and the reinforcements built up in increments of .013 to .017 in thickness, providing a gradually increasing strength down towards the base where the stress levels were highest.

A Winchester shotshell of 1884 was disassembled and examined in detail to create the figure. The date can be established by the head and base wad improvements, and the fact that it was not yet waterproofed. The technical achievements of the 1880s, particularly in working the

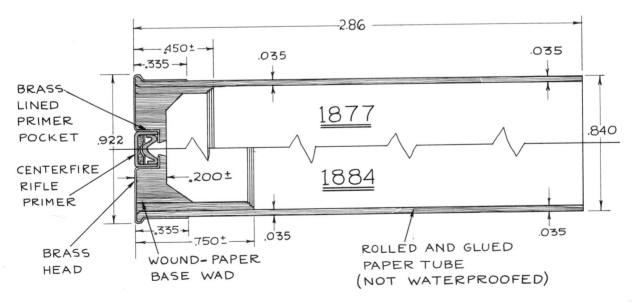

Figure 8-8 Winchester paper shotshells of 1877 and 1884. ╳

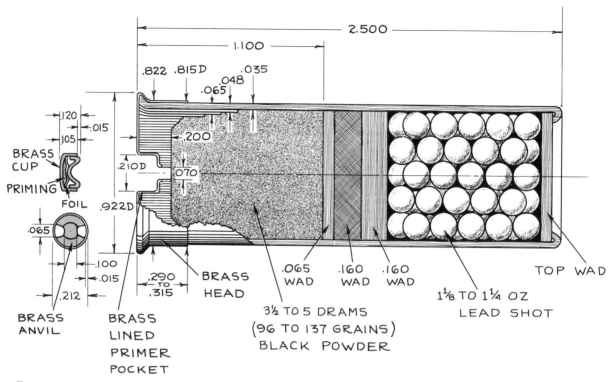

Figure 8-9   Typical loaded paper shotshell of the 1880s.

brass head of the shotshell, are impressive. A metallic primer pocket was formed from the brass head material and swaged into the paper base wad. This construction accepted the standard large rifle primer which is shown on the left side of the illustration. Because of the early machinery and techniques, the head was left untrimmed, and the height of the base varied from .290 to .315 around the circumference of the shell.

The primer is sophisticated, for the priming material was contained in a small pocket of tinfoil which is still bright and shiny after nearly 90 years. The primer is made of brass and the anvil is a very early design flanged up to form a cup which was a press fit in the primer cup. Two vents .065 inches in diameter were punched into the anvil to allow primer flame to pass into the main charge. In later years the design of the anvil was simplified until it resembled a conical three-legged stool. The three legs are sprung outwards to be an interference fit in the primer cup.

Black powder was relatively easy to ignite and burned at low pressure, so the same primers could be used for centerfire rifles, large pistol cartridges, and shotshells. Modern primers differ a great deal. Large rifle primers must have thick, hard cups to stand chamber pressures over 50,000 psi.

Pistol primers must have thinner cups to ignite with the weaker pistol firing pins. Modern shotshell powders are so difficult to ignite properly that they require an enormous priming charge, about double that for centerfire rifles, and a design known as the "battery cup" shotshell primer was created to meet these requirements.

The loading procedure for these shotshells was as follows:

1. Seat the large centerfire rifle primer in the head of the shotshell.

2. Measure a charge of 3½ to 5 drams (95.7 to 137 grains) of black powder and drop this in the shell.

3. Insert a hard ¹⁄₁₆-inch-thick wad and press it down on the powder charge, slightly compressing the charge.

4. Add two wads .160 inches in thickness to cushion the acceleration of the shot.

5. Measure 1⅛ to 1¼ ounces of soft lead shot and drop into shell.

6. Retain the shot with a thin top wad.

7. Spin over the end of the paper tube to retain the top wad.

During the 1870s and 1880s 10 gauge was the standard size. During the 1890s smaller gauges became popular such as 12, 14, 16 and 20.

BALLISTICS OF BLACK POWDER SHOTSHELLS

The first serious ballistic testing in the United States was performed at Washington Arsenal in the 1840s by a gifted Major of Ordnance, Alfred Mordeacai. These tests utilized a ballistic pendulum to measure bullet velocity. During the 1880s improved instrumentation was developed particularly the leBoulange chronographs and Schultz chronographs developed in Europe. Still, it was difficult to measure the performance of shotshells by any techniques available in the nineteenth century, so this area of ballistics was pretty well ignored.

It was not until the late 1960s that Winchester Group Research finally performed some load and development tests to establish what black-powder shotshell loads would be equivalent to current 12-gauge trap loads. The first tests were performed with commercial 12-gauge trap loads containing 23 grains of No. 450 LS Ball Powder. From a historical standpoint it was fortunate that these tests employed paper shotshells which closely simulate 19th-century black-powder shotshells.

There were minor differences, of course, for modern shells are assembled with a "cup wad," a heavy, waxed cardboard cup with the exposed edges facing the powder cavity. Gas pressure drives these edges outward, forming a better gas seal than the plain wads used in 19th-century shotshells. Cup wads were used in these tests immediately over the powder. Above the cup wad were assembled two conventional molded fiber wads, one ⅜ of an inch thick and one 7/16 of an inch thick. One and one eighth ounces of No. 7½ shot were loaded in the shell and a check showed that this constituted 400 pellets. The firing tests gave an average muzzle velocity of 1200 feet per second and a peak chamber pressure of 9,600 psi.

An equivalent black-powder shotshell load was developed to give the same velocity. Since the black powder required much more volume, the case was assembled with a cup wad plus a ⅜ inch molded fiber wad and again 1⅛ ounces of No. 7½ shot. It required 82 grains of FFFg black powder to give the same velocity. The peak chamber presure was 4,900 pounds psi.

The specifications and performance of both the smokeless and the black-powder shotshells are shown in the following table:

	3-1⅛-7½ Winchester Trap Load	3-1⅛-7½ Black Powder Shotshell
Propellant	21.0 Grains WC-450-LS (Ball Powder)	82.0 Grains DuPont FFFg (Black Powder)
Weight of Shot Charge	1⅛ Oz. (492 Grains)	1⅛ Oz. (492 Grains)
Shot Size	7½	7½
Weight of Wads	27 Grains	27 Grains
Muzzle Velocity (Average)	1202 Ft./Sec.	1205 Ft./Sec.
Peak Chamber Pressure Average	9600 Lb./In.²	4900 Lb./In.²
Kinetic Energy of Shot Charge	1579 Ft.-Lbs.	1587 Ft.-Lbs.
Efficiency (Ft.-Lbs. of Muzzle Energy Per Grain of Propellant)	79.3	20.4

The data on this table explains some of the enormous improvements in shotshell efficiency during the past few years. With the same amount of shot and wads loaded into the same type of shotshell a black-powder charge of 82 grains was required to duplicate the performance of 21 grains of modern smokeless ball powder. The ballistician measures these differences in terms of "propellant efficiency." This is defined as the number of foot-pounds of muzzle energy developed by each grain of the propellant charge. In both cases the kinetic energy of the shot at the muzzle is close to 1580 foot-pounds. The propellant charge actually has to accelerate both shot and the wads and the total energy delivered at the muzzle is 1,665 foot-pounds. This amount of energy means that each grain of the smokeless powder is developing 79.3 foot-pounds of muzzle energy.

The black powder is only one-quarter as efficient. The muzzle energy of the shot charge and the shot charge plus wads is the same for the smokeless powder load, but 82 grains of propellant is required to achieve this energy level. This calculates out to only 20.4 foot-pounds of muzzle energy per grain of black powder.

These figures are pretty consistent with the performance of 19th-century black-powder rifle ammunition. For example, the .58-caliber muzzle-loading rifles of the Civil War used a 60-grain powder charge to accelerate a 510-grain bullet to a muzzle velocity of 960 feet per second. This works out to 17.5 foot-pounds of muzzle energy per grain of propellant. Large cartridge rifles such as the Winchester .50-95-300 used a 90-grain powder charge to accelerate a 300-grain bullet to 1,557 feet per second for an efficiency of 18 foot-pounds of muzzle energy per grain of propellant. About the most efficient of the early black-powder firearms was the old .45-70 developed in 1873 after years of experimentation. A 67-grain black powder charge accelerated a 405-grain bullet to 1,318 feet per second for an efficiency of 23.3 foot-pounds of muzzle energy per grain of propellant. Almost every black powder rifle cartridge provided an efficiency between 15 and 23 foot-pounds of muzzle energy per grain of propellant.

Modern shotshell loads represent the most efficient ammunition in wide use today. Most rifle cartridges deliver efficiencies of 45 to 60 foot-pounds of muzzle energy per grain of propellant. The performance of the 21 grain ball powder charge in the shotshell listed in the table above at almost 80 foot-pounds of energy per grain represents close to the absolute peak of efficiency for modern ammunition. This extraordinary efficiency is due to these factors:

1. Initial burning of the propellant occurs within an insulated plastic chamber which minimizes heat loss.

2. The use of a solid plastic compression-formed base construction and paper or plastic cup wads to prevent gas leakage along the barrel means that almost all the pressure generated is used to accelerate the shot column.

3. The friction of the shot charge, wrapped in a plastic polyethelene sheet, along the bore gives much lower friction than a rifle bullet, which must be engraved by the rifling and is then in intense metal-to-metal contact with the barrel as it moves up the bore.

4. The large diameter of shotgun barrels allows the powder gas to expand to a very great extent before the shot leaves the muzzle. This could best be contrasted with a cartridge such as the .220 Swift where a powder charge twice as large must be burned in a barrel with only $\frac{1}{10}$ of the inside volume of a 12-gauge shotgun barrel. To burn the propellant in the .220 Swift the pressure must run over 50,000 pounds per square inch and the gas still has a pressure of over 10,000 pounds per square inch when the bullet leaves the muzzle. In a shotgun barrel, with its enormous internal volume, the propellant gas can expand only to about 500 pounds per square inch of pressure remaining at the time the shot charge leaves the muzzle.

A second series of tests were performed to load shotshells of equivalent pressure. The starting point was a black-powder shotshell load containing four drams (109 grains) of duPont FFFg black powder. A cup wad and molded fiber wad were assembled on top of the powder and $1\frac{1}{8}$ ounces of No. $7\frac{1}{2}$ shot was poured in. Since the black powder required so much volume in this load, the researchers were forced to hand load into a 3-inch compression-formed plastic shotshell. They used a cup wad, a single molded-fiber wad between the propellant and shot, and then closed the mouth of the case with a modern type of star crimp. The peak chamber pressure achieved by this load was 6,900 pounds per square inch.

Development of an equivalent smokeless-powder load required quite a bit of experimentation. The loads were developed in paper cases with a cup wad and two $\frac{1}{2}$-inch thick molded fiber wads over the propellant. It was found that WC-450 LS ball powder gave the best performance and that a charge of only 16 grains of ball propellant gave the equivalent pressures of 6,900 to 7,000 pounds per square inch.

This information is highlighted in the table below:

	$2\frac{1}{2}$-$1\frac{1}{8}$-$7\frac{1}{2}$ Modern Handload	4-$1\frac{1}{8}$-$7\frac{1}{2}$ Black Powder Shotshell
Propellant	16 Grains WC-450-LS Ball Powder	109 Grains DuPont FFFg Black Powder
Shot Weight	$1\frac{1}{8}$ oz.	$1\frac{1}{8}$ oz.
Shot Size	$7\frac{1}{2}$	$7\frac{1}{2}$
Muzzle Velocity (fps) (Average)	Unknown	Unknown
Peak Chamber Pressure (psi) (Average)	6900	6900

A comparison of the pressure-time curves of smokeless and black-powder shotshells is shown in Figure 8-10. These shells were loaded at a different time and it was found that a propellant charge of 18.5 grains of ball powder gave the equivalent muzzle velocity. The radically different characteristics of the pressure-time curves are apparent. The modern smokeless shotshell load is difficult to ignite. In fact, *shotshell primers normally require twice the priming charge of centerfire ammunition.* Even with the hot primer, ignition is slow and the pressure rises to only 1,500 psi at the end of a quarter of a millisecond. Pressure rise is then quite rapid to 8,800 psi at .7 milliseconds. The pressure then declines to ap-

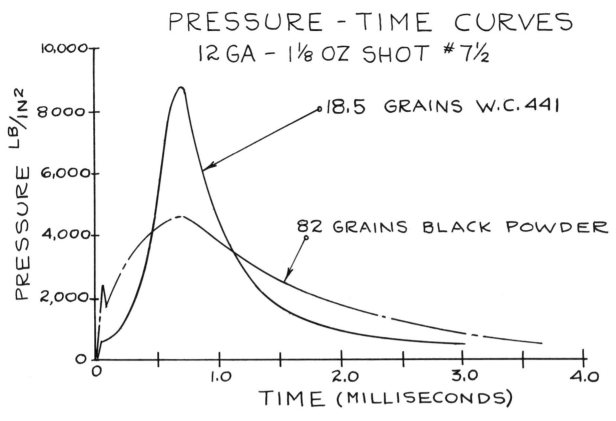

Figure 8-10 Pressure-time curves of black powder and smokeless shotshells.

proximately 500 psi at muzzle exit of the shot after 3 milliseconds.

The characteristics of the black-powder load are quite different. Ignition of black powder is relatively easy and the hot modern primer gave an extremely rapid pressure rise to about 2200 psi in less than $\frac{1}{10}$ of a millisecond. The pressure then fell back to 1,800 psi and then rose to its peak value of 4,700 psi. This characteristic of a sharp pressure rise (due to primer ignition) and then a decline as the main charge begins to burn is characteristic of many modern types of ammunition. It is seen in small-arms ammuntion and in cannon ammunition in the 20- to 30-millimeter range. The pressure-time characteristics of black powder has a much smoother profile to the curve with a low peak pressure and a much slower pressure decline. Since the shot is not accelerated as fast during the early phase of burning, it takes longer for the shot to reach the muzzle. While the bore time was 3 milliseconds with the smokeless load it is 3¾ milliseconds with the black-powder shotshell.

These curves show a very important thing. Since black-powder shotshells gave such low peak pressures they were quite safe in 19th-century shotguns with Damascus barrels or with longitudinally-welded plain shotgun barrels. A little thought shows that such shotguns could be extremely dangerous with modern high-pressure loads, which will develop twice the chamber pressure of the old black-powder designs.

EARLY SMOKELESS SHOTSHELLS

Black powder gives off a large quantity of dense gray smoke on each shot. For the wildfowl hunter this was a major nuisance for he could not tell whether his shot was high or low or even if the bird was hit until after the smoke rolled away. Soldiers had the same problem. Battlefields were enveloped in dense black-powder smoke and opposing armies could approach to suicidal ranges of 30 to 50 yards at least partly because after the first volley the soldiers simply couldn't see where the enemy was, and they continued to reload and generally blast away with very inaccurate results. There is a graphic description in *The Red Badge of Courage* of a battlefield scene in the American Civil War with the soldiers standing enveloped in the smoke of their own weapons, loading, aiming and firing with only the occasional red stab of an opposing shot to indicate where the enemy might be.

During the 1880s French chemists developed the first really practical smokeless propellants. Such experiments had been going on for centuries and some experimental ammunition using semi-smokeless propellants had even been assembled during the American Civil War. But by the 1880s the French introduced a radically new type of military ammunition, the 8mm Lebel cartridge, loaded with a smokeless propellant. This French cartridge was so advanced that it immediately made all other military ammunition obsolete and an enormous scramble was on to modernize and re-equip the world's armies with this new improvement. By the turn of the century every major army had followed the French lead, dropping their standard caliber from .45 to .30 and incorporating smokeless propellants.

The first propellants used in shotshells were known as "bulk smokeless." They were deliberately designed so that three drams of bulk smokeless would give the same performance as a three dram black-powder charge. This was a deliberate degrading of the performance of smokeless powder. Experiments performed by Winchester Group Research in the 1960s showed that modern smokeless propellants deliver approximately four times as much energy as black powder shotshells. Even

with the less efficient smokeless powders of the 1880s a three-dram charge of rifle powder would blow up most nineteenth-century shotguns. The solution was deliberately to add volume to shotgun smokeless powders so that they were safe with the measuring equipment used with black powder.

An early smokeless-powder shotshell is shown in Figure 8-11. It was designed to be the finest shotshell that could be manufactured with the technology of the 1890s. In order to prepare for the successful introduction of smokeless-powder ammunition Winchester had added a chemical laboratory to their ballistic laboratory, already equipped with the latest velocity measuring instrumentation. A young scientific graduate from Yale University was added to the staff to head the new laboratory and cope with the complex problems presented by this new and radically different propellant.

The Winchester "Leader" shotshell was loaded with either "EC," "Schultze," "S.S.," or "American Wood" smokeless bulk powder. The shells were furnished in five different loadings in 10 gauge, nine loadings in 12 gauge and one in 16 gauge. By 1900, 8-gauge and 20-gauge sizes had been added. Figure 8-11 shows a 10-gauge shell—the

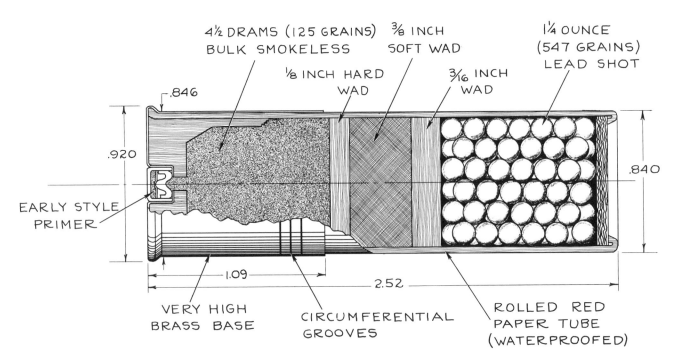

Figure 8-11 Smokeless shotshell of 1894.

most popular 19th-century size. The wound-paper base wad was extremely strong, tapering much further up the base than the earlier shotshell designs. The comparison can be seen by close examination with Figures 8-8 and 8-9. In addition, the brass head extended a full 1.09 inches up from the base of the shotshell, enclosing almost the entire powder cavity. The brass head was still extensively worked to form a brass primer pocket in the head of the shell, allowing the use of a rifle style primer. A ⅛-inch thick hard over-powder wad was rammed down onto the powder and this was backed up with a ⅜-inch soft wad and a ³⁄₁₆-inch soft wad. Leader shells were normally loaded with 1¼ ounces of soft lead shot topped by an over-shot wad. The red paper tube was then rolled over the end to retain the top wad.

A small but significant improvement had been added to the head construction. The Superintendent of the ammunition plant had found by experimentation that shallow grooves rolled into the brass head would greatly assist in locking the head to the paper tube. The grooves did not need to be deep; as gas pressure expanded the paper tube from the inside, they provided locking edges and helped prevent separation of the head from the tube.

Hand loaders found many problems with smokeless powder. Some powders were so difficult to ignite that the hand loaders would insert a booster charge of black powder over the primer and then add the charge of smokeless on top of the black. Some sophisticated hand loaders even went so far as to introduce a tube about ¼ inch in diameter immediately over the primer and filled this tube with black powder. They then poured in the smokeless-powder charge and withdrew the tube. This gave a column of black powder right up through the center of the smokeless, giving excellent ignition. This same principle has been used for the successful ignition of the tough smokeless powders in artillery shells for the past 90 years.

By the 1890s the shotshell situation was chaotic. Remington, Winchester and other leading manufacturers sold empty brass shotshells for about ten cents apiece. Empty paper shotshells could be purchased for about 1¼ cents apiece. Custom handloaders, such as Montgomery Ward in Chicago and VonLengerke and Detmold in New York, were custom loading millions of shotshells per year. In first-class paper cases, such as Winchester Leader, they were sold for about 2½ cents apiece. Cheap hand loads could be procured for about 2 cents apiece using weaker cases and less wadding. The real cut-throat manufacturers actually marketed loaded shotshells that were barely strong enough for safety for 1.6 cents per shell. Custom loading of shotshells was a business of many local sporting-goods stores who saw a chance to have a profitable sideline and make up special loads to the specifications of their good customers. Then there were the millions of American sportsmen who simply continued to hand load their own ammunition.

AMMUNITION OF THE EARLY 20TH CENTURY

The beginning of the 20th Century saw an enormous variety of shotshell designs on the American market. Paper shells were offered in hundreds of different combinations by such major manufacturers as Remington, Winchester and the Union Metallic Cartridge Company. Smaller firms loaded new shotshells, manufacturing some components themselves and purchasing the remainder from major manufacturers or specialty houses, such as lead-shot manufacturers. In addition, there was a flourishing business reloading shotshells.

The top-quality shells put out by the major manufacturers were excellent. Such a shell might be typified by the Winchester "Leader" shotshell of the turn of the century, shown in Figure 8-11. Premium shells of slightly different design were offered by other major manufacturers. The Winchester Leader had a brass head; tube and base were "consolidated" into a permanent assembly under very high pressure by an assembly machine punch. On carefully manufactured high-quality shells, this assembly was excellent. Where the manufacturers skimped on the quality of the paper tube or the brass head or the construction of the base wad, gas pressure would penetrate to the base of the shell and expand the brass head to the point where "head splits" or "rim "blowthroughs" occurred. Some manufacturers, including Remington, bypassed this problem on premium-priced shells by fitting the base wad into a steel cup and then inserting the cup and base-wad assembly into the paper tube. When this assembly was consolidated, gas leakage was minimized.

Turn-of-the-century shotshells were loaded with

both black and smokeless powder. These early smokeless propellants were "single base" powders made entirely of nitrocellulose. They were usually quite porous and had irregular surfaces. Porosity and low density meant that it was easy for the propellant to pick up moisture if stored in a damp climate. Sometimes the moisture content would increase 2 to 3 percent in a moist climate and drop to below 1 percent if stored in a dry location. These variations in moisture content affected propellant performance. Generally as the moisture content went up, the shotshell velocity went down. Sometimes the burning was erratic and the shooter could notice a difference in sound. This audible difference became known as an "off sound."

In premium-priced shells gas was sealed by a column of wads. In the leader shell at the turn of the century there was a hard wad over the powder, then a ⅜" thick soft wad and a ³⁄₁₆" wad against the shot. The charge of 1¼ oz. of lead shot was held in by another thin hard wad, and the mouth of the case was rolled over to retain the top wad.

The major manufacturers and some of the minor manufacturers joined together in the 1880s in an Ammunition Manufacturers Association to develop cooperation among the manufacturers, and standardization of ammunition design so that guns and ammunition of a given gauge would be interchangeable. In 1887 all of the manufacturers in the Association sold a total of $330,000 of loaded shotshells. In that same year they did a business of $211,000 in wads alone. By 1900 the situation had shifted radically. Members of the Association sold $1,552,000 worth of loaded shotshells compared to $442,000 worth of wads. In 1901 the figures jumped to $2,211,000 for loaded shells and $611,000 for wads.[1] These sales figures highlighted a long-term trend. As ammunition became more complex, and as black powder was replaced by smokeless, there was a greater tendency for the American sportsman to buy factory-loaded ammunition that gave more reliable performance than the cheaper hand loads available. Surprisingly, the members of the Association were quite willing to sell empty shotshells, wads and primers to the small companies who then only had to purchase powder from one of the many powder manufac-

turing companies and lead shot from primary producers such as the National Lead Company. However the association was very sensitive to smaller manufacturers starting to go into the production of these key shotshell components and become integrated producers themselves. One company that made this difficult transition was the Western Cartridge Company. Eventually Western became so successful that they were able to purchase Winchester when the giant combine fell into troubled times in the early 1930s.

In 1892 the Equitable Powder Manufacturing Company was formed in East Alton, Illinois to manufacture black powder for blasting in the mines of the Midwest. But there were seasonal fluctuations in the miners' powder requirements, and in 1898 Franklin W. Olin and his associates formed the Western Cartridge Company to use their extra powder capacity for loading shotshells during the slow season. The Ammunition Manufacturers Association members sold Olin empty shotshells and wads until 1900. Olin was not a member of the Association but had developed a loading machine that did not infringe the patents of any of the Association's members. His move was interpreted as an attempt to become an integrated ammunition producer, however, and the Association cut off the supply of primers, shotshells and wads. This forced Olin either to become an integrated producer or give up the shotshell-loading business. Despite the obstacles he chose the latter. Primers were purchased from Eley Bros. in England, and, after a great deal of experimentation, the techniques for producing paper tubes, base wads and brass heads were mastered. Experiments with over-powder and shot wads led to the use of cork wads for cushioning the acceleration of the shot in some early Western shotshells. Western had to build its own shot tower in 1904, after the Association members cut off the supply of lead shot. Nonetheless Western was able to make an excellent marketing connection through a large wholesale house in St. Louis, the Simmons Hardware Company. Simmons distributed the high-quality Western shotshells to its retail outlets in the Midwest.

The Ammunition Manufacturers Association followed a somewhat similar pattern with the Peters Cartridge Company of Kings Point, Ohio. Peters Cartridge was started in 1887 to use extra powder manufactured by the King Powder Company of the same city. Peters sold their paper-shell machinery and stock to Winchester in 1889, then

[1]Harold Williamson, Winchester, *The Gun That Won the West* (New York: A. S. Barnes, 1954).

went back into business in the 1890s using different cartridge machinery. In 1892 Winchester sued for infringement, and during the 1890s Peters was forced to develop its own integrated ammunition manufacturing operations.

The Savage Arms Company of Utica, New York, purchased metallic ammunition components from the Association members starting in 1894. This continued until they too were cut off around 1900. The influence of the Association declined during the early years of the twentieth century, and in 1907 it was dissolved.

Early Western Shotshells

During the early 1900s Western Cartridge Company, becoming an integrated ammunition producer, did a lot of design experimentation. A Western 16-gauge Xpert shell from this period was disassembled and the design is shown in Figure 8-12. The primer is an early battery-cup design, probably from Eley Brothers of England. The internal construction is quite similar to a modern battery-cup primer, but the diameter of the body is .215 inches compared to .240 inches

for the modern designs. The flash hole was covered with a thin sheet of aluminum foil to prevent propellant from drifting into the primer cavity during transport. This shotshell is technically a "duplex load" with a small charge of flake smokeless propellant immediately over the primer and a much larger charge of granular propellant making up the remainder of the 32-grain charge.

Immediately over the propellant a fiber wad was inserted and compressed to a height of .145 inches. Above this was a resilient cork wad with a compressed height of .220 inches, followed by another fiber wad with a .145-inch compressed height. The total height of the wad column was slightly over ½ inch. The shot charge of 450 grains (1 ounce) was loaded into the shotshell and a thin, hard, over-shot wad pressed into the mouth of the shell, then the paper tube was rolled over to retain a tight assembly.

The basic shotshell was made up of a laminated tapered tube .030 inches in wall thickness with an outside diameter of .720 inches. A wound-paper base wad was inserted in one end of the paper tube and retained by a low-base brass head only ⅜ of an inch high. The assembly machine then

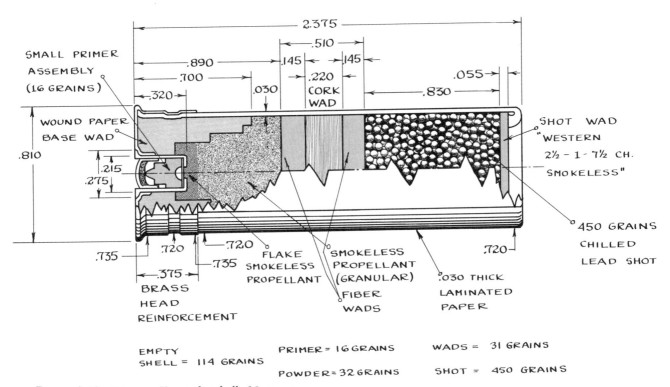

Figure 8-12 Western Xpert shotshell, 16 gauge.

swaged the brass head into the configuration shown in Figure 8-12. A groove .015 deep was rolled into the brass head interlocking the paper tube and base wads. This construction made a swaged assembly which could stand many reloadings. The center of the head of the brass case was pressed inwards to provide a metallic seat for the small battery cup primer. There was an interference fit between the .215 inch diameter of the battery cup primer, both with the fiber base wad and with the brass of the head.

The Western shotshell shows the general construction of high-quality shotshells made in the early 20th century. The use of a triple column of wads gave much better gas sealing than the single wad often used in hand loads of early shotshells of the 1870s. The gas sealing, however, was not as good as that developed with "cup wads" which became widely used in ammunition during the 1930s.

Metal-Lined Shotshells

During the late-19th century, in addition to such major manufactuerrs as Remington, Winchester, and Union Metallic Cartridge Company, many small companies purchased components from the major manufacturers in the United States and Europe and assembled shotshells for local or regional sales. Large sporting-goods houses had shotshell reloading departments that often turned out millions of rounds per year. In addition, thousands of local gunsmiths had small sideline businesses of reloading shotshells to their customers' specifications. The major manufacturers responded by providing an enormous variety of styles of ammunition. Some were manufactured with the simplest basic construction which would be safe and were designed to compete directly with the economy ammunition provided by smaller manufacturers. Good-quality shotshells were manufactured loaded with black powder, bulk smokeless powder and the new dense smokeless powders. The shells were loaded with soft and chilled shot ranging in size from very fine No. 9 up to the large buckshot and single-ball loads.

There had been persistent problems in the late 19th century of gas pressure working its way between the base wad and the paper tube and blowing out the brass rim of the shotshell. The leading manufacturers countered this problem by developing "metal-lined" shotshells, which provided strong internal reinforcement. Winchester introduced dark-green metal-lined shotshells in 1894. These were stamped with the words "Winchester," "Gauge . . ." and "Metal Lined." They were originally introduced in 10 and 12 gauge and then 4- and 8-gauge shells were added in 1897. The Winchester shells were generally assembled with a formed brass cup into which the base wad was assembled and then the entire subassembly pressed into the paper tube. Swaging on the brass head and rolling in circumferential grooves locked the paper tube securely between the inner and outer brass cups and provided extremely tough construction.

Remington manufactured similar brass-lined shotshells and on March 12, 1912, patented a construction using a steel liner. The construction is described in the 1915 catalogue:

> All "Nitro Club" shells are Steel Lined, thus making them the Strongest, therefore the Safest and Best. This form of reinforce, adopted only by us, also materially improves their shooting qualities, as shown by their superior pattern, penetration, and velocity.

Details of a Remington steel-lined shotshell are shown in Figure 8-13. The steel liner was rolled up immediately inside the wound-paper tube and extended 1.43 inches above the base giving an extremely strong head construction. This shotshell shows the ultimate in early 20th-century shotgun technology. A tough paper tube was wound of red paper. A paper base wad was wound up and then probably fitted inside the steel liner which was then formed to provide protection all the way around the base wad, then an inner rim was formed over it, completely enclosing the outer surface of the paper base wad. This subassembly was fitted inside the paper tube and then a very high brass base, 1.050 inches in length, was swaged in place to form a permanent assembly. The Remington trademark was rolled into the outside of the brass head, which locked the paper tube between the brass head and the inner steel liner. The shotshell head construction was completed by adding a large battery cup primer which had the basic .240 inch body diameter used on modern shotshell primers.

The Remington Nitro Club shotshells were available with an enormous variety of smokeless propellants. These included DuPont, Schultze, E. C., Dead Shot, Empire, Wolf, Mullerite, Lafflin and Rand Infallible, Ballistite, Walsrode, and for an extra charge of $2.50 per thousand shells

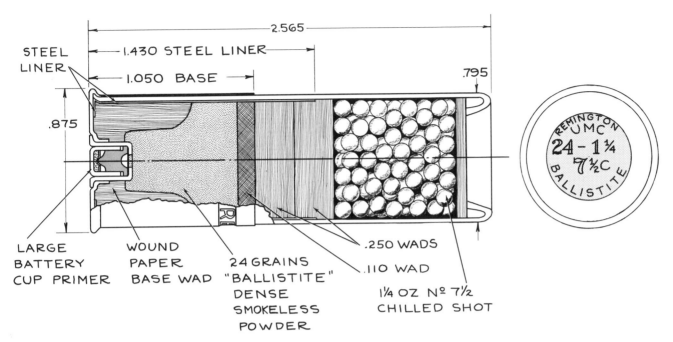

STEEL LINER

2.565

1.430 STEEL LINER

1.050 BASE

.875

.795

STEEL LINER

LARGE BATTERY CUP PRIMER

WOUND PAPER BASE WAD

24 GRAINS "BALLISTITE" DENSE SMOKELESS POWDER

.250 WADS

.110 WAD

1¼ OZ № 7½ CHILLED SHOT

REMINGTON UMC 24-1¼ 7½C BALLISTITE

Figure 8-13   Remington steel-lined shotshell.

the shooter could order Curtis and Harvey's diamond-grain smokeless powder which apparently had some magic properties. In addition, these shells were also available in most of these same brand names with bulk smokeless powders. The particular shell examined to make this illustration was loaded with 24 grains of Ballistite dense smokeless powder and 1¼ ounces of No. 7½ chilled shot. Gas sealing was provided by a very hard .110-inch thick over-powder wad and two softer ¼-inch thick wads to cushion the acceleration of the shot column. The shot was held in place by a thin over-shot wad and the mouth of the case was spun in to retain the shot in place. That the shell was loaded with dense smokeless powder can be told by the marking on the mouth. The figure "24" refers to the powder charge of dense smokeless in grains. If this were loaded with a bulk smokeless powder it would be marked with the dram equivalent marking. The steel-lined shell is a good example of the highest-quality early 20th-century shotshells.

PROPELLANTS

By 1920 three types of powder were being used in shotshells. Some traditionalists were still insisting on black-powder shotshells but most American hunters were demanding clean-burning smokeless powders. In addition to the bulk smokeless powder shown in Figure 8-11, a new type of dense

double-based smokeless powder was coming into use for shotshells. Some of the experiments were ingenious; for example, the Western Cartridge Company was trying to get into a position to manufacture their own smokeless propellants. Their technique was to grind and screen 30-caliber military rifle propellant from World War I, and blend this with a quick-burning double-based propellant, such as Hercules Bull's Eye, to provide proper ignition and burning. An excellent powder known as "Minimax" was developed in the 1930s by reprocessing the fine residue of ground-up cannon powder and by agglomerating this mixture into a propellant suitable for shotshells. Other approaches were the development of "pyro bulk propellant" made from pyro cotton purchased as World War I surplus from Picatinny Arsenal. Dense bulk powders were manufactured by grinding up World War I cannon powder, reworking it, gelatinizing the mixture and agglomerating the powder into a size suitable for shotgun propellant.

Similar wide-ranging experiments were performed by many manufacturers in the search for better wads and better gas sealing. In the early 20th century felt wads were used almost exclusively, but wads punched out of cork sheet were used in some loads, and in 1923 Western introduced a "composition" wad which was manufactured by grinding up cork and then using an oil binder which was polymerized to form a tough structure. Similar experiments were being performed by other manufacturers with the goal of achieving light-weight wads that would provide sufficient resistance that the smokeless propellants would burn properly and yet would cushion the acceleration of the shot so that minimum deformation of the shot occurred. These were conflicting requirements and were never completely solved until the development of the one-piece plastic wad and shot protectors of the 1960s.

Dense Smokeless Powders

The great advantages of smokeless powders are the elimination of the heavy residue in the bore of the firearm and of the dense cloud of smoke out the muzzle. There was a second advantage for centerfire cartridges. Since the propellant was so much more powerful than black powder, ballistics could be substantially improved. In the late 1880s and 1890s most leading nations changed from a black-powder cartridge firing a .45-caliber soft-lead bullet at approximately 1,300 feet a second to a .30 caliber smokeless-powder cartridge firing a jacketed-lead bullet at 2,200 feet per second. During the early 20th century further improvements in smokeless propellants were made and bullets were changed from round-nosed designs of slightly over 200 grains to a sharp or "spitzer" pointed bullet of approximately 150 grains. Velocities jumped from about 2,200 feet per second to the range of 2,700 feet per second. The use of dense smokeless propellant was however dangerous for the shotgun hand loader. If the hand loader accidentally put in a bulk charge of 125 grains of dense smokeless as shown in Figure 8-11, his shotgun would be shattered and he would probably be injured.

The bulk smokeless powders, which were deliberately reduced in power level to be equivalent in volume to black powder, were hygroscopic and varied in ballistic performance as humidity changed. Early in the 20th century ammunition companies began loading dense smokeless powders in shotshells under very careful factory control. These powders were of a concentrated type, requiring much smaller volume and much smaller weight of powder for equivalent ballistic performance. To keep the situation clear companies listed ammunition loaded with bulk smokeless as a "dram load." In other words, the 125 grains of bulk smokeless propellant shown in Figure 8-11 corresponded to 4½ drams of powder. The dense smokeless propellants were listed by the actual charge weight in grains. This practice was continued through 1929.

On January 2, 1930, all the manufacturers adopted a uniform designation of "dram equivalent." This means that whatever the type of propellant used it was equivalent to the performance of three drams of bulk smokeless powder. While it is a difficult system for the layman to understand, what it really means is that shotshells are loaded to achieve certain velocity and pressure levels. All double-base propellants require much lower propellant charges than the old bulk smokeless loads. Propellants with high nitroglycerin content normally burn hotter and require lower propellant charges than powders with a low nitroglycerin content. The type and weight of propellant is therefore varied to achieve standard results.

PRIMERS

Nineteenth-century shotshells were assembled with the same type of primers as used in centerfire ammunition. Early primers of the mid-century often used a priming mix known as Sharps Mixture which contained the following ingredients:

SHARPS PRIMING MIXTURE
Mercury Fulminate	25%
Mealed Black Powder	50%
Powdered Glass	25%

The mercury fulminate was an unstable primary explosive, and as it was crushed against the sharp jagged edges of the powdered glass friction and heat would develop causing ignition. The finely ground black powder was ignited and provided a flash of flame into the main black-powder charge in the cartridge case. There was a disadvantage to this mix since the mercury amalgamated with the zinc in the brass cartridge cases causing embrittlement. Collectors of early cartridges often notice that copper primers were used in 19th-century ammunition because the copper was not attacked by the mercuric fulminate.

In the late black-powder period a typical priming mix consisted of:

Mercury Fulminate	35.5%
Potassium Chlorate	15%
"Gummed Water"	4%
Powdered Glass	45.5%

These types of priming compounds were continued in early 20th-century shotshells, despite two disadvantages. One was that fulminate of mercury tended to deteriorate under conditions of high humidity or hot, dry storage. The second was that potassium chlorate attracts moisture. Minute quantities of burned primer residue were deposited in the barrel on each shot, and if the gun was not cleaned with water to dissolve the salt, these traces of potassium chlorate would attract moisture and rust the rifle or shotgun barrel. The obvious answer was to clean the gun after each shooting session with water, and then dry the bore and protect it with oil. Unfortunately this was one of the main reasons that American sportsmen wanted to get away from black powder. They were sick and tired of the endless cleaning involved after coming home from a day's shoot.

Remington took a leading role in developing noncorrosive priming in the United States. Early in 1924 a chemist, James E. Burns, stopped in at the Remington plant on his way to Florida. Burns had recently worked for the United States Cartridge Company but had quit and was heading south for a winter vacation. Burns had a flair for the dramatic, and when he called on two old friends in the Remington Research Department, he pulled out a revolver loaded with blanks and proceeded to fire six shots in their office. He then asked them to put the revolver away in a damp place without cleaning until he returned from vacation. A month later when Burns returned, the gun was taken out of storage, and the exterior had started to rust. Burns ran a cloth through the chambers of the revolver and the bore which were perfectly bright with no traces of rust. A dramatic way to apply for a job, but it was successful. He was hired on the spot.

It took years of research on the part of the Remington staff to turn Burns' home-workshop experiments into a commercially feasible priming, utilizing a new type of primary explosive known as "lead styphnate." Remington finally had to send technicians to Europe to purchase foreign patents and bring back foreign technicians to set up a manufacturing operation to produce lead styphnate at the Remington plant. In the late 1920s the new Remington "Kleanbore" priming was introduced on the American market and was an enormous hit. The "Kleanbore" trademark became so well identified with noncorrosive priming that Remington has continued to use it to the present day.

In 1930 Western Cartridge Company introduced a noncorrosive fulminate of mercury priming based on German developments of the late 1920s. At the same time Western introduced their #209 battery cup primer, which allowed the insertion of more priming mix than the old "#3 cap." The noncorrosive fulminate of mercury priming proved highly satisfactory in commercial ammunition.

During the 1930s Winchester centerfire and rimfire ammunition was loaded with a noncorrosive, nonmercuric priming of the "diazole" type. The ingredients in these primers are listed below:

Diazo-di-nitro-phenol
Tetrazene (Primary Explosive)
Antimony Sulphide
Barium—Potassium-Nitrate
Powdered Glass

Shotshells continued to be loaded by a dry-mix process in which the primary ingredients were fulminate of mercury and barium nitrate. Government specifications required the use of potassium chlorate for most primers, even during World War II, because of its excellent performance under adverse conditions. It was a corrosive primer, however, and rusting occurred if rifles were not carefully cleaned.

In 1945 Winchester-Western introduced a lead styphnate primer to replace the fulminate-of-mercury design. They also developed a new process utilizing wet-mixing techniques which contained the following ingredients:

Normal Lead Styphnate
Tetrazene
Barium Nitrate
Aluminum
Antimony Sulphide
P.E.T.N. (High Explosive)

This was so satisfactory that the process was adopted by Frankford Arsenal during the 1950s and became known as the Frankford Arsenal No. 956 mix and is widely used in military ammunition.

Since World War II the major manufacturers have continued research into better priming compounds. This is an extremely tricky field, for priming materials are primary explosives and dangerous to handle. The usual technique is to do all of the final blending and formulation under water where the priming materials remain insensitive. The lead styphnate mixes, for example, are made up as a dough the consistency of a sloppy putty. This mixture is spread over a thin brass plate with a rubber squeeze. The priming mix flows into holes drilled in the plate and is scraped off the upper surface of the brass plate. The thin brass plate is then flipped over on a hinge and the holes filled with priming compound are exactly positioned over a series of empty primer cups. Punches are brought down which push the wet priming mix out of the holes and drop them as soggy pellets into the bottom of the primer cup. The cups then move on and have a thin paper or metallic foil placed over the wet priming compound and the anvil is inserted in the base of the primer. Primers are then baked in an oven which dries off the moisture. As the compound dries, it becomes more and more sensitive. The dried primers are then fed through automated loading machines and loaded into ammunition.

In shotshell primers the construction is slightly more complex, for the battery cup consists of an outer-flanged copper tube which fits outside of the primer cup and supports the anvil. In the base of the battery cup a second piece of foil is fitted over the flash hole to prevent any fine propellant from sifting into the primer cavity and increasing the pressure in this crucial area.

Since World War II the major manufacturers have concentrated on improving the formulations of the lead styphnate priming compounds to give improved uniformity of ignition. Major research has been performed to identify entirely new priming compounds which may offer improved performance in the future. During the 1960s such a breakthrough was achieved in Winchester Group Research, with the synthesis of a new family of priming compounds patented under the name "Stabanate" after the inventor, Edward Staba. The basic explosive is a new double salt of lead styphnate. Commercialization of these improved priming compounds has been difficult and the first commercial application has been in the caseless ammunition introduced to power Ramset industrial tools. The Stabanate priming has also been used in experimental caseless military ammunition ranging from 5.56mm to 25mm in size. New experimental machinery and equipment is still under development for commercial applications.

SHOTGUN CHOKES

The origins of shotgun choke are clouded in history. There are some indications that choke-bored shotguns were experimented with and forgotten a number of times. The first patent for choke boring was for a detachable muzzle device by Sylvester Roper on April 10, 1866. An Englishman, Mr. Pape of Newcastle, England, also patented a shotgun choke in 1866, but there is no evidence that he reduced his design to practice. His claim was to reduce the shotgun barrel from 12 to 13 gauge at the muzzle, thus giving a fairly strong constriction of the shotgun bore. Americans generally credit the invention of choke to Fred Kimball, a market gunner and outstanding American shooter who operated along the Illinois flyway. Kimball's experiments with shotgun chokes have been described earlier. He claimed that his muzzle-loading single-barrel shotgun eventually gave a pattern so tight that it kept all of the shot in a 30-inch circle at 40 yards. This pattern was so small that even for a skilled shooter such as Kimball it was difficult to hit flying game and it took him a long time to use it successfully. Kimball disclosed his invention to a gunsmith named Tonks of Boston, Massachusetts, who manufactured choke-bored guns during the 1870s.

While the real inventor of choke boring may never be known, there is little question that Fred Kimball in the United States and W. W. Greener in England were responsible for bringing its advantages to the sporting public on both sides of the Atlantic. By 1875 choke boring versus the traditional cylinder bore had become such a hot issue in sporting circles that the leading British sporting magazine, *The Field*, held a series of trials to test choked guns against cylinder-bore models. These trials showed that choked guns gave a full 40% more shot in a 30-inch circle at 40 yards. During this past century there has been an increasing emphasis on choke-bored shotguns. In modern times most shooters make the error of demanding too much choke rather than too little.

Choke has a very strong effect on the shot column. This is dramatically shown in Figure 8-14. The upper illustration shows a shot package emerging from the muzzle of a cylinder-bore shotgun. As the shot cloud moved a short distance from the muzzle the lateral dispersion of the shot, due to air resistance, is beginning to have a significant effect.

The action of shot passing through a full-choked shotgun barrel is different. In a 12-gauge gun, such as was used for these tests, the barrel is constricted from .730 inches in diameter down to .694 inches in the choke area, a reduction of .036 of an inch. This represents a reduction of almost 10 percent in the cross-sectional area of the barrel

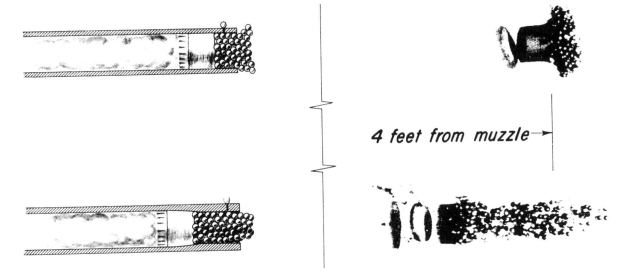

4 feet from muzzle →

Figure 8-14 The effect of choke on the shot column.

and forces the shot column to be constricted in diameter and increased in length to pass through the choke. The effect of the full choke is shown quite markedly in the lower right illustration—the shot column is lengthened, has retained its smaller diameter and tends to fly towards the target as a much tighter package of shot than the cloud from the cylinder-bore gun. This change in performance is of course due to the fact that the outer layers of shot are given an inward acceleration as they pass through the choke area thus tending to hold the shot column as a compressed package for a great distance from the gun muzzle.

Modern shotguns are bored with a variety of chokes. Shotguns for skeet shooting and upland game are generally bored very open, for the targets are fast moving and at short range a broad pattern is best. Shotguns for trap shooting, fast shooting at birds or duck hunting over decoys are usually full choked shotguns. Full choke is actually a rather difficult gun to handle and the beginning shooter is well advised to choose an open-bored gun, such as improved cylinder or modified, until he develops skill in aiming. My first repeating shotgun was an Ithaca Model 37 in modified choke and it was amazing the number of shots at rabbits and flying targets that were missed simply because the pattern was far too tight for my shooting skill.

The performance of choke is measured as the percentage of shot which is placed in a 30 inch circle at 40 yards. The traditional percentages are as follows:

SHOTGUN CHOKE
Percentage of Shot in 30-Inch Circle at 40 Yards

Full Choke	65-75 percent
Improved Modified Choke (¾ Choke)	55-65 percent
Modified Choke (½ Choke)	45-55 percent
Improved Cylinder or Skeet #2 Choke (¼ Choke)	35-45 percent
Cylinder or Skeet #1 (No Choke)	25-35 percent

These traditional percentages have changed somewhat by improvements in shotshell design. The use of one-piece wad construction, such as the Winchester-Western double A wad or the Remington power piston, tends to give approximately 10 percent better patterns with large shot sizes such as BB's or No. 2 shot. This can push the pattern percentage with a full-choke shotgun well over 80 percent. The improvement in pattern performance becomes less significant with smaller shot sizes. The performance with No. 9 shot is quite equivalent to the pattern percentages listed in the chart.

The amount of barrel constriction required to give these pattern percentages is highlighted in Figure 8-15. A full-choke barrel in 12 gauge is constricted .036 of an inch in diameter in the choke area. The amount of constriction declines in the smaller gauges. In 12 gauge the full choke represents a reduction in cross-section area of the barrel of about 10 percent. This declines to 8 percent in the 20 and 28 gauges but jumps to a 14

NOMINAL BORE AND CHOKE DIMENSIONS

Gauge	Choke	Bore diameter (inches)	Choke constriction (inches)	Percentage reduction of bore area
12	Full	.730	.036	10%
	Improved Modified	"	.022	6%
	Modified	"	.012	3%
	Improved Cylinder or Skeet #2	"	.007	2%
	Cylinder or Skeet #1	"	.0	0
16	Full	.670	.030	9%
	Improved Modified	"	.019	6%
	Modified	"	.012	4%
	Improved Cylinder or Skeet #2	"	.007-.009	2%
	Cylinder or Skeet #1	"	.0	0
20	Full	.615	.025	8%
	Improved Modified	"	.017	5%
	Modified or Skeet #2	"	.011-012	4%
	Improved Cylinder or Skeet #1	"	.007	2%
	Cylinder	"	.0	0
28	Full	.550	.023	8%
	Improved Modified	"	.015	5%
	Modified or Skeet #2	"	.010-.011	4%
	Improved Cylinder	"	.006	2%
	Cylinder	"	.0	0
.410 Bore	Full	.410	.020	14%
	Modified or Skeet #2	"	.010	5%
	Cylinder	"	.0	0

Figure 8-15 Choke characteristics.

percent reduction in 410. Improved modified choke provides a 5 to 6 percent reduction in cross-sectional area. Modified choke represents a 3 percent reduction in 12 gauge, 4 percent in 16, 20 and 28 gauge, and 5 percent in 410. In all of these cases the choke constriction represents only .010 to .012 of an inch below bore diameter. This is extremely small and it is amazing that so slight a constriction can increase the pattern percentage from an average of 30 percent with a cylinder-bore shotgun to 50 percent with a modified choke. The fact that the shot column is so sensitive to these small changes in diameter as well as to the shape of the choke makes it obvious that the crudely bored shotguns of 200 years ago

could hardly be expected to give effective choke performance. Manufacturers of even a century ago would have had great difficulty in controlling the bore diameter to within .010 inch from breech to muzzle. With muzzle-loading shotguns the breech end of the shotgun was commonly constricted much more than this small dimension just due to the limitations of the tooling available for boring long barrels.

Tight, uniform patterns require that everything be carefully controlled in the shotgun and ammunition. The shot must be uniform in diameter and round. The bore of the shotgun must be uniform in diameter and free from circumferential rings, which will tend to deform the shot. The use of a shot protector, such as a Mark V collar, a Power Piston or a Double A wad, helps a great deal in reducing the percentage of deformed shot. The shape of the choke itself is important; for many years the chokes in Winchester shotguns were machined in an arc with a 17-foot radius. This design was selected so that the initial inward acceleration of the shot, as it was constricted by the choke, would be extremely gentle. This helps the shot column to move as a fluid into its longer, more constricted configuration rather than hammering the outer shot through an abrupt change in diameter. The results of all these efforts is that the shotgunner can expect consistent and predictable pattern performance. Under special circumstanes, for extra-long-range shooting with large-shot sizes, pattern percentages exceeding 80 percent of the shot in a 30-inch circle at 40 yards can regularly be achieved.

EXTERIOR BALLISTICS OF SHOTSHELLS

There are two major problems in extending the range of shotguns. One is the dispersion of the shot which reduces the pattern density to an unacceptably low level beyond 50 or 60 yards. The second is the rapid deceleration of lead shot, which reduces its effectiveness after relatively short distances. A sphere has a large cross-section area relative to its weight. This means that the air resistance is high and the energy to overcome that air resistance relatively low. Obviously a .30-caliber sharp-nosed bullet that weighs 150 grains will retain its velocity far better than a .30-caliber (No. 1 Buck) lead shot that has a rounded shape and weighs only 40 grains. The magnitude of the problem is highlighted in Figure 8-16, which shows the results of some recent tests performed for the Sporting Arms and Ammunition Manufacturers Institute (SAAMI) with No. 4 and No. 6 shot. Initial velocity was measured with coils at a distance of 3 feet. These velocities correspond to a muzzle velocity of slightly over 1,350 feet per second. At a range of only 30 yards the velocity of both types of shot had declined over 500 feet per second. At 65 yards, or just under 200 feet, the velocity of the No. 4 shot had declined by almost 800 feet per second and the No. 6 shot by 830 feet per second. In addition to the velocity decline there is a drastic decline in pellet energy. Each pellet of No. 4 shot weighs only 3.2 grains. It starts off with just under 13 foot-pounds of muzzle energy. At 30 yards this energy has

EXTERIOR BALLISTICS OF LEAD SHOT

Velocity (ft/sec)	#4 Shot (.130" diameter)	#6 Shot (.110" diameter)
At three feet (coil measurement)	1336	1337
At 30 yards	842	804
40 "	740	701
45 "	698	658
50 "	660	620
55 "	626	584
60 "	594	550
65 "	563	518

Energy, per pellet (ft-lbs)	#4 Shot	#6 Shot
At 30 yards	5.10	2.61
40 "	3.94	1.98
45 "	3.50	1.75
50 "	3.13	1.56
55 "	2.82	1.38
60 "	2.53	1.22
65 "	2.28	1.08

Figure 8-16 Exterior ballistics of lead shot.

declined to only 5.1 foot-pounds and at 65 yards the energy is down to 2.28 foot-pounds. The analysis of data by the Winchester Group Research indicated that approximately .40 foot-pounds of muzzle energy is required just to penetrate the feathers and skin of medium-sized birds such as ducks. This further reduces the amount of pellet energy available to clobber a flying bird.

No. 6 shot provides a much denser pattern. For example, a 1¼ ounce shotshell loaded with No. 4 would hold 170 pellets where the same shotshell with No. 6 shot would hold 280 pellets. The effect of this denser pattern is largely offset by the lower velocity and energy in the No. 6 shot. Each pellet of No. 6 weighs only 2 grains and starts off with a muzzle energy of 7.9 foot-pounds. At 30 yards this has declined to 2.61 foot-pounds and at 65 yards the energy is slightly over one foot-pound per pellet. Considering that .4 foot-pounds of energy is required to penetrate feathers and skin you can see that the No. 6 shot would have virtually no effective punch on flying game at 65 yards.

The weight of the various sizes of shot pellets is shown in Figure 8-17. The finest shot, No. 12,

Shot size	Diameter (inches)	Weight (grains)	Number of shot in 1 ounce
12	.050	.18	2385
11	.060	.32	1380
10	.070	.50	870
9	.080	.75	585
8	.090	1.07	410
7½	.095	1.25	350
6	.110	1.94	225
5	.120	2.57	170
4	.130	3.24	135
2	.150	4.86	90
Air rifle	.175	8.0	55
BB	.180	8.75	50
No. 4 buck	.240	20.6	21
No. 3 buck	.250	23.3	19
No. 1 buck	.300	40.0	11
No. 0 buck	.320	48.2	9
No. 00	.330	53.8	8

Figure 8-17 Weight of shot pellets.

has a diameter of only .050 of an inch. It takes five pellets to weigh a single grain. Obviously such tiny shot averages extremely low energy levels even at muzzle velocity. With a weight of only ⅕ of a grain it simply hasn't enough mass to provide the force to overcome air resistance in its flight to the target. Heavy shot such as No. 2 and No. 4 are widely used for long-range shooting. With weights of 3¼ to nearly 5 grains, these pellets have a lot of energy at launch and retain enough energy at 65 yards so that the pellet will effectively penetrate such large birds as turkeys and geese. Even with relatively large shot, such as No. 4, the energy dissipates rapidly compared to rifle projectiles. Thus the launch energy of 11 foot-pounds per pellet has declined to less than half this value at only 30 yards of range. Even at 65 yards the No. 4 pellets retain 2¼ foot-pounds. With .4 foot-pounds required to penetrate feathers and skin, this still leaves over 1¾ foot-pounds of energy to knock the bird down. Obviously this energy is extremely small, even compared to the standard velocity .22 short bullets which retain 62 foot-pounds of energy at 65 yards range.

The difference between the performance of a spherical lead pellet and a bullet of the same weight may be made by comparing a No. 1 buckshot load with a .22 long-rifle cartridge. Both are 40 grain projectiles, but the buckshot has a diam-

eter of .300 inches (.30 caliber) compared to the rimfire bullet diameter of .224 inches. Even if both are launched at a muzzle velocity of 1,350 feet per second the much larger cross-section area of the No. 1 buckshot pellet, and its blunter ballistic shape, causes the velocity to decline much faster than with the bullet. At 50 yards, for example, the bullet would be travelling at 1,175 feet per second, the pellet at 862 feet per second. At 100 yards the bullet is still humming along at 1,045 feet per second while the No. 1 buckshot is loping at 633 feet per second. These formulas for the calculation of remaining velocity of shotshell pellets hold within the range of 500 feet per second to 1,650 feet per second. Above and below these velocity levels different physical forces are involved with pellet deceleration and modified formulas must be applied.

RIFLED SLUG LOADS

The construction of an American rifled slug load of the 1920s is shown in Figure 8-18. Such designs were the outgrowth of German research about the time of the First World War. The use of buckshot and single ball loads in smoothbore guns dates back almost 600 years. Single-ball loads have always been inaccurate, whether fired from a shotgun or a military musket. In a shotgun the ball must be small enough in diameter to pass through a full choke. In a 12-gauge shotgun the choke is .695 of an inch in diameter, while the basic bore diameter is .730. The ball rattled from side to side during its passage up the barrel, bounced off the choke and headed in the general direction of the target.

The Germans developed an alternate design consisting of a cylindrical column with a lead slug in front and a series of wads that were held to the column by a long screw. Often the lead slug was given a conical point and had rifling grooves cast into its outside surface. These slugs were marketed in the United States under the "Brenneke" trademark and were both effective and expensive. Their accuracy was much better than the old single-ball load.

American manufacturers came up with the simpler design shown in Figure 8-18, typical of the design of Remington, Peters, Winchester or Western. The rifle-slug loads were high powered and almost invariably were loaded with a high brass base shell. The shotshell shown in the illustration has a brass base .350 inches high with four

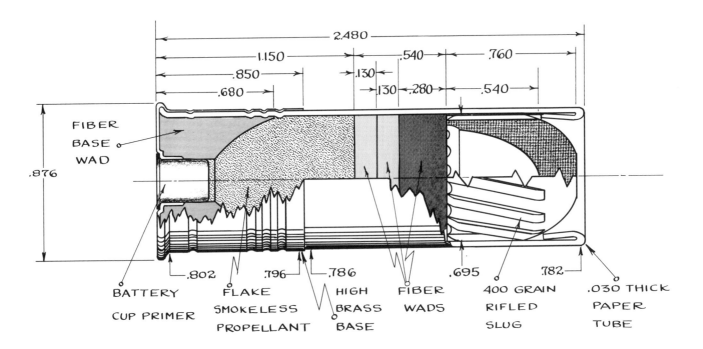

Figure 8-18 Early rifled slug load.

grooves rolled into the outside surface to lock it to the paper tube and base wad. Instead of a stepped design, the base wad was wound out of a spiral sheet of paper which gave a gradually increasing height from the center to the outer surface. A large-diameter battery cup primer with a body diameter of .240 inches was pressed in through the brass head reinforcement and base wad. The shell was loaded with a flake smokeless propellant, which was relatively easy to ignite and quick burning. This type of propellant is extremely important in shotshells, for smokeless powder in general is hard to ignite and until a high pressure is developed the flame can simply quench out. In a shotshell the resilient wad column and the large-bore diameter mean that the volume increases rather rapidly and a high priming charge and fast-burning propellant are required to prevent the flame from simply sputtering out.

Above the propellant two fiber wads were loaded with a compressed height of .130 inches each. Above this a 5/16 inch fiber wad was loaded and compressed to a height of .280 inches. The rifled slug was carefully worked out so that its weight of 400 grains was slightly under one ounce and it had a hollow cavity in the base placing its center of gravity well forward. This design tends to make the projectile stable in flight. In addition angled ridges were swaged into the outer surface of the slug. As these ridges contacted the bore of

the shotgun, and as air passed over the curved surfaces, a force was developed to spin the projectile just as if the barrel were rifled. Although the slug had to be of sufficiently small diameter (.695 inches in 12 gauge) to pass through a full-choked barrel, the accuracy was tremendously improved over the old single-ball load. With a muzzle velocity of 1,470 feet per second in 12 gauge, the rifle-slug load had a muzzle energy of 2,000 foot-pounds. The remaining velocity at 100 yards is 1,120 feet per second with a remaining energy of 1,165 foot-pounds. The high retained velocity and energy of the rifled-slug load, together with the large cross-section area of the slug, make it an effective hunting load at reasonable ranges.

BUCKSHOT LOADS

The design of a Winchester-Western Mark 5 buckshot load from the 1960s is shown in Figure 8-19. If this is compared with the rifled-slug load, many design changes can be seen. One of the most important changes was the use of double cup wads to seal the powder chamber. This design was a result of research on high-powered shotshells performed at the Western Research Laboratories in East Alton, Illinois. The idea was to form cup wads of a tough waxed laminated paper which served to seal the powder gases. The lower cup wad was perforated in the center and

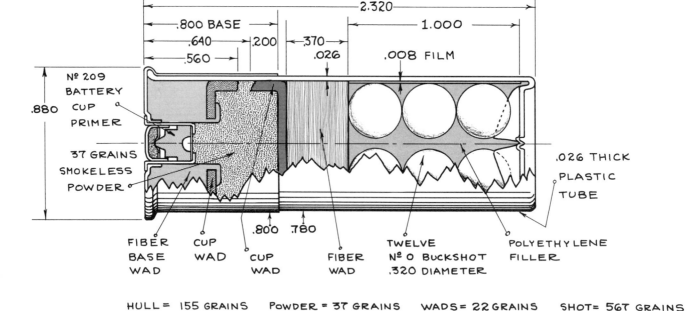

Figure 8-19   Winchester Mark 5 buckshot load of the 1960s.

was held in place by riveting over a small section of the base wad. Gas pressure tended to drive the lip of the cup wad outwards, providing a gas-tight seal against the inner wall of the paper or plastic tube. A second cup wad, placed over the powder, was held in place by a fiber wad with a compressed thickness of .370 inches. Ignition was provided by the No. 209 battery cup primer which has the large body diameter of .240 inches. The 37-grain charge of smokeless powder was ignited by the hot primer and immediately started to drive the cup and fiber wad forward. Gas pressure drove the lips of the cup wads outwards, providing a good seal against the inside of the plastic tube. As the heavily waxed cup wad passed through the forcing cone at the mouth of the chamber the flexible lips on the wad could adjust to the diametrical changes, providing much better gas sealing than was possible with a cylindrical wad.

Buckshot has been an important ammunition lead for hundreds of years. However, there has always been a problem with buckshot dispersing too rapidly in its flight through the air. Two design improvements are shown in this shotshell to minimize the rate of dispersion. One was the use of a wrapper of thin polyethylene .008 inches thick surrounding the column of a dozen buckshot. The second improvement was the use of ground polyethylene as filler in between the buckshot tending to cushion the acceleration of the

.320-inch diameter lead balls and reduce deformation due to gas force. The polyethylene film wrapper prevented direct contact between the buckshot and the barrel of the shotgun, thus greatly reducing flattening during passage up the bore.

This illustration shows the construction of the Winchester-Western design using a Reifenhauser bi-axially extruded polyethylene tube. This type of head construction and the use of a double-cup wad had been in use in Winchester-Western ammunition for over 20 years in paper shotshells, and then for a short time with plastic tubes. This is a transitional shotshell, for by the late 1960s all the powerful high-based shotshells were converted to use the stronger compression-formed one-piece plastic head construction.

LIGHT SHOTSHELLS OF THE 1960s

The design of a typical light shotshell of the mid-1960s is shown in Figures 8-20 and 8-21. This is an Xpert 3-1-8 load for use on upland game. If it is compared with the 16-gauge Xpert shotshells shown in Figure 8-12, the design progress of 40 years can be seen. The volume required for propellant is much less in the modern shotshell and so the height of the base wad has been greatly increased. Brown paper is wound up to form a hollow plug which is a slight press fit into the Reifenhauser tube. The inner windings of the plug are longer than the rest, thus forming a short

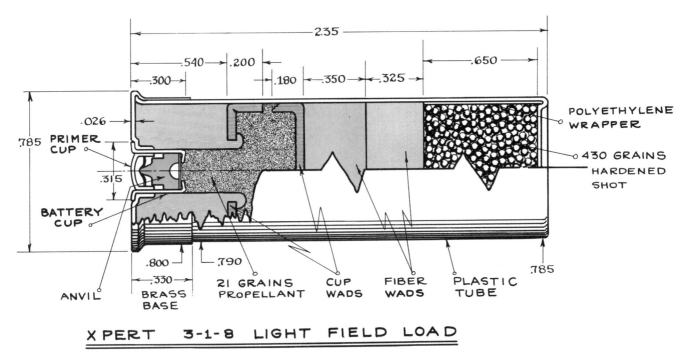

XPERT 3-1-8 LIGHT FIELD LOAD

Figure 8-20 Construction details of typical light shotshell of the 1960s.

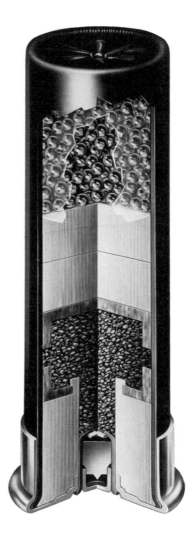

Figure 8-21 Cutaway of typical light shotshell of the 1960s.

inner tube. A heavy waxed-paper cup wad is fitted over this inner tube which is then riveted over to retain the cup wad in place.

The entire head is locked into a unified structure by the addition of a brass head reinforcement. This is .350 inch in length, thus leading to the nickname "low-base shotshell." As the brass head reinforcement is swaged into place, the paper base wad forces the end of the Reifenhauser tube to flare outward into the rim cavity so that base wad, tube and head reinforcement are locked into one permanent assembly.

Loading Operations

Low-base shotshells are primed with the same No. 209 battery cup primer as the more powerful loads. After this is pressed into the head of the cartridge, a charge of 21 grains of WC-410 ball powder was placed into the case. While the nominal powder charge is 21 grains, two disassembled shotshells had charges of 20.9 and 21.1 grains, averaging exactly on the nominal charge weight. A heavy waxed cup wad of .045-inch thick brown-paper stock was then inserted in the case to seal the powder chamber. This was followed by two fiber wads which measured approximately ⅜ of

an inch after removal from a loaded cartridge. A .012-inch thick polyethylene collar was inserted into the shotshell and a one-ounce charge of hardened lead shot was inserted in the shell. The mouth of the shell was then crimped and heat sealed to form a water tight assembly.

Interior Ballistics

The interior ballistics of the Western Xpert shotshells is shown in the third group in Figure 8-22. The total weight of the shot and wads averaged 470 grains and was launched at a muzzle velocity of 1,284 feet per second by the 21-grain powder charge. This was achieved at a peak pressure of only 11,086 pounds per square inch. The efficiency of this cartridge is exceptionally high at 81.9 foot-pounds of muzzle energy per grain of propellant. This is probably due to two factors. One is that the gas sealing of the powder cavity, with the two cup wads facing each other, provides an efficient burning of the propellant in an insulated chamber. The second is that the expansion ratio is high, leading to an efficient thermodynamic system. The expansion ratio is found by calculating the volume of the interior of the shotgun barrel plus the volume inside the empty shot-

INTERIOR BALLISTIC SHOTSHELL PERFORMANCE

Load	Weight of shot and wads, grains	Muzzle velocity ft/sec	Muzzle energy ft-lbs	Powder charge grains	Peak pressure avg. of 5 shots	"Efficiency"	Muzzle impulse lb-sec	Free recoil velocity of 7 lb shotgun ft/sec
4½ -1½ -2 Winchester Super Speed Magnum Mark 5 Lot 056BH5M WC-530 Propellant	674	1263	2390	36.1 Actual (37. nominal)	12,470	66.2	4.3	19.7
Winchester Super Speed 3¾ -1¼ -6 Mark 5 Lot V113BN2M WC-490 Propellant	570	1308	2166	30.8 Actual (32. nominal)	11,680	70.3	3.75	17.3
Western Xpert 3-1-4 Lot D3CC-1M WC-410	470	1284	1719	21.0 Actual (21. nominal)	11,086	81.87	3.0	13.7

Figure 8-22 Interior ballistics of shotshells.

shell and dividing this total by the volume of the powder chamber before the propellant starts burning. On this shotshell the expansion ratio is fourteen times as great as on the current 7.62 NATO (.30 caliber) centerfire rifle cartridge.

THEORETICAL AND ACTUAL PERFORMANCE OF SHOTSHELLS

There are many analytical tools available to assist in developing a better understanding of the performance of modern ammunition. One of the most valuable techniques is the careful analysis of the actual pressure-time curve generated by a shotshell with the assistance of computer programs. This was done for the Xpert 3-1-4 load. Five pressure-time measurements for each type of ammunition were recorded. One pressure-time trace from the oscilloscope was selected in which muzzle velocity and peak pressure were closest to the average measurements of the five shots. The photograph of the oscilloscope trace was then measured using Vernier calipers, and the pressure readings for each time interval used as an input to a computer program. A print-out of the computer calculations is shown in Figure 8-23, and a graphical representation is shown in Figure 8-24. The left-hand column of Figure 8-23 shows the

```
     AREA   WEIGHT  TRAVEL   DT PRESCAL TIMECAL TEXIT    N
     SQ IN     GRS      IN   CM  PSI/CM   MS/CM    CM
    0.4185   481.00   27.00 0.20   5799.   0.500  5.20   28


0.00 0.15 0.39 1.10 1.70 1.90 1.58 1.20 0.96 0.77
0.60 0.50 0.41 0.35 0.30 0.26 0.24 0.21 0.20 0.19
0.16 0.15 0.13 0.13 0.12 0.11 0.10 0.00


MUZZLE EXIT CONDITIONS ARE                 CF=
    2.59         0.      1277.    27.00  0.805     1585.    33.50


   12 GAUGE   XPERT   3-1-4                     08-11-70
```

TIME MS	PRESSURE PSI	CORR.VEL FT/SEC	CORR.TRAV INCHES	VELOCITY FT/SEC	TRAVEL INCHES
0.00	0.	0.	0.00	0.	0.00
0.10	875.	6.	0.00	7.	0.00
0.20	2261.	27.	0.01	34.	0.02
0.30	6378.	96.	0.08	119.	0.10
0.40	9858.	227.	0.27	282.	0.34
0.50	11018.	396.	0.65	492.	0.80
0.60	9162.	556.	1.22	690.	1.52
0.70	6958.	683.	1.97	847.	2.45
0.80	5613.	782.	2.85	970.	3.54
0.90	4488.	861.	3.84	1069.	4.76
1.00	3479.	924.	4.91	1146.	6.10
1.10	2899.	974.	6.05	1209.	7.51
1.20	2406.	1016.	7.25	1261.	8.99
1.30	2041.	1051.	8.49	1304.	10.53
1.40	1768.	1081.	9.77	1341.	12.12
1.50	1536.	1107.	11.08	1374.	13.75
1.60	1397.	1130.	12.43	1402.	15.42
1.70	1252.	1151.	13.79	1428.	17.12
1.80	1159.	1170.	15.19	1452.	18.85
1.90	1101.	1188.	16.60	1474.	20.60
2.00	968.	1204.	18.04	1494.	22.38
2.10	898.	1219.	19.49	1513.	24.19
2.20	782.	1232.	20.97	1529.	26.01
2.30	753.	1244.	22.45	1544.	27.86
2.40	713.	1256.	23.95	1559.	29.72
2.50	672.	1267.	25.47	1572.	31.60
2.60	620.	1277.	27.00	1585.	33.50

Figure 8-23 Computer printout of interior ballistics.

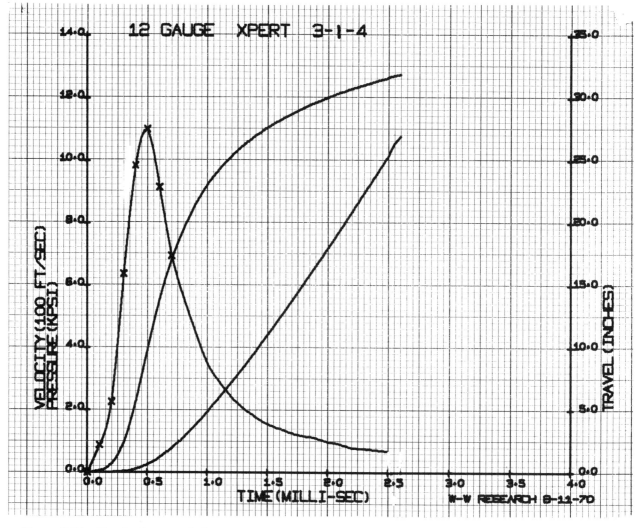

Figure 8-24 Graph of interior ballistics.

time intervals of the pressure-time trace in thousandths of a second. Measurements have been taken each one tenth of a millisecond. In the second column the corresponding pressure measurement at each time interval is printed. The second column from the right shows the velocity build up of the shot column if no friction were present. These calculations indicate that at the end of 2.6 thousandths of a second the shot column would reach a theoretical velocity of 1,585 feet per second (fps) and would have traveled 33.5 inches.

The computer automatically adjusts the computations to the actual travel distance of the shot charge in the barrel. In this case the actual travel is approximately 27 inches. A ratio of 27 divided by 33.5 gives a correction factor of .805. Both the velocity and travel of the shot charge are then recalculated by the computer using this correction factor. This computes out to a predicted muzzle velocity of 1,277 fps which corresponds

closely to the average measured velocity of 1,284 fps.

The graphical results of these calculations is shown in Figure 8-24. The curve farthest to the left is the pressure-time curve, which is a replot of the pressure-time curve on the oscilloscope. The middle curve is the velocity-time curve and shows the very high rate of acceleration during the high-pressure phase, and a relatively small rate of velocity increase as the barrel pressure declines below 4,000 psi. The right-hand curve shows the travel of the shot charge versus the time in milliseconds. The scale for this curve is on the right-hand margin, whereas the scale for the other two curves are on the left-hand side. The distance-time curve shows that at the end of one millisecond the shot charge has traveled about 5 inches. In this short distance the chamber pressure has declined to 3,500 psi and the shot charge has already achieved a velocity of 920 fps. An additional 20 inches of travel through the barrel adds only another 350 fps to the velocity.

The initial acceleration of the shot column is extremely high. For example at the end of ½ millisecond, the shot column has moved less than ¾ of an inch and yet the velocity has already reached 400 fps. This is approximately at peak pressure of slightly over 11,000 psi. At muzzle exit the gas pressure in the barrel has dropped slightly over 600 psi and the velocity has reached a measured 1,288 fps.

Theoretical Prediction of Muzzle Velocity

During 1970 Winchester Group Research developed a small analytical computer program to predict the muzzle velocity of modern ballistic systems. This formula, developed by George Lehto, was programmed into a small computer, and also into the medium-sized research computer. The purpose was to calculate the theoretical maximum velocity that will occur if all of the propellant were burned at peak chamber pressure and then allowed to expand as the projectile travels up the bore. Seven input variables are utilized to model many facets of the ballistic system. The Western 3-1-4 was analyzed using this predictive computer program, in the hope it might give additional insight into shotshell performance. The results of this analysis are shown in the top line of Figure 8-25. The predicted maximum velocity for the Xpert 3-1-4 field load was 1,508 fps, relatively close to the theoretical velocity predicted by the computer program working from actual data, but neglecting bore friction. The actual measured velocity of 1,284 fps for the Xpert loads represents 85 percent of the theoretical maximum value.

REMINGTON PLASTIC SHOTSHELLS

Remington pioneered in three important aspects of modern shotshell technology. They were the first to introduce non-corrosive "Kleanbore" lead styphnate priming in the mid-1920s. In the late 1950s they were the first to introduce plastic shotshells using a specially strengthened polyethylene tube instead of a wound-paper tube. And they also introduced the one-piece molded plastic "power-piston" in loaded shotshells which combined the features of a cup wad for sealing, a resilient spring member to cushion the acceleration of the shot and a polyethylene cup to protect the shot from rubbing against the inside of the shotgun barrel all in one molded component.

The construction of a modern Remington shotshell is shown in Figure 8-26. Peters shotshells are also manufactured by Remington and are of similar construction. The basic elements in this shotshell include a molded-plastic base wad with a thin lip at the forward edge which mates with the specially strengthened polyethylene plastic tube that has been longitudinally extruded and contains a number of fine grooves. The plastic tube is fairly transparent, so that the contents of the shotshells are readily visible to the shooter. The molded base wad and tube are formed into a permanent assembly by the addition of a brass-

THEORETICAL MUZZLE VELOCITY OF SHOTSHELLS

Shotshell	Weight of propellant (pounds)	Weight of wads and shot (pounds)	Theoretical velocity (fps)	Actual velocity (fps)	Ratio of actual to theoretical
Xpert 3-1-4	.003	.06708	1,508	1,284	85%
Super Speed 3¾-1¼-6	.0044	.08143	1,601	1,308	81.7%
Magnum 4½-1½-2	.00516	.09634	1,578	1,263	80.0%

Figure 8-25 Actual and theoretical maximum muzzle velocity.

Figure 8-26 Cutaway of modern Remington shotshell.

plated steel head which is swaged and grooved to lock the elements together. A large battery cup type primer with a body diameter of .240 inches and containing non-corrosive lead styphnate priming is pressed into the head of the shotshell forming a gas-tight seal with the molded-plastic base wad.

Remington is closely affiliated with I. E. du-Pont de Nemours, and Remington shotshells are loaded with DuPont propellants. A fine flaked powder is shown in Figure 8-26. Shotshell propellants must be fast burning and easy to ignite. Normal centerfire propellants are so difficult to ignite that the flame would quench out and give incomplete burning in a shotshell. The propellant is slightly compressed by the one-piece molded polyethylene "power-piston." The power-piston is a tight fit in the inside of the plastic tube and the skirt is designed to provide a good gas seal when expanded radially due to the propellant pressure. The final loading steps include placement of the measured charge of shot of the proper size and crimping over the mouth of the case using an eight-segment folded crimp.

The operating sequence of the shotshell and barrel is shown in Figures 8-27 and 8-28. The upper illustration of Figure 8-27 shows the shell just before the firing pin strikes the primer. All of the elements are in the configurations shown in Figure 8-26. The lower illustration of Figure 8-27

shows the situation within the shotshell after ignition has occurred and as the shotshell propellant is zooming towards 10,000 pounds-per-square-inch pressure. The primer has ignited the propellant which is partially burned (not fully burned as shown in the illustration). The gas pressure has moved the cup wad forward at a high rate of speed, compressing the plastic spring members between the cup wad and the charge of shot. The shot container has moved forward slightly, breaking open the seal at the mouth of the shotshell. The shot charge then continues forward, having the violent acceleration cushioned by the spring members, and being protected from contact with the shotgun bore by the molded polyethylene cup which surrounds it.

Figure 8-28 shows the performance of the power-piston near the muzzle of the shotgun barrel. In the upper illustration the shot column is being radially squeezed by the bore of the shotgun. As this occurs the polyethylene cup is forced inwards causing a radial inward force upon the shot column, lengthening it slightly forward of the top of the cup wad. The situation as the shot clears the muzzle is shown in the lower illustration. The molded polyethylene shot container has four longitudinal splits and as the shot charge clears the muzzle, air pressure acting on these exposed lips, bends them into the deflected position shown. This action does two things: first it moves

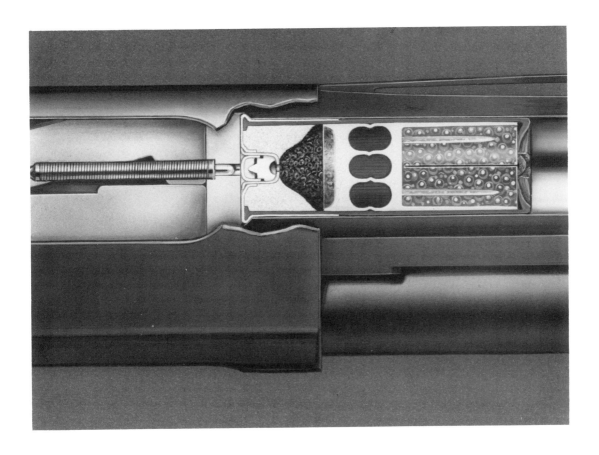

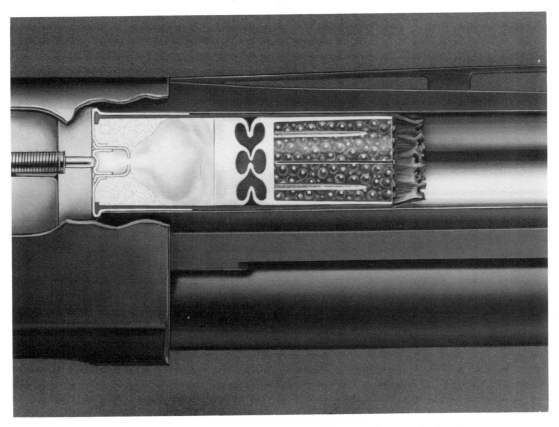

Figure 8-27 Remington shotshell just before ignition and approaching peak chamber pressure.

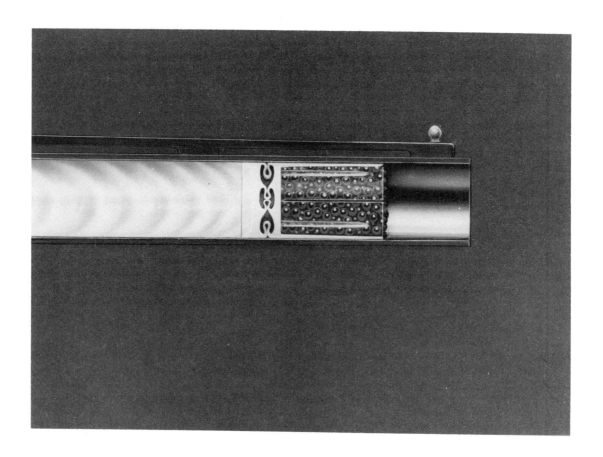

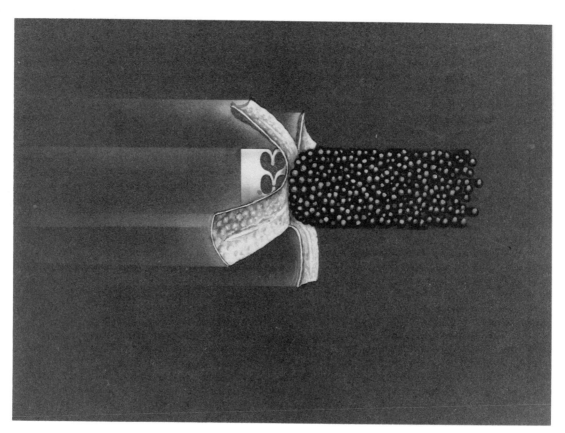

Figure 8-28   Remington shotshell at the muzzle, showing action of power-piston.

the polyethylene radially outwards away from the shot column, thus releasing the shot cloud without disrupting the pattern. Second, the arms spread in the position shown in the lower illustration causing a high air resistance so that the power-piston decelerates rapidly and quickly falls to the ground.

Remington shotshells utilizing power-pistons are available in high-base long-range loads in 12, 16, 20, 28 gauge and 410 bore. Powder charges vary from 4½ drams equivalent in the 12-gauge shotshells down to 2¼ drams equivalent in the 28-gauge shotshell. Pellet sizes from BB to No. 9 shot are offered. The Peters high velocity loads are available in the same gauges and shot sizes. Both Remington and Peters also offer lower-powered field loads which are identified by a lower base wad. These are marketed under the "Shur Shot" load in the Remington line and the "Victor" load in the Peters line, and are offered in 12, 16 and 20 gauges. Special trap and skeet loads are offered in both lines under the "All American" load. Trap loads are available in 12, 16, 20 and 28 gauges and the Skeet loads are available in all gauges including 410.

WINCHESTER-WESTERN PLASTIC SHOTSHELLS

In the late 1950s the shotshell industry underwent a quiet revolution that lasted for a decade. Most major manufacturers in the United States and Europe had been experimenting with injec-

tion-molded plastic shotshells in the years following World War II. When I joined Winchester in 1953, research into injection-molded shotshells of ethyl cellulose plastics was in high gear, and one of my first assignments, as a shotgun designer, was to convert Model 12 and Model 97 shotguns to handle very short 12-gauge shotshells molded from this material. Unfortunately, ethyl cellulose contains an ingredient called plasticizer. When loaded rounds assembled with shells fabricated of ethyl cellulose were stored under very hot conditions, this plasticizer migrates into the powder. As a result, the powder was adversely affected and partial burning of propellant (squibs) were encountered. In the mid-1950s Winchester-Western abandoned this approach.

During the same period research began into polyethylene and other thermo-plastic materials that might be suitable for injection-molded shells. Injection molding utilizes a closed die which has the exact shape of a shotshell. Hot, melted plastic under thousands of pounds per square inch of pressure is injected into this die. The die is water cooled and maintained at a carefully controlled temperature so that the plastic material solidifies rapidly and maintains the shape of the die after it is opened and the plastic component ejected. With all of the plastics available in the 1950s, test results were the same. Typical results are shown in Figure 8-29. At high temperatures the plastic material softened slightly and as the shot charge was accelerated forward by the wad column, the shot tended to expand laterally and gripped the

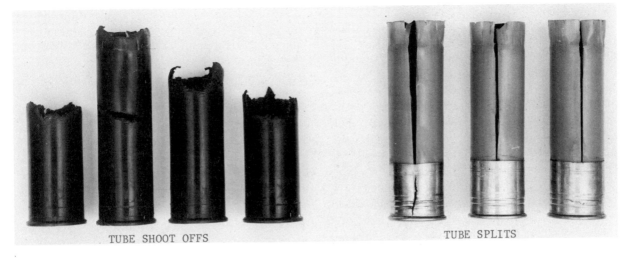

Figure 8-29   Results of tests with early plastic shotshells.

wall of the shotshell. With a strong, heavily waxed paper tube this was no problem, but with injection-molded plastic the shot pellets dug into the tube wall and tended to tear off the front half of the shotshell.

At cold temperatures another problem occurred. The plastic became harder and more brittle and tended to split under the firing pressure, as shown on the right hand side of the illustration. Winchester-Western was finally led to conclude that these defects were symptomatic of the basic nature of the injection-molding process. The characteristics of the available plastic materials were such that when formed by this process it was impossible to give them sufficient strength to withstand the high pressure and violent forces to which a shotshell must be subjected. In particular the tensile strength was too low and the very nature of the material made it highly sensitive to extremes in temperature. Research was forced to conclude that a shotshell meeting all the performance requirements could not be produced by the injection-molding process. The availability of new higher-strength plastic materials, such as the polycarbonate resins in the late 1960s, caused another flurry of activity in injection-molded shotshells. Even this material, which has been highly successful in many demanding requirements, has not provided fully satisfactory shotshells.

The failure of the injection-molding process did not mean that plastic materials were unacceptable. However, the material had to be formed in a way which would give it added strength. Such techniques were available and were used in the manufacture of mono-filament fishing lines, which possess many times greater longitudinal strength than does the basic plastic from which it is fabricated. Also, thin films made from plastics are often many times stronger than the basic strength of the material, due to the extensive "working" of the material during the manufacturing process. Winchester research reasoned that if these techniques could be applied to a plastic shotshell it could give the necessary strength in a longitudinal direction to prevent cutoffs, and sufficient circumferential strength to prevent tube splits.

During the late 1950s extensive research was performed to explore these possibilities and they were eventually successful. A German technique, the Reifenhauser process, was adopted to shotshell manufacture. The highlights of the technique are shown in Figure 8-30. Granules of polyethylene resin are shown in the plastic jar in the upper-left

corner. This resin in the pellet form was blended with a coloring agent and fed into a conventional plastic extrusion machine. The resin was melted and then forced through a ring die at high pressure to form a tube approximately $11/16$ inches in diameter (close to 12 gauge) with a heavy wall thickness. During the extrusion process air pressure was injected inside the tube and then the tube was drawn through a cooling bath to solidify the plastic resin. After the tube was cooled somewhat, it passed into a long heating bath utilizing liquid chemicals to heat the polyethylene to within a few degrees of the melting point. The liquid on the outside of the tube was also pressurized to balance the air pressure on the inside. The tube was then stretched by the machine to six times its normal length. Both the wall thickness and the outside diameter of the tube were drastically reduced as shown in the second illustration of Figure 8-30. During this process the tensile strength of the resin was increased from its original level of 4,500 psi to approximately 18,000 psi in the longitudinal direction. This increased strength prevented tube shootoffs at high temperature levels.

The long, thin tube, which had just been heated to a few degrees below its melting point, still retained air pressure internally. Suddenly the tube was pulled from the confined heating bath into the open air and immediately this internal air pressure expanded the soft tube circumferentially forming a "bubble." This circumferential expansion oriented the molecular structure in that direction and increased the radial strength of the tubing, preventing tube splits at low temperature. Thus the overall process provided increased strength in two directions, which is known as a "bi-axial orientation" of the molecular structure. The expansion of the plastic tube due to the internal air pressure is shown in the third illustration down in the figure. The process was controlled so that the tubing expanded to slightly over 12 gauge in outside diameter, and was then pulled through a sizing die which controlled the outside diameter of the final tube and chilled the material curbing further expansion by internal pressure. The final tube, exactly sized to the outside diameter of a 12-gauge shell, is shown in the lowest illustration.

Winchester-Western spent years of research on this process and introduced plastic shotshells utilizing Reifenhauser tubing in the early 1960s. Shotshells such as the Xpert load shown in Fig-

Figure 8-30 The Reifenhauser process.

212

ures 8-20 and 8-21 utilized the bi-axial oriented tubing.

Compression-Formed Shotshells

Because of the importance of modern shotshells, Winchester-Western Research was also pursuing a second, independent line of technical study during the 1950s and 1960s which blended the injection-molding process with the strength increases of axial orientation. This research led to the "compressed-formed" shotshell.

In developing a compression-formed shotshell, a research team tried to apply metalworking processes to the fabrication of plastic shotshells. The "cup-and-draw process" has been used for a century in the manufacture of metallic ammunition

and the "impact-extrusion process" has been used in the metalworking industry nearly as long. The research attempts to form plastic shotshells by similar processes met with mixed results. Some experiments were total failures while others showed some improvement in tensile strength, although the improvements were only a small percentage of those that were needed. None of the processes showed any significant evidence of being a satisfactory procedure to obtain the shape and strength needed in a one-piece shotshell.

Finally a new approach, which became known as "compression forming," was evolved. Highlights of the technique are shown in Figure 8-31. Ground polyethylene resin was blended with coloring material, as shown in the upper-left illustration. This material was run through a regular injection-

Figure 8-31 The compression forming process.

molding machine and "preforms" were molded in gang dies 40 at a time. These preforms looked somewhat like a short stubby shotshell, but they were almost solid plastic material with only a conical cavity in the top and a central hole $\frac{2}{10}$ of an inch in diameter through the head. After injection molding the preform was heated close to melting temperature and inserted in a die similar in design to those used for making centerfire cartridge cases. A punch was introduced into the die with a pilot, which passed through the $\frac{2}{10}$-inch diameter hole in the preform. As continued pressure was exerted against the punch it drove the tough polyethylene material upwards into the thin circumferential space in the die to form the side walls of the shotshell. This "compression forming" or forced flowing of the polyethylene from the preform takes place in both the longitudinal and circumferential directions, a two-directional flow resulting in the desired "bi-axial orientation." After years of process development and innumerable experiments on plastic resins, die designs and temperature controls, it was found that the thin .030 inch walls of the compression-formed shell that had received a great deal of "working" in this process had tensile strengths as high as 35,000 pounds per square inch. This compares with an original tensile strength of injection-molded polyethylene of 4,500 to 6,000 psi. The compression-formed shell after this operation is shown in the third illustration from the left in Figure 8-31 and a cross section of the formed shell is shown in the right-hand illustration. After the forming operation the shell was trimmed to proper length, as shown in the lower left hand illustration, and then a brass head was swaged into place. A completely loaded compression-formed shotshell is shown in the third illustration from the left in the bottom row. Years of tests and endless experimentation with resins were required before the combination of tough physical properties and good cosmetic appearance was achieved. This was followed by testing extending over several years at 120° F., at –20° F., and under hot, humid conditions to test long-term stability. Extensive firing tests indicated that the brass head was not needed for basic strength. Attempts to market the shells in Italy without the brass head were a failure, however, for both American and European sportsmen are convinced the metallic head adds greatly to the strength of shotshell construction. In actual fact only a metallic rim is required to reinforce the shell against the highly localized forces which oc-

cur in the cartridge cutoffs and in the extractor and ejector of modern automatic shotguns.

One major question about compression-formed shells was how they would stand up to hand loading. Using regular-production 12-gauge compression-formed shells and reloading with the normal $1\frac{1}{8}$-ounce trap load, Winchester Research found that the shell would stand reloading from 25 to 30 times. Surprisingly, the part that invariably failed was the metal head. Upon reaching this stage in the reloading test, the researchers removed the worn-out brass head, replaced it with another and continued reloading. In many cases the all plastic shell continued to stand up under continued reloading until a total of 50 reloadings had been accomplished.

During the late 1960s a research program was carried out to find out just how tough these shells really were. Normally shotshells are loaded to a peak pressure of 12,000 lbs. psi. Proof shells are loaded up in the range of 17,000 lbs. psi. Special experimental shells were loaded at 30,000 lbs. psi, then 35,000 and 40,000 lbs. psi. When these tests were passed successfully, additional shells were loaded at 45,000, 50,000 and 55,000 lbs. psi. At these pressure levels the head of the shells deformed so that they could not be reloaded, but none blew when fired in Model 1200 Winchester shotguns. Finally shotshells were loaded at a range of 60,000 to 65,000 lbs. psi, when failure finally occurred. The unsupported area of the head extruded into the extractor groove, blowing a hole in the head of the shell and blowing out the extractor.

Such extraordinary tests do not in any way mean that it is safe to hand load compression-formed shotshells to such high-pressure levels. The tests were carried out under laboratory conditions and the guns were always fired by remote control, using a long lanyard in a barricaded room. That the shells themselves are safe does not mean that the average shotgun has a barrel which is strong enough to withstand this enormous chamber pressure. Split and bulge barrels, excessive head space in the locking area and other serious and dangerous damage can be anticipated if normal shotguns are fired with excess pressure loads.

One rather strange problem occurred with the early compression-formed shotshells. The tensile strength of the compression-formed shell, particularly in the thin wall at the forward end of the case, is extremely high. The strength is so great upon firing that the pressure remaining in the

214

shell while the shot and wads were traveling down the barrel was insufficient to hold the shell mouth against the chamber wall. The hot gas passed down the outside of the shotshell discoloring the first half inch of the case mouth. This discoloration had no effect upon reloadability or subsequent performance, but the shells did look dirty and it was felt that customers would feel that gas leakage had occurred. Eventually it was found that the regular soft polyethylene collar was not transmitting the full lateral force of the shot column to the tube wall. It was absorbing sufficient force so that the tough mouth of the case was not plastered hard against the chamber wall during early motion of the shot up the barrel. This problem was solved by substituting a polyethylene-coated paper (which was a much harder surface) and this did firmly hold the shotshell mouth

against the chamber wall. Research on compression-formed shotshell technology continued all during the 1960s. A typical skeet and trap load reflecting later technology is shown in Figure 8-32. There are three differences from the early shells. The first was a minor change to the inside of the case near the primer where a ring groove was compression-formed into the polyethylene around the mouth of the No. 209 battery cup primer. It was found that gas pressure entering this groove would drive the lip inward against the mouth of the battery cup primer, eliminating a rare tendency for primer leaks. The second change, of a more major nature, was the result of years of seeking to reduce the taper of the inside wall of the shotshell. A comparison with Figure 8-33 will show that the inside wall of the modern compression-formed shell is much more uniform

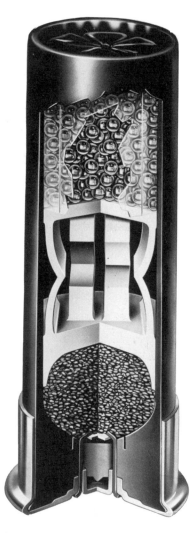

Figure 8-32 Compression-formed skeet shotshell.

Figure 8-33 Early Winchester compression-formed shotshell.

in diameter than the more heavily tapered early shotshell construction.

The third major change was the use of a one piece "AA" cup wad and shot protector instead of the earlier four piece design. The one piece AA wad was first introduced on skeet and trap loads where its improved performance was valuable in raising the scores of expert shooters. Essentially the AA wad consists of three parts. A deep-molded cup wad served to contain and seal gas pressure developed by the propellant. Above this, four arched polyethylene ribs were formed which served as compression spring members to give more gentle acceleration to the shot charge. The upper end of the AA wad was formed into a polyethylene cup with lines of weakness deliberately molded into the polyethylene walls.

After the shot charge was placed into the shell, the mouth of the shell was crimped over with a pie-shaped crimp and heat-sealed hermetically in the center. The functioning of the AA wad is similar to the sequence shown with the Remington "Power Piston" in Figures 8-27 and 8-28. The violent acceleration caused by the rapid pressure rise of the propellant is absorbed by the spring members, which drastically compress and then gradually transmit the force to the shot column. Since the shot has spherical surfaces, pushing the bottom of the shot column causes it to expand laterally, which in turn expands the shotshell mouth against the chamber walls. The crimp is broken open and the shot column and wads start moving down the barrel. Millions of dollars of research in the 1960s had eliminated the problem of dirty case mouths and the all-polyethylene shot protector functions very well.

During the late 1960s and early 1970s there was a gradual expansion of the use of compression-formed shotshells throughout the Winchester and Western lines. Many research and manufacturing problems had to be overcome before this construction could be adopted across the board. An example of this is the 410 compression-formed shotshells shown in Figure 8-34. While the layman might think that once the process was developed it would be easy to adopt it to various gauges, this little monster turned out to have incredible technical problems. Because of the small diameter and great length of the shell (a 3 inch 410 is one of the longest shotshells manufactured) the ratio of sidewall to base material is far higher on the 410 than on any other shotshell. Years of patient research and process development were required

before success was achieved. Because the ¾-ounce shot charge requires a great length of internal volume, the wad column had to be modified from the normal AA construction. This in turn required careful tailoring to provide smooth acceleration of the shot column without the spring members provided by the AA wad or the Remington power-piston construction.

Super Speed Shotshells

The construction of a compression-formed Winchester Super Speed shotshell is shown in Figure 8-35. In order to create this illustration, shotshells used in the ballistic testing for computer modeling the Model 1400 shotgun mechanism were analyzed. After the ballistic testing was completed,

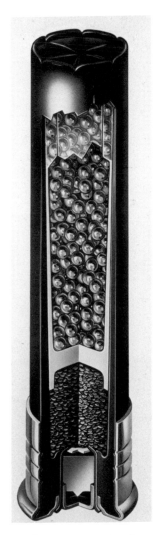

Figure 8-34 410-bore compression-formed shotshell.

216

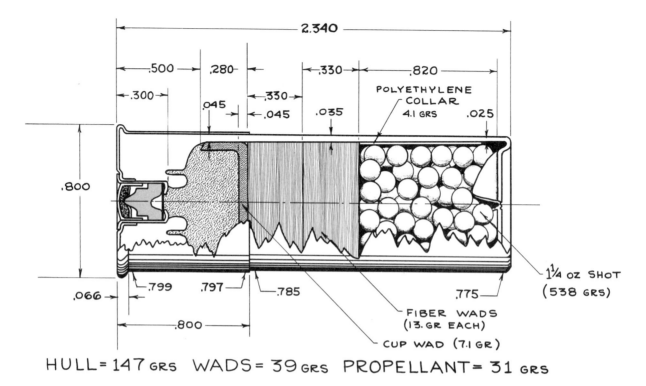

HULL=147 GRS WADS=39 GRS PROPELLANT=31 GRS

Figure 8-35 Winchester Mark 5 shotshell.

several shells were carefully sectioned, using a knife so that no material was removed. The location of the internal elements was measured and is recorded in the figure. Internal parts were then removed and weighed. The compression-formed plastic hull with primer and head reinforcement weighed 147 grains. The cup wad and two ⅜-inch fiber wads (compressed height of .330 inches) weighed 39 grains. The average weight of propellant was 31 grains. The shot charge was 1¼ ounces of No. 6 shot contained inside a thin polyethylene collar which weighed only 4.1 grains.

Some interesting things were discovered during this analysis. Due to the processing techniques, the thickness of the brass head varied considerably. The flat surface of the head measured .027 inch, while the mouth of the reinforcement which surrounds the shotshell was only .010 inch. The brass reinforcement had a maximum diameter of .880 inch over the rim, and the body tapers very slightly from .800 inch just forward of the head to .797 inch at the forward edge. The center section of the head reinforcement is pierced at the center and driven inward, forming a short brass sleeve to receive and reinforce the battery cup primer assembly.

Primer Assembly

The shotshell ignition is provided by a No. 209 battery cup primer. This consists of the large outer cup, formed out of a red-brass alloy with a basic diameter of .240 inch, and a flange at the open end which flares out to a diameter of .314 inch. The cup is slightly over .300 inch deep and the closed end has a small hole punched in the center to allow the flame to pass through to the propellant cavity. A flat anvil is punched from cartridge brass alloy sheet. It is designed to be a light press fit inside the battery cup. A thin disc of paper foil is dropped into the bottom of the battery cup, and the anvil press fitted down on top of the paper. This construction prevents any of the ball propellant from sifting into the battery cup primer during transportation.

A primer cup is then punched from cartridge brass alloy and nickel plated. A nominal priming charge of .83 grains of lead styphnate tetracene-type non-corrosive priming mixture is placed into the primer cup and covered with a disc of white Kraft paper coated with shellac. The primer cup is then press fitted into the battery cup to complete the primer assembly. Primer mixture is handled in a damp condition for safety, and sensitivity is achieved by drying the finished primer assembly at elevated temperatures to reduce moisture content. The primer assembly is press fitted into the head of the empty shotshell, forming an interference fit with the brass head reinforcement and also with the polyethylene which forms the base of the propellant cavity.

Final Loading Operations

After priming, a charge of 31 grains of WC-490 ball propellant is measured by volume and dropped into the empty shotshell. The exact powder charge is varied slightly to compensate for minor differences in propellant strength. The powder charge is selected to achieve the specified muzzle velocity within the allowable pressure limits.

The propellant is sealed in place by a cup wad made of laminated, waxed paper .045-inch thick, which is formed with a cylindrical skirt facing downwards into the propellant cavity. The skirt is so formed that it retains considerable outward pressure against the inner walls of the plastic shell, and this force is tremendously amplified by the gas pressure as the ball powder is ignited. Two $\frac{3}{8}$-inch fiber wads are then loaded into the shell and pressed firmly down onto the cup wad. In a completely loaded shell the fiber wads are compressed to a thickness of approximately .330 inch each.

The assembly of three wads performs two important functions. One is to act like the cork in a bottle, providing an initial resistance against the propellant pressure and promoting better ignition and burning. The second is to cushion the acceleration of the shot column so as to minimize the deformation of the shot.

The next step in the loading process is to insert a .012 inch polyethylene-paper collar into the shotshell. This collar, weighing only 4.1 grains, protects the shot column all the way to the muzzle of the shell. Experimentation showed that a polyethylene-paper collar provided a fairly slick surface and absorbed considerable wear. Examination of these collars after firing showed that the contact points between the paper and the spherical shot were often worn completely through during passage up the barrel.

A charge of 1¼ ounces of hardened spherical No. 6 lead shot was dropped into the shell at the next station in the loading machine. The shot column is slightly over 8/10-inch long. It is retained in the shell by extensively working the front end of the polyethylene tube into a sharp 180° bend. The polyethylene is sufficiently strong so that the interior radius of the bend is less than the thickness of the polyethylene wall. Special forming dies create six pie-shaped segments and the folded material forms a skirt which is shown extending down into the shot column in the upper half of Figure 8-35. A water-tight seal is achieved by a slight spinning operation which heat-seals the very center of the folded head crimp. The shell then goes to a printing station which prints the trademark and designation of the shotshell, 3¾ —1¼ —6. The 3¾ marking refers to the propellant charge which is equivalent to an old black-powder charge of 3¾ drams (103 grains of black powder). The 1¼ designation refers to the weight of the shot charge in ounces. The "6" refers to the size of the shot (.110 inches in diameter, with 225 pellets to the ounce). Several shells were disassembled and the propellant charge weighed. The actual charge averaged 30.8 grains of WC-490 ball propellant. This compared with a nominal loading weight of 32 grains of this propellant. The difference, 1.2 grains, indicated that this particular lot of powder was so efficient it did not require the full nominal charge to achieve the specified ballistics. Weight of the shot charge and wads was 570 grains and the measured muzzle velocity was 1,308 feet per second. This calculates out to a muzzle energy of the shot of 2,166 foot-pounds. Although the shot is the only useful muzzle energy, the propellant has to accelerate both the shot and the wad column.

Ballistics of the Super Speed Shotshell

The interior ballistics of this shotshell are shown in Figure 8-36. It is an extremely efficient shell in terms of propellant efficiency, providing 70.3 foot-pounds of muzzle energy for each grain of propellant. This high efficiency is achieved because the propellant is burned within an insulated plastic chamber so that the heat transfer losses are far lower than they are to a cold brass case wall, as in a centerfire or rimfire cartridge. The second factor adding to the high efficiency is the extreme expansion ratio which occurs. The particular shells utilized in this test series achieved an average muzzle velocity of 1,308 feet per second with an ejected mass of wads and shot of 570 grains. This corresponds to a muzzle energy of 2,166 foot-

AREA	WEIGHT	TRAVEL		DT	PRESCAL	TIMECAL	TEXIT	N
SQ IN	GRS	IN	CM		PSI/CM	MS/CM	CM	
0.4185	585.00	26.00	0.20		5795.	0.500	5.20	27

```
0.00 0.15 0.27 0.58 1.41 1.97 1.96 1.73 1.46 1.18
1.00 0.80 0.67 0.56 0.47 0.42 0.36 0.32 0.28 0.25
0.23 0.20 0.18 0.16 0.14 0.13 0.12
```

MUZZLE EXIT CONDITIONS ARE   CF=

2.59	701.	1295.	26.00	0.815	1588.	31.89

12 GAUGE SUPER SPEED 3 3/4- 1 1/4--6   11-12-70

TIME	PRESSURE	CORR.VEL	CORR.TRAV	VELOCITY	TRAVEL
MS	PSI	FT/SEC	INCHES	FT/SEC	INCHES
0.00	0.	0.	0.00	0.	0.00
0.10	875.	5.	0.00	7.	0.00
0.20	1593.	20.	0.01	25.	0.02
0.30	3361.	50.	0.05	61.	0.06
0.40	8170.	127.	0.15	156.	0.19
0.50	11416.	260.	0.38	319.	0.47
0.60	11358.	411.	0.79	504.	0.97
0.70	10025.	551.	1.37	677.	1.68
0.80	8460.	673.	2.10	826.	2.58
0.90	6838.	773.	2.97	948.	3.65
1.00	5795.	856.	3.95	1050.	4.85
1.10	4636.	924.	5.02	1134.	6.16
1.20	3882.	980.	6.17	1202.	7.57
1.30	3268.	1027.	7.37	1260.	9.04
1.40	2723.	1066.	8.63	1308.	10.59
1.50	2433.	1100.	9.93	1350.	12.18
1.60	2103.	1130.	11.27	1386.	13.82
1.70	1860.	1156.	12.64	1418.	15.51
1.80	1622.	1178.	14.04	1446.	17.23
1.90	1495.	1199.	15.47	1471.	18.98
2.00	1332.	1217.	16.92	1494.	20.76
2.10	1176.	1234.	18.39	1514.	22.56
2.20	1089.	1249.	19.88	1532.	24.39
2.30	961.	1262.	21.39	1549.	26.24
2.40	857.	1274.	22.91	1563.	28.11
2.50	770.	1285.	24.45	1577.	29.99
2.59	701.	1295.	26.00	1588.	31.89

Figure 8-36 Interior ballistics of Super Speed shotshells.

pounds and the "muzzle impulse" is quite high at 3.75 pounds-seconds. Muzzle impulse is a very useful quantity for gun designers and ballistics experts. The main usefulness lies in the fact that Newton's third law of motion states that for every action there is an equal and opposite reaction. The muzzle impulse, or momentum of the shot cloud, the wads, and the propellant gases in a forward direction, will be exactly balanced by the rearward momentum of the shotgun against the shooter's shoulder. This is not true of the muzzle energy. For example, the shotshell has over 2,000 foot-pounds of muzzle energy coming out the muzzle, but only about 28.3 foot-pounds of muzzle energy are delivered to the shooter's shoulder. If energy equivalent to the muzzle energy of the shotshell were delivered to the shooter, he would be knocked head over heels.

The muzzle impulse is useful, however, in explaining how the shotgun will behave. For example, the Super Speed load has a muzzle impulse of 3.75 pound-seconds indicating that it would give much higher recoil than the standard 7.62mm NATO cartridge fired in the M-14 rifle which has a muzzle impulse of 2.7 pound-seconds, and far more recoil than the 5.56mm cartridge used in the M-16 rifle which has only 1.24 pound-seconds of muzzle impulse. If a seven-pound shotgun were hung from thin slender wires and allowed to freely recoil when fired with the Super Speed load, it would recoil with a velocity of 17.3 feet per second. Of course it never really achieves this velocity, for it is in contact with the shooter's shoulder and after a very slight initial motion, gun and shoulder recoil together. But nonetheless this measurement of 17.3 feet per second free-recoil velocity gives a measure of the recoil intensity. Normal skeet and trap loads in a seven-pound shotgun would give only about 14 feet per second free-recoil velocity.

The pressure-time curve which most closely represented the average performance of the 3¾—1¼—6 shot shells was selected and the pressure for each .10 milliseconds of time was measured utilizing vernier calipers and a magnifying glass. This technique is laborious and there are opportunities for error if the measurements are not carefully taken. During the early 1970s a completely integrated computer setup has been developed which will automatically take the output signals from the Piezo-electric gauge (which is an "analog" signal) and convert to a "digital" signal which can be fed directly into a computer. With this new setup the output information is the same but the accuracy is slightly better and the speed enormously increased.

The measured pressure and time measurements for Super Speed shotshells are shown in the left hand two columns of Figure 8-36. The information required to convert these measurements into a calculated velocity and travel are shown as the input information in the upper two blocks of numbers in the figure. The computer program then chews away on the input information and calculates the velocity that the shot charge would achieve with no friction in the system. This calculated information, shown in the right-hand two columns of the figure show that the shot charge would travel 31.89 inches during the measured 2.59 milliseconds that the shot charge is in the barrel. Theoretical calculations also indicate that a muzzle velocity of 1,588 feet per second would be achieved. The actual travel of the shot charge is 26 inches and so the computer program automatically recalculates a corrected velocity and corrected travel utilizing the ratio of 26 inches over 31.89 inches as a multiplication factor. The corrected velocity and corrected travel are shown as the middle two columns in the figure. The predicted output velocity of 1,295 feet per second checks extremely closely with the average measured velocity of 1,308 feet per second.

The information is then replotted in graphical form, in Figure 8-37. The left-hand curve is the pressure-time curve which duplicates the measured information shown on the oscilloscope. The middle curve shows the velocity relationships of the shot charge. For example, at the end of .5 milliseconds (1/2,000th of a second) the shot charge is traveling at 260 feet per second. At the end of one millisecond it is moving at 856 feet per second. At the end of two milliseconds it has reached a velocity of 1,217 feet per second.

The right-hand curve shows the travel of the shot charge compared with time. This is a replot of the information contained in the fourth column from the left in Figure 8-36. It shows that the shot charge at first travels very slowly, moving over only .80 inch by the time the propellant has reached peak pressure. At the end of one millisecond the pressure in the chamber has declined to 5,800 pounds per square inch pressure and the shot charge has still moved only 4 inches. At this point the velocity of the charge is up to 856 feet per second. From there to the muzzle the shot charge has an average velocity of 1,000 feet per

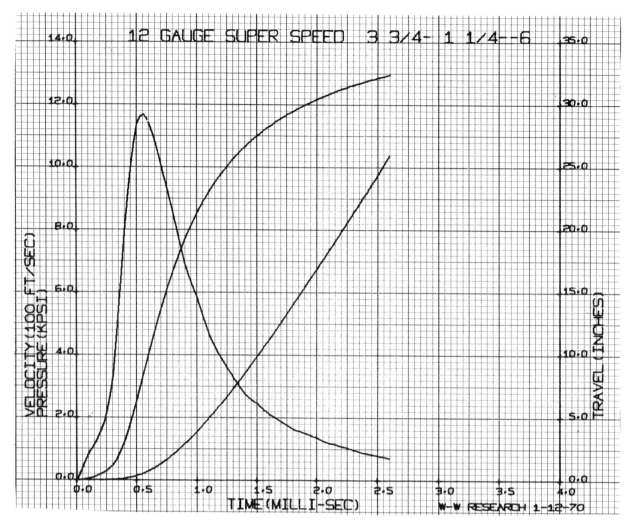

Figure 8-37 Graph of interior ballistics of Super Speed shotshell.

second and hums right along exiting from the muzzle after a total time of 1/400 of a second at a velocity of 1,308 feet per second.

Winchester Magnum Shotshells

The construction of Winchester-Western Magnum shotshells has been virtually identical to that of the Super Speed loads as shown in Figures 8-31 and 8-33. The 1/12-ounce charge of shot requires a length of nearly one inch in the shell which is achieved by using two thinner fiber wads of about .250-inch thickness each.

Magnum shotshells were also analyzed as part of the test program. Highlights of the interior ballistic performance are shown in the upper part of Figure 8-22. The weight of the shot and wads totaled 674 grains and were driven at a muzzle velocity of 1,263 feet per second by a propellant charge of slightly over 36 grains of WC-530 ball

propellant. This particular lot of propellant was slightly more powerful than normal, for it required one grain less than the nominal powder charge to reach the velocity specifications. The WC-530 propellant is a slower-burning propellant than the WC-490 loaded in the Super Speed shotshell and both are slower propellants than the WC-410 used in the light Western 3-1-4 load.

The propellant charge of 36 grains in the Magnum shell is heavy compared to the 21 grains required to reach the same velocity in the Xpert field load. Even though the powerful propellant charge was used to drive a heavy load of shot, the propellant burning characteristics were carefully tailored so that the peak pressure averaged slightly under 12,500 pounds per square inch. Muzzle energy was high at just under 2,400 foot-pounds. Another measure of the power of this cartridge is the muzzle impulse of 4.3 pound-seconds. This high power level would give a free recoil velocity, in a seven-pound gun, of just under 20 feet per second, far above the 15 feet per second established by the British as a tolerable level of gun recoil. Most shooters would agree that shooting rounds of skeet or trap with Magnum shot shells would be extremely unpleasant at these recoil levels. Since most hunting conditions call for only a few shots at a time, these enormously powerful cartridges can be handled by American sportsmen. Most skilled shooters who use a lot of Magnum shotshells will tend to select a heavy shotgun (around 9 pounds) to minimize the recoil velocity and the recoil impact on the shooter's shoulder.

The computer analysis of the 12-gauge Magnum shotshell is shown in Figure 8-38. The theoretical velocity with no bore friction is 1,376 feet

```
      AREA    WEIGHT   TRAVEL   DT PRESCAL TIMECAL TEXIT    N
      SQ IN      GRS       IN   CM  PSI/CM   MS/CM    CM
     0.4185   692.00    28.00 0.20   5766.   0.500  5.40   28


 0.00 0.18 0.84 2.07 2.17 1.95 1.58 1.31 1.08 0.90
 0.75 0.64 0.55 0.48 0.41 0.35 0.31 0.28 0.25 0.22
 0.20 0.18 0.16 0.15 0.14 0.12 0.11 0.10


 MUZZLE EXIT CONDITIONS ARE                 CF=
     2.69      605.     1246.       28.00  0.905       1376.      30.90


    12  GAUGE MAGNUM MARK 5   4 1/2-1 1/2-2           11-12-70
```

TIME MS	PRESSURE PSI	CORR.VEL FT/SEC	CORR.TRAV INCHES	VELOCITY FT/SEC	TRAVEL INCHES
0.00	0.	0.	0.00	0.	0.00
0.10	1055.	3.	-0.00	4.	-0.00
0.20	4843.	36.	0.01	40.	0.01
0.30	11935.	147.	0.12	162.	0.13
0.40	12512.	299.	0.39	331.	0.43
0.50	11243.	447.	0.84	493.	0.92
0.60	9110.	572.	1.45	631.	1.60
0.70	7553.	675.	2.20	745.	2.43
0.80	6227.	759.	3.06	838.	3.38
0.90	5189.	830.	4.02	916.	4.44
1.00	4336.	888.	5.05	981.	5.58
1.10	3742.	938.	6.15	1036.	6.79
1.20	3188.	981.	7.30	1083.	8.06
1.30	2767.	1017.	8.50	1123.	9.38
1.40	2398.	1049.	9.74	1158.	10.75
1.50	2046.	1077.	11.02	1189.	12.16
1.60	1810.	1100.	12.33	1215.	13.61
1.70	1620.	1122.	13.66	1238.	15.08
1.80	1458.	1141.	15.02	1259.	16.58
1.90	1308.	1158.	16.40	1278.	18.10
2.00	1153.	1173.	17.80	1295.	19.65
2.10	1066.	1187.	19.21	1310.	21.21
2.20	957.	1199.	20.64	1324.	22.79
2.30	876.	1210.	22.09	1336.	24.39
2.40	807.	1221.	23.55	1348.	26.00
2.50	697.	1230.	25.02	1358.	27.62
2.60	680.	1238.	26.50	1367.	29.26
2.69	605.	1246.	28.00	1376.	30.90

Figure 8-38 Interior ballistics of 12-gauge Magnum shotshell.

per second and the calculated travel is 30.9 inches. The calculated muzzle velocity is 1,246 feet per second utilizing a corrected shot travel of 28 inches. The actual muzzle velocity of 1,263 feet per second represents 92 percent of the velocity which would be achieved with no friction.

The performance of the Magnum shotshells is shown in graphical form in Figure 8-39. The left-hand curve is a replot of the pressure-time curve shown on the oscilloscope. The middle curve shows the velocity buildup of the shot column under the accelerating force of the gas pressure. Peak pressure is achieved at the end of .4 milliseconds (1/2,500 second). Although the shot charge has moved only 4/10 of an inch, it has already achieved a velocity of 300 feet per second. At the end of the incredibly short time of one thousandth of a second the shot charge has trav-

eled slightly over 5 inches and has reached a velocity of 888 feet per second. From this point until muzzle exit at 2.69 milliseconds, the shot charge is slowly accelerating from 888 feet per second to the muzzle velocity of 1,246. The average velocity over this time span is 1,100 feet per second.

The right-hand curve shows the relationship of travel versus time. It has a slight upward curvature as the gas pressure continues to accelerate the shot charge, and the shot column covers a greater distance with each increment of time as it nears the muzzle.

Magnum shotshells pose the most difficult problems in research and production. The extremely heavy shot charge must be contained within the confines of the standard sized shotshell. Normal propellants would run the peak pressures way over the safe shotgun maximum of 12,500 psi to

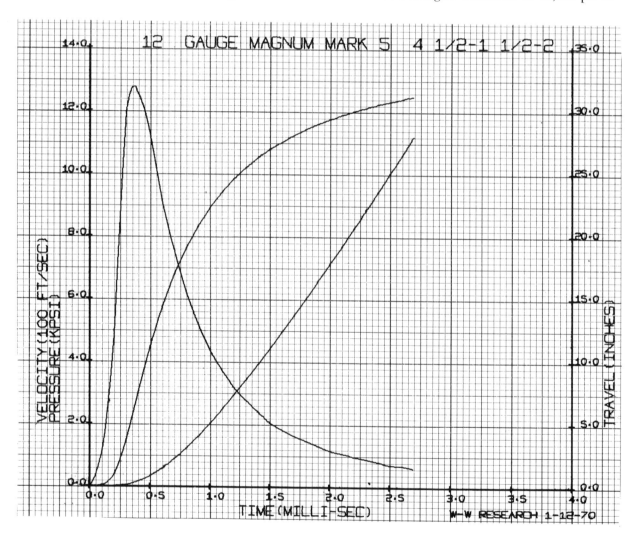

Figure 8-39 Graph of interior ballistics of Magnum shotshell.

achieve muzzle velocities close to 1,300 feet per second. Propellant characteristics are carefully tailored, utilizing all the tricks of the trade to provide the unique combination of good ignition, high muzzle velocity and a moderate peak pressure. Some of these tricks include flattening the ball propellant grains and then adding special "deterrents," which slow down the initial burning rate of the propellant grains till the flame has burned through the deterrent coating. By this time the propellant has passed peak pressure and the rate of gas generation is increased as the flame eats into the basic ball propellant beneath the deterrent coating.

Magnum shotshells truly represent the maximum-performance package that can be squeezed into a standard-sized shotshell.

FEDERAL SHOTSHELLS

The Federal Cartridge Corporation of Minneapolis is an independent ammunition manufacturer whose strongest offerings are in the shotshell and rimfire types of ammunition. My first shooting as a boy in the early 1940s was with Federal Monark rimfire cartridges marketed through Sears, Roebuck. Since my major source of income was digging and hauling sand at a nickel a wagon load, the cost of ammunition loomed large in my budget. By saving for several weeks, I could get together $1.70, which allowed me to purchase a carton of 500 rounds of Federal standard velocity .22 short cartridges. This works out to an incredible 17¢ for a box of shells. At that time the Remington and Winchester ammunition was considerably more powerful than Federal and cost 25¢ a box. Not only was the Federal ammunition cheaper, it was much quieter—a major consideration in the suburban community where I grew up. Federal has continued to market ammunition both under their own trademark and through major sporting-goods houses during the past 40 years.

In the early 1970s the Federal line of shotshells was in transition. The high-base shotshells marketed under the "Hi-Power" trademark and the low-base shotshells marketed under the "Field Load" were manufactured with semitransparent plastic cases similar to that used in the Remington and Winchester-Western Reifenhauser shotshells. On top of the propellant a stack of two molded fiber wads were assembled and then a molded polyethylene cup which held the shot, rather similar to the front section of a Winchester-Western AA

wad. Twenty-eight gauge and 410 high-power shotshells were still loaded in paper tubes. Federal also marketed an economy line of "Monark" target shells which were loaded in paper tubes in 12 and 16 gauge and 410 bore, and in plastic hulls in 20 and 28 gauge. The top of the Federal shotshell line are the 12-gauge Champion II target loads. These include a new one-piece plastic hull. After the polyethylene is formed into the basic hull structure, a brass head is swaged in place and a Federal battery cup primer pressed into the head. The propellant charge of flake powder is measured and placed into the case and then the Federal "pellet protector wad" pressed into the mouth of the case and compressed down on the propellant charge. The pellet protector wad consists of two parts. A molded cup wad is made like a disc with a flange at the edge to provide gas sealing. The second component is the entire forward assembly, consisting of the shot cup and a long central post extending from the shot cup back to the cup wad and the cylindrical outer surface, which is in contact with the inside of the shot shell. After the hardened lead shot charge is dropped in the shotshell the mouth of the case is formed over, using a pie-shaped crimp to retain the shot.

Actual photographs taken 12 inches from the muzzle show four petals of the polyethylene shot cup beginning to fold back and release the shot. The gas-sealing cup wad has been driven forward by the acceleration of the gas, compressing the center post and the polyethylene ring to one-half its original height. A photograph 36 inches from the muzzle shows the petals of the shot protector completely folded back and the plastic cup wads separated into two pieces and traveling about an inch away from the rear of the shot column.

PERFORMANCE OF MODERN SHOTSHELLS

The intense competition in the field of shotgun ammunition has caused a great deal of research and engineering to develop better shotshells. First the black powder was replaced with bulk smokeless, then the bulk smokeless replaced with dense smokeless, and more complex construction adopted to provide improved performance. But what did these improvements do for the shooter? Certainly one reading the advertising copy of the early 20th century would come to the conclusion that the ultimate in shotshell construction had already been achieved and that no further improvements were possible.

During the early years of the 20th century most of the changes were concerned with developing more durable, more reliable, cleaner-burning shotshells. During the past 40 years there have been substantial improvements in pattern performance. These changes are highlighted in Figure 8-40. One of the most competitive fields of shotshell technology are trap loads, since very minor differences in pattern performance can decide a championship between extremely skilled shooters. Another reason that trap loads are a good indicator of performance is that they are designed to be fired in full-choke shotguns. Shooters have become more skilled and handicap distances longer and the ability to provide a tight, uniform pattern has been a consistent research and production objective.

In the mid 1930s the average pattern was about 65 percent. More damaging than this average percentage was the phenomena known as "blown patterns," where the percentage would be under 40 percent of the shot in a 30-inch circle at 40 yards. This phenomena would occasionally occur with any of the ammunition loaded up to the 1930s because the top wad would occasionally remain in the center of the pattern and decelerate due to the air pressure. If this happened the shot would flow around the top wad, causing a lateral acceleration of the shot and a large open space in the center of the pattern. This type of "blown pattern" could be disastrous to a top trap shooter for he could lose a bird in a tightly fought match with no error on his part. Another cause for blown patterns was the escape of gas around the side of the wad column, allowing hot gas to fuse some of the shot together and causing a deflected pattern. This can be understood by considering the construction of an average shotgun chamber. The chamber diameter must exceed .800 of an inch in 12 gauge in order to take the body of the shotshell. It then has a tapered section known as the "forcing cone" which tapers to the bore diameter of .730 of an inch. During firing, the wad column passes from the .730 of an inch inside diameter within the shotshell through the tapered section of the forcing cone and back to the .730 of an inch diameter in the barrel. During passage through the forcing cone, gas occasionally got around the wad column causing serious performance disruption and a blown pattern.

In the late 1930s Remington introduced a fold-type top crimp to replace the roll crimp with its over-shot wad. The end of the shell itself was folded in a pie-shaped pattern, and once this crimp opened up there was nothing ahead of the shot column to disrupt the pattern. Winchester-Western followed suit with this important improvement in 1938. This change increased the average percentage pattern from 65 percent to 68 percent, and made a significant improvement in the excepted minimum percentage pattern which might be encountered in a occasional shotshell.

In 1946 Winchester-Western made a major improvement in shotshells through the development and patenting of the "cup wad," which is shown in Figures 8-19 and 8-20. Use of the cup wad significantly reduced gas leakage around the wad column and brought the average performance of the trap loads to 72 percent pattern at 40 yards. More significantly, by eliminating almost all of the gas leakage, there was a great improvement in the expected minimum shot pattern, which jumped to 60 percent.

In the early 1960s another major improvement came with the introduction of the W-W Mark 5 plastic wrapper around the shot. This feature again had a significant effect on performance by reducing the deformation of the shot against the interior surface of the barrel, upping the pattern percentage to 77 percent and causing another slight increase in the minimum expected pattern—to about 62 percent. During the 1960s Remington developed two significant improvements which have had a major effect on shotshell technology. First was the development of the oriented polyethylene tube. Remington's special manufacturing techniques made polyethylene material sufficiently tough to withstand the firing forces and they received an important patent that covered both design and manufacturing techniques for plastic shotshells utilizing plastic tubes. Later in the 1960s Remington introduced its unitized "power piston," and Winchester-Western introduced the A-A wad. The effect of the one-piece wads is shown in the right-hand side of Figure 8-40. The average pattern percentage rose to 80 percent and the expected minimum pattern rose to 65 percent.

The effect of these changes over the past 40 years has been dramatically illustrated in the games of skeet and trap. During the 1930s there would be 3 or 4 men who had a perfect run of 100 straight during a match. In modern times there is greatly increased participation in skeet

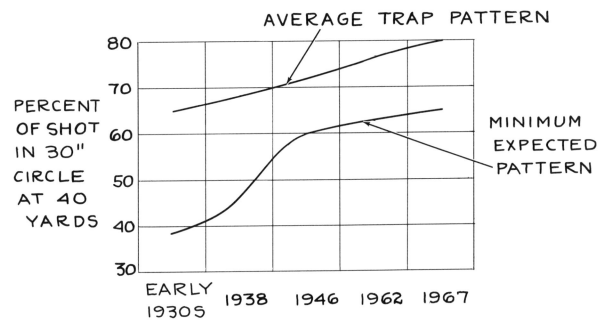

Figure 8-40   Graph of improvement in trap patterns.

but there are hundreds of men breaking 100 straight during the big matches. Similarly, in trap shooting the maximum handicapping distance during the 1930s and the early postwar years was the 25 yard line. This meant that your top-rated shooter would stand 25 yards from the trap so that even a fast shooter would have to break birds at a distance between 30 and 45 yards. With the improved shotshells of the postwar years so many shooters were able to break all of their targets from the 25 yard line that the rules had to be revised and a new 27 yard handicapping distance established. While the lower pattern percentages and occasional blown patterns of 25 years ago would eliminate many competitors, the tight and uniform modern patterns of modern loads have led to intense and hard-fought competition among the 63,000 registered trap shooters of the present day.

Chapter 9

FUTURE SHOTGUNS AND AMMUNITION

The future is always difficult to predict, but there are trends in military and commercial firearms and ammunition that give us clues as to the direction we are going in. During the 1960s there was tremendous interest in caseless ammunition for use in military and sporting firearms. Caseless ammunition from .22 caliber up to extremely powerful 25mm-cannon ammunition for use on supersonic jet fighters was designed and tested. From a military standpoint, caseless ammunition has one extremely important advantage: approximately 50 percent of the total weight of a cartridge consists of the brass case which is used once and thrown away. The brass case is a complex component to manufacture, requiring multimillion-dollar machinery and careful control over metallurgy and heat treatment to provide the proper combination of tensile strength and ductility to perform in automatic military weapons. Cartridge brass is basically an expensive material, consisting of 75 percent copper and 25 percent zinc. Copper is in short supply throughout the world, and in times of emergency the supply becomes even more critical. The supply of copper became so crucial in Germany during World War II that the 7.62 Kurz ammunition introduced in 1943 was manufactured entirely with mild-steel cartridge cases. In addition, much of the standard German 7.9mm Mauser rifle and machine gun ammunition was manufactured with steel cartridge cases, even though such manufacture wears out tooling rapidly and the cases must be protected from corrosion by a coating of lacquer. Experimental programs in the United States during and since World War II have investigated steel and aluminum cartridge cases as substitutes for brass. Aluminum is gaining favor as a material for the future.

The requirements for modern military ammunition are difficult to meet. Finished ammunition certified to meet Government specifications is kept in Government warehouses such as Rock Island Arsenal in Illinois, or Frankford Arsenal in Philadelphia, to await shipment to field forces on demand. It may have to endure shelf storage for 10 to 20 years in peacetime before being called upon to perform perfectly in an emergency. Some of the ammunition used early in World War II had been manufactured at the close of World War I. For many years the author used twenty-year-old World War II ammunition in rifle matches, and it performed beautifully. When military ammunition is withdrawn from storage it cannot always receive the gentlest of treatment. It may be hurriedly loaded into aircraft, shipped thousands of miles and then dropped by parachute to beleaguered forces holding an isolated position. Despite heavy impact with the ground and years of storage, the troops rightfully expect to tear the ammunition cans open, feed the ammunition into a hot machine gun and secure flawless performance.

Both military and commercial ammunition is designed to function under enormous temperature variations. Military ammunition must function properly at −65° F. in an Arctic blizzard, but must be able to withstand storage under high-humidity jungle conditions or perform properly in the desert, where ammunition temperatures may reach 140° F. Aircraft ammunition may sit in the loaded magazines of a parked jet aircraft baking in the sun at 120° F. and five minutes later be subjected to the icy blast of −60° F. air in a dogfight at 50,000 feet.

While commercial shotshells do not have to meet quite such rigorous conditions, they are regularly tested for performance at −40° F. and 120° F., as well as under high-humidity and extended-storage conditions. Shotshells are often used under very damp conditions and sometimes are completely immersed in water. It is a tribute to the millions of dollars of research and development and production experience by industry and the Government that American ammunition is considered to be the finest in the world. It will perform under incredible operating conditions.

If the weight of military ammunition could be cut in half by the elimination of a cartridge case, there are enormous advantages all the way through the logistics chain. For example, the aircraft delivering ammunition to isolated troops could carry twice as much. The fighter plane, with its stringent requirements, could double the magazine capacity of its cannon. These factors led to large research and development programs in the 1960s and the 1970s to explore the potential of caseless military ammunition.

The first experimental work was done with the .30-caliber (7.62mm) caseless ammunition since this is the standard NATO cartridge. During the late 1960s the standard U. S. infantry rifle was the M-14 chambered for this ammunition. A comparison of the weight of the components in the 7.62mm cased and caseless ammunition is shown in the table below. Although exactly the same projectile is used in both rounds of ammunition, the overall weight is cut almost exactly in half. The ballistic performance of the ammunition was virtually identical.

	7.62mm (30-cal.)	
	NATO Standard brass cased ammunition	7.62mm caseless ammunition
1. Bullet weight	149 grains	149 grains
2. Propellant weight	42	45
3. Cartridge case weight	190	0
4. Primer weight	5	1
5. Overall cartridge weight	386 grains	195 grains
6. Muzzle velocity (ft/sec)	2700	2700

Experimental work was performed at Springfield Armory to convert M-14 rifles to fire the caseless ammunition. The modifications included a redesigned bolt and chamber. The bolt had a cylindrical extension forward of the locking lugs which had several piston rings for gas sealing. The firing pin also had a gas-sealing system built in. These rifles were successfully fired for thousands of shots, but there were persistent problems with gas leakage and dirt buildup on the sealing surfaces. Gas sealing is, of course, extremely crucial in a caseless rifle, for a flashback into the magazine area would cause a serious fire and spill a stream of burning cartridges out the bottom of the magazine. One excellent characteristic of modern smokeless propellants is that they will *not* develop high pressure unless they are confined.

In the late 1960s and early 1970s research programs were performed to develop caseless ammunition in 5.56mm. A comparison of the standard 5.56mm brass cased and caseless ammunition is shown in Figure 9-1. The brass-cased ammuni-

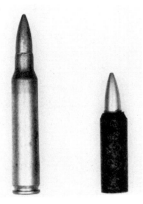

Figure 9-1   Comparison of cased and caseless 5.56mm ammunition.

tion contains a 55-grain bullet with a lead core and a gilding metal jacket. (Gilding metal is 90 percent copper and 10 percent zinc.) The case is loaded with 28½ grains of propellant and launches the bullet at a velocity of 3,250 ft/sec. A caseless 5.56mm cartridge, developed by Frankford Arsenal, is shown on the right side of the illustration. This uses exactly the same 55-grain bullet and has the same muzzle velocity. The overall cartridge weight is cut about in half.

A cross section drawing showing the difference in internal construction between the 5.56mm cased ammunition and experimental caseless ammunition is shown in Figure 9-2. The brass-cased ammunition has a hard "outer shell" enclosing all of the fragile components such as the propellant and primer mix. Primer mix is contained in the shallow brass priming cup and then seated flush with the head of the cartridge. Even if the ammunition is dropped from a great height, it is extremely rare that a primer will be struck exactly

right and ignite. Even if it does, the characteristics of smokeless propellant are such that sufficient pressure will be built up to eject the projectile from the case or split the sidewall of the case open, and then generally the remainder of the propellant will remain unburned. The brass case is an excellent container to hold all the components in proper configuration.

Construction of caseless ammunition is very different. The basic structure consists of a cylinder made of the same type of propellant as used in the cased ammunition but it is treated with solvents so that it becomes a semi-plastic mass, which is then forced into a die and molded into the shape shown in the illustration. Hard pressure in the die squeezes out much of the solvent, and then the cylinders are placed in an oven where the remaining solvent is baked out. The result is a very tough molded-plastic cylinder. Inside this a second cylinder, made of an amber-colored nitrocellulose propellant, was placed. The thin

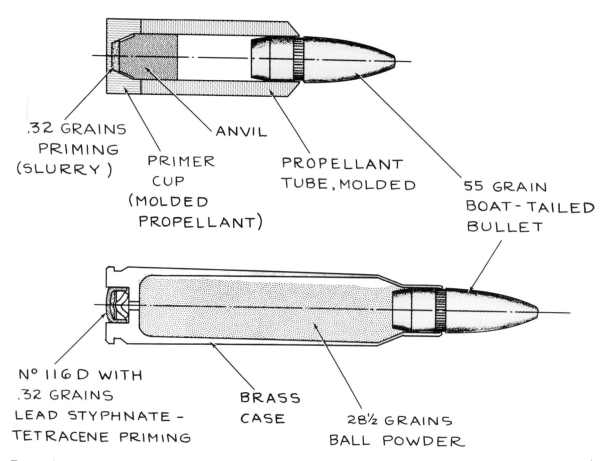

.32 GRAINS PRIMING (SLURRY)

PRIMER CUP (MOLDED PROPELLANT)

ANVIL

PROPELLANT TUBE, MOLDED

55 GRAIN BOAT-TAILED BULLET

Nº 116 D WITH .32 GRAINS LEAD STYPHNATE - TETRACENE PRIMING

BRASS CASE

28½ GRAINS BALL POWDER

Figure 9-2 Cross section of cased and caseless 5.56mm ammunition.

inner cylinder had an inside diameter of .224 inches, the same diameter as the projectile. After the two cylinders were assembled the bullet was pressed into the inner cylinder and glued in place.

The priming assembly was contained in a separate plug of .224-inch diameter which was molded with a priming cavity. Damp priming mixture was placed into this cavity and then "consolidated" under pressure. A thin sheet of purple-colored paper was glued across the top of the priming compound to give a measure of environmental protection. A separate plug of nitrocellulose propellant was compacted and inserted into the center of the propellant tube and the priming assembly was glued in place. The purpose of the separate plug was to bring the overall weight of the propellant charge up to the specification figures so that proper velocity levels would be achieved.

The tough tube of nitrocellulose propellant is fairly difficult to ignite and the performance of some of the early primer designs was not totally satisfactory. Other priming designs were investigated including the use of a second priming cup with an additional priming charge inside the plastic tube. Other designs were developed which provided better protection for the priming compound.

Tens of thousands of rounds of caseless ammunition of 5.56mm and 7.62mm have been successfully developed and tested. This ammunition has been demonstrated in military rifles and machine guns in full automatic fire but substantial technical problems remain. Ammunition used by the infantry may be given such rough treatment on its way to the front lines that extra packaging precautions are required with caseless ammunition. Problems of heat build up within the tiny seals in the gun mechanisms and the danger of flashback causing fire in the magazines were all problems which led to a temporary suspension of caseless ammunition research for small arms in the early 1970s. Advancing technology will find solutions to these problems but caseless small-arms ammunition will probably not come until the 1980s.

CASELESS AMMUNITION

There is an application where caseless ammunition has enormous benefits. Air fighters need to shave every possible pound from the weight of their aircraft so that they can out accelerate, out-speed, and outmaneuver their opponents. United States jet aircraft have compiled an enormously successful record in aerial dogfights since World War II. During the Korean War our standard first-line jet aircraft was the F-86 Sabre, armed either with 6 50-caliber machine guns each firing at a rate of approximately 1,200 rounds a minute, or with 4 M-39 20mm cannon. The M-39 each had a single barrel but a five-shot cylinder, just like a revolver. This design was an outgrowth of German research during World War II. The advantage of the revolver concept is that the five chambers allow the ramming and extraction of the large 20mm rounds of ammunition at reasonable speeds even though the firing rate was as high as 1,400 shots per minute.

In the period since the Korean War the Air Force has changed over to a 6-barrel "Vulcan" cannon which is driven by an electric or hydraulic motor. These 20mm cannon provide firing rates up to 6,000 shots per minute and extraordinarily high reliability. This M-61 aircraft cannon developed by General Electric under government contract is used by all the first-line United States fighters. It, too, has compiled an enormously successful record of aerial combat against Soviet-made aircraft, which are armed with 23mm and 30mm single-barreled cannon of traditional design which fire at much slower rates.

For the next generation of American fighter aircraft to be used in the late 1970s and 1980s the Air Force is developing a radically new 25mm cannon utilizing caseless ammunition. Details of this new ammunition are classified, but in general terms it is somewhat similar to the caseless ammunition shown in Figure 9-1 except that the high-explosive projectile is buried completely within the propellant tube. The objectives of this program are to provide high-velocity ammunition that will have greatly increased power and range over the present 20mm design and yet not have a great increase in weight. These characteristics are important in a dogfight with the high speeds and fast twisting motions of modern jet aircraft. The projectiles are launched at high velocity and are designed to retain high velocity during their flight through the air. These design features make for a short time of flight between aircraft and target. With both planes twisting violently in the air this short time of flight can make the difference between a hit and a miss. The requirements for high power with minimum weight can justify great complexity in ammunition design and manufacturing procedures. The construction must provide for carefully programmed propellant-burning rates while the designs look simple to the casual observer. The technical problems are very difficult and millions of dollars in research and development are required to successfully develop this radically new aircraft ammunition.

The decade of the 1960s and the early 1970s were periods of intense interest in caseless ammunition for sporting uses. Caseless ammunition to replace .22-caliber rimfire cartridges and centerfire ammunition were investigated. The Daisy Manufacturing Company, long a major manufacturer of air rifles, became interested in a European process for caseless .22-caliber ammunition which consisted of a lead bullet with a molded chunk of nitrocellulose propellant glued and mechanically bonded to its base. The rifle was designed with a powerful spring that drove an air piston. When the trigger was pulled, the piston moved forward under the urging of the powerful drive spring and compressed a column of air, which impacted the base of the propellant. The air column was heated to the point where it ignited the ·propellant which then burned and accelerated the projectile down the barrel. Check valves prevented gas from leaking back into the compression chamber. Daisy placed this gun and ammunition on the market during the late 1960s but it was soon found that the cost of the ammunition was about equal to that of regular rimfire cartridges.

One of four ammunition concepts from a Winchester patent application is shown in Figure 9-3.

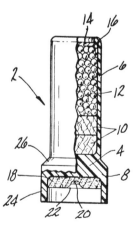

Figure 9-3 Patent drawing of Winchester caseless shotshell.

The concept was created by William B. Woodring who holds many inventions in the ammunition field. The shotshell design basically consists of a molded-plastic carrier which contains all of the elements of the shotshell. A long cylindrical skirt (24) is molded on the back of the caseless shotshell. Into this cavity a compressed pellet of fibrous-nitrocellulose propellant is press fitted in place. There are many approaches to making a compressed pellet of powder. The approach used in most military ammunition is to soften the propellant grains in a solvent and then compress the sticky mass in a die which forms the pellet to the exact shape desired. Winchester Research has used this approach for military ammunition ranging in size from .22 centerfire (5.56mm) up to the 25mm caseless ammunition for the Air Force. For commercial caseless shotshells and experiments with .22-caliber ammunition a fibrous, pure nitrocellulose propellant is often used, since the hairy fibers can be compacted dry in a Stokes-type press making the pellet as shown in the patent application. (Stokes presses are used to make aspirin tablets and other compacted pills of this shape.) Special additives are required in the propellant to eliminate the possibilty of a build up of static electricity during the manufacturing process and the possibility of an occasional detonaton of a powder pellet. Compression pressures on the pellets are high—often in the order of 5,000 to 10,000 pounds per square inch. The result is a dense structure with a high degree of mechanical strength.

The pellet is formed with a depression (shown as No. 22). A small quantity of slurry priming is placed into this depression (shown as No. 20). The combination of slurry priming and fibrous nitrocellulose is a good one, for the wet priming mixture interlocks with the fibers of the compressed-powder pellet locking the priming in place. The slurry priming consists of a patented priming mixture with the basic ingredient a double salt of lead styphnate. The ingredients are ground extremely fine and are carried as a suspension in the water solution. Primed pellets are baked to drive off the water, leaving a highly consolidated primer in the center of the pellet. The fact that the priming is well below the surface of the pellet makes it safe to handle and the primed pellets can be press fitted into the base of the caseless shotshell.

In the design shown in this patent application, two fiber wads (No. 10) were pressed into the mouth of the case to cushion the acceleration in the shot column. Then the shot charge (No. 12) was measured and poured into the case. The mouth of the case was closed with a frangible plastic disk (No. 14) and then the mouth of the case rolled over to retain the frangible disk in place (No. 16).

A gun designed to fire the caseless shotshells is shown in Figure 9-4. This is one of four illustrations contained in a Winchester research patent issued in August, 1972. The design work on both guns and ammunition was performed in the middle and late 1960s. The drawing shows a caseless shotshell in place in the chamber and the gun locked and ready to fire. The shotshell has two basic diameters conected by a conical surface which is shown as No. 26 in the ammunition drawing. As the gun is closed and fully locked, the bolt presses the shotshell tightly against the conical surface in the chamber so that the shell is well supported. As the cartridge is fired this interference fit gives good support for the priming material against the firing pin below. The firing pin tip is designed to penetrate the priming materal and give a stab-type ignition. This means that instead of the priming being crushed between a firing pin and a fixed metal anvil, the heat is generated by the motion of the tapered firing pin's point penetrating the priming material, thus causing sufficient friction for ignition. The priming in turn is sufficiently violent to break up the compressed powder pellet and start ignition of the nitrocellulose.

When the gas pressure builds up the entire caseless shotshell is accelerated forward. For it to pass up the barrel of the shotgun the entire larger diameter back end of the shell must be swaged down to bore diameter. This action gives "shot start" resistance which is important to get adequate burning of the propellant. As the shotshell is accelerated up the barrel, the acceleration forces cause the frangible disk, which closes the mouth of the shell, to break. The design of this frangible disk is tricky. It must be sufficiently strong and tough to withstand normal handling and shipping forces yet must fracture into small fragments under the violent acceleration which occurs during propellant burning. In a full-choke gun there is an additional force tending to fracture this disk due to the circumferential compres-

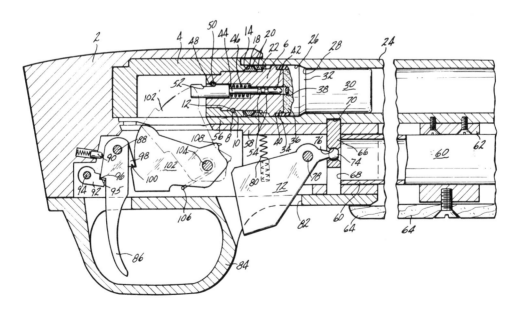

Figure 9-4 Patent drawing of action for caseless shotshells.

sion of the entire shotshell passing through the choke. After the shell leaves the muzzle of the gun, air pressure tends to slow down the plastic carrier while the heavy lead shot holds its velocity much better. The result is a separation of the shot cloud from the plastic carrier a few feet from the muzzle of the gun. The shot cloud then continues unhampered in its flight to the target.

The shotgun shown in Figure 9-4 contains several features to adopt it to caseless ammunition. The bolt slides a long distance inside the chamber of the shotgun. The firing pin has a long, close-fitting cylindrical seal in the bolt (No. 42). In addition two gas-sealing grooves were cut into the firing pin (No. 54). Experience has shown that gas escaping along the sides of a close-fitting pin gets confused when it gets to a groove and swirls into a turbulent flow. The pile up of this turbulent gas tends to block additional gas flow and provides improved sealing of the firing pin. The front surface of the bolt was cylindrical and designed to be a slight interference fit with the inside skirt of the caseless shotshell. It is not clearly shown in the illustration. The skirt of the shotshell is actually a tight fit on the bolt and a slightly loose fit in the chamber. This feature is for unloading the shotgun. If the gunner changed his mind, all he needed to do was to open the action and lift the shotshell off the bolt with his fingers. This feature was also useful if a misfire occurred. Misfires are rare in production ammunition. They do occur with some frequency in the early stages of an experimental program, particularly when different formulations of priming, propellant, firing pin and initial volume are being explored. We found that with extremely light priming charges it was sometimes possible for the firing pin to ignite the priming and the pellet would remain intact with merely a black smudge in the center of the pellet showing that the priming had burned. On other occasions the firing-pin impact and the burning of the light priming charge caused the pellet to fracture but did not cause the full ignition.

The bolt assembly also contained split sealing rings. These are shown to the rear of the bolt head near the end of the chamber. Nos. 14, 18, 20 and 22 all point to various aspects of the sealing system. The basic idea was that the gas pressure striking the front split ring expanded it outwards sealing off the gas flow between the sealing ring and the chamber. As this ring drove to the rear it rode up the sloping surface on the rear split ring, driving it inwards and sealing the gas path between the ring and the bolt. Very sophisticated instrumentation was used at times to check the efficiency of the sealing systems. A special device which looked like a camera was pointed at the breech end of the gun. A container was filled with liquid nitrogen, which exists at a temperature very close to absolute zero. When the shot was fired the heat-sensitive camera would blink its eye rapidly looking at the temperature of the breech sealing area and then looking at the temperature of the liquid nitrogen. As it jumped back and forth between these two temperature extremes it would develop an electrical signal which was plotted on an oscilloscope giving an exact temperature versus time reading of the breech area. Experiments with different types of sealing systems showed that the split-ring seals are an excellent approach for the late 1960s.

The remainder of the shotgun would be equally well adapted to caseless or conventional ammunition. The barrel slid forward to open the gun. It was locked in a rear position by a locking block (No. 70) which was controlled by the locking lever (No. 72). To open the gun the trigger finger was simply moved forward of the trigger guard, lifting the lever which unlocked the gun and allowed the barrel to be slid forward.

Although both Winchester and Remington have successfully developed caseless shotguns and ammunition, such a radical change in ammunition design had to demonstrate a highly significant improvement for the shooter to be successful in the market place. Modern shotshells have been refined through many millions of dollars of research and development into economical ammunition designs that give superb performance. In the late 1960s, caseless shotguns and ammunition simply did not offer sufficient improvement over conventional ammunition to justify the multimillion dollar programs of additional research, development and production that would be required to market it. With evolving technology in the 1970s and 1980s, however, caseless shotguns and ammunition may well become a reality for the sportsman as the century nears its close.

ELECTRIC IGNITION

Electric ignition of ammunition has been a fascinating field for inventors for many years. Patents date back into the 19th century. During World War II the development of electric-primed ammunition became important for an unusual reason. Late in the War powerful aircraft were fitted with turrets which carried twin .50-caliber machine guns, and some extremely large aircraft, such as the B-29, carried twin 20mm cannon. The post-war aircraft such as the B-36 were designed with installations containing several 20mm cannon in a single turret. The turrets had to track enemy aircraft at high speed and with great precision because of the high aircraft speeds and great distances involved. If one cannon in the turret fired slightly ahead of the other the result would be a twisting force on the turret which would deflect the aim of both guns and cause misses. The best solution to this problem was to develop electrically primed ammunition. The guns cycled normally, but only when both guns were closed and locked could the single firing circuit be energized which would send a jolt of electricity to ignite both cartridges simultaneously. This approach eliminated the twisting force. For this reason the 20mm aircraft ammunition used in United States aircraft at the present time is all electrically primed.

There are two styles of electric primers. The type often used in military ammunition is known as "bridge-wire" primer. In this design the firing pin is actually an electrode that contacts the center of the primer. The center portion of the primer is insulated from the rest of the cartridge case. Fine nicrome wires lead from the insulated center through priming mix and are grounded to the outer surface of the primer assembly. When the jolt of electric current passes through the firing pin into the center of the primer assembly, the fine wires heat up rapidly, igniting the primer mix which in turn ignites the propellant.

This same type of ignition has been investigated for shotguns. A French firm, Rouby, designed and manufactured a double-barreled shotgun utilizing a battery pack in the butt stock to provide electric ignition. The shotshells are conventional in appearance as shown in Figure 9-5 but they contain an electric bridge-wire primer. There are many advantages to an electric-ignition shotgun. The trigger is simply a switch so that the pull may be made as light or as short as is desirable. In an ordinary shotgun after the trigger is pulled there is a significant time delay (usually about 6 to 10 milliseconds) while the hammer falls, strikes the firing pin, crushes the primer mix and starts off ignition. In the electric ignition system as soon as the switch is closed power flows to the bridge-

Figure 9-5   Rouby electric shotshells.

wire primer igniting the shotshell. This small difference in timing would not be significant to the average shooter, but it does provide a slight improvement to the really skilled top-flight hunter or skeet or trap shooter. The big problem to date is that bridge-wire primers are expensive to manufacture. Very fine wires must be soldered or crimped from the center electrode to the ground at the edge of the primer assembly, and it must be done in such a way as to give good electrical contact even with the kind of low voltage which occurs with battery power. The usual procedure is to solder the bridge wires, but this involves expensive hand assembly and inspection operations.

Another approach to electric ignition is to use an "electric-resistance" primer mix. With this approach the center electrode might be considered as a rod extending into a special priming material. As the jolt of electricity moves down the firing pin into the center rod, it must travel outward through the special priming mix to reach the negative side of the circuit at the edge of the primer cup. If the priming mix is formulated just right, there will be sufficient heat buildup to cause ignition without the use of a bridge wire. Such priming mixes are suitable for both cased and caseless ammunition, and have been widely used in military 20mm ammunition.

Whether electric ignition will become practical depends to a large extent on research being performed in the priming laboratories throughout the world. At the present time the trend even in military ammunition is to move away from electric and back to percussion ignition. Even though our 20mm aircraft ammunition has been electrically

234

primed for 30 years, the next generation of ammunition now in research and development will use percussion primers.

ALUMINUM AMMUNITION

As stated, the 1960s was a period of research in the field of caseless ammunition. By 1970 it became apparent that caseless ammunition would not be significantly cheaper than cased ammunition when all aspects of the system are considered, and that the problems outweighed the advantages for small-arms applications.

Instead, in the field of small arms the trend has been in the direction of aluminum ammunition. There was a great burst of activity in aluminum ammunition during the 1950s, but this quieted down while caseless ammunition was being investigated. Now aluminum is coming back with greater strength than ever before. The Army has developed a medium-powered 30mm aircraft cannon shell for use on helicopter armament known as the "WECOM-30." The design is shown in Figure 9-6. It is designed with a straight, belted aluminum case and projects a dual-purpose high-explosive projectile weighing 3,000 grains at a velocity of 2,200 feet per second. The term "dual purpose" means that this projectile is designed both for armor penetration and high explosive effect in a single design. It does this by a specially designed fuse and a "shaped-charge" configuration in the high-explosive charge. WECOM-30 ammunition is operational and gives excellent performance.

Another application for aluminum ammunition is in the 40mm grenade launcher widely used in Southeast Asia. This is unusual ammunition, in allowing the foot soldier to fire a 40mm grenade at ranges out to 375 yards without excessive re-

coil. This is accomplished by the use of a "high-low" ballistic system shown in Figure 9-7. A small propellant charge is burned in the high pressure chamber at a pressure of about 35,000 pounds per square inch. The gas bursts through small holes into the main cavity of the case and exerts a pressure of about 3,500 pounds per square inch to gently accelerate the grenade at a velocity of 250 feet per second. Modern propellants are rather difficult to ignite and will not burn properly at pressures as low as 3,500 psi. The use of the high-low system is a technique to get uniform clean burning of the propellant and still provide the low pressure required for gentle acceleration of the grenade.

The use of aluminum ammunition has also been investigated in shotshells. Winchester Research performed an extensive research and development program for aluminum shotgun ammunition. One of the goals was to try and achieve 12-gauge shotshell performance in a gun that would be the size of a 20-gauge shotgun. Two styles of shells evolved. The lighter load is shown in Figure 9-8. This carried 1⅛ ounces of shot and was ballistically equivalent to a 12-gauge field load. Because the aluminum walls are so thin, the overall shell was extremely compact and could easily fit in a 20-gauge shotgun action. The effect was to have a light, compact shotgun but with a barrel 14 gauge in size and excellent ballistic performance. There was a request for even more powerful ammunition, and a 14-gauge aluminum shell carrying a full 1¼ ounces of shot was developed. This design is shown in Figure 9-9. Both designs used a fiber cup wad for gas sealing and a heavy fiber wad to buffer the force between the propellant charge and the shot. The lighter load had a spherical crimp which opened up to release the shot

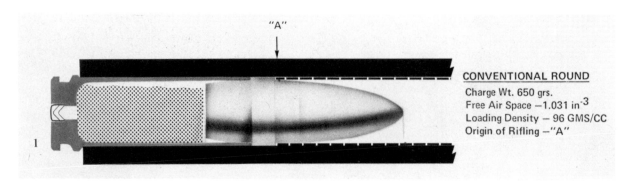

Figure 9-6 WECOM-30 aluminum-cased 30-cal. ammunition.

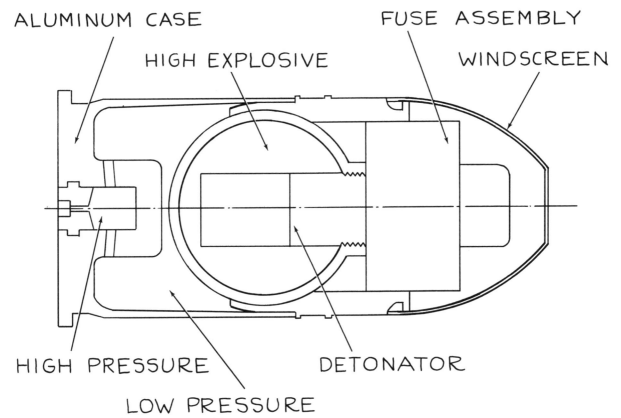

Figure 9-7   40mm aluminum ammunition.

Figure 9-8   14-gauge 1⅛-ounce aluminum shotshell.

Figure 9-9 14-gauge 1¼-ounce aluminum shotshell.

To get a full 1¼ ounces of shot into this compact overall size it was necessary to put on a thin top wad and then roll the thin aluminum lip over slightly to retain the wad in place.

The research and development work was successfully performed and hundreds of thousands of shells were manufactured and tested before the program was suspended in favor of the development of plastic shotshells in conventional gauges which would not require the hunter to purchase an entirely new firearm. The 14-gauge shotshells tended to give excellent patterns because the thin aluminum walls have virtually no "forcing cone" at the front of the chamber. Aluminum shotshells were also developed in 12 gauge, but the very thin side walls meant that aluminum shells needed a different chamber configuration than paper or plastic shells, even in the same gauge. Further research also showed that plastic shotshells, if compression formed, or made of bi-axially oriented polyethylene, would function very well in conventional chambers and could be reloaded many more times than aluminum shotshells.

SHOTGUNS OF THE FUTURE

Consumer surveys indicate that most sportsmen would be interested in an auto-loading shotgun which was light in weight, inexpensive, never got dirty and required little maintenance. Manufacturers have gone a long way towards meeting these demands but further research can lead to even better products in the future.

Shotguns pose a unique problem because the cartridge case is relatively weak compared to a centerfire cartridge, and the shotgun action must successfully handle an enormous range of power levels. If all the shotgun was called upon to handle was ammunition loaded with 25 grains of propellant and 1¼ ounces of shot, it would be a relatively simple matter to design a gun that would function reliably under wide temperature ranges and other adverse conditions. The problem becomes enormously more complex when this same shotgun must handle a shotshell loaded with 20 grains of powder and 1 ounce of shot on an icy cold wet day in a salt marsh and then be carried to another part of the country to fire 1½ ounce magnum loads carrying a 40-grain-propellant charge when the temperature stands at 100°. It is a miracle that any single shotgun design can meet this enormous range of operating conditions. The best candidates so far are the long-recoil and gas-operated actions. Only time and ingenuity will tell if other types of action can successfully meet all of these conflicting conditions.

One approach to a future shotgun design is shown in Figure 9-10. A one-piece stock has been designed which has a four-shot magazine in the forearm. A carrier mechanism is tied in with the trigger mechanism and this is inserted through the underside of the stock. The receiver is tubular and contains a compact locking mechanism known as the "collet locking" system. As the name implies, the collet lock works similarly to the collet gripping system used in lathes to hold cylin-

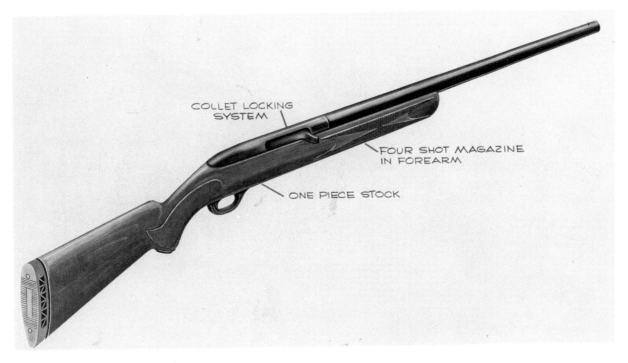

Figure 9-10 Collet-locking shotgun.

drical work pieces. The design includes 6 to 10 locking fingers which are cammed out into recesses on the closing motion of the bolt. The beauty of this system is that it provides locking completely around the circumference of the locking ring, so that the radial engagement can be relatively small. As the action is operated the bolt slide moves slightly to the rear which allows the collet locking pieces to rotate inwards out of the locking recess. The entire assembly then moves to the rear functioning for the remainder of the operating stroke similarly to any modern auto-loading shotgun.

A second design approach is shown in Figure 9-11. This might be termed an "over-under" auto-loading shotgun. The design includes a one-piece stock which would probably be molded of a glass-reinforced thermosetting high-strength plastic. Although it has the appearance of an over-under shotgun the upper barrel is in fact the magazine tube and a barrel buffer assembly. Shotshells would be loaded through the loading port in the top of the action and pushed forward into the magazine tube. The barrel is the lower tube and is allowed to recoil within the stock. A powerful return spring and buffer assembly is installed in the forward part of the upper magazine tube. As the barrel recoils to the rear the buffer assembly absorbs the energy, buffering the barrel to a stop and returning it to a fully forward position. This

type of design would probably be most practical with a short-recoil type of action which could take advantage of the barrel motion to operate the auto-loading mechanism. The fired shells would be ejected from the bottom of the mechanism so that the gun would be equally useful to right- and left-handed shooters. A tang safety has been designed, since this is the most natural position from a human engineering standpoint.

Another advanced shotgun concept is shown in Figure 9-12. The idea is to bring the line of recoil as low as possible, so that the shotgun moves in a straight line against the shooter's shoulder. The action is in effect upside-down, with the breech and chamber on the bottom. The magazine tube is on top of the forearm and the shells are loaded through what would normally be the ejection port. Ejection is downwards out the bottom of the action. The gun could easily be made as a gas-operated design by simply placing the gas system in the area forward of the magazine tube. This concept includes a narrow rib resting on top of the barrel which provides a clean line of sight from breech to muzzle. It is well known that skilled shooters always fire the lower barrel of an over-under shotgun first since this gives minimum disturbance of aim. This shotgun takes advantage of this idea and would allow a faster recovery time than conventional shotguns with barrel on top.

Which of these designs will become reality by

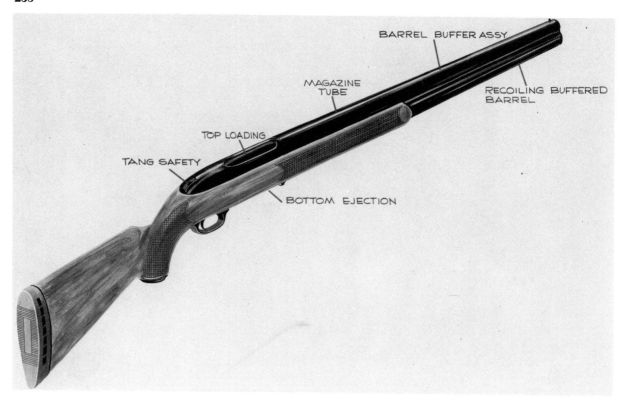

Figure 9-11   Over-under auto-loading shotgun.

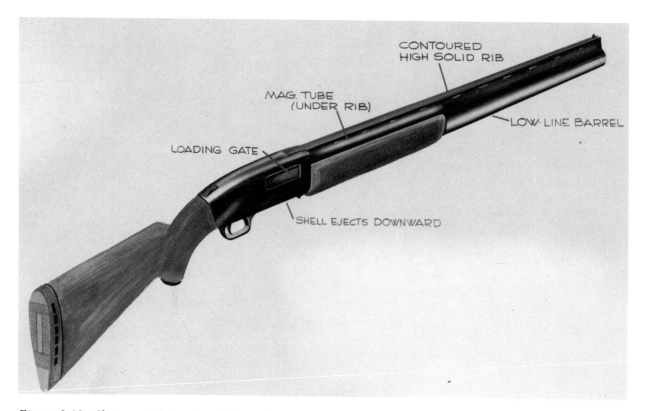

Figure 9-12   Shotgun with low barrel line and magazine at top.

1990? To a surprising extent it depends on the mood of the American sportsman. Although Americans go for flashy cars and clothes they tend to be relatively conservative in firearms design. Except for special commemorative models the American sportsman generally seems to like solid-steel receivers and barrels, well-machined components and wooden stocks and forearms. If large numbers of American sportsmen are willing to move away from tradition towards radical styles of shotgun design then manufacturers will be glad to fill the demand. It is the author's opinion that the American sportsman is keenly aware of quality, is very style conscious and is willing to try new ideas *if* they lead to better performance. My guess is that shotguns such as the one shown in Figure 9-12 will become a reality before the new century dawns.

Index